Placing Parties in American Politics

DAVID R. MAYHEW

Placing Parties in American Politics

ORGANIZATION, ELECTORAL SETTINGS,
AND GOVERNMENT ACTIVITY IN
THE TWENTIETH CENTURY

PRINCETON UNIVERSITY PRESS
PRINCETON, NEW JERSEY

Copyright © 1986 by Princeton University Press

Published by Princeton University Press, 41 William Street,
Princeton, New Jersey 08540
In the United Kingdom: Princeton University Press, Guildford, Surrey

All Rights Reserved

Library of Congress Cataloging in Publication Data will be
found on the last printed page of this book

ISBN 0-691-07707-X
ISBN 0-691-02249-6 (pbk.)

This book has been composed in Linotron Sabon and Gill Sans
Clothbound editions of Princeton University Press books are printed on acid-free paper, and
binding materials are chosen for strength and durability. Paperbacks, although satisfactory for personal collections, are not usually suitable for library rebinding

Printed in the United States of America by Princeton University Press
Princeton, New Jersey

To my colleagues and teachers

Bob Dahl, Bob Lane, and Ed Lindblom

CONTENTS

MAPS

FIGURES

TABLES

ACKNOWLEDGMENTS

A great many people helped me in this enterprise. Robert Lane gave important encouragement at the start. Thomas Brown, Stanley Kelley, Jr., Frank J. Sorauf, Bruce Stinebrickner, and Philip Williams read the entire manuscript and supplied valuable criticism. Christopher Achen, James Fesler, David Johnston, James March, John McCarthy, Douglas Rae, Steven Rosenstone, Rogers Smith, Steven B. Smith, Michael Taylor, Sanford G. Thatcher, and Edward Tufte helped me think about setting up arguments and using evidence. I profited from conversations some years ago with John H. Fenton. Roy Behr, Mark Hansen, Christopher Jarvis, Miles McNiff, David Schwartzbaum, Ronald Seyb, Daniel Starr, and Patricia Sykes contributed great skill and industry as research assistants. The following generously supplied useful evidence or helped me try to find it: Christopher Achen, Christopher Arterton, David Broder, Henry P. Brubaker, Walter Dean Burnham, David A. Caputo, James Chubbuck, Lida Churchville, Alan L. Clem, Don Collat, Martha Derthick, Robert B. Dishman, Richard R. Dohm, Ralph Eisenberg, Ina Ewing, Thomas A. Flinn, Donald L. Fowler, Gregory Fullerton, Hugh Davis Graham, Jack D. Haley, Mark Hansen, Marvin Harder, Richard Hofstetter, Charles S. Hyneman, Kenneth Janda, Malcolm E. Jewell, Peter Keisler, Marvin Krislov, Tom Lindenfeld, Seymour Martin Lipset, Michael Margolis, Robert E. McCarthy, Clifton McCleskey, Robert McClure, Thomas Milch, Austin Ranney, Ross R. Rice, Dawn Rossit, Richard M. Scammon, Mildred Schwartz, James Scott, Rogers Smith, Michael W. Traugott, John W. Wood, and Belle Zeller. I had students in class whose work helped along my own: Daniel Biser, Steven Calabresi, Thomas Cavanagh, Judith Center, Theodore Eismeier, Jeffrey Kampelman, Richard L. McCormick, Mark Smith, Raphael Sonenshein, Bruce Stinebrickner, and Hector E. Vela. Against odds Nancy Delia, Roberta Dulong, Sandra Nuhn, and Gretchen Oberfranc turned my handwriting into typescript. The text profited from superb copyediting by Elizabeth Gretz. I had valuable fellowship support at pertinent times from the National Science Foundation, the Guggenheim Foundation, the Hoover Institution, and Yale University, and I drew on the outstanding resources and services of the Littauer Library at Harvard, the Green Library and Hoover Institution Library at Stanford, the Library of Congress, and especially Sterling Memorial Library at Yale. All the misconceptions, misreadings, and other sorts of mistakes in the pages following are of course mine.

Placing Parties in American Politics

Political parties assume importance in some lines of scholarship because of competition or cleavages that occur *between* them, as evidenced in patterns of election returns. In investigations initiated by V. O. Key, Jr., close (as opposed to one-sided) electoral competition between parties in the American states has been held to foster a particular policy result—government solicitousness toward society's "have-nots." Parties fighting close elections are induced to cater to them.[1] "Party realignment" theory, as advanced by Walter Dean Burnham, makes claims about election returns and time: the American public is said to abandon a routinized interparty electoral cleavage every few decades and create a new one (as in 1896 or in the early 1930s), at once expressing itself with something like maximum genuineness and bringing about exceptionally important government policy making.[2]

Parties take on importance in other traditions of scholarship largely because of what occurs *within* them; the concern is with their structure. A familiar European literature that concentrates on socialist "movement" parties includes Robert Michels's work in 1911 pointing to a growth of intraparty oligarchy and Maurice Duverger's in 1951 offering "cadre," "branch," "cell," and "militia" as a typology of party organization rooted more or less in social class.[3] Concern with relationships between class and party structure and (potentially at least) between party structure and state programmatic activity animated both works. Of course the main tradition of work on American party structure has centered not on socialist movements but on a home-grown product: the country's elaborate system of local, state, and national patronage organization that took shape and gave politics and government a distinctive character in the nineteenth century and then settled into a long irregular decline during the twentieth (though the

[1] Key seems to have laid the base for this scholarship in political science in Chapter 14 of his *Southern Politics in State and Nation* (New York: Vintage, 1949).

[2] See, e.g., Walter Dean Burnham, *Critical Elections and the Mainsprings of American Politics* (New York: Norton, 1970).

[3] Robert Michels, *Political Parties: A Sociological Study of the Oligarchical Tendencies of Modern Democracy* (New York: Free Press, 1962); Maurice Duverger, *Political Parties: Their Organization and Activity in the Modern State* (New York: Wiley, 1963), pp. 17-40.

Chicago organization and others still carry on). Most activity by American citizens addressing parties in the last hundred years has zeroed in on this type of organization—notably in campaigns against city machines—and scholars from James Bryce and Moisei Ostrogorski around the turn of the century through Harold Gosnell in the 1930s and Edward C. Banfield and James Q. Wilson in the 1960s have written on its various pluses and minuses, causes, characteristics, and consequences.[4] One argument on consequences emerges nicely in Stephen Skowronek's recent work documenting the difficulty of building bureaucracies (and thus of making available what they were capable of doing) in the American national government of the late nineteenth century, which was largely staffed by the parties' patronage appointees.[5]

This work is a discussion of structure *within* parties—more specifically a what, why, when, where, and so what treatment of American party structure at the local level in the twentieth century. It dwells on traditional patronage organizations though it considers other structural forms, and it occasionally goes beyond the local level to take up the state and national. Like much other work on parties and elections, it assumes the importance of electoral politics, government activity, and elite actors, and its aim is to suggest some particular causal relations between elite actors' activity in electoral politics (the causes) and government activity (the effects). *Electoral politics* means nominating or general election processes or both. *Government activity* refers to outcomes generated by public officials (or official processes), including government policies, policy stands, projects, graft, appointive government jobs, and other valued things officials might somehow have access to and give out. *Elite actors* are organizations or people (leaving aside voters as such) who try to exercise influence in electoral politics in order to influence government activity. They might in principle include such diverse entities as candidates for office (whether or not incumbents), party organizations of various kinds, good-government associations, reform movements, referendum movements, newspapers, farmers' groups, labor unions, private corporations, newspapers, and political

---

[4] James Bryce, *The American Commonwealth* (New York: Putnam's, 1959), vol. 1, part 3; Moisei Ostrogorski, *Democracy and the Organization of Political Parties*, vol. 2 (New York: Macmillan, 1902); Harold F. Gosnell, *Machine Politics: Chicago Model* (Chicago: University of Chicago Press, 1968); Edward C. Banfield, *Political Influence: A New Theory of Urban Politics* (New York: Free Press, 1961); Edward C. Banfield and James Q. Wilson, *City Politics* (Cambridge: Harvard University Press and M.I.T. Press, 1963); James Q. Wilson, *The Amateur Democrat: Club Politics in Three Cities* (Chicago: University of Chicago Press, 1966).

[5] Stephen Skowronek, *Building a New American State: The Expansion of National Administrative Capacities, 1877-1920* (Cambridge: Cambridge University Press, 1982).

action committees. I give at least passing attention to instances of all of these. The ways elite actors might try to exercise influence in electoral politics range from packing nominating caucuses to mobilizing or manufacturing public opinion. The routes to influencing government activity, once electoral influence is gained, might include taking over elective government positions, "sending messages" or generating "mandates," and persuading or bargaining with public officials. In principle the causal relations I seek to detect might be either links intended by the pertinent elite actors (the winning party organization gets the cable TV franchise) or links not intended (the Republican party in 1860 helped to cause a bloody war).[6]

Its structural focus notwithstanding, this enterprise began as a blend of reflections on substance and also on data and methodology that was brought on by both the between- and within-parties traditions of scholarship and contrasts between them. As a matter of methodology approaching philosophy, I admired a great deal the post-Key and Burnham schools' reach for what might be called empirical extensiveness in studying American politics—the gathering and analysis of vast comprehensive stocks of election returns over space (the cross-state studies) and time (the "realignment" studies). There is much to be said for data analysis. But otherwise I had doubts about both schools' methods and premises. Particularly in the cross-state research positing government policies as a function of close versus one-sided party competition, there was something dubious about routinely construing parties to be artifacts of election returns—voters who happened to join in various November mixes—without reference to party structure. Did close electoral competition thirty years ago between party slates of organization politicians in, say, New Jersey have the same meaning and effects as close races between loose assortments of politicians who shared party labels in Oregon?

Perhaps the whole enterprise of betting so much on patterns of party competition was misconceived in any case. What if the more fundamental policy-related distinction in the American party sphere of the last century or so has indeed had to do with structure rather than competition, as other scholarships and much public activity suggest: namely, the basic structural distinction between having traditional patronage organizations and—what? Having weak Progressivized struc-

---

[6] I seldom take up the possibility of causation running the other way. Thus, for example, the CIO in the 1940s helped cause government activity, but government in the mid-1930s helped cause the CIO (and perforce its electoral activity). In general I think I have the arrow going in the right direction on matters I address, though some relations undeniably display elements of reciprocal causation.

tures instead? It is difficult to say precisely, but I began with the thought that a simple having versus not having dichotomy might be a useful approach. Could new light be shed on this old subject of traditional organization and its alternatives, perhaps by bringing to it some empirical extensiveness? The idea of looking into American party structure at the local level all around the country came to seem attractive; I might do justice to the subject of structure by aiming for a large universe of local information. It happens that several forms of party structure, including American patronage organizations, loose Progressivized parties, European socialist movements, and, for that matter, James Q. Wilson's amateur Democratic club movement of the 1960s, all generate visible outcroppings at the local level that perform or foster theoretically interesting activity—city machines conducting their distinctive business, for example, free-swinging direct primaries allowing easy entry into politics, socialist "branches" enrolling and educating members, and amateur clubs accommodating issue raising and participation by middle-class activists.[7] Having one of these forms forecloses having others. And, as it happens, the American dichotomy of having versus not having traditional patronage organization divides reality over time (nineteenth century versus twentieth, especially at state and national levels) but also over space. At the local level much of the country's formation of patronage organizations carried on quite well as late as the 1960s, standing in relief against a residual assortment of generally weaker party forms in other places and inviting comparative analysis across geography. An eye could be kept open in such analysis for American forms that approach the European socialist pattern—not an alertness likely to yield a great deal, but parties energized by unions, for example, might merit special attention.

The data search induced by these thoughts resulted in Part I, which is a disciplined setting out of voluminous information; the thoughts themselves resulted in Part II, a variously historical, speculative, and otherwise generalizing treatment of Part I's information. Part I amounts to a detailed map of a national political universe expressed in prose. In principle it is a comprehensive documentation of American city- or county-level party structure, presented state by state, as of the late 1960s—or at least party structure examined for whether it did or did not consist of specifiable kinds of party or partylike organizations that acted consequentially in nominating processes. I thought it crucial to investigate nominating activity to try to get a fix on traditional patronage organizations at the local level; whatever else they do, they try

[7] The source on the clubs is Wilson, *The Amateur Democrat*.

to get their candidates nominated. Such patronage enterprises are given careful attention, a reasonably clear operational definition, and a precisely used label ("traditional party organizations") in Part I, and each state is assigned a summary score to gauge, for its local electoral environments, the overall incidence and prominence of such organizations. I try to track other sorts of consequential nominating organizations, also.

The late 1960s is a good time to inspect because it both closes and samples fairly well a long twentieth-century span between the second and third of three major periods of structural change in American parties—the first being the Jacksonian period, the source of the nineteenth century's characteristic party system; the second, the Progressive period (and a bit before), during which national, state, and local parties were substantially overhauled with the effect of producing a hybrid twentieth-century system; and the third, the last decade and a half or so, during which local party organizations have decisively declined and telecommunications processes, candidate organizations, and capital-intensive party organizations have become central features of a distinctive new electoral politics. The long intermediate twentieth-century span is my chief concern here. The present I comment on directly at the very end of the concluding chapter, but my more general objective is to try to frame it, illuminate it, to some degree account for it, and by implication to appraise it and suggest its potential by analyzing the past.

Data availability made focusing on the late 1960s practical. My sources for Part I are other people's writings—works by political scientists, historians, journalists, and others who have been alert to party or partylike organizations active in nominating processes as they supplied careful accounts of electoral environments at lower levels of office around the country. I searched through books, articles, dissertations, shorter unpublished manuscripts, and newspaper stories written in the 1950s, 1960s, 1970s, and early 1980s for information, often given in passing, about electoral politics. Good material turned up in works of widely varying content and purpose, though the well-developed scholarships of the 1950s on state politics and the 1960s on city politics proved especially useful. The single most valuable set of materials was a series of reports on twenty-one large cities prepared by the Joint Center for Urban Studies at M.I.T. and Harvard University in 1959-1963. It scarcely needs saying that I fell short of finding material on all the lower-level political units around the country. In practice, given the sources, the reports I make are a blend of general, undiscriminating evidence on the lower-level electoral environments of whole states, and particular evidence on cities and counties that are large enough or whose politics has otherwise been eye-catching enough to draw the attention of writers. The overall mix of sources made the late 1960s an appropriate standard time to try to register organizational readings for, either directly from textual reports about that time or by suitable interpolation or extrapolation from reports about earlier or later times.[8]

Part I as prepared is an exceptionally large dose of facts for a work of political science, and I should say why I am presenting such detailed geographic material and suggest how to handle it.[9] There are three reasons for presenting it in such volume and form. First, my data readings for (in principle) the late 1960s pick up, for the most part, durable rather than short-term political phenomena (a point elaborated in Chapter 8). In general, local patterns of "traditional party organization" or its lack go back to the turn of the century and before. They are

[8] Before putting together the national data base described above, I assembled an entirely different data base similar to it in important features and also geared to finding out about local party structure via nominating activity. This was a collection of returns from primary elections for the late 1960s (in principle and more or less in practice), for the offices of state representative, state senator, and U.S. Representative, gathered for all fifty states and (incidentally) most of the country's major metropolitan counties. Through some intricate statistical manipulation of these data I produced for each geographic unit two separate readings that indexed the level of competition among candidates in its primaries (one value having to do with numbers of candidates competing, the other with scatter of the vote). The idea behind this was that readings on primary competition might give, by inference, readings on the prominence of party organization: the lower the level of competition the more prominent the hand of party organization in structuring the primary vote. The logic of this is reasonable enough, and I know now that in general the results of the actual calculation do square in interesting ways with the reality of party organization. But they square in complicated ways, and analysis of the primary returns alone presented new puzzles: in many geographic particulars the readings on competition accommodated what I already otherwise thought I knew about organization, but in others they decisively did not. And once put together, the readings on primaries seemed disappointingly bloodless, farther removed from real politics than I wanted to be. Hence, after soldiering through it, I came to regard the work on primaries as a warmup exercise and moved on to the prose data discussed above that underpin the finished book. In some respects the readings based on primary returns are worth comparing with the material gathered later, and for this reason I present them and draw a brief comparison in Appendix A. The best time to inspect this appendix is just after reading Part I, but it is not essential to the argument of the book.

[9] Three works on American politics come to mind that follow comparable principles of geographic comprehensiveness in setting out information: Key's *Southern Politics*, which sketches mid-twentieth-century politics in each of the eleven Southern states; Richard P. McCormick, *The Second American Party System: Party Formation in the Jacksonian Era* (New York: Norton, 1966), which gives accounts of party cleavage and structure in twenty-three states; and Kevin P. Phillips, *The Emerging Republican Majority* (New Rochelle, N.Y.: Arlington House, 1969), which discusses patterns of party cleavage at the grass-roots level around the country.

durable and also very likely important. I came to think of American lo-
cal-level electoral environments (in their structural aspects) as enduring
independent variables, so to speak, settings capable of outlasting
events, issues, individual politicians, ethnic groups, unions, and private
corporations operating in politics, and even particular political parties,
and able to shape to an appreciable degree what happens in politics and
government as these things or actors happen, operate, or come and
go.[10] The thrust here may call to mind and in fact owes something to
Fernand Braudel's principle of partitioning history by duration, in
which patterns or constraints of the middle or longer run channel or
shape the short run and are accorded corresponding care and importance.[11]

Second, I thought a data presentation might in general serve the
cause of doing empirically extensive research on twentieth-century
structure. Writing on American party structure has overwhelmingly
been intensive rather than extensive—case studies of locales are the
norm—and the better-known results are spotty (we may understand
Chicago, but how about Baltimore or Louisville?), not readily comparable, and overtold (here come the Boss Plunkitt stories again). The
subject of party structure suffers from an odd problem of undercumu-
lation, and it seemed to me that what needed cumulating and also presenting was some accurate, standardized, and geographically comprehensive information (rather than, say, "findings," as is the common
assumption in political science). My own research hardly required me
to look into all features of local party structure, but I did track some—
particularly organized nominating activity. I devised decision rules for
tracking nominating activity (see Chapter 1) that are sensitive to "traditional party organization" versus its absence, but also to other sorts
of consequential organization that turn up here and there in its absence—in areas that for the most part have not had much important
nominating organization at all. Many, though not all, such nonstandard forms are discussed in Part II. The result in Part I is a kind of
organization census that takes note of not only "traditional party organizations" but also, for example, Minnesota's unusual Democratic-

[10] To give two good examples of outlasting particular parties: ward politicians' practices and many of the resourceful politicians themselves jumped from one party to the
other as Pittsburgh and Philadelphia shifted from being Republican to Democratic machine holdings in the 1930s and 1950s, respectively. See Chapter 2.

[11] See Fernand Braudel, "History and the Social Sciences," ch. 2 in Peter Burke (ed.),
Economy and Society in Early Modern Europe: Essays from "Annales" (New York:
Harper and Row, 1972), pp. 13-21; J. H. Hexter, *On Historians: Reappraisals of Some
of the Makers of Modern History* (Cambridge: Harvard University Press, 1979), pp. 93-
100.

Farmer-Labor (DFL) party, the now-defunct Byrd apparatus in Virginia, Manhattan's amateur Democratic clubs, Houston's Harris County Democrats (HCD, a liberal-labor alliance), Dallas's Citizens Charter Association (CCA, a municipal businessmen's party), and such good-government organizations as Cincinnati's City Charter Committee and Kansas City's Citizens' Association.

Third, to present a full universe of rather spare and formulaic structural data may help shake loose American party structure from an encrustation of theories, concepts, and generalizations it might better do without. This is a subject where, for example, structure is often taken as sufficient evidence of function (a city machine carries with it an underground welfare state); structure, Michels and Ostrogorski notwithstanding, is cloudily defined in terms of worthwhile function (parties are "linkage devices" that "fulfill functions" or "serve as channels of representation"); structures do frictionless service in visions of party competition ("let us assume a party . . ."); and structural patterns are often thought to be inferable from levels of party competition (this is a one-party area so democracy must have gotten displaced into contested primaries) or efficiently indexed by statutes (having officially nonpartisan elections means not having party organizations). In marshaling material I have tried first of all to leave aside such ideational baggage by presenting individual data readings cleanly free of it. Yet second, in some particulars anyway, I have sought to allow better exploration of whether or under what conditions such baggage should be carried by determining what in fact covaries with what in a large data universe. In the same spirit I shied away from sorting the considerable diversity of American party structure into a few imposed categories, my "traditional party organization" category aside, and in this one variant that was coded for, I have taken care to show where its decision rules run up against blurry cases in the real world. Additional categories would probably darken rather than illuminate. The overall result is a large set of stripped-down data that offers openings rather than closure, conveys rather than resolves many of its dissonances and anomalies, and adds up to an invitation to pillage and speculate.

The state-by-state accounts in Part I are as terse as I could make them and still supply a sense of how I use evidence, an element of texture, and some particulars to be discussed later on. They average three paragraphs per state (the longer treatments in general come early). Still, the total amount of material is considerable and it may help to suggest three alternative ways of dealing with it. The first is to read the text and also the numerous footnotes referencing and often elaborating it; the combination amounts to, among other things, a bibliographic essay.

This I recommend to serious students of parties. The second is to read just the text, which is designed to be autonomous in itself and supply a relatively quick tour. Either of these courses permits a kind of systematic musing in going through the material, a consideration of what goes with what—as for example on the relation between having nonpartisan electoral systems and not having "traditional party organizations." How close is the association in fact? The third option is to sample Part I, go on to Part II to see the use I make of state-by-state material, and then circle back and read more fully. As a sampling strategy I recommend reading Chapter 1; the sections on Rhode Island, New Jersey, and Pennsylvania in Chapter 2 (these three states are more or less typical of the chapter); the introduction and sections on (more or less typical) West Virginia, Maryland, and Indiana in Chapter 3; the introduction and sections on (anomalous) Louisiana, (more or less typical) Alabama and Florida, and (anomalous) Virginia and Texas in Chapter 4; the introduction and sections on (more or less anomalous) Massachusetts and Michigan, (more or less typical) Wisconsin, (anomalous) Minnesota, (more or less typical) Nebraska, and (anomalous) Oklahoma in Chapter 5; the section on (more or less typical) Montana, (anomalous) New Mexico, and (more or less typical) California and Washington in Chapter 6; and Chapter 7, which summarizes Part I and introduces new material only in its last paragraph.

Part II, written in essay style, is a mixture of treatments beginning with Chapter 8, which casts back through American history for antecedents or causes of the geographic pattern of party structure evident in the late 1960s. I focus mostly on antecedent structural patterns, taking up briefly the scantily documented early nineteenth century (touching on New York's Albany Regency, for example) and then the much better documented period around 1900—much of the best work is recent—where I stop to take note of local structure and also of the impressive family of state party organizations of the time (Platt's in New York, Quay's in Pennsylvania, the Gorman-Rasin organization in Maryland, and Elkins's extraordinary combine in West Virginia are examples). In general I document and emphasize the considerable place-specific continuity in forms of local party structure over the last century or (in some particulars) century and a half, and take up in addition the relationship between local and state forms around 1900. I look into the overall geographic incidence of city machines, which have been far from universal. On causes of geographic structural patterns I think I have better luck suggesting when and where they might be sought than pinpointing them myself, though I briefly examine such familiar matters as the relative size of immigrant populations (not very helpful), urban versus rural environments (it helps), the move to nonpartisan elections in cities (probably much less consequential than it looks), past patterns of two-party electoral competition (probably a washout), and political culture (hard to get a handle on it). The impressive thing is the structural continuity.

Chapter 9 is a speculative, cross-sectional inquiry into relations between twentieth-century geographic patterns of party structure and such patterns in other phenomena. Thirteen "organization states" (ones having especially prominent "traditional party organizations" in the late 1960s) stand against the rest in a dichotomy capturing party structure. What used to be called "pressure politics"—a variety of free-wheeling pressure group activity—seems to have had a low incidence in organization states. I briefly consider the "pluralist" and "community-power" traditions of studying urban politics, locating the sorts of places they study in respectively organization and nonorganization territory. I make a case that "issue density" may run low in the electoral processes of organization states, and that labor unions, demagogues (suitably defined), and ideology-based mass organizations have on the whole operated in electoral politics more effectively outside organization territory. Around the middle of the century social class cleavages in voting (the South aside) seem to have been more pronounced outside organization territory.

Chapter 10 shifts to cross-sectional statistical analysis, investigating relations between electoral structure and the sizes of states' "public economies" in the 1950s, 1960s, and 1970s, defined as ratios of state and local revenue or expenditures to personal income received (or, in one calculation, to income produced). The chapter includes a series of figures (drawings), each of which presents state-by-state ratio data on revenue or expenditure for a specified year as well as data on party structure, and also a series of corresponding tables that present the results of equations based on data displayed in the figures. The figures, which permit examination of particulars, are especially informative.

Apart from New York, "organization states" used to run exceptionally small public economies, a relation I speculate about by introducing five hypothetical causes: their party organizations' incentive structures, their relative lack of openness to interest groups, low "issue density" in their electoral politics, their relative inhospitality to bureaucracy, and political cultures grown up around their electoral and governmental processes. Particular settings or instruments touched on in this chapter, all in the interest of exploring relationships between electoral structure and "public economies," include New York's reform-vs.-regulars tradition and the state's Rockefeller governorship of 1958-1973, North

Dakota's Nonpartisan League, Minnesota's Farmer-Labor party, Louisiana's Long family, Virginia's Byrd regime, New Hampshire's *Manchester Union Leader*, Massachusetts's Brahmin tradition, California's recent Proposition 13 movement, Philadelphia's once-dominant Republican machine, and Chicago's century-old political economy built on "tax-fixing" by ward organizations.

Chapter 11 considers more generally the American connection between electoral structure and assertive government during the twentieth century. Attention is given to the Progressive period, the Democratic New Deal coalition, and briefly the present. I concentrate on the intellectual side of Progressivism (amended in scope enough to include Ostrogorski's work in 1902), taking up the effort by Herbert Croly and others to rethink electoral politics in a setting where political parties (nineteenth-century patronage parties at all levels) seemed to have become an impediment to both democracy and government. The arguments of this remarkable endeavor have dropped from the repertoire of post-1932 political scientists captivated by parties, even though the Progressive statement probably remains as good a normative-cum-analytic guide to American twentieth-century subnational government (which it helped lay the basis for) as anything else. In treating the New Deal coalition (from the mid-1930s through roughly the late 1960s) I concentrate on political structure and activity rather than on theory, in particular on the extraordinary turnabout of local patronage parties in Roosevelt's first term—something like a change of signs—as they moved from being Progressivism's targets to Democratic Presidents' pillars of support, from enemies of assertive government to—at the national level anyway—its collaborators. Political science followed not more than a decade behind, supplying notably Key's and E. E. Schattschneider's visions of parties as engines of government in which the Progressive hostility toward received American party organization hardly made an appearance. It was as if Croly and Ostrogorski had never written. Doing full justice to the role of traditional party organizations in the Democrats' national Roosevelt-through-Johnson coalition would probably take a full book, so what I have to say should be put down as surmise or conjecture. But at any rate my claim is about structure: that the national Democratic combination of these decades was to a significant degree a structural arrangement among Presidents, local party organizations, and also unions that is insufficiently understood—as are its policy effects—by dwelling on parties as voter alignments. I close with comparable assertions about the present.

A Geography of Organization
in the Late 1960s

CHAPTER I

Forms of Organization

The objective of Part I is to identify and characterize party or partylike organizations that were operating consequentially in American nominating processes at lower levels in the late 1960s. "Traditional party organizations" will receive the most attention, but the net has been cast more widely in order to pick up scattered instances of other sorts. This is done to identify some nonstandard forms of organization worth discussing later in Part II, and also to complicate a bit, in the interest of accuracy and texture, the basic American twentieth-century dichotomy between having strong party organization (the traditional patronage variety) and, at least at the nominating level, having little or no organization at all in environments where candidates are supplied for the most part by uncontrolled primaries.

I should begin by defining some terms. In the case of *organization* it will be useful to start with a broader construction than "party" implies, then retreat back through forms I note only episodically in the state-by-state reports, and end with forms I try to track systematically.[1] Let us say that an "organization" is a group of people who consciously coordinate their activities to achieve an end, and that the pertinent end in this case is the nomination of a candidate or candidates for public office.[2] Entities meeting these requirements include, first of all, candidate organizations—groups devoted to the advancement of just one candidate—which are the most widespread form of organization specific to

[1] A number of political scientists have presented definitions of party and partylike entities. Sources especially useful in the framing of the discussion in this chapter were: Edward C. Banfield and James Q. Wilson, *City Politics* (Cambridge: Harvard University Press and M.I.T. Press, 1963), chs. 9, 10; Frank J. Sorauf, *Party and Representation: Legislative Politics in Pennsylvania* (New York: Atherton, 1963), ch. 3; David M. Olson, "The Structure of Electoral Politics," *Journal of Politics* 29(1967), 352-367; *ibid.*, "Toward a Typology of County Party Organizations," *Southwestern Social Science Quarterly* 48(1968), 558-572; *ibid.*, "District Party Organization and Legislative Performance in Congress," *Journal of Politics* 36(1974), 482-486.

[2] This draws on James Q. Wilson's definition of "party organization" in *Political Organizations* (New York: Basic Books, 1973), pp. 95-96.

American electoral environments.[3] Some of the more interesting of these will be noted, but for the most part I regard candidate organizations as unremarkable and leave them alone. Perhaps also meeting the requirements, strictly read, are organizations dealing chiefly in other things but incidentally in elections—in particular, newspapers, private corporations in general, and unions. I document some of the more obvious and consequential ventures into nominating politics by such organizations, but otherwise I pass them by.

Left over after this narrowing are organizations I do in principle try to track systematically—that is, organizations specific to the electoral sector and devoted to advancing a number of candidates for a number of offices (rather than a single candidate for one office). To these the label "party" or "partylike" reasonably applies. More precisely, I try to track such organizations in instances where they seem to exercise influence in nominating processes and in which the nominations at issue are worth winning—that is, in parties that are dominant or at least respectably competitive in local and district elections and hence are generators of public officials (Democrats in Brooklyn, both parties in Indianapolis, but not Republicans in Brooklyn). It will come as no surprise that getting a sure handle on organization in many of the country's nominating environments is close to a hopeless task even when good accounts are available: the softer forms of party or partylike organization, perceivable as nods, nudges, and rumors, are hard to distinguish from nothing at all and act as a minimal constraint on individual candidates. I pick up what I can of these. But a number of forms are fairly easy to follow, including traditional party organization.

By *nominating processes*, another general term that needs discussion, I mean primaries, caucuses, and conventions that confer official party nominations, but I include also the processes of nonpartisan elections—the familiar system used by most American cities and sometimes by other jurisdictions in which a first-round election is ordinarily followed by a runoff, the ballots have no party labels, and the vote is open to all, regardless of party registration. Nonpartisan elections are of course not a direct equivalent of partisan nominating processes, but they achieve the comparable effect of converting fields of potential candidates into small sets of real candidates. And, as a practical matter, nonpartisan elections offer the same sort of opportunity that standard partisan primaries do to organizations who wish to promote sets of

[3] For a treatment of candidate organization see *ibid.*, pp. 115-116. Joseph A. Schlesinger's essay entitled "Political Party Organization," ch. 18 in James March (ed.), *Handbook of Organizations* (Chicago: Rand McNally, 1965), is mostly about candidate organization.

candidates. In both cases a lack of widely available information that might be used to sort or identify either potential candidates or candidates appearing in an undifferentiated list on a ballot (in the nonpartisan instance, ballots at both stages) invites unofficial slating or endorsements. In fact some kinds of organizations confine their activities to one type of process or the other, but traditional party organizations have operated indiscriminately in both, promoting candidates wherever the opportunity arises.

Finally, the special term *traditional party organization* is needed since no other has quite the right meaning. This term, its shortened form "traditional organization," and its acronym "TPO" will be used interchangeably in the following chapters to refer to any organization at the level of county, city, city ward, township, or other local jurisdiction about which all five of the following statements can be made:

(1) *It has substantial autonomy.* It is not the creation of, nor does its maintenance depend on the internal incentive structure of, a separate organization that operates mostly outside electoral politics—in particular a corporation or a labor union. It may derive a significant part of its resources from public officials or party organizations at higher governmental levels (particularly the state level), but it nonetheless has the capacity to act as a substantially independent power base in dealing with such officials or organizations.

(2) *It lasts a long time.* Its life span is measurable in decades or generations rather than in months or years. It can survive leadership changes. A qualification here, to be elaborated later, is that in some environments what persists is a pattern of organization rather than a set of specifiable organizations.

(3) *Its internal structure has an important element of hierarchy.* Its leader or leaders exercise a good deal of influence in organization activities, including the promotion of candidates, and are widely recognized as party leaders in their locales. In fact, TPOs are commonly referred to by the names of their leaders, as in "the Smith organization," "the Smith-Jones organization," or sometimes even "the Smith-Jones-Brown organization."

(4) *It regularly tries to bring about the nomination of candidates for a wide range of public offices.* The range ordinarily includes county, state assembly, state senate, and (often nonpartisan) municipal offices; sometimes judgeships; sometimes congressional and statewide offices. The effort takes the form of at least "endorsing" candidates, and ordinarily in cases of local and district offices the stronger form of "slating" or "putting up a slate" of candidates. "Slating" carries an implication of generating or adding to an official field of candidates by inducing

people to enter it, and perhaps also limiting it by inducing others to stay out.

(5) *It relies substantially on "material" incentives, and not much on "purposive" incentives, in engaging people to do organization work or to supply organization support* . This draws on James Q. Wilson's typology of incentive systems that organizations use to maintain themselves.[4] TPOs have relied substantially on what Wilson calls "individual material" inducements—that is, "tangible rewards: money, or things and services readily priced in monetary terms," of kinds that can be assigned to particular individuals.[5] These may include appointive or elective positions in government, contracts or other preferments supplied by government, economic opportunities that result from working in or around government, and exemptions from strict law enforcement on such matters as vice and taxes.[6] Benefits may go to supporters outside the organization—for example, voters and contributors of money—as well as to workers within it, though the distinction between outsiders and insiders is blurry. Probably most TPOs have relied also to a substantial degree on "solidary" inducements, either of a "specific" kind—for example, honorary appointments conferring prestige—or of a "collective" kind—for example, the enjoyment that comes from working together with other people.[7] But TPOs have not depended significantly on "purposive" inducements—that is, they have not counted very much on workers or supporters inspired to activity by issues, principles, causes, or ideologies.[8]

Organizations that satisfy these five conditions routinely turn up in American settings of the late 1960s, which gives confidence that the five belong together in a definitional set. Still, the country's local environments have generated a lot of inventive organizational forms, and it will be important to try to take a close look at phenomena that meet the conditions ambiguously or meet some but not all of them. Ambiguity can arise, for example, on the matter of organizational autonomy: in rural plantation areas that support the practice of multiple-office slating, it is often hard to tell whether political organization operates independently of economic organization or as just another expression of it. And a number of settings support lavish patronage transactions but lack any trace of party or partylike organizations ca-

---

[4] Wilson, *Political Organizations*, ch. 3 on organizations in general, ch. 6 on political parties.

[5] *Ibid.*, pp. 33, 36-39, 97-101, quotation at p. 33.

[6] This borrows heavily from *ibid.*, p. 97.

[7] *Ibid.*, pp. 33-34, 39-45, 110-115.

[8] *Ibid.*, pp. 34-35, 45-51, 101-110.

pable of boosting people into office; individual officeholders, once they somehow reach office on their own, use government jobs to build their own personal electoral bases. Near misses or anomalies of these and other sorts will be noted.

Is "traditional party organization" just another label for a "machine"?[9] In the usage here the answer is no. "Machine" ordinarily refers to a party organization that exercises overall control over government at a city or county level.[10] "Traditional party organization" has a broader reference. All "machines" at the local level are TPOs: the term "machine" will be used strictly hereafter (except in quotations) to refer to a TPO in control of a city or county government. But not all TPOs are machines. An organization might meet all five conditions set out above and thus be a TPO, yet not have overall control of a government. It might slate for a broad set of offices yet normally win nominations and elections in only one city ward or a set of wards. It might control a set of citywide or countywide offices but not the major executive offices. It might help put people in office yet lose control of them once they get there—losing access to the jobs, contracts, and other resources that officeholders can dispose of. This happens occasionally with mayors. Moreover, a TPO might control a central government sometimes but not usually or always—the old Tammany Hall pattern—thus at times adding up to a "machine," strictly speaking, and at times not. And a TPO might have to coexist in its city or county with one or more other TPOs. We shall come across instances of locales where Democrats and Republicans each field a TPO, and instances where one major party accommodates two or more TPOs by itself. These last cases, which stretch the terminology to its limits, will require special definitional attention.

In the ensuing sketches each state is given a score gauging the prominence of TPOs in its politics in the late 1960s on a 1-to-5 scale. In principle the score for each state is an average of scores for each of its lower political units (counties in most states) weighted appropriately according to population size, and each contributory score for a lower unit registers the incidence and influence of TPOs in its own electoral politics: minimal scores for locales with no TPOs at all, somewhat higher scores

[9] Some especially useful treatments of the term "machine" may be found in *ibid.*, pp. 97-101; Banfield and Wilson, *City Politics*, ch. 9; and Raymond E. Wolfinger, *The Politics of Progress* (Englewood Cliffs, N.J.: Prentice-Hall, 1974), pp. 99-106.

[10] This is in the spirit of Wallace S. Sayre and Herbert Kaufman's discussion of Tammany Hall—of the times, and by what rough criteria, Tammany "can be said to have exercised dominant supervision over" the New York City mayoralty. See *Governing New York City: Politics in the Metropolis* (New York: Norton, 1965), pp. 688-689.

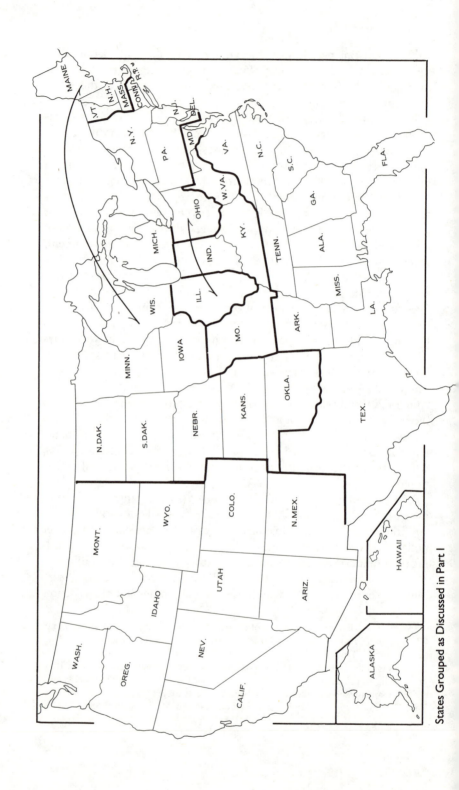

States Grouped as Discussed in Part I

for locales where TPOs have exercised decisive influence in nominating processes for some lower-level offices some of the time (and where the TPO nominees have subsequently won election), and on up to maximal scores for locales where TPOs have exercised decisive influence in nominating processes for major and minor offices year after year (and again the nominees have won election). This is the plan in principle. In practice, given the evidence, it is impossible to be anywhere near so exact. My fallback procedure is to circumvent the arithmetic and make scoring judgments about states as wholes, basing them on whatever evidence there is but staying as close as possible to the logic of positing scores for locales and then weighting and averaging them. Scoring by state makes sense: states have in fact varied as states in the prominence of their TPOs. Of course many states have varied internally also, since TPOs as a rule have been more of a presence (if a presence at all) in metropolitan areas than in rural areas. But cities located in the same state almost always bear a family resemblance to each other in organizational forms, and most states with urban TPOs have had some rural TPOs also. The typical state assigned a 5 on the TPO scale for the late 1960s is a predominantly metropolitan state with influential TPOs operating in most or all of its metropolitan and some of its rural areas.

The fifty states will be discussed one by one, with each assigned a TPO score at the end of its sketch. They are grouped as follows (see map). Considered first, in Chapter 2, are eight "organization" states that run from Rhode Island west through Illinois (but skipping Indiana). Next are five "persistently factional" states that run from Maryland west through Missouri (Chapter 3), then the eleven ex-Confederate Southern states (Chapter 4), then a heterogeneous group of thirteen states that extend from northern New England west along the Canadian border and south through the Midwestern plains (Chapter 5), then finally the thirteen states of the mountain region and Pacific West (Chapter 6). The 1970 population of each state, county, and municipality will be given as it is introduced.

Regular Organization States

A traditional party organization that operates without sustained opposition inside its own party from any other organization of the same kind—the party may nonetheless contain a "reform" opposition—is often called a "regular" organization. Such "regular" apparatuses are the chief concern of this chapter. An efficient way to detect these, as well as other sorts of units that back candidates for nomination, is to look carefully at accounts of direct primaries—the process almost all states have used to nominate local and district officials since early in the twentieth century. Candidates in nearly all states today, once they pay fees or submit lists of petition signatures, can enter primaries and in principle compete as equals. But the exceptions include Rhode Island and Connecticut, the first two states to be discussed.

RHODE ISLAND (949,723) _____

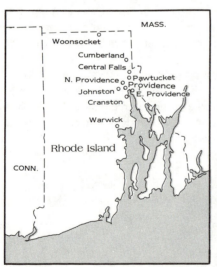

Direct primaries date back only to 1947 in Rhode Island, and candidates officially endorsed by party committees receive first-place listing on the primary ballot and asterisks beside their names. This used to be a tight system; until the 1970s all but a handful of candidates for the state legislature won nomination without primary challenges, and in the dominant Democratic party only one challenger ever defeated an official endorsee in a primary for congressional or statewide office—Claiborne Pell in his first run for the Senate in 1960.[1]

[1] "Senate," "Senator," and "Senatorial" will be used to refer to the U.S. Senate; when

These rules and patterns do not reveal whether the state has supported "traditional party organizations," though they suggest an environment in which such enterprises might flourish. In fact they have flourished. Providence (179,116), the state's metropolis, has supported a Democratic machine equaling Chicago's in control over city affairs during most of the last half-century. From 1941 through 1974 only three people (including two strong party leaders) held the mayoralty and only two—each doubling as head of the Department of Public Works—served as Democratic city chairman. Providence had no civil service requirements in the 1960s; party leaders distributed some 2,800 jobs in the public sector more or less equally by ward, ensuring the allegiance of city councillors, ward committeemen, and other subordinates. Members of ward committees, according to a report on the city's Fox Point area, "were responsible for the orderly distribution of patronage jobs, of neighborhood improvements, [and] of a wide range of preferential treatments consisting of contract awards, ticket-fixing or protecting numbers running."[2] Organization leaders used the endorsement system to exercise control over Democratic nominations. From 1948 through 1968, in 540 instances of nomination for mayor or city council, only four resulted in victories by challengers over organization endorsees (two occurred when a regular endorsee got mixed up in a scandal over a stolen car ring). This is an outstanding, perhaps unparalleled, record of slating effectiveness.[3]

---

lowercased, these words will refer to state senates. Sources on primary contesting in Rhode Island are Duane Lockard, *New England State Politics* (Princeton: Princeton University Press, 1959), pp. 187-190, 205; Elmer E. Cornwell, Jr., "Rhode Island: The 'Long Count' and its Aftermath," part 3 in George Goodwin, Jr., and Victoria Schuck (eds.), *Party Politics in the New England States* (Durham, N.H.: New England Center for Continuing Education, 1968), pp. 26-27; Elmer E. Cornwell, Jr., et al., *The Rhode Island General Assembly* (Washington, D.C.: American Political Science Association, 1970), p. 140; Richard A. Gabriel, *The Political Machine in Rhode Island* (Kingston: Bureau of Government Research, University of Rhode Island, 1970), p. 12.

[2] Rita Moniz, "The Portuguese of New Bedford, Massachusetts and Providence, Rhode Island: A Comparative Micro-Analysis of Political Attitudes and Behavior" (Ph.D. dissertation, Brown University, 1979), p. 240. The report here at pp. 236-241, based on interviews in 1977-1978 with Fox Point committee members who were reflecting back on several decades of experience, gives a good picture of a strong and industrious ward organization.

[3] The source of most of this paragraph's material on Providence is Gabriel, *Political Machine in Rhode Island*, pp. 11-16. The source on civil service and tenure of city leaders is John A. Perrotta, "Machine Influence on a Community Action Program: The Case of Providence, Rhode Island," *Polity* 9(1977), 483-485. Perrotta on contracts: "Other kinds of patronage—such as municipal contracts—also are available to the machine. Municipal procedures are sufficiently flexible to permit machine leaders to circumvent bidding regulations and award contracts on the basis of favoritism" (p. 484).

Elsewhere in the state, a 1959 source refers to Democratic machines in a number of smaller cities,[4] and a 1970 source points to "the continued existence of machine style politics in most of the older urban centers of the state," specifying Providence and three cities with formally nonpartisan elections—Pawtucket (76,984), Woonsocket (46,820), and Central Falls (18,716)—but goes on to say that organizations in the last three differed in their ability to discipline members.[5] A 1977 source tells of strong Democratic organizations in these same three nonpartisan cities that sometimes fielded "regulars" against slates of "insurgents" in municipal elections; of a Democratic machine electing slates of nominees and distributing patronage jobs in North Providence (24,337); of a Democratic "Hayden organization" in control of local government and nominating processes since World War II in Cumberland (26,605); and a pattern of competitive slating among organization Democrats, reform Democrats, and Republicans in formally nonpartisan East Providence (48,207), a prosperous suburb.[6] All the locales discussed here, including Providence, are located in the northeastern section of the state, a Democratic area of cities, suburbs, and mill towns where a majority of the state's population resides. Republicans evidently used to operate a number of traditional organizations in both rural and urban areas—a strong Republican machine ran Pawtucket, for example—before the party lost its important local bases during the New Deal.[7]

In the 1940s and 1950s, notably during the governorship of Dennis J. Roberts (1950-1958),[8] the state's local Democratic organizations served as building blocks for an organization at the state level exercising extraordinary control over nominations and government. Roberts's considerable authority as leader of the state Democratic party,

[4] Lockard, *New England State Politics*, p. 203.

[5] Gabriel, *Political Machine in Rhode Island*, p. 3.

[6] Steven G. Calabresi, "Rhode Island Politics" (Yale course paper, 1977), pp. 8-12.

[7] Lockard, *New England State Politics*, p. 172; Gabriel, *Political Machine in Rhode Island*, pp. 4-6. In the early 1930s a Republican machine in Pawtucket "considered the best in the state" gave way neatly and quickly to an eye-catching Democratic machine that ruled until the early 1950s. See Matthew J. Smith, "The Real McCoy in the Bloodless Revolution of 1935," *Rhode Island History* 32(1973), 67-70, quotation at p. 70; and Joseph Kelly, "Boss Rule and Reform in Pawtucket, Rhode Island," pp. 19-22 in Robert W. Sutton, Jr. (ed.), *Rhode Island Local Government: Past, Present, Future* (Kingston: Bureau of Government Research, University of Rhode Island, 1974).

[8] Roberts won his first gubernatorial election in 1950; his immediate successor first won election in 1958. The practice here will be to refer to public officials' time in office by years of election rather than years of inauguration. Hence, for example, 1952-1960 for President Eisenhower.

according to one account, was "based upon his control over the Providence Democratic organization, a power he did not relinquish when he ceased being the city's mayor and became governor."[9] But no state leader achieved Roberts's influence during the 1960s, and the results of two well-publicized Democratic primaries in the mid-1970s suggested that the party was losing its capacity to slate for higher offices: in 1974 a party-endorsed incumbent Congressman lost a primary to Edward P. Beard, a house painter who came across well on television and "campaign[ed] vigorously and issu[ed] a constant stream of proposals"; and in 1976 a party endorsee for Senator lost to Richard P. Lorber, a Cadillac-Pontiac dealer who introduced expensive media techniques.[10] In addition, the Providence organization split in half in 1974 as the result of a spirited personal feud between the mayor and party chairman— nothing to do with issues or programs seems to have been involved— and the mayoralty went to a Republican.[11] Still, an overall TPO score for the state in the late 1960s: a solid 5.[12]

CONNECTICUT (3,032,217) _____

In Connecticut, as in Rhode Island, direct primaries came in late (1955), party units at various levels of office formally endorse candidates, endorsees challenged in primaries earn asterisks and first-place listing on the ballot, and a sizable majority of endorsees wins nomina-

[9] Lockard, *New England State Politics*, p. 203, and in general on state party organization, pp. 203-206. The builder of the state organization was J. Howard McGrath in the early 1940s. See Jay S. Goodman, *The Democrats and Labor in Rhode Island, 1952-62: Changes in the Old Alliance* (Providence: Brown University Press, 1967), pp. 82-83.

[10] On the 1960s see Cornwell, "The 'Long Count,' " p. 27. On Beard: *Congressional Quarterly Weekly*, August 31, 1974, p. 2379 (source of quotation); and September 14, 1974, p. 2527. On Lorber: *ibid.*, September 18, 1976, p. 2533; and September 25, 1976, p. 2608.

[11] Calabresi, "Rhode Island Politics," pp. 10-11; Perrotta, "Machine Influence," pp. 484-485; Neal R. Peirce, *The New England States: People, Politics, and Power in the Six New England States* (New York: Norton, 1976), pp. 174-176. Democratic organization control of nominations for the state legislature fell off in Providence in the early 1970s. See Victor L. Profughi, "Rhode Island: The Party Is Sick But It Isn't Dead—Yet," in Josephine F. Milburn and William Doyle (eds.), *New England Political Parties* (Cambridge, Mass.: Schenkman, 1983), pp. 75-76.

[12] Profughi, "Rhode Island," provides a brief general account of loosening organizational hold on Rhode Island's Democratic nominations at various levels of office in the 1970s. See pp. 75-78. Organizational influence may have gotten restored a bit by a shift to closed primaries (registered Democrats only) in 1978, but media technology was nonetheless very clearly bringing about a politics of individual candidacies in elections for high offices. See pp. 78-79, 83-87, 92-93.

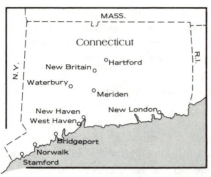

tion without being challenged in primaries. Party leaders or committees in rural and suburban as well as urban areas have a record of seeking out and appraising candidates before making endorsements. That is, they have recruited, and according to a recent study were still doing so in 1980.[13] At the level of governor and Senator only five Connecticut party endorsees (three Republicans and two Democrats) have ever had to compete in primaries, and only one has lost—in 1970 a Democratic Senatorial endorsee lost to challenger Joseph E. Duffey, an anti–Vietnam War activist and national chairman of the Americans for Democratic Action. As in the Rhode Island case, these Connecticut rules and patterns reveal nothing conclusive about "traditional party organizations," but in fact the state's urban centers have supported them.

The best-documented local environment is New Haven (137,707) of the late 1950s, then dominated by a Democratic organization run by John M. Golden and Arthur T. Barbieri in alliance with Mayor Richard C. Lee, or—perhaps another plausible way of looking at it—headed by all three. Party leaders presided over the selection of candidates for aldermanic, citywide, and state legislative offices. For aldermen, "ordinarily the initiative for recruiting suitable candidates lies in the wards, but party leaders often intervene directly, and usually they have no difficulty either in getting their own candidates accepted by the ward committee or in denying nominations to hopefuls they find objectionable."[14] Leadership control over nominating processes and the city

---

[13] On recruiting activity see, e.g., James D. Barber's treatment of state legislative nominating in *The Lawmakers: Recruitment and Adaptation to Legislative Life* (New Haven: Yale University Press, 1965), pp. 26-29, 72-76, 122-129, 169-174, 237-240. For treatments of primary contesting for lower offices in the first decade of the challenge primary see Duane Lockard, *Connecticut's Challenge Primary: A Study in Legislative Politics* (New York: McGraw-Hill, Eagleton Case #7, 1960), p. 24; and National Municipal League, *Ten Years of Connecticut's Challenge Primary* (New York: National Municipal League, 1966). The report on recent years is Barbara Burrell, "Local Party Committees in Connecticut: Membership, Task Performance and Party Vitality," paper delivered at the 1980 conference of the Northeastern Political Science Association.

[14] Robert A. Dahl, *Who Governs? Democracy and Power in an American City* (New Haven: Yale University Press, 1961), p. 112 and more generally pp. 104-114. See also Wolfinger, *Politics of Progress*, pp. 204-211; and Lockard, *New England State Politics*, pp. 301-302. The only reference on state legislative slating is a brief mention in Lockard, but there is no doubt it regularly took place.

government (notably the board of aldermen) depended heavily on the particularistic distribution of material goods—notably contracts, insurance accounts, and favorable tax assessments in exchange for campaign contributions and other support, and several hundred patronage jobs in exchange for salary kickbacks, party support, and party work.[15] An upper stratum of party leaders is said to have gained a good deal of indirect material profit from operating in and around government. For example, "a contractor hoping to build a new school would be likely to do business with John M. Golden, . . . senior partner in a bond and insurance agency."[16] The regime of Lee, Barbieri, and Golden prevailed without much electoral opposition until Lee retired as mayor in 1969, after which a stripped-down "Barbieri organization" won a series of close mayoral elections against an alliance of reform Democrats before losing the mayoralty and going into decline in the mid-1970s.[17]

Traditional party organizations regularly appear in less comprehensive accounts of other Connecticut cities.[18] In Hartford (158,017) of the 1950s and 1960s, the "Bailey organization," based on patronage and headed by local, state, and national leader John M. Bailey, seems to have dominated Democratic nominating processes and to have endorsed candidates with considerable success in the city's nonpartisan municipal elections. The opposition in the latter was a good-government group called the Citizens Charter Committee (CCC), led by, among others, Abraham Ribicoff, later Democratic governor and Senator with Bailey's support.[19] "The Bailey machine," according to one

[15] Wolfinger's treatment of New Haven in *The Politics of Progress* (Englewood Cliffs, N.J.: Prentice-Hall, 1974), pp. 74-87, 92-99, and 104-105, gives an exceptionally rich picture of material incentives and transactions in an organization environment.

[16] *Ibid.*, p. 80. "The income that some party leaders received directly from the public treasury was dwarfed by trade from people who hoped to do business with the city or wanted friendly treatment at city hall, and thus sought to ingratiate themselves with the influential."

[17] For an account of patronage dealings in the Bartholomew Guida mayoralty of 1969-1975 see Michael Johnston, "Patrons and Clients, Jobs and Machines: A Case Study of the Uses of Patronage," *American Political Science Review* 73(1979), 385-398.

[18] The best general guide is Judith A. Center, "Reform's Labours Lost: Two Eras of Party Change in Connecticut and Massachusetts" (Ph.D. dissertation, Yale University, 1981), pp. 78-91, covering the years 1969-1976.

[19] Clear pieces of evidence are that the organization narrowly defeated the CCC in a hard-fought council election in 1953, and that regular, patronage-oriented Democrats ran the council in 1968. Hartford switched from partisan to nonpartisan elections in 1947 and later back to partisan again starting in 1969. Sources on Hartford are Joseph I. Lieberman, *The Power Broker: A Biography of John M. Bailey, Modern Political Boss* (Boston: Houghton Mifflin, 1966), pp. 74-82, 101, 114-115, 160-165 (on the 1953 council election), 260-261, 335; Everett C. Ladd, Jr., *Ideology in America: Change and Response in a City, a Suburb, and a Small Town* (Ithaca: Cornell University Press, 1969), pp. 122-130, 298-300 (on the 1968 council), 310-319; and Clyde D. McKee, Jr., "Con-

report, was "a traditional one in its commitment to organization maintenance more than to substantive programs, in its pragmatism, in its
fear of issues, in that it does not see in politics an instrument for social
change."[20] Democratic "powerhouses"—the local idiom for machines—are said to have operated in the 1960s in Waterbury (108,033)
and Meriden (55,959); the former evidently erupted in acrimony along
ethnic lines as its organization eroded in the 1970s.[21] Norwalk
(79,113) has been an exception among the state's cities in its lack of
traditional organization, or it was at any rate in the 1970s, when
loosely organized reform Democrats ran successfully in municipal elections against three other parties.[22] At least two Democratic machines
ran at full steam as recently as the late 1970s—in West Haven (52,851),
where Harold Allen, Jr., in league with the mayor and the mayor's
brother, slated candidates and distributed patronage from a base in the
health department; and in Bridgeport (156,542), where Mayor John C.
Mandanici (1975-1981) exercised conspicuous control over party
nominations and the city government until brought down by an em-
broilment with the Federal Bureau of Investigation and an election defeat in 1981. The latter was notable for firebombings of both sides during the campaign and Mandanici's carting off thousands of agency
documents when he left office.[23]

---

necticut: A Political System in Transition," in Milburn and Doyle (eds.), *New England Political Parties*, pp. 32-34. On Ribicoff: Lieberman, pp. 99-100, 164-165.

[20] Ladd, *Ideology in America*, p. 130. When the city council arranged a reception for federal Model Cities money in 1968, "few observers doubted the party had any other objective in its action than keeping control of mammoth patronage possibilities" (p. 299). On techniques: "Rather than challenging the theory of nonpartisanism, Bailey merely used the procedures within the theory to build power for an urban Democratic machine. He recruited candidates for the city council, assumed responsibility for circulating their petitions, paid their filing fees, raised campaign funds, and recruited party workers" (McKee, "Connecticut," p. 33).

[21] Information supplied by Judith A. Center.

[22] Center, "Reform's Labours Lost," pp. 86-90; Paul Bass, "Third Parties Feel Lure of Grass Roots," *New York Times*, August 18, 1985, pp. CN1, 6-7.

[23] On West Haven: Robert Palm, "The Bully of Campbell Avenue," *Connecticut*, February 1980, pp. 39-41, 88-89. Palm's characterization of West Haven: "One of the most highly politicized cities anywhere, one with a long reputation for cronyism and bossism, a sort of miniature Chicago" (p. 39). On Bridgeport: "In the Common Council, where the Mayor brings the semimonthly meetings to order with a huge gavel, all 20 aldermen are Democrats, and almost all the votes are unanimous, with no public debate. Bridgeport's delegation to the General Assembly in Hartford also votes as a bloc, as do its representatives in Democratic Party gatherings. . . . Members of the Common Council and other city bodies all praise Mr. Mandanici; according to opponents that is a prerequisite for membership" (Matthew L. Wald, "Bridgeport Is Struggling With Its Image and Reality," *New York Times*, December 22, 1978, p. B3). Other sources on Bridgeport are

The Democratic organizations of Bridgeport, New Haven, Hartford, and Waterbury, all now weak or nonexistent, presented a decisive alliance in state Democratic politics in the 1950s and 1960s as the core of John Bailey's celebrated organization at the state level—once discussed by Duane Lockard under the title "Democratic Party Organization: The Dominance of City Machines."[24] Bailey, to the "big-city barons . . . was never boss but always broker. He was first among equals. He led, but together they decided on candidates. They gave him absolute legislative support, but he gave them patronage and places on the state ticket."[25] The combination was formidable: in a well-publicized though unsuccessful challenge to Bailey in 1958, a labor-oriented liberal who was trying to win a statewide congressional nomination had to seek convention delegates in the small towns.[26]

Connecticut probably deserves a TPO score of 5 for the late 1960s, given the strength and character of its Democratic organizations as well

---

Richard L. Madden, "Mayoral Races Are Focus of Connecticut's Voters," *New York Times*, November 1, 1981, p. 50; Robert E. Tomasson, "Bridgeport's New Mayor Finds Some Bare File Cupboards," *New York Times*, November 20, 1981, p. B1; Leonard J. Grimaldi, "Ex-Mayor Plans a Comeback," *New York Times*, August 22, 1982, p. CN8; and information supplied by Judith A. Center. The Mandanici administration is said to be "remembered, among other things, for 19 indictments and 15 convictions—a remarkable performance, even by Bridgeport standards" (John Birchard, "Bridgeport Broil," *Connecticut*, October 1983, p. 36).

[24] A general comment on the decline of the state's urban organizations appears in Richard L. Madden, "Parties' Clout Eroded," *New York Times*, November 11, 1979, p. CN1. On Hartford, a recent treatment deals with the Kinsella family, "fixtures in Hartford and stalwarts in its Irish political machine, long run by Thomas J. Spellacy, John P. Kelly, and John M. Bailey. . . . The Bailey machine, like Frog Hollow and the other South End Irish neighborhoods that were its bulwark, has long since disappeared" (David Margolick, "Impeachment Move Sets Precedent in Connecticut," *New York Times*, May 3, l984, p. B1). On Bailey's state organization: Lockard, *New England State Politics*, pp. 257-266. "Although there are rivalries and dissension in all these organizations, in most convention battles the top men of the city machines usually manage to present a solid front for bargaining purposes. With their local power and patronage, the city bosses cooperate with the state leaders only as it seems convenient" (p. 258). Lockard mentions "a dozen or more city bosses" at one point but emphasizes the role of the four organizations listed above (pp. 257-258).

[25] Lieberman, *Power Broker: John M. Bailey*, p. 340. Blocs from the same four cities gave Bailey his core of support in the legislature (pp. 130-131).

[26] Joseph P. Lyford, *Candidate* (New York: McGraw-Hill, Eagleton Case #9, 1960). Lyford, himself the candidate, recalled: "By and large, delegates from the big cities are not expected to exercise independent judgment. They are handled like poker chips by their local political leaders." "In the past the small-town delegates had never been as effective as those from the larger cities because they acted as individuals and usually refused to be 'delivered' in blocs and coordinated into working coalitions" (pp. 2, 19). See also Lieberman, *Power Broker*, pp. 216-219.

as its overall Democratic orientation. Still, the score is assigned with misgivings because the state's Republicans, significantly more successful in controlling sizable towns and cities than their Rhode Island counterparts, have generated little evidence of traditional party organization; at least little appears in standard scholarly and journalistic accounts. In particular, the several large Republican towns in suburban Fairfield County seem to have lacked the strong organizations of comparable Long Island towns just to the south.

NEW YORK (18,241,266) _____

Because New York's party organizations have always attracted a good deal of interest and coverage, this sketch will offer few surprises. An especially good treatment of local parties in the mid-1960s, by Stuart K. Witt, reports that local organizations regularly slated candidates for a range of public offices everywhere in the state; the distribution of patronage jobs was an important organization activity in rural and suburban as well as urban settings; and with notable exceptions powerful party leaders (county leaders in particular) exercised considerable influence in the selection of candidates and other organization affairs.[27] The exceptions were Democratic reform organizations working to implement principles of intraparty democracy in New York City and relatively nonhierarchical parties in upstate rural areas.[28] Other sources flesh out these generalizations with specifics.

In New York City (7,895,563), twentieth-century electoral politics through the 1950s had these components: a natural Democratic ma-

[27] Stuart K. Witt, "The Legislative-Local Party Linkage in New York State" (Ph.D. dissertation, Syracuse University, 1967), especially ch. 3 ("Local Party Organization"). The dissertation is based on interviews conducted in 1966 with a sample of thirty-three members of the lower house of the state legislature, and also with party leaders and activists in the assemblymen's locales, party leaders in the assembly, and staff personnel in the legislative and executive branches of the state government. On organization slating: pp. 49-62. On the thirty-three assemblymen: "All the legislators were initially nominated with the assistance of their local party organization or a party faction that later came to control the organization. And prior to their becoming legislative candidates they all participated in the life of the party" (p. 98). On patronage jobs: pp. 63-68. On strong leaders: pp. 36-38, 52-61. Organizations with strong leaders operated according to what Witt calls a "leadership principle": "a norm that prevails in varying degree among active party members such that they expect that their party organization shall be represented by a single voice, not necessarily that of the formal leader, which, once having spoken, is binding on matters of organizational policy" (pp. 37-38).

[28] On New York City: *ibid.*, pp. 54-55. On upstate areas: "In none of the rural organizations surveyed did the county chairman appear to occupy an indisputable and unambiguous role in the pre-primary recruitment process" (p. 59).

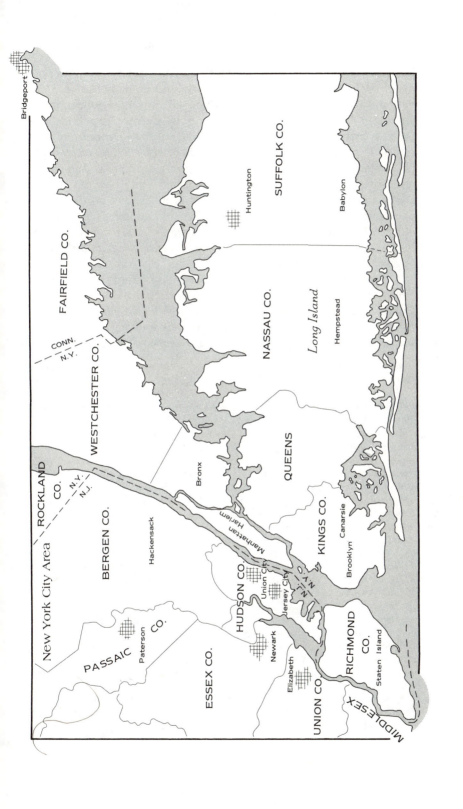

New York City Area

Bridgeport

FAIRFIELD CO.

CONN.
N.Y.

WESTCHESTER CO.

ROCKLAND CO.

N.Y.
N.J.

BERGEN CO.

Hackensack

PASSAIC CO.

Paterson

ESSEX CO.

HUDSON CO.

Union City

Jersey City

Newark

Elizabeth

UNION CO.

RICHMOND CO.

Staten Island

MIDDLESEX

Manhattan

Harlem

Bronx

QUEENS

KINGS CO.

Canarsie

Brooklyn

NASSAU CO.

SUFFOLK CO.

Huntington

Babylon

Long Island

Hempstead

jority in the electorate; independent Democratic organizations in each of the city's five boroughs (counties), notably Tammany Hall in Manhattan, a rival organization in Brooklyn, and a strong organization beginning in the 1920s in the Bronx; party clubs as centers of political and social activity at the assembly district level; effective organization control of Democratic nominations and hence access to most public offices; a lack of interest by the party organizations in broad public policy; close and chronic contesting for the mayoralty between regular Democrats, put up by the borough organizations, and reform candidates entered by "fusion" coalitions of Republicans, minor parties, and independents; and the three-term administration of reform mayor Fiorello La Guardia (1933-1945), who significantly weakened the borough organizations by taking away much of their patronage.[29]

A decisive break away from organization control occurred in the 1960s in Manhattan (1,539,233). Tammany Hall, never very strong among blacks in Harlem, had to contend with a postwar in-migration of white professionals who took an exceptional interest in issues and sought to pursue it by participating in the Democratic party.[30] The re-

---

[29] On the individual borough organizations see e.g., Warren Moscow, *Politics in the Empire State* (New York: Knopf, 1948), pp. 94-101, 125-136. The classic treatment of party clubs is Roy V. Peel, *The Political Clubs of New York City* (New York: Putnam's, 1935). See also Wallace S. Sayre and Herbert Kaufman, *Governing New York City: Politics in the Metropolis* (New York: Norton, 1965), pp. 137-138. The best source on control of nominations is *ibid.*, ch. 5. On lack of interest in broad public policy: "The most distinctive characteristic of the party leaders as participants in the city's political process is their relative neutrality toward the content of public policy. In the main, they are interested most often in exceptions to policy or program rather than in its broad alteration. They seek procedural exceptions—a higher priority for their petitioner, an amelioration of the rules in behalf of their client, an individual advantage in a complex system, a dispensation of mercy rather than impersonal justice—more often than they seek a change in basic public policy or program" (*ibid.*, pp. 474-475). On Brooklyn in particular: "The organization's survival depends on a kind of workaday responsiveness, but neither ideology nor social vision are essential to it" (Hendrik Hertzberg, " 'Hi, boss,' said the judge to Meade Esposito," *New York Times Magazine*, December 10, 1972, p. 84). On contesting for the mayoralty see Sayre and Kaufman, *Governing New York City*, pp. 174-202, 684-689. On La Guardia: "No one before La Guardia's time had ever figured on a reform administration succeeding itself, and while the machines had been able to stand his first four years in office, with their carry-over appointees, the last eight years were ruinous" (Moscow, *Politics in the Empire State*, p. 97).

[30] On Harlem: James Q. Wilson, "Two Negro Politicians: An Interpretation," *Midwest Journal of Political Science* 4(1960), 349-355. Demographic change is said to have been already an important ingredient in regular Democratic congressman John O'Connor's primary defeat in 1938 on the middle East Side—Franklin Roosevelt's chief victory in his move to purge anti–New Deal Democrats from Congress that year. See Richard Polenberg, "Franklin Roosevelt and the Purge of John O'Connor: The Impact of Urban Change on Political Parties," *New York History* 49(1968), 310-316.

sult was a well-publicized series of slating contests between Tammany regulars and reform Democrats in which the reformers emerged victorious. Carmine DeSapio, Tammany's last traditional boss, lost his party leadership position in 1961, the last organization congressmen lost primaries to reformers in 1960, 1962, and 1970, and offices at lower levels fell away.[31] To a student of parties the most interesting development in Manhattan in these years was the reform Democrats' familiar effort to construct durable slating organizations radically different from those of the traditional parties. These were district reform clubs, run according to democratic principles and largely dependent on "purposive" incentives to get people to join and do party work.[32] For a while they were a success; with the struggle against "bossism" as an inspiration in the 1960s, they attracted and held members and slated candidates with considerable authority.[33] In the late 1970s their endorsements still counted for something in primaries and candidates still tried to win them, but the earlier enthusiasm was gone, meetings drew fewer people, and memberships were down.[34] In fact, Manhattan party organizations of all kinds seem to have decayed or disappeared by the late 1970s.[35] Herman D. Farrell, Jr., elected Democratic county leader in

[31] The reform-regular warfare of the 1950s leading up to DeSapio's defeat is covered in James Q. Wilson, *The Amateur Democrat: Club Politics in Three Cities* (Chicago: University of Chicago Press, 1966), ch. 2; and in John F. Davenport, "Skinning the Tiger: Carmine DeSapio and the End of the Tammany Era," *New York Affairs* 3(1975), 72-93.

[32] The authoritative treatment of this effort is Wilson, *The Amateur Democrat*. Wilson's comment on organizations of the kind set up by Manhattan reformers: "Generally speaking, clubs of amateur politicians are examples of 'purposive' organizations. Most people belong because of the goals they feel the clubs serve rather than from any hope of material gain or because they enjoy the sociability the clubs provide" (p. 164).

[33] For a good account of Democratic slating in Manhattan of the mid-1960s, part regular and part reform, see Edward N. Costikyan, *Behind Closed Doors: Politics in the Public Interest* (New York: Harcourt, Brace and World, 1966), chs. 7-9.

[34] On continuing endorsement activity: Daniel R. Biser, "The Amateur Democrat Revisited: Reform Club Politics in New York City" (Yale course paper, 1977). One reason for the persistence of the clubs' slating influence has to do with the law; New York election statutes are so complicated and petition requirements so stiff that a candidate needs the help of clubhouse lawyers and signature gatherers to reach the primary ballot and stay there (pp. 14-18). On reform clubs' decline see, e.g., Warren E. Farrell, "Political Clubhouses Lose Importance in Elections," *New York Times*, June 9, 1969, p. 41; Frank Lynn, "Most Political Clubs in City Are Losing Their Power," *New York Times*, November 27, 1971, p. 33; Frank Lynn, "A Race with Few Rooters: Democratic District Leaders," *New York Times*, August 22, 1977, p. 29.

[35] A 1977 report: "A clear signal of the decline of the Democratic organization in New York City is that district leaders will be elected in next month's primary in Manhattan but that very few voters and even politicians say they care. The collective yawn over the district leaderships markedly contrasts with the politics of 10 and 20 years ago" (Lynn,

1981, inherited "an organization that few now take seriously."[36] The decline of party organizations has paved the way for increasingly prominent candidate organizations—in recent judgeship primaries, for example, and in an expensive 1977 primary for borough president in which Andrew J. Stein drew on a family fortune to defeat Robert F. Wagner, Jr., who was backed by the reform clubs.[37]

In the city's other large boroughs, the organization in the Bronx (1,471,701) survived the 1960s in weakened condition; the ones in Queens (1,987,174) and Brooklyn (2,602,012) were in somewhat better shape though declining.[38] The Bronx organization under Charles Buckley (1953-1967) and Patrick J. Cunningham (1967-1978) had to wage a long defensive war like Tammany Hall's in Manhattan against reformers.[39] Its public offices fell away—two congressional seats at once in 1964, the borough presidency, a number of senate and assembly seats—producing by the early 1970s an exaggerated dependency on judicial nominations and court patronage.[40] Since then its hold on the

---

"A Race with Few Rooters," p. 29). A 1972 sounding turned up only one healthy club of the old Tammany type in the large area between the Battery and 125th Street. See Tom Buckle, "As Hell's Kitchen Changes, So Does McManus," *New York Times*, June 20, 1972, p. 41.

[36] Maurice Carroll, "3d 'Irish' Entry Complicates Tammany Leadership Race," *New York Times*, April 26, 1981, p. 50. See also Maurice Carroll, "Tammany Hall Has a New Chief and a Bigger Mortgage Than Ever," *New York Times*, May 3, 1981, p. E6.

[37] On the Stein-Wagner primary: Biser, "Amateur Democrat Revisited," p. 18. On judicial primaries: E. J. Dionne, Jr., "Surrogate-Race Upset Tied to Trend," *New York Times*, September 10, 1977, p. 17; E. R. Shipp, "Democratic Primary Campaign for Manhattan Surrogate Intensifies," *New York Times*, September 12, 1982, p. 52.

[38] Frank Lynn makes the comparison in a detailed treatment of the borough organizations in the early 1970s: "Disagreements Mark Decline of County Leaders in the City," *New York Times*, May 25, 1972, pp. 47, 49.

[39] A 1968 description based on information supplied by Bronx party activists: "Since about 1960, the Reform clubs have been challenging the regular Buckley organization in a fight to the death. . . . Each faction places a complete slate against the other in every Democratic primary. Each side views the primary as a contest for power. Each side recruits candidates, registers voters, staffs polling places, and campaigns, not only to elect 'good men' to office but to capture the party organization" (David M. Olson, "Toward a Typology of County Party Organizations," *Southwestern Social Science Quarterly* 48(1968), pp. 565-566). For a later treatment of the continuing struggle see Frank Lynn, "Bronx Insurgent Democrats Challenge Cunningham's Post as County Leader," *New York Times*, February 12, 1976, p. 35.

[40] On the loss of offices: Martin Tolchin, "Democratic 'Bosses': Mechanics of Power," *New York Times*, June 1, 1970, p. 27. On the early 1970s: Lynn, "Disagreements Mark Decline," p. 49. A good account of the role of the Bronx organization in slating judicial candidates is Glenn Fowler, " 'Making' of Judges: How Rare Method Works in New York," *New York Times*, October 10, 1977, pp. 1, 48. In 1976 a state prosecutor accused party leader Cunningham of selling judgeships but failed to make the charge stick. In

judiciary seems to have loosened as well, and Cunningham's successor
as party leader seems reduced at times to a role of one power broker
among many in the Democratic party's confusing, multicandidate primaries.[41] Queens and Brooklyn supported "the strongest of the county
organizations" in the early 1970s, still in control of "virtually every
public office nomination, including Borough President, Congressional
seats, the Legislature, City Council and the judiciary"—though not
very influential in primaries for higher office.[42] The Brooklyn organization headed by Meade H. Esposito (1969-1984), centered in the
Thomas Jefferson Democratic club in Canarsie, accumulated influence
by placing people in elective posts and also in several hundred appointive jobs at county and district levels (though few in the central city
administration)—in the courts, where some four hundred jobs went to
clerks, administrative aides, law secretaries, etc.; in the countywide offices of borough president, surrogate, and district attorney; in lesser instruments such as the county's board of elections and marriage-license
bureau and as marshals and pothole inspectors; and later on in the
1970s in community planning boards and the city's newly decentralized school system.[43] The model career of a Brooklyn politician pro-

---

1982 a federal court found Cunningham guilty of tax evasion while leader in the mid-
1970s. The prosecution argued "that Mr. Cunningham was splitting fees that came from
judges who are elected in the main through party endorsement" (Marcia Chambers,
"Government's Case Is Summed Up In Cunningham Tax-Evasion Trial," *New York
Times*, June 12, 1982, p. 1). See also Marcia Chambers, "Cunningham Found Guilty On
Tax Count," *New York Times*, June 19, 1982, pp. 27, 51.

[41] On the state of the organization in 1977: Frank Lynn, "Loss of Power By Cun-
ningham Is in Evidence," *New York Times*, March 13, 1977, p. 31. On the judiciary:
Frank Lynn, "Cunningham to Quit in May as Leader of Bronx Democrats," *New York
Times*, April 6, 1978, p. A22; and Wayne Barrett and Joe Conason, "A Reform Judge
Beats Friedman," *Village Voice*, September 17-23, 1980, pp. 5-6. On a Bronx primary in
the regime of party leader Stanley M. Friedman: Wayne Barrett and Joe Conason, "The
Bronx: Friedman's Wild Rule," *Village Voice*, August 24, 1982, p. 5.

[42] Lynn, "Disagreements Mark Decline," pp. 47, 49, quotation at p. 49. The Queens
organization, normally given only scanty attention by writers, drew some coverage when
Geraldine Ferraro won her Vice-Presidential nomination a decade later in 1984. A summary appraisal at that time: "The Queens Democratic organization is not the all-pow-
erful political entity of the past. But, like its counterparts in other boroughs in this city or
old cities such as Chicago and Baltimore, it still doles out judgeships, low-level city jobs,
spots on the Democratic ticket and money-making assignments at the courthouse to the
party faithful." Leaders of some forty clubhouses served as "funnels for the patronage
system." Margaret Shapiro, "In Ferraro's Queens, Old-Time Patronage Is Still Boss,"
Washington Post National Weekly Edition, September 10, 1984, pp. 10-11 (quotations
at p. 10). Ferraro nonetheless won her first House nomination in 1978 without organization support.

[43] On the Jefferson club: "The club's operation is a model of well-run machine politics.
It avoids controversial issues, services various contracts and complaints for its constitu-

gressed through an assortment of elective and appointive offices to end in a judgeship, of which the organization controlled some seventy.[44] In the early 1980s Esposito's organization still figured regularly in Brooklyn's electoral activity, though its supply of public offices had shrunk: three dependable congressional seats were lost in primaries to insurgents Elizabeth Holtzman (1972) and Stephen J. Solarz (1974) and itinerant Bronx reformer James H. Scheuer (1974); a number of judgeships and assembly seats fell to insurgents; and, worst of all, Holtzman won the district attorney's office in 1981 despite an all-out organization drive to stop her. "She'll send us all to jail" is said to have served as the campaign's "gallows humor."[45]

Of the suburban jurisdictions outside New York City, the one with the most influential organization is Nassau County (1,428,838), adjoining Queens.[46] Nassau has been run during the last six decades almost without pause by a Republican machine centered, at least in recent times, in the immense "town" of Hempstead (801,592). Leadership passed from G. Wilbur Doughty—the man Robert Moses had to deal with when he built parkways in the 1920s on Long Island—to J. Russel Sprague, and in the late 1960s to Joseph M. Margiotta.[47] Under

---

ents, employs the power of patronage and perquisites to extract loyalty from its workers and election district captains, extends community influence through inter-linking position-holding in the synagogues and community organizations, and mobilizes a tightly controlled electorate consisting of its three thousand dues-paying members" (Jonathan Rieder, "Danger and Dispossession: The Making of Middle America in Canarsie, 1960-1976" [Ph.D dissertation, Yale University, 1979], pp. 47-48). The club is treated in Hertzberg, " 'Hi, boss,' said the judge to Meade Esposito," pp. 33, 74-88. On the Brooklyn organization's patronage sources: Tolchin, "Democratic 'Bosses,' " p. 27; Frank Lynn, "To Brooklyn Democratic Party Belong the Power and the Spoils," New York Times, April 15, 1974, pp. 33, 62; Marcia Chambers, "How a Judge Is Made in Brooklyn: Case of Borough President Leone," New York Times, January 3, 1977, pp. 1, 10; and Marcia Chambers, "An Embattled Esposito Stands Firm in Brooklyn," New York Times, February 17, 1979, pp. 3, 26.

44 See Chambers, "How a Judge Is Made in Brooklyn."

45 On judgeships: Chambers, "An Embattled Esposito," p. 26. On assembly seats: Wayne Barrett and Joe Conason, "Meade Esposito's Final Days," Village Voice, September 17-23, 1980, p. 5. On the Holtzman victory: Maurice Carroll, "Is There a Brooklyn Clubhouse After Liz Holtzman?" New York Times, September 27, 1981, p. E6.

46 The best general sources on Nassau County are Frank Lynn, "Nassau Republicans March to Beat of Powerful Drumming by Margiotta," New York Times, December 8, 1972, pp. 47, 50; Samuel Kaplan, The Dream Deferred: People, Politics, and Planning in Suburbia (New York: Seabury, 1976), ch. 11; and Frank Lynn, "D'Amato and G.O.P. on L.I. Share Common Toughness," New York Times, September 29, 1980, pp. B1, B4.

47 On Moses and Doughty: Robert A. Caro, The Power Broker: Robert Moses and the Fall of New York (New York: Knopf, 1974), pp. 208-212. Moses found that Doughty was delighted with the idea of having big construction contracts to work with. On

Margiotta, said to be "ambidextrous ideologically," the organization had little trouble controlling party nominations for offices at all levels, local to congressional; one result was a delegation to the state legislature known as "Margiotta's marionettes."[48] In 1977 Margiotta had a falling out with the county's top executive official and easily purged him in a primary.[49] Patronage jobs have been "an accepted and expected reward for party work."[50] A 1972 report noted that three-quarters of the county's some 1,800 Republican committeemen held appointive jobs on the public payroll. In the early 1970s the party raised over a million dollars a year for organization use, some of it coming from over 17,000 county and town employees "encouraged" to turn over one percent of their salaries, some from middle-level party leaders directed to produce $400 for each of the county's 961 election districts.[51] Another source of funds was kickbacks to the party from town and county insurance commissions, an old practice raised to a new efficiency by Margiotta that drew in $685,000 over a decade and brought him a prison term, ending his reign as party leader in 1983.[52] On Nas-

Sprague see Moscow, *Politics in the Empire State*, pp. 137-138; and Kaplan, *Dream Deferred*, pp. 140-141.

[48] On Margiotta's ideology: Lynn, "D'Amato and G.O.P.," p. B4. Some sources on Republican slating in Nassau are Kaplan, *Dream Deferred*, pp. 138-143; Witt, "Legislative-Local Party Linkage," p. 56; Dennis S. Ippolito and Lewis Bowman, "Goals and Activities of Party Officials in a Suburban Community," *Western Political Quarterly* 22(1969), 576; and for an account of a county nominating convention, *New York Times*, March 26, 1972, p. 38. On the marionettes: Wayne Barrett, Joe Conason, and Jack Newfield, "Al D'Amato and the Shame of the Suburbs," *Village Voice*, October 8-14, 1980, p. 1.

[49] Frank Lynn, "There's a Fight in Nassau: Politically, the Suburbs Are Not Unlike the Big City," *New York Times*, March 13, 1977, p. IV:8; Irvin Molotsky, "Nassau Democrats Given Chance for a New Image," *New York Times*, August 29, 1977, p. 31; "Margiotta Didn't Run, But Won Big," *New York Times*, September 11, 1977, p. E5; Alan Eysen, "The Race Behind the GOP Race," *Newsday* (Long Island), September 6, 1977, pp. 1-3 of "Nassau County Voters Guide."

[50] Dennis S. Ippolito, "Political Perspectives of Suburban Party Leaders," *Social Science Quarterly* 49(1969), 809. Study based on interviews with Nassau party committeemen conducted in 1966.

[51] In addition the leaders were "expected to support a $500-a-plate dinner, a $125-a-person cocktail party and the $125-a-person Joseph M. Margiotta Invitational Golf Tournament." Some of the proceeds went into a $30,000 salary and chauffeured Cadillac for Margiotta. Lynn, "Nassau Republicans," p. 47. All the material on the early 1970s is from *ibid*. For a recent report about the mid-1970s see John T. McQuiston, "Nassau G.O.P. Made Employees Donate Funds, Jury Finds," *New York Times*, September 5, 1985, pp. A1, B4.

[52] Frank Lynn, "The Margiotta Case and Splitting of Insurance Fees," *New York Times*, December 26, 1981, p. 26; Frank Lynn, "At Last, a Last Hurrah for Margiotta?" *New York Times*, May 8, 1983, p. E6; *United States v. Margiotta*, 688 F.2d 113-119 (1982).

sau's Democratic side regulars and reformers clashed in the 1970s in Manhattan fashion, but the party ordinarily managed to slate candidates without holding primaries and sometimes won elections.[53]

Elsewhere in the suburbs, information is fragmentary on Westchester County (894,406) though good on Suffolk County (1,127,030). Both supported strong Republican organizations like Nassau County's until about thirty years ago and Republicans in both carried their slating power into the early 1970s. Democrats, however, have been making inroads and neither county has generated a recent Republican leader as influential or eye-catching as Margiotta.[54] The old Westchester organization seemed more or less withered away in one report of the mid-1970s.[55] In Suffolk County, however, a 1980 study turned up unmistakable traditional organizations in both parties in the sizable towns of Babylon (203,570) and Huntington (200,172)—a familiar pattern of strong leaders, leadership control of nominations, little interest in issues, and distribution of patronage to ensure party work and disci-

[53] On regulars vs. reformers: Kaplan, *Dream Deferred*, pp. 141-142; Ippolito, "Political Perspectives," pp. 808-809. On Democratic slating in general see Ippolito and Bowman, "Goals and Activities," p. 576; Witt, "Legislative-Local Party Linkage," p. 56. An account of a slating convention: *New York Times*, April 16, 1972, p. N42. An account of a primary: *Newsday*, September 11, 1974, p. 21.

[54] Suffolk's last strong Republican leader was W. Kingsland Macy, who ran the county organization for about three decades. See Caro, *Power Broker*, p. 217; Moscow, *Politics in the Empire State*, p. 139. Macy's counterpart in Westchester was William L. Ward, who ran things for nearly four decades (*ibid.*, p. 138). "The era has passed when the late William L. Ward could rule Westchester as a benevolent Republican despot from his roll-top desk in Port Chester. . . . He filled county offices without hesitation, sometimes quite informally as he sat on the spacious porch of his home on a Sunday morning" (Clarence Dean, "Disunity in G.O.P. Reflects New Structure of Suburbs, *New York Times*, June 1, 1964, pp. 1, 21). In 1935 Roy Peel made an interesting point about the suburbs in his study of New York City's political clubs. In fact the terrain of the old clubs included Westchester and Nassau counties and at least the urban parts of Hudson and Essex counties in New Jersey, not just New York City proper. "Only on the fringes of the metropolitan area—in Putnam [N.Y.], Rockland [N.Y.], Passaic [N.J.] and Monmouth [N.J.] counties—do we encounter radically different types of political organizations." (Peel, *Political Clubs*, p. 301). He said nothing about Suffolk County or Connecticut's Fairfield County. On Westchester in general: Witt, "Legislative-Local Party Linkage," p. 57. For an account of Republican nominating in a small Westchester town: Mark K. Adams, *A Report on Politics in New Castle, New York* (Cambridge: Joint Center for Urban Studies, M.I.T./Harvard, 1961), pp. II:16-24. For an instance of Republican slating activity in Westchester: "Westchester Republicans Set to Designate Vergari to Oppose Reid," *New York Times*, March 29, 1972, p. 25. On slating in Suffolk: Frank Lynn, "Suffolk Republicans Facing First Primary Challenge," *New York Times*, September 5, 1979, pp. B1, B6.

[55] David S. Broder, "GOP Yielding Ground to Suburban Democrats," *Washington Post*, June 14, 1975, pp. A1, A4. This is a feature story on politics in Westchester County.

pline.[56] "The consensus [among interviewees in the study] was that nominations normally filtered down from the party elders with few floor challenges or primaries and committee people typically acquiescing to or endorsing the candidate choices of their leaders";[57] "no more than 20 percent of either elites or committee people identified political philosophy or issue positions as nominations criteria, thus confirming once again the non–programmatic orientation of these party organizations."[58] The organizations drew strength from patronage positions in town, county, and state governments (summer jobs for teenagers were highly prized) and the Suffolk County Off Track Betting Corporation—"the Suffolk County parties have agreed to divide O.T.B. jobs 50-50 to town committee members, their relatives, friends or constituents"—and evidently from kickbacks in sewer construction and insurance.[59]

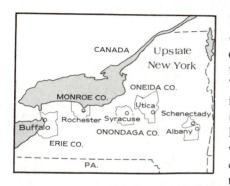

Of New York's upstate urban counties running west to east from Buffalo to Albany, only Albany has inspired detailed writing about its parties. The picture is nonetheless sufficiently clear in Buffalo (462,768) and its parent unit, Erie County (1,113,491), where a conspicuous Democratic organization run by Peter J. Crotty starting in 1953, and by his successor Joseph F. Crangle since 1965, has drawn sustenance from city and county patronage and channeled candidates into a range of judicial, state legislative, county, and municipal offices—including the mayoralty in 1965, 1969, and 1973, though not in 1977 or since.[60] In a 1970 study Democratic politicians in Buffalo were found

---

[56] Richard F. Koubek, "The Intra-Party Uses and Influences of Personal Resources Distributed by Suburban Party Elites" (Ph.D. dissertation, City University of New York, 1980), especially chs. 2-6. The study is based on interviews with 103 party leaders and lower-level activists in Babylon and Huntington in 1978-1979. Babylon Democrats supported a reform opposition as well as party regulars.

[57] *Ibid.*, p. 108. More generally on party leadership: pp. 59-72, ch. 5.

[58] *Ibid.*, p. 145. On issues more generally: pp. 74-77, ch. 4, pp. 143-145.

[59] Quotation at *ibid.*, p. 153. On patronage more generally: pp. 64-65, 71, 73-74, 88-90, 103-104, ch. 6. Summer jobs for teens had cachet also in Nassau County in the late 1960s, according to Bruce Stinebrickner (pers. comm.).

[60] On the Crangle organization in 1970: Tolchin, "Democratic 'Bosses,' " p. 27. On the state of the organization and loss of the mayoralty in 1977: Frank J. Prial, "Crangle's

to climb the same kind of party-controlled career ladder as regular Democrats in New York City.[61] Evidently the Republicans have also operated a traditional organization in Erie County.[62]

Rochester (296,233) supported an impressive Republican machine around the turn of the century, but George Eastman, of Eastman Kodak, broke its control of city administration in the 1920s by ushering in a city-manager plan.[63] Weaker organization of some sort—probably based on county patronage—was nonetheless evident in newspaper coverage in 1970: "Mrs. Arthur Cropsey, the Republican organization-backed candidate, held a scant lead over conservative James R. Sims early today in the primary race for city school board nomination. . . . The Monroe [County] Democratic organization lost two out of three ward committee primaries, but Democratic County Chairman Robert J. Quigley claimed it would have little effect on his leadership. The organization lost the 14th and 3rd Wards, while retaining the 5th Ward control of Robert Lesczinski, a political protege of Sam Solone, retired 7th Ward leader."[64]

Control of Erie County Democrats at Stake in Buffalo Primary," *New York Times*, August 15, 1977, p. 31; Frank J. Prial, "Black Activist Confounds Experts In Upset in Buffalo Mayoral Race," *New York Times*, September 10, 1977, pp. 1, 17; "Crangle Backs Eve For Buffalo Mayor In a Surprise Move," *New York Times*, September 14, 1977, p. D22; Paul Carton, "A Black Man Runs for Mayor: The Extraordinary Campaign of Arthur O. Eve," *Afro-Americans in New York Life and History* 4(July 1980), 8-12. (In fact a white independent, not Eve, ended up in the mayoralty.) The most useful general source on organization in Buffalo and Erie County politics is Walter A. Borowiec, "Politics and Buffalo's Polish Americans," pp. 16-39 in Angela T. Pienkos (ed.), *Ethnic Politics in Urban America: The Polish Experience in Four Cities* (Chicago: Polish American Historical Association, 1978), at pp. 23-35.

[61] Barbara Greenberg, "New York Congressmen and Local Party Organization" (Ph.D. dissertation, University of Michigan, 1973), pp. 31-33. Based on material from 1970 interviews and questionnaires.

[62] On the Erie County Republican party and Polish-American politicians: "The average Polish Republican must be a loyalist. If he is a ward chairman or party functionary, he may depend entirely on the party for his job. And since the party does not endorse mavericks, the Polish Republican who hopes to be endorsed for an office which is competitive must be loyal. He must tend to ward committee work, attend fund-raisers, campaign for other endorsed candidates and be ready to run as a 'sacrificial lamb' in areal contests" (Borowiec, "Buffalo's Polish Americans," p. 28, and more generally pp. 27-30). Republicans held the top executive office in Erie County from 1965 through at least 1979. See Maurice Carroll, "County Executive's Race Spices Election in Buffalo," *New York Times*, October 29, 1979, p. B2.

[63] See Clement G. Lanni, *George W. Aldridge: Big Boss, Small City* (Rochester: Rochester Alliance Press, 1939), *passim*, pp. 130-133 on Eastman; and Philippe Dressayre, "Pouvoirs sur la Ville: Les 'Machines' de Rochester (New York)," *Revue Française de Science Politique* 30(1980), 776-798.

[64] *Rochester Democrat and Chronicle*, June 24, 1970, pp. 1, 3.

Further east, a 1961 study of Syracuse (197,297) described a cohesive Republican party in control of the city and its parent unit, Onondaga County (472,835), but said nothing about nominations or incentives.[65] Clues about the latter appeared in a 1978 newspaper story entitled "Onondaga Official Admits Illegal County G.O.P. Conspiracy on Employee Kickbacks," concerning party officials on trial for an apparently long-standing practice of soliciting money for the party from county employees—assistant district attorneys, for example, were supposed to kick back $25 for each $1,000 of their salaries.[66] Democratic nominations in Oneida County (273,037) are said to have been managed until the mid-1960s by the "Elefante organization" centered in Utica (91,611).[67] And both the city (77,958) and county (161,078) of Schenectady were dominated through the mid-1960s by a patronage-based Republican organization heavily dependent on an Italian-American vote.[68]

In Albany, both the city (115,781) and the county (286,742), site of the strongest upstate party organization during most of this century, Daniel P. O'Connell and his brothers took over the county's Democratic party in the early 1920s. "Uncle Dan" ran it by himself from 1939 until his death in 1977, sharing control of the city beginning in 1941 with Erastus J. Corning II, mayor then and mayor still when he died in 1983.[69] In the last three decades the organization has drawn occasional primary challenges and Republicans have won some offices,

[65] Roscoe C. Martin et al., *Decisions in Syracuse* (Bloomington: Indiana University Press, 1961), pp. 42-46, 227-229, 306-307.

[66] *New York Times*, November 19, 1978, p. 36. See also Jill Smolowe, "Onondaga to Mark Start of an Inquiry," *New York Times*, November 23, 1980, p. 37. Ultimately a special prosecutor brought indictments against thirty-nine Onondaga party officials and officeholders (almost all Republicans) and as of November 1980 had won conviction of eighteen, most apparently for soliciting but some for taking bribes on county contracts.

[67] Witt, "Legislative-Local Party Linkage," pp. 60-61. No report on Oneida Republicans.

[68] James A. Riedel, "Boss and Faction," *Annals of the American Academy of Political and Social Science* 353(1964), 14-26. In 1960, 79 of 278 Republican county committeemen had jobs on the public payroll (p. 22). In the early 1960s old-line organizations in both Schenectady parties came under attack by reform factions, Republican and Democratic, which "drew heavily from the silk-stocking wards, the towns, and those sections still able to muster some civic spirit. Both appealed to the intellectuals and idealists. The 'old guard' factions, while in both cases backed by the more conservative business element, drew most heavily on the plight of the insecure and impoverished" (p. 23).

[69] For a good book-length treatment see Frank S. Robinson, *Machine Politics: A Study of Albany's O'Connells* (New Brunswick, N.J.: Transaction Books, 1977). Other good general sources: Ralph Blumenthal, "State Study Finds Albany 'Fleeced' by Machine's Rule," *New York Times*, December 26, 1972, pp. 1, 29; Frank Lynn, "Political Machine Grinds On in Albany City Hall," *New York Times*, February 10, 1973, pp. 33, 64.

but the machine still had firm control of the city in 1980.[70] An interest-ing and well-documented feature of Albany politics (of the recent past if not of the present) is the organization's record of distributing nearly everything a city government has command of in ad hoc, particularistic fashion: jobs and promotions in the police department, city jobs in gen-eral, city contracts, city purchases of goods and services, parking tick-ets, tax assessments ("they played the whole matter of taxes like a fine violin"), real estate tax delinquencies, and enforcement of laws on gambling, prostitution, and dope peddling.[71] O'Connell himself was a sober and circumspect businessman in his role as boss: "Not until his eighty-fifth birthday did he ever consent to be interviewed on televi-sion. He is not a man to be encountered anywhere but in his own home, limiting his public appearances to only one a year, the annual meeting of his organization. Between meetings he runs it by telephone."[72] Nevertheless, "favors were still doled out by Dan O'Connell person-ally, even into his eighties. . . . He frequently has seen up to fifty people a day in his home."[73]

This ends the tour. If the state is considered as a whole, the most striking change in New York organizational patterns during recent dec-ades has been, without much doubt, the Democratic county organiza-tions' nearly complete loss of control over nominations for higher of-

---

[70] Robinson, *Machine Politics*, chs. 21-24; Richard Meislin, "Albany's Mayor Is in a Primary Fight—His First in 36 Years in Office," *New York Times*, August 28, 1977, p. 45; Maurice Carroll, "Corning of Albany Still Thriving in Job," *New York Times*, May 13, 1980, pp. B1, B8. "As head of President Carter's campaign here, Mayor Erastus J. Corning 2d was asked to send state headquarters a list of Albany officials who were sup-porting the President in the Democratic primary. Someone in his office sent along a di-rectory of the city government. You misunderstood, Carter headquarters said. What we wanted was a list of just the Carter supporters. No, *you* misunderstood, was the reply from Albany. That *is* the list of Carter supporters" (*ibid.*, p. B1).

[71] On the police department: Robinson, *Machine Politics*, pp. 199-200. See also James Q. Wilson, *Varieties of Police Behavior: The Management of Law and Order in Eight Communities* (Cambridge: Harvard University Press, 1968), pp. 237-238. On city jobs in general: "Citizens seeking city jobs first obtained 'white slips'—notes or scraps of pa-per from county Democratic headquarters that cleared them for employment" (Blumen-thal, "State Study," p. 1). See also Robinson, pp. 165-170. On contracts: Robinson, pp. 170-176; Blumenthal, p. 1. On city purchases: Robinson, pp. 170-175; Blumenthal, p. 1. On tickets: "Fixing parking tickets . . . is a way of life in Albany. Tickets are taken to the ward leader, who passes them on to party headquarters" (Robinson, p. 201). On tax assessments: *ibid.*, pp. 133-140, quotation p. 133. On real estate taxes: *ibid.*, pp. 140-143. On law enforcement: *ibid.*, pp. 110, 203-206. There are elements of standardization in enforcement. Prostitutes used to pay $20 a week at Democratic headquarters to stay in business (p. 203).

[72] *Ibid.*, p. 106.

[73] *Ibid.*, p. 109.

fices.[74] In New York City's congressional delegation, the proportion of Democrats owing their initial victories to organization slating has gone from almost all in 1960 to just a few today.[75] New York City mayoral nominations have receded from the regulars' grasp. The decisive juncture was Mayor Robert F. Wagner's inspired abandonment of the county organizations in 1961: after receiving important backing from them in 1953 and 1957, he won renomination for a third term as the anti-Tammany candidate of the reform clubs and civil service unions.[76] No mayor after 1961 except Abraham Beame (1973-1977) has had much to do with the regular organizations, and their influence in the mayoral primaries of 1977 and 1981 was negligible. And organization control of statewide nominations has come to an end. Before 1967, in the state's previous convention system, a handful of county leaders managing blocs of delegates could often choose Democratic nominees for governor and Senator, but no organizations have exercised much influence in the crowded primaries since then except the candidates' own.[77] By the early 1980s Republican statewide nominating had come to look the same.[78] Even so, New York of the late 1960s was probably still enough of an organization state to deserve a TPO score of 5: only two unquestionable machines remained (the Nassau Republican and

[74] Frank Lynn makes the point well in his 1972 piece, "Disagreements Mark Decline," p. 47.

[75] Evidence is decisive that the city's Democratic House members used to be put into office by the county organizations. See Alan Fiellin, "Recruitment and Legislative Role Conceptions: A Conceptual Scheme and a Case Study," *Western Political Quarterly* 20(1967), 281-282. "It seems clear that the 'loyal Democrat' on his way up in New York works to get the 'nod,' the 'promotion.' Following the 'rules of the party faithful' would seem to be the major qualification" (p. 282).

[76] See Theodore J. Lowi, "Machine Politics—Old and New," *The Public Interest*, Fall 1967, pp. 89-90.

[77] An event important in firing up reform Democrats for their last drive against Tammany was the Buffalo convention of 1958, in which six county leaders from Erie County and New York City decided a Senate nomination. See Costikyan, *Behind Closed Doors*, chs. 11-13. On recent statewide primaries see for example Neal R. Peirce, *The Megastates of America: People, Politics, and Power in the Ten Great States* (New York: Norton, 1972), pp. 55-56. Under the law a statewide party committee still has the power to "designate" (endorse) candidates, but from 1968 through 1982 all nonincumbent Democratic "designees" for governor and Senator drew challengers and only one of the seven survived a primary. For a general treatment of New York's statewide nominating processes over the last century or so see Howard A. Scarrow, *Parties, Elections, and Representation in the State of New York* (New York: New York University Press, 1983), ch. 2.

[78] See Frank Lynn, "New York's G.O.P. Is a Grand New Party," *New York Times*, December 28, 1980, p. E6; Frank Lynn, "G.O.P. Puts 3 Candidates for Governor in Primary," *New York Times*, June 17, 1982, p. B6.

Albany Democratic) and Tammany had just about disappeared, but in general the traditional county organizations were still quite alive.

NEW JERSEY (7,168,164) _____

The flavor of New Jersey's nominating politics of the late 1960s comes across well in newspaper coverage of primaries. A headline on Middlesex County, for example: "Light Turnout Helps Organization."[79] On Ocean County: "Regular Ocean Democrats Triumph."[80] On Hudson County and its Democratic leader: "Kenny Remains King of the Hill in Hudson Politics."[81] A story on Bergen County: "The six Regular Democratic Organization Assembly candidates were front runners in the Assembly race in Bergen County."[82] A story on Cape May County: "Beech Fox, Republican organization candidate for sheriff against incumbent A. Hubbert Heil, won by better than two to one."[83] On Atlantic County: "Dunbar's victory represented a defeat for the long entrenched Democratic organization headed by City Commissioner Arthur W. Ponzio, Jr."[84] And on Mercer County: "Democrat Kenneth Wooden and Republican Lester Allen, insurgents in Mercer's primary election for Assembly, have suffered the usual fate of those who take on entrenched political organizations."[85]

The best overall source on New Jersey's organizations is a 1975 discussion by John Blydenburgh.[86] As in New York, organizations at the county level have ordinarily been the important units and county leaders the important figures.[87] The county organizations have traditionally stockpiled influence by distributing material goods (or entitlements convertible into material goods) in particularistic fashion—county and municipal jobs, for example, government contracts, and municipal zoning variances.[88] A 1957 canvass of fifty-seven party leaders pro-

[79] *Trenton Evening Times*, June 4, 1969, p. 14.
[80] *Ibid.*
[81] *Newark Star-Ledger*, June 4, 1969, p. 18.
[82] *Ibid.*, p. 19.
[83] *Philadelphia Inquirer*, June 4, 1969, p. 61.
[84] *Ibid.*
[85] *Trenton Evening Times*, June 4, 1969, p. 2.
[86] "Party Organizations," ch. 5 in Alan Rosenthal and John Blydenburgh (eds.), *Politics in New Jersey* (New Brunswick, N.J.: Eagleton Institute of Politics, Rutgers University, 1975).
[87] See *ibid.*, pp. 134-136; Ralph C. Chandler, "The County Chairmanship in New Jersey: A Comparative Study of Selected States" (Ph.D. dissertation, Columbia University, 1970), p. x; Richard P. McCormick, "An Historical Overview," ch. 1 in Rosenthal and Blydenburgh (eds.), *Politics in New Jersey*, p. 25.
[88] Blydenburgh, in "Party Organizations," pp. 119-130, considers in detail the incen-

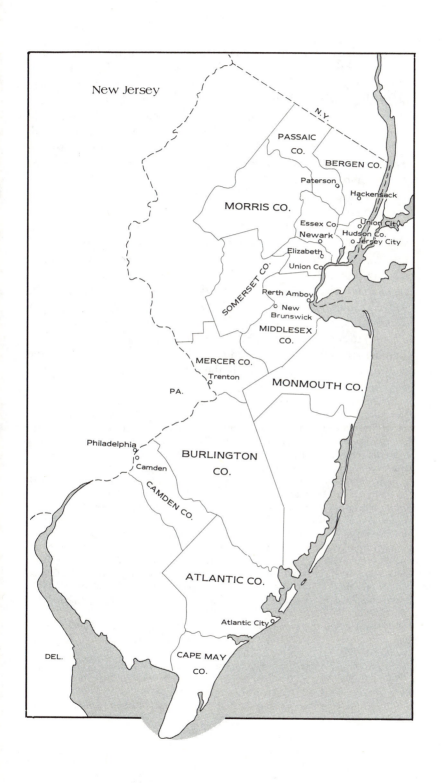

duced a plausible result: "Ninety-four per cent of the leaders interviewed said that they help get persons jobs on the public payroll, and
83 per cent said that they had 'a pretty good understanding' with these
job holders for contributions to the party's expenses."[89] Organization
"screening committees" at the county and municipal levels have traditionally slated candidates in party primaries, evidently still with considerable success in the 1960s.[90] Organizations in the larger counties, for
example, used to follow a practice of cycling people in and out of the
state assembly.[91]

Blydenburgh discusses twelve county organizations that observers
have thought to be especially "strong" in recent times (in the 1960s;
some declined in the 1970s).[92] A "strong" organization is evidently one
with a recognized leader, clear internal lines of authority, good control
of its party's nominations for public offices voted on countywide and
possibly municipal positions, and good control of its county's or at
least a major city's government. These are stiff requirements. Six of the
twelve strong organizations are Republican: in Atlantic County
(175,043), site of Atlantic City (47,859); in rural Cape May County
(59,554) in the far south; in Burlington County (323,132) in the Philadelphia suburbs; and in Bergen (897,148), Somerset (198,372), and
Monmouth (461,849) counties in the New York City area's suburban

---

tive arrangements that have induced people to participate in party activity in New Jersey.
One conclusion: "Nonmaterial, private benefits probably play a greater role in motivat-
ing political participation than material private benefits. On the other hand, participants
who receive material benefits probably work harder. Material incentives do play a very
important role in political party organization in New Jersey and elsewhere; but in relative
terms, nonmaterial benefits motivate the largest number of participants in party politics"
(p. 123). But the "nonmaterial" benefits Blydenburgh writes of are all, in James Q. Wilson's terminology, "solidary" benefits: either "collective solidary" benefits—for example, the pleasure of associating with other people—or, more important in Blydenburgh's
account, "specific solidary" benefits—for example, the prestige that comes with getting
appointed to a position, getting nominated for a position, serving as a poll watcher, or
even having a license plate with a low number on it. Blydenburgh nowhere mentions
"purposive" incentives. On county and municipal jobs: pp. 124-125, 126-128, 129; for
specific evidence on the suburban municipalities of Camden County: Bruce T. Stinebrickner, "Representative Government and Partisanship in Suburban School Districts" (Ph.D.
dissertation, Yale University, 1974), p. 278. On government contracts: Blydenburgh, pp.
129-130. On zoning variances: *ibid.*, pp. 128-129.

[89] Richard T. Frost, "Stability and Change in Local Party Politics," *Public Opinion
Quarterly* 25(1961), 234. The fifty-seven were a selection of leaders in eight New Jersey
counties.

[90] Blydenburgh, "Party Organizations," pp. 114-115.

[91] John C. Wahlke et al., *The Legislative System: Explorations in Legislative Behavior*
(New York: Wiley, 1962), pp. 44, 98. Data gathered in 1957.

[92] The material in this paragraph is from Blydenburgh, "Party Organizations," pp.
130-134.

sprawl. The other six are Democratic, all but one operating in urban counties with large cities: Essex County (932,299), site of Newark (381,930); Hudson County (609,266), site of Jersey City (262,545); Mercer County (303,968), site of Trenton (104,638); Passaic County (460,782), site of Paterson (144,824); Camden County (456,291), site of Camden (102,551); and the exception, Middlesex County (583,813), site of a number of smaller cities including Perth Amboy (38,798) and New Brunswick (41,885). The twelve organizations' counties together include about three-quarters of state population. Most of the state's other nine counties are relatively small and outside the greater New York and Philadelphia areas.[93]

On the Republican side, Somerset County's organization is said to have been the state's strongest in the mid-1970s—"an urban machine in a suburban setting." At the time Somerset was the only New Jersey county without civil service rules.[94] Bergen County, a suburb of New York City like Nassau and Westchester counties, supported a strong Republican organization until the mid-1960s that was said to have its "heart . . . in Hackensack [36,008], the county seat where traditional machine politics dominated."[95] It might be noted that affluence does

---

[93] The chief exception here is Union County (543,116), site of Elizabeth (112,654). Union County has probably supported traditional organizations at municipal and county levels even if no "strong" county organization exists by Blydenburgh's standard. It certainly has had regular organizations that slate candidates. See for example "A Triumph for Kinneally; Regular Democrats Take It All," a report on primaries in the *Newark Star-Ledger*, June 4, 1969, p. 19. Suburban Morris County (383,454), a Republican stronghold, is said to have a distinctively individualistic style of politics. County organization is weak and candidates have traditionally run for office using their own resources. See Maureen Moakley and Gerald Pomper, "Party Organizations," ch. 4 in Richard Lehne and Alan Rosenthal (eds.), *Politics in New Jersey*, rev. ed. (New Brunswick, N.J.: Eagleton Institute of Politics, Rutgers University, 1979), p. 96.

[94] Blydenburgh, "Party Organizations," pp. 130, 134.

[95] A feature of New Jersey's Republican primary in 1965 was "the easy victory in Bergen County of the organization-backed ticket over an insurgent slate for the State Legislature, county freeholders, and state committee. The results left no doubt of the continued control by the county leader, Walter H. Jones." And in the primary for governor: "Mr. Jones was again a key figure in this primary. . . . He threw the weight of his big-county machine into the primary and the result was a substantial margin in Senator [Wayne] Dumont's favor in that county." Walter H. Waggoner, "Jersey Primary Won by Dumont," *New York Times*, June 2, 1965, p. 42. But the Jones regime came to an abrupt end in November 1965, when Democrats took over almost all Bergen's state legislative seats and "even won control of the Board of Chosen Freeholders, which operates the county and dispenses patronage" (Walter H. Waggoner, "Republican Rule Ended in Jersey," *New York Times*, November 3, 1965, p. 31. On Bergen in general see also Blydenburgh, "Party Organizations," p. 133. The reference to Hackensack is from Moakley and Pomper, "Party Organizations," pp. 95-96, which discusses the condition of the county's weakened Republican organization in the late 1970s.

not rule out having traditional party organizations: of 344 American counties with populations over 100,000 in 1970, Nassau, Westchester, Bergen, and Somerset counties ranked third, seventh, tenth, and twelfth in median family income. The Atlantic County Republican organization, run by Enoch L. "Nucky" Johnson from 1909 until his indictment for tax evasion in 1939, and then by Frank S. "Hap" Farley until federal prosecutors closed in on the party's local contract dealings in 1971, used to stand out both for its corruption and for its exceptional influence in state party affairs. Both Johnson and Farley relied on a core vote in formally nonpartisan Atlantic City—under Johnson, at least, substantially a black vote.[96]

In New Jersey's Democratic party, the most important unit during most of the twentieth century has been the Hudson County organization, normally centered in officially nonpartisan Jersey City, led by Frank Hague from 1917 through 1949 and John V. Kenny from 1949 through 1971.[97] Probably the Hague machine controlled Jersey City as completely as a party organization has ever controlled an American city. It was noted for its command of city and county jobs, its considerable money income, its model ward and precinct structure, and its slating power in nonpartisan elections and Democratic primaries.[98]

---

[96] On Atlantic County under Johnson: Dayton D. McKean, *Pressures on the Legislature of New Jersey* (New York: Columbia University Press, 1938), p. 33; "Enoch L. Johnson, Ex-Boss in Jersey," *New York Times*, December 10, 1968, p. 47. On Farley and the events of the early 1970s: Peirce, *Megastates of America*, p. 225; "Records Subpoenaed by U.S. in Atlantic County Corruption Inquiry," *New York Times*, August 15, 1971, p. 58; "An Old Pro Is Beaten in South Jersey," *New York Times*, November 3, 1971, p. 31; Joseph F. Sullivan, "Ex-Atlantic Aide Convicted of Extortion," *New York Times*, November 25, 1972, p. 67. According to the last account a former Atlantic County Engineer, on trial for extorting $250,000 from contracting and engineering firms, "testified that the money he had collected went to the Atlantic County Republican organization." A good capsule treatment of the Johnson and Farley regimes appears in George Sternlieb and James W. Hughes, *The Atlantic City Gamble* (Cambridge: Harvard University Press, 1983), pp. 31-38.

[97] This seems to be the only New Jersey organization anyone has done a detailed study of. There are five good monographic treatments: Dayton D. McKean, *The Boss: The Hague Machine in Action* (Boston: Houghton Mifflin, 1940); Chandler, "The County Chairmanship," ch. 3 ("Profile of a Chairman at Work: The Municipal Monarchy of Frank Hague"), a summary account based partly on interviews with Kenny; Richard J. Connors, *A Cycle of Power: The Career of Jersey City Mayor Frank Hague* (Metuchen, N.J.: Scarecrow Press, 1971), with an epilogue, pp. 202-211, covering the Kenny era; John Kincaid, "Political Success and Policy Failure: The Persistence of Machine Politics in Jersey City" (Ph.D. dissertation, Temple University, 1980), ch. 7 on the Hague machine, ch. 8 on the Kenny machine and its aftermath; and William Lemmey, "Boss Kenny of Jersey City, 1949-1972," *New Jersey History* 98(1980), 9-28.

[98] On jobs see McKean, *The Boss*, pp. 121-132; Connors, *Cycle of Power*, pp. 62-67.

Hague could mobilize enough Hudson County votes in the 1920s and 1930s to swing the outcomes of Democratic primaries for governor and even to exercise influence in state Republican primaries.[99] Kenny is said to have headed after 1949 "a loosely led payroll army: Irish, Italian and Polish in composition and tied to himself by personal loyalties, patronage and contract handouts." Patronage jobs were drawn from both city and county (including some 2,000 in the city medical center), and income issued from a Rice Pudding Fund that assessed 3 percent of public employees' salaries and from union funds, gambling, contract kickbacks, and evidently business shakedowns and organized crime. Organization candidates usually prevailed in Jersey City elections and Democratic county and state legislative primaries.[100] In 1970 a federal indictment of Kenny and the mayor of Jersey City brought to light a record of extraordinary thievery, and the city turned to a reform mayor for six years as a result.[101] But Thomas F. X. Smith, elected mayor in

---

On income sources: McKean, ch. 7, pp. 145-149. On ward and precinct structure: *ibid.*, pp. 132-137; Connors, pp. 57-62, 69-71. On slating power: McKean, pp. 84-85, 137-144; Connors, ch. 5.

[99] McKean, *The Boss*, pp. 47-55, 67-77; Connors, *Cycle of Power*, pp. 49-52, 108-109.

[100] Source of quotation: Connors, *Cycle of Power*, p. 203. On patronage: Lemmey, "Boss Kenny." On patronage and sources of money: Kincaid, "Political Success," pp. 502-503, 511-514. On salary assessments: Ronald Sullivan, "Employes of Jersey City Now Balk at Political Tithes," *New York Times*, October 10, 1971, p. 76. On slating power see Connors, pp. 202-211. In the 1960s Kenny shifted the location of his ward committeemen's jobs from city to county government (Lemmey, pp. 20-24).

[101] "Here's how a federal court described the Kenny-led extortion ring: 'At the head of the scheme was J. V. Kenny, who, the evidence suggests, ruled the political life of both (Jersey) City and (Hudson) County. He effectively determined who would hold public office in (city or county) government, and he organized a system to ensure that all contractors working on a public project would kick back a percentage of the contract price (about 10%) to a designated bagman. Generally speaking, members of the city government would collect kickbacks from city contractors, and members of the county government from county contractors.'" (Stanley Penn, "A New New Jersey? Once a Corrupt Haven, State Is Shaken Up By Federal Prosecutors," *Wall Street Journal*, June 30, 1972, p. 23.) "The trial unveiled a spectacular array of contract schemes and kickbacks involving millions of dollars and approximately 186 corporations. In one instance, the defendants had demanded seven percent ($2.8 million) of a $40 million reservoir contract. The company withdrew its bid. The usual rate was ten percent and contractors 'lined up' in the County Chairman's office to make so many deals that the Chairman often lost track of the money and simply stored it in ashcans in his basement" (Kincaid, "Political Success," p. 520). "Probably the most shocking disclosure concerned Mayor Thomas Whelan and City Council President Thomas Flaherty. The two officials maintained joint numbered accounts at a Florida bank, which had deposits of over $1,200,000, all in cash or negotiable bonds purchased for cash. The businessman's mayor, who fired cleaning women and handicapped personnel from the Medical Center, the war hero who urged

1977, again briefly put into effect the traditional formula of slating and patronage in city and county, even successfully purging an incumbent Democratic congressman in 1978 in order to advance an organization nominee.[102] More recently Union City (58,537), another Hudson County jurisdiction, came to notice as a decades-old machine city on the occasion of Mayor William V. Musto's imprisonment for racketeering.[103]

Elsewhere in the Democratic party the Middlesex County organization, built by David T. Wilentz in the 1930s on bases in New Brunswick and Perth Amboy, maintained some of its considerable authority in the early 1970s, still under Wilentz, though not much was left by the early 1980s.[104] "As county organizations in New Jersey go, the Wilentz ma-

---

the city to strive for moral behavior, turned out to be one of the city's biggest thieves" (Lemmey, "Boss Kenny," p. 26). For a treatment of the regime of reform mayor Dr. Paul Jordan see Stephen R. Weissman, "White Ethnics and Urban Politics in the Seventies: The Case of Jersey City," *Polity* 9(1976), 182-207; and Kincaid, "Political Success," pp. 521-546.

[102] See Brian O'Reilly, "Tommy Smith's First Hurrah," *New Jersey Magazine*, March 1979, pp. 17-19, 49-53; Kincaid, "Political Success," pp. 539-549; Moakley and Pomper, "Political Organizations," p. 94. The 1978 purge repeated an achievement of 1958, when the Kenny organization took on Congressman Alfred D. Sieminski and defeated him easily in a primary. See Alfred E. Clark, "Hudson Approves a Record Budget," *New York Times*, March 1, 1958, p. 17; George C. Wright, "Williams, Kean Win Jersey Vote," *New York Times*, April 16, 1958, p. 26. In 1978 Congressman Joseph A. LeFante withdrew without bothering to contest a primary when Smith's Hudson organization decided to slate Frank J. Guarini, Jr., instead (*Congressional Quarterly Weekly*, February 25, 1978, p. 472, and May 27, 1978, p. 1325). Guarini won 81.9% of the vote in a three-way primary, 75.3% of the major-party vote in the November election, then two months later a position on the House Ways and Means Committee.

[103] Alfonso A. Narvaez, "Stakes High in Election for Musto's City Office," *New York Times*, July 31, 1982. Mayor William V. Musto was one of thirteen figures indicted as of February 1983 as the result of a federal investigation of corruption in Hudson County. See Joseph F. Sullivan, "The Trials of Hudson Corruption Cases," *New York Times*, February 27, 1983, p. E6. A side product of the Musto trial was "a 35-page memo from the U.S. attorney's office that paints Hudson County politics as a circus of influence peddling, racketeering, organized crime, and murder" (Sue Warner, "Hudson County: A Sordid Look," *Bergen Record*, April 18, 1982). On the Musto machine: "Hudson County also became the second largest Cuban settlement outside of Miami, with most of the Cubans settling in Union City where Mayor Musto's thirty-year-old Italian machine welcomed them with bilingual education programs, good gambling, and a share of the patronage pool" (Kincaid, "Political Success," p. 527).

[104] A 1979 report: "Until recently, it might have been characterized as a machine organization, but demographic shifts and other factors have produced something closer to a coalition where power is dispersed and loyalty is diffuse" (Moakley and Pomper, "Party Organizations," p. 94, and more generally pp. 94-96). See also McKean, *The Boss*, p. 56; and Blydenburgh, "Party Organizations," pp. 132-133. A strong Democratic machine still ran New Brunswick in the early 1980s. See Kay Lawson, Gerald Pomper,

chine is unusually enlightened, reasonably liberal and moderately honest," one observer commented in 1970.[105] The Mercer County organization, entrenched at ward and district levels in officially nonpartisan
Trenton, ranked as one of the state's strongest in the 1970s: "Large
Democratic pluralities out of the thirteenth legislative district and patronage resources from the state capital at Trenton enable the Demo-
cratics to control the county government."[106] A Democratic organization run by Alfred Pierce dominated the city of Camden in the 1960s,
and, as a byproduct, Camden County; leadership passed in the mid-
1970s to Mayor Angelo J. Errichetti of later Abscam notoriety.[107]

Essex County's Democratic organization had solid control of nominations for the state legislature in the early 1960s, and evidently its
leadership and patronage connections survived the decade in good condition.[108] The surprise in Essex County is the political texture of Newark. Party organizations have routinely controlled municipal elections
in other officially nonpartisan New Jersey cities (Jersey City and Atlantic City in particular), but evidently not in Newark. One author contrasts Jersey City's elections dominated by Hague in the 1920s and
1930s with Newark's "loosely structured free-for-alls."[109] Another de-

---

and Maureen Moakley, "Party Linkage at the Base: Middlesex County, New Jersey," paper presented at the 1983 convention of the American Political Science Association, p.
10.

[105] Ross K. Baker, "A Machine Hangs on in Jersey," *Washington Post*, June 21, 1970,
p. B1.

[106] Moakley and Pomper, "Party Organizations," p. 98 (includes quotation); Blydenburgh, "Party Organizations," pp. 130, 131. The Mercer organization is the youngest of
the state's major Democratic organizations, dating back only to the late 1940s.

[107] Don DeMaio, "Green is a primary color," *New Jersey Magazine*, June 1979, pp.
24-32; Harry Kendall, "Angelo Errichetti: Atop the Slippery Pole," *New Jersey Magazine*, November 1978, pp. 9-12, 39-43. On Camden County's nonpartisan municipalities
in the early 1970s: "There are no primaries and both Democratic and Republican organizations regularly field identifiable slates of candidates. Although candidates unaffiliated
with either major party need not fulfill formidable requirements to earn a place on the
ballot, they have almost no chance of being elected. Party organization support—endorsement, financing, literature, and scheduling—forms the basis for almost every successful campaign" (Stinebrickner, "Representative Government," p. 270).

[108] On the early 1960s: Gerald Pomper, "Ethnic and Group Voting in Nonpartisan
Municipal Elections," *Public Opinion Quarterly* 30(1966), 91-93. On the 1960s in general: Blydenburgh, "Party Organizations," p. 131; Alfonso A. Narvaez, "Essex Chief, at
26, Holds New Power," *New York Times*, November 27, 1978, pp. B1, B9. A Democratic organization sagging during the 1970s in notional Tyrone County, portrayed in a
recent piece, seems to be the Essex County Democratic organization in disguise. See Gerald M. Pomper, Rodney Forth, and Maureen W. Moakley, "Political Parties: Another
Machine Withers Away: For Better? For Worse?" ch. 5 in Allan P. Sindler (ed.), *American
Politics and Public Policy: Seven Case Studies* (Washington, D.C.: CQ Press, 1982).

[109] Connors, *Cycle of Power*, p. 113-114.

scribes a "largely individual, disorganized, and incoherent" Newark election in 1962 in which nineteen candidates sought four at-large city council positions in general without making alliances with each other or carrying organizational endorsements, though a black "machine" did some slating in one ward.[110] Newark's Kenneth Gibson, elected mayor in 1970, evidently showed little interest, at least in his early years in office, in building his own Democratic city organization or dealing with county leaders on patronage.[111]

In general, New Jersey's traditional organizations, like others elsewhere, have been losing control of their electorates.[112] At the level of statewide primaries, the Republican county organizations used to exercise influence in the 1960s that has largely drained away since.[113] On the Democratic side, the Hudson County ascendancy gave way in the 1950s and 1960s to small coalitions of county leaders; Mercer and Middlesex leaders, for example, took the initiative in slating Richard J. Hughes for governor in 1961.[114] But in the 1970s, though the Hudson organization still had to be reckoned with, the state's Democratic primaries for governor and Senator came to look like typical American contests among candidate organizations.[115] A new law providing state

[110] On 1962: Pomper, "Ethnic and Group Voting," pp. 79-97, quotation at p. 93. The best source on Irvine Turner's ward organization, which operated throughout the 1960s, is Fred Barbaro, "Newark: Political Brokers," *Society* 9(September-October 1972), 42-54. Raphael Sonenshein, in "Mayor Kenneth Gibson's Newark" (senior thesis, Woodrow Wilson School of Public and International Affairs, Princeton University, 1971), pp. 10-50, gives an account of Newark municipal elections in 1954 through 1970 in which the only significant slating organization of a traditional sort was Turner's.

[111] Blydenburgh, "Party Organizations," p. 131.

[112] See Maureen Moakley, "New Jersey," ch. 10 in Alan Rosenthal and Maureen Moakley (eds.), *The Political Life of the American States* (New York: Praeger, 1984), pp. 236-238.

[113] On the 1960s see for example George C. Wright, "Jersey Will Hold Primary Tuesday," *New York Times*, April 16, 1961, p. 41. In 1978 Jeffrey Bell's victory over Senator Clifford Case in the Republican Senate primary was a triumph of a model candidate organization.

[114] George C. Wright, "Hughes' Naming Due Tomorrow," *New York Times*, February 12, 1961, p. 53; George C. Wright, "Democrats Name Hughes in Jersey," *New York Times*, February 14, 1961, p. 1. In 1958 the Hudson organization backed a loser for the first time in decades in a statewide Democratic primary, but its power was evident even in the loss. Former Senator Harrison Williams, who won his first nomination that year in a three-way primary, had the support of all the county leaders but Hudson's and won 64.6% of the total vote and a 84,495 plurality over the runner-up in the twenty counties outside Hudson; in Hudson County he got 7.7% of the total vote and trailed the state runner-up by 71,747; 37.9% of the total state vote was cast in Hudson County. See George C. Wright, "Williams, Kean Win Jersey Vote," pp. 1, 26.

[115] On the Hudson organization see e.g., *Congressional Quarterly Weekly*, May 27, 1972, p. 1200; June 11, 1977, p. 1144; June 10, 1978, p. 1446. Successfully using a can-

subsidies for candidates in primary campaigns produced free-for-alls among thirteen Democrats and eight Republicans in the primaries for governor in 1981.[116] Two sets of actors in particular contributed to the organizations' decline: liberal activists, notably in Bergen, Essex, and Passaic counties, who challenged the party regulars in primaries at all levels in the 1960s and 1970s; and, probably more important, federal prosecutors, who have done considerable damage during the last two decades to the Atlantic, Hudson, and Essex county regimes.[117] Landmark events took place in 1977-1979 in Essex County. As prosecutors closed in on Democratic party chairman Harry Lerner, preparing an indictment for racketeering, conspiracy, bribery, and extortion, a reform movement redesigned the structure of the county's government, evidently cut off its patronage, and elected to the new post of county executive a twenty-six-year-old assemblyman who claimed a record of legislative accomplishment on utility rates, tenant rebates, generic drugs, and anti-redlining.[118] This association of a New Jersey county government with an interest in issues was something of a novelty. But a TPO score for the late 1960s is easy to assign: a solid 5. In fact if the states were ranked from 1 to 50 according to the prominence of their TPOs, New Jersey might well rank first.

PENNSYLVANIA (11,793,909) _____

Press reports on Pennsylvania's primaries read like New Jersey's. A Philadelphia report of the late 1960s: "Louis G. Hill, Democratic organization-backed candidate, overwhelmed his opponent, Benjamin L. Long, in primary voting here Tuesday to win his party's nomination to

---

didate organization, Bill Bradley won his 1978 Senate primary without any help from the county organizations. See *ibid.*, May 27, 1978, pp. 1322-1323; June 10, 1978, p. 1446.

[116] Joseph F. Sullivan, "Turning off Party Machines Turned on the Candidates," *New York Times*, March 8, 1981, p. E6. This is a good overall treatment of the decline of county organization influence in statewide nominating.

[117] On liberal activists see for example Blydenburgh, "Party Organizations," pp. 118-119, 132.

[118] On Lerner: Alfonso A. Narvaez, "Essex Sheriff and 2 Aides Indicted With a Former Democratic Chief," *New York Times*, August 24, 1979, pp. A1, B2. On the reform movement: "Old Order Changeth in Essex Politics," *New York Times*, June 11, 1978, p. E6; Joseph Sullivan, "Essex Disassembles Its Machine," *New York Times*, June 25, 1978, p. E7; and Narvaez, "Essex Sheriff," p. B2. On the new county executive, Peter Shapiro, as reported in Narvaez, p. B2: "Part of Mr. Shapiro's campaign focused on county employees and he issued a 'bill of rights' for them, which included the right to be free from political harassment and from alleged demands and requests by superiors for contributions to political parties."

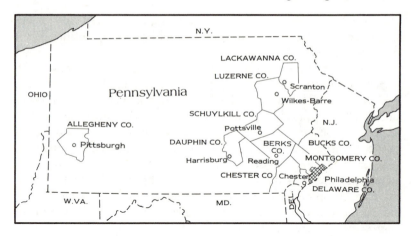

the State Senate. . . . Of the 16 contests for the State House of Representatives in the city, only three non-organization candidates were victorious."[119] A headline on Delaware County: "Organization-Backed Candidates on Top in Delaware GOP Vote."[120] On an incumbent assemblyman losing a primary in Montgomery County: "He failed to seek organization backing and ran as an independent Republican."[121] A story on Bucks County: "Bucks County's Republican organization suffered a major setback Tuesday night as State Sen. Marvin V. Keller was defeated."[122] A headline on Lackawanna County: "Party-Backed Candidates Win Nominations for Legislature."[123] A story on Allegheny County (Pittsburgh area) Democrats: "Twenty organization candidates for the House had a fight on their hands from non-endorsed candidates. Nine had no contests in their bids to face Republican opponents in the November general elections."[124]

Pennsylvania's parties have indeed resembled New Jersey's and New York's. The best general post–World War II guide is Frank J. Sorauf's treatment of electoral politics at the state assembly level in the late 1950s.[125] "Old-style political machines, with their armies of committeemen and party workers, prevail in many small towns and cities, as

[119] *Philadelphia Inquirer*, May 18, 1966, p. 21.
[120] *Ibid.*
[121] *Ibid.*, May 20, 1970, p. 5.
[122] *Ibid.*
[123] *Scranton Times*, May 20, 1970, p. 1.
[124] *Pittsburgh Post-Gazette*, May 18, 1966, p. 16.
[125] Frank J. Sorauf, *Party and Representation: Legislative Politics in Pennsylvania* (New York: Atherton, 1963). Study based on interviews with some five hundred politicians and community informants around the state.

well as in the metropolitan centers of the state"—though in general cities, not surprisingly, had stronger organizations than rural areas.[126] "The tradition of politics as a system of immediate and direct rewards lives on and attracts to both party banners workers who openly seek those rewards. . . . The tradition of politics as personal gain perforce means that Pennsylvania politics are nonideological and often issueless."[127] In general the organizations in Sorauf's account were hierarchies centered at the county level that exercised impressive control over nominations for the state assembly within their jurisdictions.[128] One gets the sense from other sources that the state's organizations were somewhat weaker but still very much in business in the late 1960s.

A brief survey of the state can begin with Philadelphia (1,950,098), one of the major machine cities of American history.[129] From the Civil

[126] Source of quotation: *ibid.*, p. 14. In Chapter 3, Sorauf presents an A-B-C-D scale of party organizations. An "A" organization is an "old-style 'machine'; consistent, almost full-time committee work, determined internal discipline, and centralization of authority mark its hierarchy"; and a "D" organization is a "minimum" outfit: "in most cases a paper organization in which a handful of activists keep alive a substantially disorganized and demoralized party" (pp. 46-47). In both parties, but notably the Democratic, organization type varied with density of population: of the thirty-five assembly districts relatively high in density (over 1,000 people per square mile) thirty were dominated on their Democratic side and sixteen on their Republican by county organizations of A or B type; for the forty-one districts lower in density, the comparable figures for A or B type were nine on the Democratic side and seven on the Republican. See pp. 47-50. Of course a lot of these districts were in one-party areas, where one would not expect the minority party to have much of an organization. Witt, in his 1967 study of New York, sorted his data by the rules of Sorauf's classification and found more or less the same relation in New York between population density and organization type. See Witt, "Legislative-Local Party Linkage," pp. 82-85.

[127] Sorauf, *Party and Representation*, p. 14.

[128] On hierarchy: "Primary responsibility for recruiting and ticket-building rests generally with the party chairman, although he may share it with informal leaders, party insiders, or party executive committees. In only ten of these 156 constituency parties [Democratic and Republican parties in 78 assembly districts] did the recruitment power rest with special party caucuses or selection committees" (*ibid.*, p. 57). On counties as the important centers of organization: pp. 50-51. On the nominating process: pp. 52-58, ch. 5. Sorauf's summary statement: "The political party in Pennsylvania exercises enormous control over the business of picking state legislators. It has been able to absorb the direct primary into its domination of the selection process, and it has largely been able to exclude nonparty groups from significant influence in it" (p. 120). To what end? "Finally, for what it reaffirms about Pennsylvania politics, party leaders only infrequently mentioned ideological criteria for candidates. Either general ideological standards ('liberal' and 'conservative') or those allied to party ('party principles' and the like) figured in the criteria listed by less than 10 per cent of the local party leaders interviewed" (p. 110).

[129] City and county of the same name have identical boundaries. The best general sources on electoral politics in post-1950 Philadelphia are James Reichley, *The Art of Government: Reform and Organization Politics in Philadelphia* (New York: Fund for

War through the 1940s the dominant organization was Republican, but it crumbled in 1951 in a spell of weak leadership combined with uneasy voter attachment to an anti–New Deal and anti–Fair Deal party, and gave way to a Democratic organization different in label but identical in kind.[130] Hundreds of Republican ward and precinct leaders—especially in the "controlled wards"—defected to the Democrats in 1951 through 1955, taking along whatever voters they could.[131] By the late 1950s a stable Democratic organization presided over the city's considerable patronage network and a ward and precinct apparatus that copied the Republicans' though it better penetrated the city's growing black population.[132] Organization leaders ordinarily controlled nominations for municipal judgeships and congressional, state legislative, and city council seats.[133] In a study of North Central Phila-

---

the Republic, 1959); Robert L. Freedman, *A Report on Politics in Philadelphia* (Cambridge: Joint Center for Urban Studies, M.I.T./Harvard, 1963); Conrad Weiler, *Philadelphia: Neighborhood, Authority, and the Urban Crisis* (New York: Praeger, 1974), ch. 8; and Joseph R. Daughen and Peter Binzen, *The Cop Who Would Be King: Mayor Frank Rizzo* (Boston: Little, Brown, 1977).

[130] See Reichley, *Art of Government*, pp. 5-24; Freedman, *Politics in Philadelphia*, pp. II:20-24.

[131] Reichley, *Art of Government*, pp. 97-100; Freedman, *Politics in Philadelphia*, pp. II:48-49. How much these leadership changes affected the city vote for higher offices is an intriguing question, though not an easy one to answer because Philadelphia's long-run trend was in a Democratic direction anyway. Still, the figures are interesting: in Presidential voting the city never voted over 5.1% more Democratic than the country as a whole in the four Roosevelt elections; in 1948 it voted 2.0% more Republican than the country; in 1952 and 1956 it voted 13.8% and 14.8% more Democratic than the country. Truman in 1948 carried the city by 6,737 votes; Stevenson in 1952 carried it by 160,478 votes. Charles A. Ekstron has shown, in a study of Philadelphia municipal elections, that Republican mayoral candidates won their highest percentages in wards lowest in socioeconomic status in the elections of 1947 and 1951. The relation holds separately within the set of white wards in 1947, black wards in 1947, white wards in 1951, black wards in 1951, and also white wards in 1943. (In 1943 there were not enough dominantly black wards to make the comparison.) It went away after the Democrats came to power. See "The Electoral Politics of Reform and Machine: The Political Behavior of Philadelphia's 'Black' Wards, 1943-1969," ch. 6 in Miriam Ershkowitz and Joseph Zikmund II (eds.), *Black Politics in Philadelphia* (New York: Basic Books, 1973).

[132] On patronage: Reichley, *Art of Government*, pp. 23-24; Freedman, *Politics in Philadelphia*, pp. II:40-42, 47-50. On ward and precinct organization: Reichley, pp. 97, 100-107; Freedman, pp. II:38-39, 46-52; III:4.

[133] On Congress: Freedman, *Art of Government*, p. II:33; on organization control of the city's state legislative delegation, and by inference their nominations: Edward F. Cooke and William J. Keefe, "Pennsylvania: The Limits of Power in a Divided Government," ch. 8 in Malcolm E. Jewell (ed.), *The Politics of Reapportionment* (New York: Atherton, 1962), p. 154; on the city council: Freedman, pp. II:8, 50-51; on judgeships: Freedman, pp. II:11-13, 18-19.

delphia in the early 1970s everything was still in place—precinct operatives, patronage, slating—an overall party domination of political
life.[134]

One office the city's Democratic organization has never controlled is
the mayoralty. All four Philadelphia mayors in 1951 through 1979
won election at least once backed by supporting Democratic coalitions
independent of the organization; all four began office cooperating with
the organization but ended up fighting it. Joseph S. Clark (1951-1955)
and Richardson Dilworth (1955-1962) led reform coalitions; James H.
J. Tate (1962-1971) began office as an organization man, but like New
York's Mayor Wagner six years earlier built a constituency in civil service unions and created his own electoral base in 1967; and Frank L.
Rizzo (1971-1979) won office on a law-and-order appeal to whites
("I'm gonna make Attila the Hun look like a faggot after this election's
over").[135] Rizzo took to patronage dealing himself in the mid-1970s,
won over a few ward leaders, put up a primary slate against the regular
organization and defeated it, and installed his own Democratic city
chairman.[136] This was unsettling to an organization already declining
in influence, like most others elsewhere in the 1970s, as were the convictions of leading party regulars in well-publicized Abscam and
"ghost-workers" trials in 1977 through 1980 (the latter followed a
crackdown on the custom of hiring campaign workers on state money
in "no-show" jobs).[137] Some things go on and on: recent reports tell of
ward leaders in South Philadelphia, the organization's traditional base,
pursuing particularistic neighborhood routines that probably date
back 150 years.[138] But organization candidates lost three out of five at-
large council nominations in the city's Democratic primary in 1979, encountering stiff competition from a coalition of liberals and blacks and

[134] Stanley B. Greenberg, *Politics and Poverty: Modernization and Response in Five
Poor Neighborhoods* (New York: Wiley, 1974), pp. 64-71.

[135] On Clark and Dilworth: Freedman, *Politics in Philadelphia*, pp. II:30-32. On Tate:
Weiler, *Philadelphia*, pp. 166-167. On Rizzo: Daughen and Binzen, *The Cop Who
Would Be King, passim*, statement from 1975 campaign at p. 8.

[136] *Ibid.*, ch. 14, pp. 325-326. See also James T. Wooten, "Rizzo Solidifies Power in
Philadelphia," *New York Times*, May 26, 1976, p. 11.

[137] See Wendell Rawls, Jr., "The Making of Some Political Careers in Philadelphia,"
New York Times, February 8, 1980, p. B4; William Robbins, "3 Are Found Guilty in
Patronage Fraud," *New York Times*, October 26, 1980, p. 26; and Albert R. Hunt, "A
Political Machine Faces a Challenge: The Abscam Scandal," *Wall Street Journal*, April
18, 1980, pp. 1, 32. "They were talking a lot about Abscam even in the controlled
wards," one politician is said to have mused (p. 32).

[138] See Karen De Witt, "Philadelphia Councilman Excels in the Politics of Favors,"
New York Times, December 2, 1979, p. 32; and Leslie Bennetts, "South Philadelphia
Hears an Old Refrain: 'Do Me a Favor,' " *New York Times*, April 23, 1980, p. B9.

also from other endorsing groups in a wild contest generating 101 candidates for the five positions.[139] And journalists have managed to produce detailed stories on the Democratic mayoral primaries of 1979 and 1983 without giving attention to the regular organization—a precedent-setting oversight that says something about its current influence.[140]

Charles E. Gilbert, writing in the mid-1960s on three Republican counties in the Philadelphia suburbs—Bucks (415,056), Montgomery (623,921), and Delaware (601,423)—found in general "a low-pressure politics centered on careerism and organization loyalty."[141] As of 1950 each had been dominated for decades by a patronage-based, hierarchical county organization in control of Republican nominating at the county level and at least an arbiter on political matters in the townships.[142] The Bucks and Montgomery organizations were still slating candidates and handing out patronage in the early 1960s, but both (especially Montgomery's) were fragmenting and losing control as middle-class activists of both parties moved into politics. Richard Schweiker, later Senator and then Secretary of Housing and Urban Development, ran as an insurgent and won a congressional seat from Montgomery County regulars in 1960.[143] But John J. McClure, Delaware County leader from 1921 through 1965, still ran a powerful organization in the 1960s, using a small "War Board" to generate decisions on slating and patronage and tending a core electoral base among impoverished blacks in the city of Chester (56,331) for use in Republican primaries.[144] The Delaware organization, like Hudson County's in New Jersey, has a record of purging its own party's congressmen to promote new nominees: there are instances in 1948, 1964, and 1974.[145] In another Philadelphia suburb covered in a monograph by it-

---

[139] Sandra Featherman, "Ethnicity and Ethnic Candidates: Vote Advantages in Local Elections," *Polity* 15(1983), 397-415.

[140] See for example Gregory Jaynes, "Philadelphia Seen Apathetic on Vote," *New York Times*, May 8, 1979, p. 15; Gregory Jaynes, "Rizzo Spurns Both Mayoral Nominees," *New York Times*, May 17, 1979; William Robbins, "In Underdog's Role, Rizzo Sets Plans to Win 3d Term as Philadelphia Mayor," *New York Times*, December 22, 1982, p. A16; William Robbins, "Philadelphia Rivals Call Turnout Vital in Primary," *New York Times*, May 16, 1983, p. A10.

[141] Charles E. Gilbert, *Governing the Suburbs* (Bloomington: Indiana University Press, 1967), quotation at p. 62.

[142] *Ibid.*, chs. 6, 9. Summary comments pp. 73-76.

[143] *Ibid.*, chs. 7, 8. On Schweiker: *ibid.*, p. 94.

[144] On Delaware County in general: *ibid.*, chs. 9, 10. On the mid-1960s: pp. 107-109. On McClure: *ibid.*, chs. 9, 10. On the War Board: pp. 103, 110-112. On the electoral base: *ibid.*, pp. 102, 112-113.

[145] *Ibid.*, p. 106 on 1948, p. 108 on 1964. On the 1974 instance see *Congressional Quarterly Weekly*, May 11, 1974, pp. 1215-1216; May 25, 1974, pp. 1364-1365. The War Board's victor in the 1974 primary lost in November to a Democrat.

self, Chester County (278,311), yet another dominant Republican organization ran substantially on patronage in the 1960s and routinely slated nominees.[146]

Pittsburgh (520,117), like Philadelphia, is an old Republican machine city that turned Democratic, though its switchover came two decades earlier, during the New Deal.[147] In 1932-1938 in the Pittsburgh case, large numbers of lower-level committeemen abandoned the Republican organization and joined the Democratic.[148] By 1937, under the leadership of David L. Lawrence, Democrats had built an organization with an effective ward structure and impressive staying power.[149] In the 1950s and 1960s about three-quarters of the several hundred Democratic city committeemen had jobs on the government payroll.[150] A study conducted in 1966-1967 describes a hierarchical city organization controlling access to public and party offices including the mayoralty, city council posts (all at-large), judgeships, and delegations to national Democratic conventions.[151] Erosion began soon afterward: the mayoralty fell to maverick Democrat Peter F. Flaherty in 1969 and has not reverted to organization hands since, and control of city appointments and nominations for lower offices sagged in the 1970s.[152] Politics elsewhere in Pittsburgh's parent unit, Allegheny

---

[146] Earl M. Baker, "Community and Party: Perceptions of the Political Party Among Local Legislators" (Ph.D. dissertation, American University, 1971), pp. 77-78, 155. Chester County is a unit separate from and not including the city of Chester.

[147] Bruce M. Stave, *The New Deal and the Last Hurrah: Pittsburgh Machine Politics* (Pittsburgh: University of Pittsburgh Press, 1970), pp. 27-32 on the Republican machine tradition; chs. 3-6 on the switchover.

[148] *Ibid.*, pp. 34-35, 60, 173-74. "In one ward, the Third, more than half the committeemen made this shift, indicating that control of the ward remained in the hands of the same individuals, although their party label had changed" (p. 174). See also William J. Keefe and William C. Seyler, "Precinct Politicians in Pittsburgh," *Social Science* 35(1960), 29.

[149] Stave, *New Deal and Last Hurrah*, chs. 6-8.

[150] *Ibid.*, pp. 169-173; Keefe and Seyler, "Precinct Politicians," p. 28.

[151] Martin A. Levin, *Urban Politics and the Criminal Courts* (Chicago: University of Chicago Press, 1977), pp. 36-45 ("The Political System of Pittsburgh"). On hierarchy: "The Democratic organization also has a well-developed, regularized, and disciplined hierarchy. 'Waiting in line' is accepted and respectable. At times personal goals must be subordinated to those of the party, and members must accept the need to stay in a position longer than personally desired, forego a desired post, or wait one's 'turn' on the ticket in order to maintain the organization's ethnic balance" (p. 39).

[152] On the 1969 election, in which the organization did maintain solid control of the city council, see Stave, *New Deal and Last Hurrah*, pp. 189-190. Flaherty served two four-year terms and then another independent, Richard Caliguiri, defeated an organization candidate in the mayoral election of 1977. See Terence Smith, "Big-City Machines Fared Poorly, As Did Blacks, in Local Elections," *New York Times*, November 10, 1977, p. A18; and "Quiet Skills of an Unbeatable 'Grunt,' " *Time*, June 15, 1981, p. 31. On

County (1,605,133), has engendered little writing but traditional organizations seem to have operated there in the state's metropolitan style.[153]

Reports on a number of cities and counties in eastern Pennsylvania supply evidence of traditional organizations. In Reading (87,643) and its parent unit, Berks County (296,382), where an important socialist movement rose and fell earlier in the century, a faction of "old-line organization Democrats" competed against "the reform element known as the Berks Independent Democrats or BID" in the mid-1960s. One account nonetheless points to organizational weakness on both the Democratic and Republican sides in Reading municipal elections: "Each candidate has been forced (and free) to develop his own constituency of neighbors, fellow ethnics, social clubs, and city workers."[154] In Lackawanna County (234,107), site of Scranton (103,564) and various mining communities, a model Democratic machine presided over slating and patronage in the 1950s—its leader Michael F. Lawler ranked as one of the "big three" state Democrats (along with the Philadelphia and Pittsburgh leaders)—though it appears to have run out of steam during the 1960s.[155] Republicans were running an "especially

---

organization sag in the 1970s: Michael Margolis, Lee S. Weinberg, and David F. Ranck, "Local Party Organization: From Disaggregation to Disintegration," paper presented at the 1980 convention of the American Political Science Association, pp. 4-6, 21-23. By the early 1980s electoral politics up and down the line in Pittsburgh seems to have taken on a more individualistic flavor: "The loyalties of the newer [party] activists are directed more toward particular party leaders or personal ambitions than toward achievement of organizational goals. Local party organization remains vital, but transmogrified. Grass roots activity is high as ever, but it tends to be supportive only of particular candidates rather than the party slate" (Michael Margolis and Raymond E. Owen, "From Organization to Personalism: A Note on the Transmogrification of the Local Political Party," paper forthcoming in *Polity*, 1985, quotation at p. 11).

[153] See Sorauf, *Party and Representation*, pp. 51, 108, and chs. 3 and 5, *passim*; Levin, *Urban Politics and the Criminal Courts*, pp. 38-41.

[154] In Reading's Democratic primary for mayor in 1967, the old-line candidate lost to a BID candidate who went on to defeat an incumbent Republican. See David S. Broder, "A Microcosm of Politics," *Washington Post*, September 29, 1968, pp. B1, B5, short quotation at B1. On organizational weakness: John A. Gardiner, *The Politics of Corruption: Organized Crime in an American City* (New York: Russell Sage, 1970), ch. 2, long quotation at p. 12. On the earlier Socialist movement: William C. Pratt, " 'Jimmie Higgins' and the Reading Socialist Community: An Exploration of the Socialist Rank and File," ch. 6 in Bruce M. Stave (ed.), *Socialism and the Cities* (Port Washington, N.Y.: Kennikat, 1975).

[155] Kathleen Purcell Munley, "From Minority to Majority: A Study of the Democratic Party in Lackawanna County, 1920-1950" (Ph.D. dissertation, Lehigh University, 1981), Introduction, ch. 2 of part 4, and Conclusion. On the "big three": p. 354. On politics in the 1950s: "Absolute loyalty to Lawler was a prerequisite that rarely required

potent" machine in the late 1950s in Dauphin County (223,834), site of Harrisburg (68,061), which has evidently kept on placing people in office.[156] Luzerne County (342,301), site of Wilkes-Barre (58,856), changed only in recent times from a Republican into a Democratic holding; the city's government switched in 1959 and the county's in 1967.[157] A Republican machine ran at least Wilkes-Barre (no evidence on the county) in the 1950s; a Democratic machine ran both city and county in the mid-1970s, when nearly everyone in an appointive or elective city or county job is said to have received it through a party decision.[158] Finally, an interesting report tells of Schuylkill County (160,089), in anthracite coal country, where an old Republican machine continued in power in the early 1970s: no issues (except for "the most egregious outrages such as the stealing of meat from the old folks home") disturbed a patronage politics based on a core organization vote among Eastern European Catholics.[159]

Recent changes in Pennsylvania's statewide nominating patterns again resemble New Jersey's and New York's: county organizations have lost most of their influence in the last few decades. On the Democratic side, the Philadelphia and Allegheny County organizations used to take the lead in slating candidates for governor and Senator; in 1958, for example, their spokesmen engineered a Senate nomination for George Leader, and the Philadelphia chairman vetoed Richardson Dilworth as gubernatorial nominee, paving the way for David L. Law-

---

discussion. All parts of the organization depended on the Commissioner for support and patronage. Applicants for state jobs submitted their names to Lawler directly. Although each local political leader was a power in his own area, each realized that without Lawler's endorsement and approval they mattered very little because partisan support at the lower levels of political activity was intricately tied to political favors and jobs. And Lawler dispensed all political patronage. One political leader has described the Democratic Party during these years as the largest employer in the county" (p. 355).

[156] On the 1950s: Sorauf, *Party and Representation*, p. 37. For a more recent trace of the organization's slating activity: *Harrisburg Patriot*, May 20, 1970, pp. 1, 9. See also Paul B. Beers, *Pennsylvania Politics Today and Yesterday: The Tolerable Accommodation* (University Park: Pennsylvania State University Press, 1980), pp. 168-171.

[157] James L. Sundquist, *Dynamics of the Party System: Alignment and Realignment of Political Parties in the United States* (Washington, D.C.: Brookings, 1973), p. 232.

[158] On the Republican machine: Sorauf, *Party and Representation*, p. 37. On the Democratic machine: Jeffrey Kampelman, "Democratic Politics in Luzerne County" (Yale course paper, 1977).

[159] Richard L. Kolbe, "Culture, Political Parties and Voting Behavior: Schuylkill County," *Polity* 8(1975), 241-268; quotation at p. 266. Sorauf writes that a political culture hospitable to traditional organization has prevailed not only in Philadelphia, Pittsburgh, and many smaller Pennsylvania cities, but also in "the heavily populated, though unincorporated, coal-mining sections and steel-mill centers of the state" (*Party and Representation*, p. 59).

rence instead.[160] But in 1964 a reform candidate defeated a Philadelphia-Allegheny entry in a Senate primary, and independent millionaire Milton J. Shapp won primaries for governor over an organization designee in both 1966 and 1970.[161] No Democratic slating of any kind counted for much in statewide primaries of the 1970s.[162] The Republican story is more complicated, but earlier coalition-building activities by county chairmen—evident for example in 1950 and 1954—had clearly given way to candidate organizations by the 1970s. H. John Heinz III's media blitz in the Republican Senate primary in 1976 is a case in point.[163] In general, with Shapp in the governorship (1970-1978) and Flaherty and Rizzo running their idiosyncratic mayoralties, Pennsylvania politics at the top executive level took on a novel nonorganizational cast in the 1970s. But the state's TPO reading for the late 1960s is an emphatic 5.

DELAWARE (548,104) _____

In nominating for statewide office (including its congressional seat), Delaware uses a challenge-primary system in which a convention loser needs 35 percent of the delegate vote to force a primary. Conventions were said in the mid-1950s to be "nothing more than formal clearing houses for ratifying the choices of the party organizations in the counties"—the state's three counties plus separately by custom the city of Wilmington (80,386).[164] In addition the parties have a long tradition of slating candidates for state legislative, county, and some municipal offices even though endorsements have no legal standing.[165] Primaries

[160] See Reichley, *Art of Government*, pp. 40, 45; *Congressional Quarterly Weekly*, May 16, 1958, p. 615.

[161] On the Senate primary in 1964: Maria J. Falco, *"Bigotry!" Ethnic, Machine, and Sexual Politics in a Senatorial Election* (Westport, Conn: Greenwood, 1980), chs. 2, 3. On 1966: Carl Lieberman, "The Defeat of an Organization Candidate: Shapp Versus Casey," *Social Science* 43(1968), 210-216. On 1970: *Congressional Quarterly Weekly*, May 8, 1970, pp. 1232-1233 and May 22, 1970, p. 1358.

[162] See for example Walter Shapiro, "Denenberg v. Flaherty: Politics after Common Cause," *Washington Monthly*, July/August 1974, pp. 23-32; *Congressional Quarterly Weekly*, May 6, 1978, p. 1102, and May 20, 1978, pp. 1226-1227.

[163] On the 1950s: Gilbert, *Governing the Suburbs*, pp. 72-73. On Heinz: *Congressional Quarterly Weekly*, April 17, 1976, p. 896; May 1, 1976, p. 1063. See also the Republican gubernatorial primary of 1978: *Congressional Quarterly Weekly*, May 6, 1978, p. 1101; May 20, 1978, p. 1226.

[164] Paul Dolan, *The Government and Administration of Delaware* (New York: Crowell, 1956), pp. 35-36, quotation at p. 36. Wilmington is legally a subsidiary unit of New Castle County.

[165] *Ibid.*, pp. 34-35.

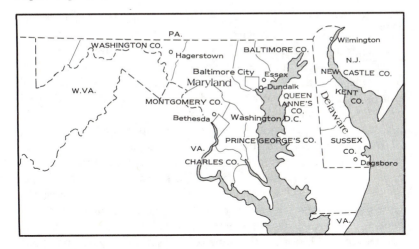

around 1970 often inspired newspaper accounts about organization slating, such as this comment on a state senate primary in New Castle County: "The Moore-Backer race was the one that generated the most interest, and many Democrats had given Moore an even chance of upsetting the Democratic organization, which brought its full resources to bear on the contest."[166] On a Republican primary for governor: "In the Buckson view, Peterson begins with the advantage of the basic organizational support in populous New Castle County. The party workers and the committeemen, controlled by the organization, are going to bring in a certain minimum vote for Peterson."[167] And on a purge that failed: "Sen. Curtis W. Steen of Dagsboro today interpreted his decisive primary victory Saturday as an indication of the dwindling popularity of Sussex County Democratic Chairman Raymond V. West."[168]

The existence of slating in Delaware is easier to establish than the kinds of organizations doing it. Monographic writing gives little help, though a source on New Castle County (385,856) in the 1960s tells of a patronage-based public labor force that was probably sufficient to flesh out a traditional county organization.[169] At the city level, news-

---

[166] *Wilmington Evening Journal*, August 19, 1968, p. 1. Moore was a maverick incumbent who in fact lost the primary.

[167] *Ibid.*, August 9, 1972, p. 27.

[168] *Ibid.*, August 19, 1968, p. 2. West had backed a challenger against the incumbent Steen.

[169] Before some reforms in the middle and late 1960s the county government was "administered in a fiercely partisan manner in which each of the 750 to 800 county jobs were delegated on the basis of political patronage" (Carol E. Hoffecker, *Corporate Capital: Wilmington in the Twentieth Century* [Philadelphia: Temple University Press, 1983], p. 213, and more generally pp. 207-219).

paper reports allow at least one solid conclusion: a moderately strong, traditional Democratic organization was operating around 1970 in Wilmington.[170] Its leader, Leo T. Marshall, characterized at one point as "the strongman in the Wilmington organization, which forms the backbone of the state party," is mentioned repeatedly.[171] Although control over the mayoralty was evidently beyond reach, the Marshall organization slated candidates for a range of public offices in the area, backed a number of successful candidates in city council and state legislative elections, and distributed patronage jobs. A 1966 election amounted to a conventional match between organization and reformers.[172] In a 1968 assembly primary, a "Black Power activist" challenged an organization candidate and lost.[173] In a 1972 state senate primary a young black community activist took on a black organization incumbent, advising voters to "take the $2 or the half-pint and then vote your conscience."[174] A story of the same year tells of the city organization's custom of circulating an "official yellow ballot" on primary day listing its designees.[175] An organization sweep drew notice in 1968: "Wilmington's Democratic organization emerged unscathed from the City Council primaries with Council President William J. McClafferty, Jr. and three at-large candidates winning handily."[176] With a traditional organization in its metropolis and county organizations that routinely slate candidates, Delaware has the appearance of a spinoff of New Jersey or Pennsylvania in party structure. A TPO score for the state: 4.

OHIO (10,652,017)

Work by Thomas A. Flinn makes it clear that lower-level party organizations exist and exercise influence in Ohio—in selecting state legislative candidates, for example, according to a study of the mid-1960s: "The overwhelming impression [is] that the party-sponsored can-

---

[170] The interpretation here is confirmed by Don Collat, an observer of Delaware politics.

[171] For example, *Wilmington Evening Journal*, July 19, 1966, pp. 1, 3; June 17, 1970, p. 3; August 14, 1972, p. 3; Curtis Wilkie, "Godfather of Democrats," *Wilmington Evening Journal*, August 6, 1972, p. 29 (source of quotation). Brief mentions of the Marshall organization appear in Hoffecker, *Corporate Capital*, pp. 174, 215.

[172] *Wilmington Evening Journal*, July 19, 1966, pp. 1, 3.

[173] "Bratten, a Black Power activist, lost the 4th Representative District run to Butcher. Although Bratten campaigned actively and had the support of several organizations in the district, which is Wilmington's West Side, he was not able to overcome Butcher's organization support." *Ibid.*, August 19, 1968, p. 2. Unlike Bratten, some challengers to the Wilmington organization during these years did win primaries.

[174] *Ibid.*, August 14, 1972, p. 3.   [175] *Ibid.*, August 21, 1972, p. 4.

[176] *Ibid.*, August 19, 1968, p. 1.

didates win in contested primaries." He says in addition: "Party is a reservoir from which candidates come, a screen through which they must pass, and an object at which their [primary] campaigns are directed."[177] At the same time one gets a sense that Ohio's county organizations (the basic units) have taken a somewhat less hierarchical form and traveled less on material inducements than have their counterparts in Pennsylvania and New Jersey.[178] Patronage jobs and other material benefits are one important set of inducements that encourage organization activity—jobs connected with county probate judgeships seem especially valuable—but organizations are said to depend also on other incentives such as a sense of "social responsibility" (though not much on "purposive" incentives of the Manhattan kind).[179] Leaders have something resembling a command relationship with committee members who are in politics for material gain, but cannot similarly control members involved for other reasons.[180]

[177] Thomas A. Flinn, "The Ohio General Assembly: A Developmental Analysis," ch. 6 in James A. Robinson (ed.), *State Legislative Innovation: Case Studies of Washington, Ohio, Florida, Illinois, Wisconsin, and California* (New York: Praeger, 1973), pp. 237-244, quotations at p. 243.

[178] The source on the nature of Ohio's county organizations is Thomas A. Flinn, "American County Political Parties: Purposes and Other Purposes," paper presented at the 1982 convention of the American Political Science Association. The study is based on participant observation, interviews with county leaders, and questionnaires addressed to county leaders and committee members; its material was gathered at a number of points between the early 1960s and early 1980s. The organizations do not seem to have changed significantly during the two intervening decades.

[179] On material "profit" as inducement: *ibid.*, pp. 13-19. On other kinds of inducement: *ibid.*, pp. 19-38.

[180] On leadership: *ibid.*, pp. 18-19, 27-33. An interesting statement on the relation between hierarchy and material inducements: "It may be said that the presence of career and job interests or purposes helps to predict and to explain some of the relationships that appear between leaders and some party members. It is the basis of an exchange or bargaining relation between leaders on the one hand who can make a contribution to nominations, elections, and to appointments and some members on the other hand who seek those objects. It is a relation unlike the one which commonly exists between the county leaders and other members which involves common purposes and the exchange of intangibles like friendship, information, and esteem. It is a relation which allows the leaders to use something like command in relation to party members as a tool of leader-

The Ohio city with the most interesting organizational past is Cincinnati (452,524), where a Republican machine influential in state affairs and usually in control of the city and of the parent unit, Hamilton County (926,018), operated for several decades through the mid-1920s.[181] A reform movement in 1925 brought to power the City Charter Committee (CCC), which has dominated Cincinnati politics much of the time since then.[182] The CCC is perhaps the most eminent of a familiar American class of slating organizations—municipal "good-government" groups with intellectual roots in the Progressive era, ordinarily support bases in business and professional communities, a distaste for patronage politics, and a commitment to efficiency in government and nonpartisanship in elections. The CCC in its prime had an impressive ward and precinct structure made up largely of middle-class housewives.[183] City reform notwithstanding, the older Republican organization endured in Hamilton County and still operated impressively in the late 1950s (for which the best monographic evidence is available): some 2,500 county patronage jobs, yielding a 2½ percent salary kickback as well as work in the party cause, underpinned an effective ward structure inside and outside the city. Party leaders presided over nominations for county and state legislative offices and slating for the city council; the party had no dissident factions of any importance, no independent ward fiefdoms run by individual politicians, and rarely any primary contests.[184] This hegemony lasted at least until the late

---

ship unlike their usual methods of leadership like guidance, suggestion and persuasion" (pp. 18-19).

[181] See Zane L. Miller, *Boss Cox's Cincinnati: Urban Politics in the Progressive Era* (New York: Oxford University Press, 1968); Ralph A. Straetz, *PR Politics in Cincinnati: Thirty-Two Years of City Government through Proportional Representation* (New York: New York University Press, 1958), pp. xi-xvii.

[182] Straetz, *PR Politics*, *passim*; Kenneth E. Gray, *A Report on Politics in Cincinnati* (Cambridge: Joint Center for Urban Studies, M.I.T./Harvard, 1959), part II. John J. Gilligan, later a liberal Democratic congressman and governor, rose in local Cincinnati politics under CCC sponsorship. See *ibid.*, p. II:13.

[183] On the CCC's incentive structure see Gray, *Politics in Cincinnati*, pp. II:29-30; Charles R. Adrian and Charles Press, *Governing Urban America* (New York: McGraw-Hill, 1968), p. 103. "Women volunteer workers in the precincts have always been the foundation of the Charter organization. . . . The reform City Charter Committee realized at an early date the importance of precinct-level campaigning and of maintaining a permanent core of workers. Without patronage (patronage is contrary to reform's principles, of course), the organization could only depend on workers who had substantial amounts of time to give and were attracted by the Charterite commodity—good (anti-machine) government. The person who most often meets these qualifications is the middle-class housewife" (Gray, pp. II:29-30).

[184] Material on the Hamilton organization is drawn from Straetz, *PR Politics*, pp. 189-193; Gray, *Politics in Cincinnati*, pp. II:9, 28-29.

1960s and, because Hamilton County is Republican territory, organization nominees for county and state legislative offices normally got elected.[185] But Cincinnati spun out its own peculiar and vigorously competitive party system in city council elections, which were formally nonpartisan. Close races occurred from the 1920s until the late 1950s between the usually victorious CCC and the Republicans' traditional organization based in the county.[186] More recently three separate slating organizations have regularly fielded candidates, with Republicans prevailing in the 1960s and a coalition of Charterites and Democrats in the 1970s.[187]

Cuyahoga County (1,721,300), parent unit of Cleveland (750,879), differs from Hamilton County in having a Democratic allegiance and also crowded primaries and decentralized party organization. But Cuyahoga's Democratic organization, like Hamilton's Republican, has figured importantly in city and county affairs. Reports on Cleveland from the early 1960s and early 1970s tell a consistent story: government patronage helped to support a stratum of veteran Democratic ward leaders, who performed election-day tasks and cleared job applicants on their home grounds; alone or in league with other party leaders they slated candidates quite successfully for county offices, seats in the state legislature, and the city's formally nonpartisan council positions.[188]

[185] The hegemony lasted at least in the case of state legislative nominations. See Malcolm E. Jewell, *Metropolitan Representation: State Legislative Districting in Urban Counties* (New York: National Municipal League, 1969), pp. 5, 8-9.

[186] On competition between Charterites and Republicans: Straetz, *PR Politics, passim*; Gray, *Politics in Cincinnati*, part II.

[187] On the 1960s: Iola O. Hessler, *29 Ways to Govern a City* (Cincinnati: Hamilton County Research Foundation, 1966), p. 67. On the 1960s and since: Howard D. Hamilton, *Electing the Cincinnati City Council: An Examination of Alternative Electoral-Representation Systems* (Cincinnati: Stephen H. Wilder Foundation, 1978), pp. 7-8, 61, 93-101; W. Donald Heisel, "Abandonment of Proportional Representation and the Impact of 9-X Voting in Cincinnati," paper presented at the 1982 convention of the American Political Science Association.

[188] Martha Derthick, "Cleveland" (unpublished manuscript prepared for the Joint Center for Urban Studies, M.I.T./Harvard, date c. 1962), pp. 11-16; Ronald J. Busch, "Party Structure: The Case of Cleveland Ward Leaders," paper presented at the 1973 convention of the American Political Science Association, pp. 4-5. In 1972 the average span of time already spent in office among Democratic ward leaders was nineteen years (Busch, p. 7). From a more recent study of Cuyahoga Democratic and Republican parties, with data from 1975 and 1981, on the subject of patronage: "The parties do . . . manage to work in and around the prevailing civil service systems. A management survey done some years ago for then Cleveland Mayor Ralph J. Perk stated emphatically that the 'civil service system . . . exists more in name than in fact.' No one contends the situation has changed very much. Cleveland city government may be something of an exception in the county, but county and state offices show evidences of the patronage system

This has not been an enterprise rivaling Chicago's; patronage is modest by comparison, and the custom in writing about Cleveland's party apparatus has been to declare it weaker than some but stronger than others elsewhere.[189] Its decentralization stands out: from one viewpoint the party looks like a county organization, from another like a set of autonomous ward organizations.[190] Yet the ward leaders do not have a history of competing with each other over candidates in citywide or county primaries. Before the mid-1960s, when Cuyahoga County state legislators all ran for nomination (and election) at large—in 1962, for example, 105 candidates pursued 17 Democratic assembly nominations on a bedsheet ballot—the organization's practice was to put up one slate of candidates and ordinarily to get them nominated.[191] As for the Cleveland mayoralty, no holder of the office since at least 1941 has relied much on the Democratic organization in winning nomination or election. Newspaper endorsements have helped, but more important has been unmediated support from racial or ethnic groups, depended on by all six mayors from 1941 through 1979—blacks in the case of Carl B. Stokes (1967-1971), more often Eastern Europeans as with Frank J. Lausche (1941-1945), Ralph J. Perk (1971-1977), and Dennis J. Kucinich (1977-1979).[192]

---

also" (Thomas A. Flinn and Ronald J. Busch, "Is Party Dead? A Study of Political Party Organization in a Large Urban County," paper presented at the 1982 conference of the Midwest Political Science Association, pp. 6-7).

[189] See Derthick, "Cleveland," p. 11; Edward C. Banfield and James Q. Wilson, *City Politics* (Cambridge: Harvard University Press and M.I.T. Press, 1963), pp. 306, 325. Other in-between statements: "It would be a mistake . . . to approach the Cuyahoga county parties as patronage parties; but it would also be a mistake not to take patronage into account and to look for its presence. . . . The attentive observer may note that relations between leaders and some members of the Democratic Party involve the unstated premise that the members want something which the leader may have to offer." And: "Parties examined here do not fall into the category of machines in that relatively few of their members are on the public payroll to take only one very important point of classification. It is also clear that they are not amateur organizations in that issue or policy orientation is not dominant or even prominent as a reason for joining or remaining in them although it is a factor among others. The Cuyahoga parties fall between machine and amateur if a continuum from one to the other can be imagined." Flinn and Busch, "Is Party Dead?" pp. 7, 38.

[190] On decentralization: Derthick, "Cleveland," pp. 12, 15; Busch, "Party Structure," p. 5; Charles H. Levine, *Racial Conflict and the American Mayor: Power, Polarization, and Performance* (Lexington, Mass.: Heath, 1974), pp. 54-55.

[191] On the Democratic organization's slating effectiveness in the old legislative primaries: Jewell, *Metropolitan Representation*, p. 8; Howard D. Hamilton, "Legislative Constituencies: Single-Member Districts, Multi-Member Districts, and Floterial Districts," *Western Political Quarterly* 20(1967), 323.

[192] For reports on Cleveland's mayoral politics see Derthick, "Cleveland," pp. 12-17;

Two other urban centers turns up in monographic accounts. Jefferson County (96,193), site of formally nonpartisan Steubenville (30,771), supported a strong party organization of a traditional sort in the early 1950s (no evidence is available since then). The county's Democratic chairman is said to have been a "virtual party dictator, once elected. He makes the real decisions about candidates, discipline, organization, and patronage, practically single-handed." Chairman Hugo Alexander presided over an elaborate precinct organization inside and outside Steubenville in 1950, keeping unions and minority groups in line with "a judicious distribution of patronage and candidates."[193] Toledo (383,818) is a nonpartisan city whose municipal elections have in fact generated matches between Republicans and Democrats.[194] For two decades through 1966 a ward and precinct organization run by John Patrick Kelly operated on the Democratic side, evidently sustained by personal loyalties and modest patronage from the party's organization in Lucas County (484,370). Kelly's organization was too weak to do much in Toledo's mayoral elections but easily strong enough to prevent the United Auto Workers (UAW) from staging a Detroit-style takeover of the party.[195]

Sampling newspapers' election coverage is the only practical way to gain information on Ohio's other urban centers. Organization seems flimsiest in Summit County (553,371), site of formally partisan Akron (275,425), where primary coverage in 1973 (the city) and 1974 (the

Levine, *Racial Conflict*, ch. 4; William E. Nelson, Jr., and Philip J. Meranto, *Electing Black Mayors: Political Action in the Black Community* (Columbus: Ohio State University Press, 1977), ch. 3. On Kucinich: William K. Stevens, "At 31, Cleveland's Mayor Elect: Dennis John Kucinich," *New York Times*, November 10, 1977, p. A19. In recent decades Cleveland's city council elections have been formally nonpartisan and mayoral elections formally partisan. Even so, the Democratic organization has exercised considerable influence in the former and very little in the latter.

[193] Fay Calkins, *The CIO and the Democratic Party* (Chicago: University of Chicago Press, 1952), pp. 37-44, quotations at pp. 39, 43.

[194] Jean L. Stinchcombe, *Reform and Reaction: City Politics in Toledo* (Belmont, Calif.: Wadsworth, 1968), pp. 43-46. See also *Toledo Blade*, September 15, 1971, p. 1.

[195] Stinchcombe, *Reform and Reaction*, pp. 49-62, 165-166. The text gives only fragmentary material on the nature of the Kelly organization and its relations with county Democrats. See especially pp. 49-50, 61-62. On dealing with the UAW: "Democratic party chairman John Patrick Kelly, anxious to protect the party from UAW captivity, has successfully excluded most union officials from executive, ward, and precinct positions, while relying on their assistance at election time. With a solid entourage of incumbent ward chairmen and precinct committeemen, the party chairman has easily disposed of occasional UAW slates in precinct races" (pp. 165-166). Useful background material on Toledo politics in the 1920s through the 1940s appears in Dennis M. Anderson, "Experiences with Proportional Representation in Toledo, Ohio," paper presented at the 1984 convention of the American Political Science Association.

county) reports "old-guard" Democrats opposing "new-guard" Democrats and local notables endorsing each other but does not refer to slates or organizations; the dominant theme is of candidates seeking office on their own.[196] In Montgomery County (608,413), site of Dayton (243,601), the local newspaper covered county and state legislative primaries around 1970 from the perspective of whether party endorsees were winning, but nothing comes through (in a quick inspection) about the nature of the endorsing organizations.[197] Dayton itself is an old nonpartisan reform city. A good-government organization called the Citizens' Committee dominated municipal elections at least through the 1950s; an apparent successor called the All Dayton Committee put up a slate in the 1969 municipal elections, but there was no sign of regular county organizations.[198] Mahoning County (304,545), site of Youngstown (140,909), provides more evidence of traditional organization. The local newspaper framed municipal primaries in 1971 as a test of how well the Democratic county organization was doing, as in: "The test of the Democratic organization's strength in the primary may be greatest in some ward council contests."[199] The primary results brought attention to "twenty-six-year-old Jerome F. McNally, a spirited campaigner, and the only candidate to upset the Democratic machine in Tuesday's council primary races."[200] Franklin County (833,249), site of Columbus (540,025), seems to run an organization politics. How well party endorsees fare has supplied the theme in coverage of state legislative and county primaries, as in a 1968 report: "Franklin County Republicans voted just about as expected Tuesday, giving endorsed candidates healthy leads in all races."[201] Columbus's nonpartisan municipal elections have in fact been contests between Re-

---

[196] *Akron Beacon Journal*, September 12, 1973, p. 1; May 8, 1974, p. 1. The flavor of the coverage: "Tuesday's balloting also ousted two Democratic ward councilmen—Richard Capron, who was beaten in Ward 7 by Herbert E. Stottler, a United Steelworkers representative, and Walter Ridge, who lost in Ward 9 to Don Plusquellic, a B. F. Goodrich salary analyst and former Kenmore High School quarterback" (*ibid.*, September 12, 1973, p. 1).

[197] *Dayton Daily News*, May 8, 1968, pp. 1, 7; May 6, 1970, p. 1.

[198] See Charles R. Adrian, "A Typology for Nonpartisan Elections," *Western Political Quarterly* 12(1959), 454; *Dayton Daily News*, November 5, 1969, p. 1.

[199] *Youngstown Vindicator*, May 2, 1971, pp. 1, 8.

[200] *Ibid.*, May 3, 1971, p. 1.

[201] *Columbus Citizen-Journal*, May 8, 1968, pp. 1, 9. Coverage of Franklin County's primaries of 1964 began as follows: "A total of 118,306 partisan voters trooped to the polls Tuesday in Franklin County in a primary election that easily earned the title of 'Organization Day.' Almost without exception voters of both parties handily elected the endorsed candidates. In a few cases 'independent' candidates gave endorsed candidates a struggle" (*ibid.*, May 6, 1964, p. 1).

publican and Democratic slates. In the first-round election in 1971, for example, four council candidates backed by the Democratic county organization outpolled two candidates of a "Democratic splinter group," one said to be a "former City Hall patronage boss," thereby progressing to the second round along with four Republicans who were also organization designees.[202]

The two Ohio parties have followed somewhat different traditions in conferring statewide nominations. State Democrats were said in the 1960s to be "an aggregation of city machines which had little or no interest in statewide elections unless the candidate was from their city."[203] Democratic primaries for governor and Senator have been wide open affairs. Republican primaries used to be quieter, one reason apparently being that the Hamilton County organization used its influence to impart some order from the mid-1930s through the mid-1960s.[204] An overall TPO score for Ohio: 4.

ILLINOIS (11,113,976)

The Democratic machine in Chicago (3,369,359) and Cook County (5,493,529) has of course supplied the organizational muscle of Illinois politics in modern times. In 1931 Anton J. Cermak broke a city tradition of autonomous ward organizations by assembling a Chicago machine, and two talented Democratic mayors kept it going—Edward J. Kelly from 1933 through 1947 (in partnership with county chairman Patrick A. Nash) and Richard J. Daley from 1955 until his death in 1976.[205] Some notable features of the Daley regime were a hierarchical

---

[202] *Columbus Evening Dispatch*, May 5, 1971, p. 1. On Democratic and Republican slating in Columbus municipal elections see also Hessler, *29 Ways to Govern a City*, p. 20.

[203] John H. Fenton, *Midwest Politics* (New York: Holt, Rinehart and Winston, 1966), p. 137.

[204] *Ibid.*, pp. 134-136.

[205] There was a time of troubles (no authoritative leader) in the interval between Kelly and Daley. On the change in organizational form in the 1930s: Alex Gottfried, *Boss Cermak of Chicago: A Study of Political Leadership* (Seattle: University of Washington Press, 1962), chs. 10-13; and Donald S. Bradley and Mayer N. Zald, "From Commercial Elite to Political Administrator," ch. 1 in Leonard I. Ruchelman (ed.), *Big City Mayors: The Crisis in Urban Politics* (Bloomington: Indiana University Press, 1969), pp. 18-25. Scholarship on Chicago is voluminous enough to allow a good look at ward-level organization in each of several decades. On the 1920s: Sonya Forthal, *Cogwheels of Democracy: A Study of the Precinct Captain* (New York: William-Frederick, 1946); the 1930s: Harold F. Gosnell, *Machine Politics: Chicago Model* (Chicago: University of Chicago Press, 1968), chs. 2-4; the early 1950s: Martin Meyerson and Edward C. Banfield, *Politics, Planning and the Public Interest: The Case of Public Housing in Chicago* (Glencoe,

(though short of dictatorial) party structure; organization control of some 30,000 city or county patronage jobs; a lack of interest in issues (thought to be "irrelevant at best and dangerously divisive at worst"); and an ability to slate candidates authoritatively for the mayoralty, most county offices, Chicago's formally nonpartisan board of aldermen, the Democratic share of the county's delegation to the state legislature, city and county judgeships, and eight or so Congressional seats.[206] Chicago leaders also dominated the selection of Democratic nominees for governor and the Senate for nearly half a century, losing only a Senate primary in 1938 and gubernatorial primaries in 1936 and

Ill.: Free Press, 1955), pp. 64-79; the 1970s under Daley: Milton L. Rakove, *Don't Make No Waves, Don't Back No Losers: An Insider's Analysis of the Daley Machine* (Bloomington: Indiana University Press, 1975), ch. 4, and Thomas M. Guterbock, *Machine Politics in Transition: Party and Community in Chicago* (Chicago: University of Chicago Press, 1980).

[206] On hierarchical relations see for example Rakove, *Don't Make No Waves*, ch. 3; Edward C. Banfield, *Political Influence: A New Theory of Urban Politics* (New York: Free Press, 1961), ch. 8. On patronage jobs: Rakove, pp. 112-117. On lack of interest in issues: Leo M. Snowiss, "Congressional Recruitment and Representation," *American Political Science Review* 60(1966), 629. Banfield's conclusion, p. 263: "Civic controversies in Chicago are not generated by the efforts of politicians to win votes, by differences of ideology or group interest, or by the behind-the-scenes efforts of a power elite. They arise, instead, out of the maintenance and enhancement needs of large formal organizations. The heads of an organization see some advantage to be gained by changing the situation. They propose changes. Other large organizations are threatened. They oppose, and a civic controversy takes place." (By "large formal organizations" Banfield means not the party organization itself but rather such organizations as newspapers, government agencies, universities and department stores.) On slating for congressional office: Snowiss, pp. 628-636. On county offices: Rakove, pp. 95-100. On judgeships: Rakove, pp. 221-232. Chicago's particularism in giving out governmental benefits has extended to the judiciary, where federal investigators recently uncovered a brisk practice of selling

1972. One of Daley's last acts was to purge an incumbent Democratic governor in the 1976 primary.[207] By this time, though, the machine's grip on Chicago had loosened. Leadership troubles ensued after Daley's death, and the secession by blacks evident in 1979 and 1980 led to Harold Washington's election as mayor in 1983 on an anti-organization platform.[208] He had interesting comments on the Democratic organization, saying it had "superimposed itself on the city, forced city employees to work for it and skimmed millions of dollars in contracts which it gave to special interests," and that the party "does not have a right any more than any other interest group to control, smother or swamp municipal government."[209]

General treatments of Illinois party structure outside Cook County are vague or spotty, but reports on particular metropolitan areas add up to a picture of heterogeneity.[210] There is no trace of traditional party organization in the city of Rockford (147,370), the home territory of John B. Anderson.[211] Peoria (126,963) ceased being a machine city

---

decisions for cash. See Andrew H. Malcolm, "Chicago Inquiry Shows The Courts' Hidden Side," *New York Times*, December 18, 1983, p. 28.

[207] On the Chicago organization's control of statewide nominating: Robert F. Sittig, "Party Slatemaking and the Direct Primary in Illinois and Other States" (Ph.D. dissertation, Southern Illinois University, 1962), chs. 5, 6; Rakove, *Don't Make No Waves*, pp. 142-155. Daley's use of Michael J. Howlett to defeat Governor Dan Walker in the 1976 primary is discussed in Len O'Connor, *Requiem: The Decline and Demise of Mayor Daley and His Era* (Chicago: Contemporary Books, 1977), pp. 55-67.

[208] On the organization's losing control of blacks: Michael B. Preston, "Black Politics in the Post-Daley Era," pp. 88-117 in Samuel K. Gove and Louis H. Masotti (eds.), *After Daley: Chicago Politics in Transition* (Urbana: University of Illinois Press, 1982). In general on the organization's decline in influence in the 1970s: William J. Grimshaw, "The Daley Legacy: A Declining Politics of Party, Race, and Public Unions," pp. 57-87 in *ibid.*

[209] Source of first quotation: Nathaniel Sheppard, Jr., "Chicago Mayor-Elect Vows Reforms," *New York Times*, April 15, 1983, p. A14. Second quotation: Andrew H. Malcolm, "Chicagoan Sees His Victory As Minority Group 'Lesson,' " *New York Times*, February 27, 1983, p. 24.

[210] No one has produced a general treatment of the state's parties like Sorauf's work on Pennsylvania or Witt's on New York. Downstate politicians have in general been "professionals" rather than "amateurs," according to Daniel J. Elazar in *Cities of the Prairie: The Metropolitan Frontier and American Politics* (New York: Basic Books, 1970), pp. 241-250 and ch. 7. One author wrote two decades ago that downstate parties commonly engaged in preprimary slating: Clarence A. Berdahl, "Some Problems in the Legal Regulation of Political Parties in Illinois," in Lois M. Pelekoudas (ed.), *Illinois Political Parties* (Urbana: Institute of Government and Public Affairs, University of Illinois, 1960), p. 25. Another author wrote that they did not: Samuel K. Gove, "Local Politics: The Illinois Experience," paper presented at the 1962 convention of the American Political Science Association, p. 5.

[211] Calvin F. Exoo, "Ethnic Culture and the Incentives of Political Party Activists in Two Midwestern Cities" (Ph.D. dissertation, University of Wisconsin–Madison, 1979), chs. 4, 5, pp. 245-246.

around 1950, and in the late 1960s a good-government group called Citizens for Representative Government seems to have been the only organization making endorsements—this may be unique—in a formally partisan system of municipal elections.[212] Republican "boss" H. L. Green is said to have dominated Champaign County (163,281) from the 1920s through the early 1950s, but the county's Champaign (56,532) and Urbana (32,800) seem to have operated without traditional organizations in the 1960s and 1970s.[213] City commissioners run their own individual patronage organizations in nonpartisan Springfield (91,753).[214] Impoverished East St. Louis (69,996) in St. Clair County (285,199) has supported the most prominent downstate machine of recent times. From 1951 through 1971 Mayor Alvin G. Fields, considered the second-ranking Democrat in the state, ran a lush patronage regime controlling the city's (nonpartisan) elective offices, city and many county appointive offices, city precinct committeemen of both parties, and a "submachine" penetrating the city's large black population.[215] A switch from Irish to black control produced a somewhat less centralized but no less corrupt politics by the late 1970s— East St. Louis in 1978 was the first city to lose its federal CETA (Comprehensive Employment Training Act) money for misusing funds. A black reform mayor, however, won election in 1979.[216] This exhausts

[212] John M. Sumansky, "Peoria: The Growth and Development of a River Town," pp. 123-141 in Daniel M. Johnson and Rebecca M. Veach (eds.), The Middle-Size Cities of Illinois: Their People, Politics, and Quality of Life (Springfield, Ill.: Sangamon State University, 1980), at pp. 128-129. On the good-government group: "Like most political organizations, CFRG based its structure on the electoral units of the political system. Besides the mass membership, ward captains were elected from each of the ten wards in the city. Those ten ward captains and the president made up the Board of Directors of the Citizens for Representative Government." CFRG endorsed in the primaries of both parties. See William K. Hall, "Taking Over City Hall—and Losing It," ch. 20 in Edgar G. Crane, Jr. (ed.), Illinois: Political Processes and Governmental Performance (Dubuque: Kendall/Hunt, 1980), quotation at p. 259.

[213] Rozann Rothman, "Champaign-Urbana: The Politics of Transition," pp. 35-67 in Johnson and Veach, Middle-Size Cities of Illinois, at pp. 44-51.

[214] James Krohe, Jr., and Cullom Davis, "Springfield: An Evolving Capital," pp. 191-213 in Johnson and Veach, Middle-Size Cities of Illinois, at pp. 203, 205-206.

[215] Dennis R. Judd and Robert E. Mendelson, The Politics of Urban Planning: The East St. Louis Experience (Urbana: University of Illinois Press, 1973), pp. 11-15, and for an account of the 1971 election, pp. 15-40; Nelson and Meranto, Electing Black Mayors, pp. 49-57, and for an account of the 1967 election, pp. 36-49; Jane A. Altes and Robert E. Mendelson, "East St. Louis: A Persevering Community," pp. 89-121 in Johnson and Veach, Middle-Size Cities of Illinois, at pp. 102-103.

[216] The organization used CETA funds to put precinct workers, party committeemen, election judges, and city officials' relatives on the public payroll. See Nathaniel Sheppard, Jr., "East St. Louis Faces Removal of Officials in Fund Inquiry," New York Times, March

the pertinent downstate information. Unfortunately no one seems to have written on the surburban Republican "collar counties" outside Chicago.[217] But no matter: Illinois's TPO score is an unproblematic 5.

25, 1978, p. 6; Nathaniel Sheppard, Jr., "Voters in East St. Louis Hope to Oust Graft," *New York Times*, March 26, 1979, p. A16. On the 1970s in general: Altes and Mendelson, "East St. Louis," pp. 102-109. On reform mayor Carl E. Officer: Nathaniel Sheppard, Jr., "East St. Louis Mayor Seeks to Reverse Decaying City's Fortunes," *New York Times*, December 19, 1980, p. A22.

[217] A work now under way by Mildred Schwartz will supply some information on these counties.

CHAPTER 3

States with "Persistent Factionalism"

The "traditional party organizations" described so far have been "regular" or, to introduce a synonymous term, "monopolistic" in form—that is, one traditional organization (if any) per party per locale. In some instances a traditional organization may compete against another sort of entity within its own party—Democratic regulars against reform clubs, for example, in Manhattan—and no doubt most traditional organizations have spells when the lines of leadership are unclear. Nevertheless, the norm in the eight "organization states" of Chapter 2 has been monopoly and ordinarily the practice has been monopolistic: we have no trouble talking about *the* Republican organization of Nassau County or *the* Democratic organization of Chicago.

Both norm and practice have differed in the states examined in this chapter. A variant species of politics appears in which two or more traditional organizations commonly operate in the same party in the same city or county, normally competing against each other in primaries for a broad range of offices, and in which few people seem to regard such intraparty rivalry as odd or exceptional. In some places both Republicans and Democrats sustain two or more traditional organizations. In some cities or counties competing organizations of the same party operate from more or less secure bases in their own wards, or sets of wards, and contend with each other for citywide or county offices; in other jurisdictions they display no such pattern of geographic anchoring. In most states of this group local organizations enter into alliances with politicians who are seeking or holding the governorship, which bolsters intraparty competition at both statewide and local levels. On the one hand, if gubernatorial candidate A forges a link with organization X in a county, candidate B of the same party can easily win support in the same county by rallying organization Y; the overall effect is an easy achievement of dualism—at a minimum—in statewide nominating. On the other hand, if organization Y is weaker than organization X but supported a candidate who becomes governor, Y can draw patronage from the statehouse to shore itself up; the overall effect, given some reasonable assumptions, is a nourishing of intraparty pluralism at the local level.

Organizations competing within a local party are often called "factions," an adequate term though its use requires consideration. In the ordinary language of politics a "faction" can be nearly anything—a politician's "personal following," for example, or even a set of people whose only connection is thinking alike on certain issues.[1] The usage here will be strict. A "faction" is a traditional organization that regularly competes for a wide range of offices against one or more other traditional organizations of the same party in the same city or county. With one qualification, all the traits of TPOs are present: a "faction" is autonomous, durable, and hierarchical; it slates for a range of offices; it relies substantially on material inducements. The qualification concerns its durability. A traditional organization of the New Jersey type can persist over generations as detectably "the same" organization. Traditional organizations of a "factional" type, even though they ordinarily endure over decades and amount to more than simply "personal followings" of politicians, often break up when their leaders die or retire. Factional reshuffles occur. In discussing factionalized settings it is best to say that *patterns* of factionalism persist over generations even if identifiable factions do not.

Although this forces factions to pass the same definitional tests as traditional organizations of a monopolistic sort do, the language may still cause uneasiness. "Factions" are *parts* of parties, are they not, rather than parties themselves? Why call them "traditional party organizations"? The answer builds on the presupposition that finding out whether organizations that display the five assigned traits take up political space is in general more important than worrying about how many of them operate per party. If this is true, a common term is needed to cover both factional and monopolistic organizations, and "traditional party organization" is used here. Still, there is no point in ignoring the distinction, and the coding scheme has been amended to accommodate it. In states where traditional organizations are commonly factional—commonly rather than uniformly, for monopolistic

[1] "A politician has a 'personal following' to the extent that people will vote for him and otherwise support him because of an attachment they feel to him as a person, or as a 'house,' and not from regard for his political principles, loyalty to the party he represents, or in expectation of material rewards. These considerations may be present, but they are not the basis of the politician's hold on his followers; they would vote for him anyway" (Edward C. Banfield and James Q. Wilson, *City Politics* [Cambridge: Harvard University Press and M.I.T. Press, 1963], p. 129).

organizations do turn up—the 1-through-5 coding formula will work as it has but its overall readings will be tagged "PF." That is, a state with a heavy incidence of factional organizations will earn a score of 5-PF. The letters stand for "persistent factionalism," a term borrowed from Edwin Rothman.[2]

WEST VIRGINIA (1,744,237)

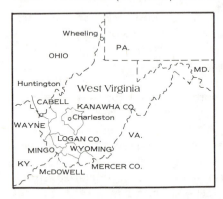

An exquisite report by Rod Harless on Kanawha County (229,515), site of West Virginia's capital city of Charleston (71,505), gives a sense of what factional politics can look like in full bloom.[3] The county is ordinarily Democratic, and he describes that party's primaries for county and state legislative offices in 1970. Three Democratic factions were operating in 1970, each already in possession of one or more county offices and therefore of a supply of patronage jobs and precinct workers. County clerk Jack Pauley and circuit clerk Jack Kinder ran one faction. A second headed by county assessor Lee Kenna held the assessor's office and also a county commissioner's seat. A third led by Sam McCorkle controlled the sheriff's office. Each of these three organizations, following local custom, designated its own slate of candidates for the full set of offices open in the 1970 Democratic primaries. This custom had a simple rationale: in every election year each faction sought to protect whatever county patronage it had and capture whatever more it could get. In 1970, at least, no faction showed much interest in issues or programs.

In the view of Kanawha's factional leaders the key electoral prize in 1970 was a county commissioner's seat. They also supported candidates for the county's fourteen at-large state assembly seats, though they cared little who won; they backed assembly candidates only to

[2] Edwin Rothman, "Factional Machine-Politics: William Curran and the Baltimore City Democratic Party Organization, 1929-1946" (Ph.D. dissertation, Johns Hopkins University, 1949), pp. 76, 179-193.

[3] Rod Harless, *The West Virginia Establishment* (Huntington, W.Va.: Appalachian Movement Press, 1971), pp. 33-51. All the material here on Kanawha is drawn from the Harless account.

give their slates geographic balance and to extract campaign funds from people they supported. To anyone trying to win a Democratic assembly nomination the importance of achieving factional support was obvious: only one candidate within memory had survived a primary without a faction's support, and in fact nobody won a nomination in 1970 without a faction's support. The factions went in for elaborate activities on primary day: each ordinarily printed up a sample ballot marking its designees and circulated thousands of copies around the county. In a Democratic primary electorate of about 25,000 people each faction was said to control about 2,500 votes—or about ten votes per factional precinct leader in each of the county's 253 precincts. In Kanawha's crowded and confusing primaries—52 Democrats sought the 14 assembly nominations in 1970—a difference of 2,500 votes was ordinarily decisive. In 1970 an assembly candidate had to pay $400 to win a place on the Kenna slate, $300 to make the Pauley-Kinder slate, and $250 to make the McCorkle slate. The pricing spread made rough sense: each faction ended up with some primary winners, but in general the slates drew votes in the order of their factions' prices. Seven victorious candidates appeared on two slates. Prices are said to have run a good deal higher in state senate primaries.

This Kanawha system has an arresting harmony to it. Other accounts make it clear that factions have flourished in much of the rest of West Virginia. One author reports that "in Democratic-majority counties two strong factions almost invariably emerge," often a courthouse group and a school board group.[4] Another notes that Republicans also generate factions and gives several examples.[5] Candidates seeking high offices run up against local factions and have to figure out how to deal with them—Ken Hechler, for example, candidate in a Democratic congressional primary in 1972 and John F. Kennedy in the Presidential primary of 1960.[6] "As the campaign got underway [Robert] Mc-Donough and Lawrence F. O'Brien, Kennedy's politicking expert, were assigned the task of courting the county organizations. They roamed the state trying to get their man slated. . . . In counties where the dominant Democratic organization would not embrace Kennedy, Mc-

[4] Robert E. Lanham, "The West Virginia Statehouse Democratic Machine: Structure, Function, and Process" (Ph.D. dissertation, Claremont Graduate School, 1971), chs. 4 and 5, quotation at p. 148.

[5] Lester "Bus" Perry, *Forty Years Mountain Politics, 1930-1970* (Parsons, W.Va.: McClain Printing Company, 1971), p. 79. Perry spent forty years watching and participating in the politics of Logan County.

[6] On Hechler: Mark Smith, "West Virginia's New Fourth Congressional District: An Analysis of the 1972 Democratic Primary" (Yale course paper, 1972).

Donough and O'Brien put their money on the strongest anti-organization faction or tried to set up their own precinct organization."[7] There are several reports of factions selling slate positions to candidates and also buying votes from voters.[8] Harless aside, most accounts of particular factional organizations deal with Democratic coal-mining counties in the southern part of the state. In the early 1970s, for example, Logan County (46,269) had a Hager faction and a Scaggs faction. McDowell County (50,666) had Camper and Hassan factions. In Wyoming County (30,095), the chief organization was evidently a school board group.[9] In Mingo County (32,780), famous for its corrupt elections, Noah Floyd ran the dominant organization but a competing faction led by Lafe Ward and Tom Chafin kept an oar in.[10] The chief factional leader in Mercer County (63,206) was said to be Shorty Simons. Politics in Wayne County (37,581), just west of the coal belt, amounted

[7] Harry W. Ernst, *The Primary That Made a President: West Virginia 1960* (New York: McGraw-Hill, 1962, Eagleton Case #26), p. 18. An oral history recollection by Miles Stanley, speaking from a background in labor politics: "So national candidates and state candidates who win elections in West Virginia go into the counties and endeavor to, what we call, 'buy in' to the strongest organization. That is, they put so much money on the line in exchange for the support of that organization which has already been built up, and from the reports which I have read and reports which I have received, the Kennedy campaign people had more money to work with, more resources—they could 'buy in' to more organizations and perhaps stronger organizations than could the Humphrey people." Matthew A. Reese, Jr., on Kennedy's victory in the 1960 primary: "I think that the President won so handily in West Virginia because we very carefully aligned ourselves with the successful slates." And on the factions' lack of ideological coloration: "Reese went on to explain that the Humphrey-Kennedy slates were not lined up with either liberal or conservative factions within the counties. In most cases no such distinctions existed at the local level so such an alignment would have been difficult if not impossible." William Lewis Young, "The John F. Kennedy Library Oral History Project, the West Virginia Democratic Presidential Primary, 1960" (Ph.D. dissertation, Ohio State University, 1982), pp. 135-141, quotations respectively at pp. 138, 137, 138.

[8] On selling positions: Harless, *West Virginia Establishment*, pp. 34, 37; Ernst, *Primary That Made a President*, p. 17. On buying votes: Ernst, pp. 16-17; K. W. Lee, "Fair Elections in West Virginia," pp. 158-168 in Frank S. Riddel (ed.), *Appalachia: Its People, Heritage, and Problems* (Dubuque: Kendall/Hunt, 1974), pp. 162-163.

[9] On Logan County: Mark Smith, "West Virginia's New Fourth Congressional District," pp. 32-33. On Logan County over several decades: Perry, *Forty Years Mountain Politics*, ch. 10. An earlier Democratic leader of the county is memorialized in George T. Swain, *The Incomparable Don Chafin* (Charleston, W.Va.: Jones Printing Company, 1962). On McDowell County: Smith, pp. 33-34. On Wyoming County: *ibid.*, p. 31.

[10] Mark Smith, "West Virginia's New Fourth Congressional District," pp. 36-37. In the Mingo County Democratic primary of 1968 the price of a vote ranged between $3 and $10. "Some enterprising voters would wait all day outside the courthouse for the highest bid" (Lee, "Fair Elections," pp. 162-163). Also on the Floyd organization and Mingo elections in the mid-1960s: Huey Perry, *"They'll Cut Off Your Project"* (New York: Praeger, 1972).

to a contest between a "Courthouse crowd" and the "Fair Elections and Good Government Committee"—a certain misnomer.[11] All these groups, again, were slate makers covering a range of offices: any Democrat trying to get anywhere in southern West Virginia politics in the early 1970s had to reckon with them.

West Virginia's governorship has carried with it a good deal of patronage, and its pre-1970s incumbents, though ordinarily neutral in other primaries, are said to have wielded considerable influence in primaries choosing nominees to be their successors. "Statehouse machine" is a common term for the governor's apparatus.[12] But for the party out of office (the governorship goes back and forth between Republicans and Democrats), the power centers in gubernatorial nominating have apparently been the counties. On the Democratic side in 1960, for example: "Attorney General W. W. Barron was clearly the man to beat for the Democratic gubernatorial nomination. Most of the tightly-controlled counties with strong organizations were behind him."[13]

An overall TPO score for the state: 4 or 5? The decision is not easy, but for two reasons 4 seems more appropriate than 5. First, it is hard to tell how much traditional organizations have amounted to outside the Charleston (Kanawha) and southern coal-mining areas. Charleston's newspaper refers to factional dealings but papers in Huntington (74,315) and Wheeling (48,188)—at least on brief inspection—do not.[14] One author says flatly that Cabell County (106,918), site of Huntington, had no Democratic organizations of any consequence in the early 1970s.[15] But second and more important, the activities of these West Virginia organizations are neither as obvious nor as public as activities of monopolistic organizations in states to the north. Any-

[11] On Mercer County: Mark Smith, "West Virginia's New Fourth Congressional District," pp. 35-36. On Wayne County: *ibid.*, pp. 28-30.

[12] On neutrality: Lanham, "Statehouse Democratic Machine," p. 164. On the role of governors in nominating see John L. Bailey, "The Direct Primary in West Virginia" (M.A. thesis, West Virginia University, 1966), chs. 2-4; Paul F. Lutz, "The 1952 West Virginia Gubernatorial Election," *West Virginia History* 39(1978), 210-235.

[13] Ernst, *Primary That Made a President*, p. 18. Barron won nomination and election.

[14] *Charleston Gazette*, May 11, 1966, p. 1; May 15, 1968, p. 1; *Huntington Herald-Dispatch*, May 15, 1968, p. 1; May 13, 1970, p. 1; *Wheeling Intelligencer*, May 13, 1964, p. 1; May 11, 1966, p. 1; May 15, 1968, p. 1; May 13, 1970, p. 1. A writer on Jersey City with a good eye for organization comments in passing that "Wheeling, West Virginia's machine came to an end as a formal organization only with the death of Bill Lias in 1970" (John Kincaid, "Political Success and Policy Failure: The Persistence of Machine Politics in Jersey City" [Ph.D. dissertation, Temple University, 1981], p. 29). But this is all, and the local newspaper is silent on pertinent occasions.

[15] Mark Smith, "West Virginia's New Fourth Congressional District," p. 26.

one, scholar or voter, could pick up a newspaper in Chicago or Phila-delphia in the 1960s and find out with certainty which candidates the local organizations were slating for nomination. This is not so in West Virginia, where factional organizations often go about their slate mak-ing so tentatively and covertly that one wonders what they are doing, whether voters know what they are doing, and sometimes whether they are doing anything at all. On occasion they seem to sell slate positions to candidates, and then pocket the money and do nothing. In a 1972 congressional primary a Mercer County faction leader is said to have split his support among all three candidates: he "wanted to be able to say that he supported the winner no matter who the winner turned out to be," an understandable aim.[16] These West Virginia organizations have exercised impressive influence in the nominating process, but the way they operate probably puts a ceiling on their influence. Overall TPO score: 4-PF.

MARYLAND (3,922,399) _____

Scholarship on parties in Maryland is excellent even though it is mostly unpublished. The major work, a 1,042-page dissertation by Henry Bain on nominating for the state legislature in four counties and a Bal-timore City district over an eight-decade period ending in the mid-1950s, is probably one of the half dozen or so most illuminating works ever done on American nominating practices.[17] Bain and other writers leave no doubt about the texture of Maryland's twentieth-century pol-itics: slating by hierarchical organization has been the typical route to elective offices at least at lower levels.[18] In the Democratic party, tra-ditionally dominant in most areas, nominating organizations in many though not all places have been factional rather than monopolistic, and metropolitan dailies have supplied good coverage of factions' slating activities. Local organizations have regularly built alliances with state-wide candidates. Until recently the typical Democratic primary for gov-ernor or Senator featured a contest between or among evenly matched

[16] *Ibid.*, p. 35.

[17] Henry Bain, "Five Kinds of Politics: A Historical and Comparative Study of the Making of Legislators in Five Maryland Constituencies" (Ph.D. dissertation, Harvard University, 1970). The study is based on documentary materials and also about 180 in-terviews conducted with political figures in the mid-1950s.

[18] Bain's summary comment on slating: "The complete control of legislative nomina-tions by political organizations is a noteworthy feature of politics in four of the [five] lo-calities" (*ibid.*, p. 982). The exception, Washington County, will be discussed in the text. On hierarchy: "Strong leadership, exercised publicly by a single person, has been the rule in the localities studied" (p. 985, and more generally on leadership, pp. 985-989).

candidates, each enjoying factional support in more or less the same array of locales: if faction X backed A, then faction Y supported B and sometimes faction Z supported C.[19] George P. "Your Home Is Your Castle" Mahoney—at one point a vigorous opponent of open housing legislation—turned up as an A, B, or C in a long series of Senate and gubernatorial primaries in the 1950s and 1960s. Mahoney, a charismatic loner of a sort organizations ordinarily shun—by one account a "wealthy paving contractor with a lust for politics, an almost magical hold on the affections of the working people, and no discernible convictions or qualifications"—usually ran with factional sponsorship and managed to win three nominations, though never an election.[20]

Four jurisdictions accommodate about 70 percent of Maryland's population—Montgomery and Prince George's counties in the Washington suburbs and Baltimore City and Baltimore County a few miles northeast. (See map of Maryland and Delaware in Chapter 2.) Baltimore City (905,759) supported a Democratic machine for over half a century after the Civil War, but settled into a new equilibrium of Democratic factionalism in the late 1920s that lasted into the 1970s.[21] The pattern's essentials during the 1950s and 1960s in particular have been documented well by Bain and others. Each of the city's six ancient legislative districts ordinarily supported a dominant home-grown faction that had to compete within its district against one or more other Democratic factions, often invasion beachheads set up by factions ascendant in other districts. The factional organizations had roots in Tammany-style political clubs. They entered into shifting, cross-district alliances, usually resulting in two groups that opposed each other in city council politics and mayoral and gubernatorial primaries, thereby ordinarily giving a dualistic cast to the city's politics. They fought over patronage, not issues. They slated candidates for all offices in reach, and it was difficult to win an elective office—nearly impossible to win a lower-level office—without being a factional designee. As organiza-

[19] On ties between local Democratic factions and statewide candidates see for example *ibid.*, pp. 119, 158, 270, 396, 434, 820-823, 869-870, 895-912.

[20] Quotation at *ibid.*, p. 158. Mahoney won Senate nominations in 1952 and 1956 and a gubernatorial nomination in 1966. On relations between Mahoney and local Democratic factions see *ibid.*, pp. 158, 396, 434, 823, 870, 876, 911-912; J. Anthony Lukas, "Boss Pollack: 'He Can't Be There But He Is,' " *Reporter*, July 19, 1962, p. 35. On the 1966 primary see *Congressional Quarterly Weekly*, September 2, 1966, pp. 1915-1916; September 16, 1966, p. 2165.

[21] On the machine: E. Rothman, "Factional Machine-Politics," ch. 1; James B. Crooks, *Politics and Progress: The Rise of Urban Progressivism in Baltimore, 1895 to 1911* (Baton Rouge: Louisiana State University Press, 1968). On the slide from monopoly into factional pluralism: Bain, "Five Kinds of Politics," pp. 816-820; E. Rothman, *passim*.

tions they took the form of hierarchies ordinarily named after their leaders.[22] Best-known of the factional chiefs from the 1940s through the 1960s was the Fourth District's James H. "Jack" Pollack, who "maintained a stronger grip on primary elections and officeholders in his district than any of the leaders in other parts of the city, had a bigger claim to jobs and favors in the various departments of the municipal government and the offices of the elected judges and court clerks, and was the most free from enduring loyalties to city wide groupings or even to the Democratic party."[23] In the early 1960s—to give a sense of the local complexity—the leading factions were said to be Pollack's in the Fourth District, Tommy D'Alesandro's in the First, the venerable Della-Wyatt organization in the Sixth, a Goodman-Cardin-Kovens group in the Fifth, a Valis-Mach-Briscoe group in the Second, and a Buffington-Coggins-O'Malley group in the Third.[24] Later, in the 1970s, the district organizations were still vibrant enough to carry on an old practice that calls to mind West Virginia: before primaries and general elections they extracted "walking-around money" from candidates for higher offices in exchange for promising to bring out a favorable vote. George McGovern's agents optimistically "walked over" $2,500 to Pollack's headquarters in the fall of 1972.[25]

---

[22] E. Rothman, "Factional Machine-Politics," chs. 3-6, deals with the 1940s but is pertinent here. Bain, "Five Kinds of Politics," pp. 820-825, 839-871, 876-919, gives an elaborate treatment of the city's politics up through the mid-1950s. Later though much briefer reports make it clear that factional patterns of the 1950s persisted through the 1960s: Robert D. Loevy, "Political Behavior in the Baltimore Metropolitan Area" (Ph.D. dissertation, Johns Hopkins University, 1963), pp. 33, 92-93; Iola O. Hessler, 29 Ways to Govern a City (Cincinnati: Hamilton County Research Foundation, 1966), pp. 24-26; David M. Olson, "Toward a Typology of County Party Organizations," Southwestern Social Science Quarterly 48 (1968), p. 566; Ronnie Goldberg, "The Politics of Local Government in Baltimore," Appendix A in Peter Bachrach and Morton S. Baratz, Power and Poverty: Theory and Practice (New York: Oxford University Press, 1970), pp. 116-118. Specifically on the clubs: Franklin L. Burdette, Election Practices in Maryland (College Park: Bureau of Public Administration, University of Maryland, 1950), pp. 18-19; Bain, p. 969. On patronage rather than issues: "The factional process does not seem to have resulted in the evolution of factions which were distinguishable in terms of public issues; factional labels appeared to be distinctively relevant only when matters of patronage or prestige were at stake. In sum, the factions, as such, were 'job-factions' rather than 'issue-factions' " (Rothman, pp. 259-260). For a detailed and masterful account of Democratic slating activities in the city's 6th legislative district in 1954, see Bain, pp. 876-919.

[23] Bain, "Five Kinds of Politics," p. 880. See also pp. 823, 879-881, and for a 1954 Pollack invasion of the 6th district, pp. 895-902; Lukas, "Boss Pollack," pp. 35-36; Goldberg, "Politics of Local Government," pp. 116-117.

[24] Loevy, "Political Behavior," p. 92. For a 1970 rundown see Baltimore Evening Sun, September 16, 1970, p. D28.

[25] See Richard M. Cohen and Jules Witcover, A Heartbeat Away: The Investigation

Baltimore County (621,871), suburban territory bordering the city on three sides but not including it, ordinarily votes Democratic in local politics, though Republicans have won some offices in recent decades. The county, like the city, used to support a monopolistic Democratic organization but—again like the city but later—switched to a new equilibrium of Democratic factionalism in the 1940s.[26] In-migration produced the shift. During World War II thousands of white blue-collar workers move from the city into the county's southeastern suburbs, and the city's political structure traveled there with them—including political clubs, hierarchical organizations, deliverable precincts, patronage transactions, and competitive factionalism. Democratic factional leaders in and around Dundalk (85,377) and Essex (38,193) emerged as influence brokers in county primaries. In the 1950s and 1960s the county's Democratic politics centered in a contest between two factional coalitions, based respectively on patronage from the state legislature and from county offices, with individual factional leaders choosing and sometimes changing sides. Newspaper coverage of primaries in 1966 gives the flavor: "The Pine-Anderson Democratic organization held strong in the eastern sector of Baltimore county and provided a narrow winning margin for county executive candidate Dale Anderson and 23 other ticket candidates." But the Pine-Anderson faction lost eighteen other nominations: "These seats were taken by the Dewberry-Kahl forces and by independents."[27] The best-known product of Baltimore County politics in modern times is Spiro T. Agnew.

Politics in Prince George's County (661,192) resembles Baltimore County's: a "highly factional, patronage-oriented Democratic party" is said to have dominated electoral politics in the 1960s.[28] Newspaper

---

and Resignation of Vice President Spiro T. Agnew (New York: Viking, 1974), pp. 45-48. In the November election of 1970 a number of Baltimore factions left off their sample ballots the name of Senator Joseph D. Tydings, a Democrat they detested. J. Glenn Beall, Jr., the Republican who narrowly defeated Tydings, is said to have distributed some $60,000 in "walking-around money" among the Democratic organizations (*ibid.*, pp. 45-46). For a treatment of cash transfers on a primary day see Michael Weisskopf, "Baltimore: Politics as Usual: Precinct Payouts Typify Election Windup," *Washington Post*, September 11, 1978, pp. A1, A8.

[26] The information here on Baltimore County is taken from Loevy, "Political Behavior," pp. 121-127, 152-174, 205. See also Cohen and Witcover, *A Heartbeat Away*, pp. 48-49.

[27] *Baltimore Sun*, September 14, 1966, p. B2.

[28] James E. Skok, "Participation in Decision Making: The Bureaucracy and the Community," *Western Political Quarterly* 27(1974), 64. See also Willard J. Hutzel, "Political Clubs in Suburbia: A Case Study of Club Politics in Montgomery and Prince George's Counties, Maryland" (Ph.D. dissertation, University of Maryland, 1966), pp. 23-28.

stories provide good information on the slating activities of Prince George's factions and their tie-ins with candidates for governor.[29] Montgomery County (522,809), the state's other and more affluent Washington suburb, supported an authoritative Democratic machine from the 1920s through the mid-1940s but by the mid-1960s it had vanished.[30] The county's Democratic politics from roughly 1950 through 1965 had much in common with politics in New York City during that time. Middle-class activists, mostly newcomers to Montgomery County, moved into the Democratic party to displace patronage-oriented regulars. Democratic primaries became routinized slating contests. Localities switched from organization to reform—Bethesda (71,621) defected first, and others in short order; the reformers succeeded in taking over the party but maintained the regulars' tradition of entering slates in primaries. By the late 1960s Montgomery County no longer supported any traditional organizations, issues animated its activists in both parties, and its government had become a "highly professionalized bureaucracy under a nonpartisan manager."[31]

Bain presents interesting material on some of Maryland's smaller counties. Queen Anne's County (18,422), a rural, Democratic, mostly white area on the Eastern shore, was the scene of a Democratic factional politics based on patronage for nearly a century between the 1870s and mid-1950s. There were three successive cleavages within the party, each between a pair of rival Democratic factional organizations, which lasted twenty-five, thirty-four, and thirty-one years; during the last it was nearly impossible to win an elective office without being slated by the George faction or its adversary the Roe faction, both heavy dealers in patronage.[32] Charles County (47,678), once a rural slave area in southern Maryland along the Potomac (which became in

---

[29] See for example *Washington Post*, September 14, 1966, p. A17; September 16, 1970, p. A13.

[30] The material here on Montgomery County is taken from Bain, "Five Kinds of Politics," ch. 9, authoritative up through 1954; Hutzel, "Political Clubs," pp. 28-31; Skok, "Participation in Decision Making," p. 64. Charles E. Gilbert's study of Republican machines in Pennsylvania's Bucks, Montgomery, and Delaware counties (see ch. 2, note 141) and Bain's study of E. Brooke Lee's Democratic machine in Maryland's Montgomery County are apparently the only elaborate treatments ever done of suburban machines. In 1970, its machine days over, Maryland's Montgomery County ranked first in median family income among the country's 344 counties that had populations over 100,000.

[31] Skok, "Participation in Decision Making," p. 64. Skok emphasizes differences between the traditional politics of Prince George's County and the reform-professionalized politics of Montgomery County.

[32] All the material on Queen Anne's County is from Bain, "Five Kinds of Politics," ch. 8.

the 1980s yet another Washington suburb), was run from the mid-1890s through the mid-1950s by a white Republican machine in control of a largely black electorate.[33] In the 1950s its leaders still obtained many votes by buying them: "All accounts agree that hard cash has remained an essential item in securing the votes of a large segment of the Negro population."[34] Washington County (103,829), a western jurisdiction where Democrats and Republicans have traditionally supplied fairly close competition in elections, used to have consequential party organizations but they crumbled during the quarter century after Maryland enacted a direct primary law in 1912.[35] By the 1950s no group in either party was slating candidates successfully in primaries. This sequence of introduction of a direct primary followed by organizational decay is probably common around the country, but Bain's work on Washington County seems to be the only detailed longitudinal study demonstrating it. A TPO score for Maryland: 5-PF, organizational decline in Washington and Montgomery counties notwithstanding.

KENTUCKY (3,219,311)

Kentucky clearly belongs in a class with Maryland and West Virginia. In the 1960s officials from the governor down relied heavily on patronage as a political currency; local politicians in the Democratic party, dominant in most places, typically lined up in competing county "factions" (though some had stayed in power a long time); local Democratic "factions" routinely entered into alliances with candidates for governor; and Democratic governors channeled patronage through a favored "faction" in each county.[36] Quotation marks are used because

---

[33] Material on Charles County is from *ibid.*, ch. 7.

[34] *Ibid.*, pp. 205-206. On Republican slating activity in 1954: "The ticketmaking procedure followed the usual lines. Thomas Mudd [party chairman] appointed a committee to propose a ticket to the county Republican committee, but, as usual, its job was simply to announce the decisions that he arrived at by consultation with the other party leaders. . . . There was little in the way of issues or ambitions to disturb the usual procedures of ticketmaking" (*ibid.*, pp. 261-262). By the early 1950s the black vote was slipping away and the Republican hold on the county had become precarious; Democrats won some important victories in November 1954.

[35] Material on Washington County is from *ibid.*, ch. 10.

[36] On patronage: Malcolm E. Jewell and Everett W. Cunningham, *Kentucky Politics* (Lexington: University of Kentucky Press, 1968), pp. 43-45, 59-60, 67-70, 71-74, 106; Douglas O. Arnett, "Eastern Kentucky: The Politics of Dependency and Underdevelopment" (Ph.D. dissertation, Duke University, 1978), pp. 59-65, 69-70. Most of Arnett's material is from the mid-1960s. The basic reference on county factions is Jewell and Cunningham, pp. 45-56. "With few exceptions the Democratic county organizations are di-

the customary Kentucky meaning of "faction" is somewhat broader than the meaning stipulated earlier. In Kentucky's rural areas some "factional" organizations have served as governors' political agents but done little else, some have settled into a few county offices without trying to expand their holdings, and many have gone about slating with the elusiveness and intrigue of their West Virginia neighbors.[37] Still, it seems appropriate to say that Kentucky has been well stocked at lower levels with traditional organizations of a factional sort. Democrats at the state level have also lined up in competing "factions"—that is, enduring rival coalitions each made up of a group of Democratic politicians holding or seeking statewide elective offices and their local allies. This was the case, anyway, from the mid-1940s through the mid-1960s when "factional" leaders Earl Clements and A. B. "Happy" Chandler kept an antagonism going. In fact the county bases of these state-level "factions" shifted considerably from election to election and from can-

vided into two clearly recognizable factions. Among the exceptions are the declining number in which a single strong faction has long been dominant" (*ibid.*, p. 55). See also Arnett, pp. 58-86 ("County Political Power Structures"). On ties with gubernatorial candidates: Jewell and Cunningham, pp. 45-56. On channeling patronage to counties: Jewell and Cunningham, pp. 47-52, 59-60; Arnett, pp. 59-65.

[37] See Jewell and Cunningham, *Kentucky Politics*, pp. 47-52, 151-155, 159. On local endorsements in statewide Democratic primaries: "Slating arrangements are carried out in an atmosphere of mystery and even intrigue, as state and local politicians maneuver at the last moment to make the deals that they believe will enhance the prospects of the particular candidate to whom they have the greatest loyalty. A comprehensive statewide study of slating in a primary would require the collection of sample ballots distributed by two or more factional organizations in every county and even modifications in the ballot made by precinct leaders in some counties" (p. 152).

didate to candidate, though some county organizations stayed loyal to one or the other "faction" over a long series of elections.[38]

Jefferson County (695,055), site of Louisville, (361,958), an old machine city, supported strong traditional organizations in both parties in the 1950s and 1960s. Republicans and Democrats shared or alternated in power.[39] Both parties used whatever they could of some 2,200 city and county patronage jobs to staff their precinct structures, and raised money by assessing patronage employees 2 percent of their salaries. Both organizations regularly slated candidates for city, county, and state legislative offices, and their designees almost always won nomination—Republicans ordinarily without opposition, Democrats over recurrent but weak opposition from local factions allied with politicians at the state level.[40] Both organizations exercised considerable influence in their parties' primaries for governor.[41] Anti-organization

[38] On factions at the state level see *ibid.*, pp. 131-147. In 1963, after bitterly opposing each other for decades, Chandler and Clements combined forces against an incumbent Democratic governor (*ibid.*, p. 137). By the late 1960s it looked as if Kentucky Democrats were falling into a conventional West Virginia pattern, with incumbent Democratic governors trying to name their successor nominees but little order beyond that at the top of the party. See *ibid.*, pp. 137-138. An elaborate rundown of what are claimed to be statewide factional lineages extending over the last several decades appears in "Brown Won Without the Machine," *Lexington Leader*, August 23, 1979, pp. A1, A4. On an "Administration Faction" persisting at the state level from 1947 through 1967 see Marc Landy, "Kentucky," ch. 9 in Alan Rosenthal and Maureen Moakley (eds.), *The Political Life of the American States* (New York: Praeger, 1984), pp. 210-211.

[39] On Louisville's machine past see William E. Ellis, "Robert Worth Bingham and Louisville Progressivism, 1905-1910," *Filson Club History Quarterly* 54(1980), 169-195. Material on Jefferson County Republicans is from Jewell and Cunningham, *Kentucky Politics*, pp. 102-107. The basic source on county Democrats is *ibid.*, pp. 70-76, 159-160. Carol L. Denning, "The Louisville (Kentucky) Democratic Party: Political Times of 'Miss Lennie' McLaughlin" (M.A. thesis, University of Louisville, 1981), chs. 3-5, deals with Democratic party organization over about half a century ending in the early 1960s.

[40] On Jefferson County's Democratic primaries see also Malcolm E. Jewell, "Party and Primary Competition in Kentucky State Legislative Races," *Kentucky Law Journal* 48(1960), 531-534. On the county's state legislators, all elected in single-member districts, see Jewell and Cunningham, *Kentucky Politics*, p. 74: "For many years the Democratic organization controlled the legislative delegation from Jefferson County, which it had selected through its endorsement procedures. The delegation held binding caucuses and voted in a disciplined fashion on local issues and on the governor's measures. The Democratic organization was able to provide those governors whom it supported with a reliable block of legislative votes, and in return it could expect favorable treatment from the governor."

[41] See Jewell and Cunningham, *Kentucky Politics*, pp. 73-75, 136, 140-142 on Democrats; pp. 107-108, 117, 120 on Republicans. On the place of Jefferson County organization in state politics early in the century: "[A Democratic governor] did not want to alienate the Louisville machine because of the important Democratic vote in the city and

suburbanites interested in issues intruded into Democratic politics in the 1960s, giving the regular organization a new kind of opposition to contend with. But the regulars maintained effective control of nominations, purging an incumbent state senator, for example, in advancing a state legislative slate successfully in 1967.[42] The county's Republican organization commonly slated blacks for elective offices in the 1960s and gave over a fifth of the party's patronage jobs to blacks.[43]

Fayette County (174,323), Kentucky's second metropolitan center and site of Lexington (108,137), supported a Democratic machine through the 1930s, and a patronage organization survived in Lexington's lower-income precincts, supplying the base, perhaps (the evidence is inconclusive), of an "Underwood faction" that had the earmarks of traditional organization and maneuvered fairly successfully in the city's nonpartisan elections in the late 1960s.[44] But evidently no traditional organization played a significant role in the county's Democratic primaries for state legislative and county offices during the 1960s.

Kentucky organizations have flourished in much of the countryside as well as in the cities—for example in Logan County (21,793) and in two other nearby agricultural counties in the southwest.[45] The state's

---

county." After 1910: "Political machines in Louisville and northern Kentucky continued to control local elections and to broker state offices." Ellis, "Bingham and Louisville Progressivism," pp. 181, 194.

[42] Malcolm E. Jewell, *Metropolitan Representation: State Legislative Districting in Urban Counties* (New York: National Municipal League, 1969), p. 24. In 1979 Louisville reformers unhappy with a Democratic regular in the mayoralty entered a slate that won a municipal primary. "The Mayor got his start in the Democratic Party as a precinct captain after World War II and worked his way up through the hierarchy. Many of his challengers in the party's liberal wing trace their political roots to neighborhood activism and civic organizations" (Iver Peterson, "Foes of Louisville Mayor Seek Impeachment Vote," *New York Times*, September 18, 1979, p. A12).

[43] Republican mobilization of the black vote is apparently an old county tradition. For an account of the Republican organization's enterprising fraudulence in the 1920s see Joseph P. Harris, *Registration of Voters in the United States* (Washington, D.C.: Brookings, 1929), pp. 372-377.

[44] Most of the material on Fayette County is from Jewell and Cunningham, *Kentucky Politics*, pp. 76-78. On the "Underwood faction" see W. E. Lyons, *The Politics of City-County Merger: The Lexington-Fayette County Experience* (Lexington: University Press of Kentucky, 1977), pp. 37-50.

[45] In the 1960s Logan County had sustained a strong Democratic organization for about fifty years. The county had a record of turning in especially lopsided vote percentages in statewide primaries. See Jewell and Cunningham, *Kentucky Politics*, pp. 53-54. The nearby counties of Trigg and Todd are said to have supported strong Democratic organizations up through the 1950s. See John H. Fenton, *Politics in the Border States: A Study of the Patterns of Political Organization, and Political Change, Common to the Border States—Maryland, West Virginia, Kentucky and Missouri* (New Orleans: Hau-

most interesting rural organizations have operated in the Appalachian hills and valleys of the southeast, an area of twenty or so of the country's poorest counties—about half coal-mining centers and half not, half traditionally Democratic and half Republican, some run by single organizations without opposition and others fought over by rival factional organizations.[46] The chief sources of local patronage in this territory turn out to be the school systems. The best way to build a factional organization has been to become a school superintendent, give out jobs to janitors, bus drivers, lunchroom clerks, and others, and then to mobilize the appointees and their families to vote and work for slates of candidates for school board, county, municipal, and state legislative offices.[47] This may be the only part of the country where husband-and-wife teams run machines. In Breathitt County (14,221), for example, Ervine Turner took over the school superintendent's job in 1924 when his brother gave it up; Ervine's wife Marie took it in 1931 and kept it until 1969. There was factional wrangling at the start, but after 1938 Marie and Ervine ran a trim Democratic organization and the county without much opposition from inside or outside the party.[48] Baxter and Mallie Bledsoe conducted a Republican regime of the same sort in Clay County (18,481); one of them held the superintendent's job all but one year between 1927 and 1974.[49] The Office of Economic Opportunity came up against these and other Appalachian organizations—a Democratic combine in Floyd County (35,889), for example—when it sent poverty workers into Kentucky's eastern counties in the mid-1960s.[50] An enterprise coming in from outside offering jobs and attempting to organize the population was an alarming incursion. The obvious recourses were either to expel the OEO locals or else to capture them, and apparently the indigenous county organizations more or less took them

---

ser, 1957), pp. 25-26, 71. All three counties are located in an old slave-owning area along the Tennessee border; their populations have been predominantly white in this century.

[46] The basic source on the southeast is Arnett, "Eastern Kentucky," pp. 58-86. In this set of twenty or so counties there is no apparent difference in political structure between counties having and not having coal mines.

[47] See *ibid.*, pp. 69-86. Arnett does not say that teachers were treated as patronage appointees, but they probably had to stay in line politically. He tells of a young Clay County teacher who poll-watched for the wrong side in a primary and soon got assigned to an elementary school reachable only on thirty miles of bad roads over mountains and up hollows (pp. 80-84).

[48] See Jewell and Cunningham, *Kentucky Politics*, pp. 54-55; Arnett, "Eastern Kentucky," pp. 70-72.

[49] See Arnett, "Eastern Kentucky," pp. 72-86.

[50] On Floyd County: Richard A. Couto, *Poverty, Politics, and Health Care: An Appalachian Experience* (New York: Praeger, 1975), pp. 76-79, 93-95.

over.[51] An overall TPO score for Kentucky is the same as West Virginia's: 4-PF.

INDIANA (5,193,669)

"Politics in Indiana is a business conducted by men who devote their lives to it and make their living at it."[52] According to Frank J. Munger's definitive account, Indiana politics as of the 1950s was emphatically an organization enterprise anchored in the inducements of state and local patronage.[53] Urban (though not rural) organization commonly took a factional form, one organization controlling a party's official structure and another in the same party struggling to take it over. City hall and county courthouse groups often supplied the contending factions, each capable of mobilizing a following of patronage workers.[54] Alliances routinely occurred between local factions and politicians who sought nomination or held office at the statewide level.[55]

---

[51] On the OEO incursion see Arnett, "Eastern Kentucky," chs. 4 and 5. The alarmed organizations appealed to both the local Republican congressman, Tim Lee Carter, and the local Democratic congressman, Carl D. Perkins. Perkins, better connected in Washington, was more helpful in getting the OEO off their backs. See *ibid.*, pp. 240-242, 248-250. The OEO ran into comparable trouble in West Virginia's Mingo County. See H. Perry, *"They'll Cut Off Your Project."* "The greatest obstacle to the elimination of poverty in Mingo was the political machine, which manipulated elections to maintain control" (Perry, p. 136).

[52] Frank J. Munger, "Two-Party Politics in the State of Indiana" (Ph.D. dissertation, Harvard University, 1955), p. 6.

[53] *Ibid.*, ch. 4 ("Party Structure: Patronage and the Hierarchy of Power").

[54] On local factions: *ibid.*, pp. 137-143, 158-160.

[55] *Ibid.*, pp. 98-99, 107, 162, 185-186. See also Frank J. Munger, *The Struggle for Republican Leadership in Indiana, 1954* (New York: McGraw-Hill, 1960, Eagleton Case #23), pp. 16-26. Until 1976 Indiana's candidates for governor and Senator were chosen by convention rather than by primary, so alliances between local factions and candidates for nomination at the statewide level manifested themselves in selection of delegates and convention voting.

Local factions fought over patronage, not issues: "Squabbles over who will get what jobs are the principal—and almost the only—cause of factional fights within the party."[56] It was common practice in urban (though not rural) areas for local organizations—one or more per party—to circulate their "slates" of candidates in advance of primaries. Indiana's "slating" had an unusually formal quality and a special meaning, because state law specified precisely what groups had to do in making up and circulating their lists of names—even though no trace of "slating" appeared on the primary ballot itself.[57] Outside the cities, low-income counties in the southern part of the state were said to excel in election fraud, strength of party organization, and value placed on patronage.[58] This is a picture of Indiana thirty years ago, but it seems to have stayed more or less the same through the 1960s.[59] In 1971 the party custom of assessing state, county, and local employees 2 percent of their salaries was still in place.[60] Newspapers covering Indiana primaries around 1970 framed stories by discussing the activities of slat-

---

[56] Munger, "Two-Party Politics," p. 177. See also pp. 5, 180, 228-229.

[57] On slating: *ibid.*, pp. 156-161.

[58] *Ibid.*, p. 146; Munger, *The Struggle*, p. 28.

[59] For evidence of tie-ins between local factions and candidates seeking nomination in state conventions see, for 1962, John H. Fenton, *Midwest Politics* (New York: Holt, Rinehart and Winston, 1966), pp. 172-173; for 1956-1962, David C. Leege, "Control in the Party Convention Nominating System: The Case of Indiana," ch. 11 in James B. Kessler (ed.), *Empirical Studies of Indiana Politics: Studies of Legislative Behavior* (Bloomington: Indiana University Press, 1970), pp. 202-209. In addition, Leege reports a pattern of high turnover among party chairmen in urban counties—a consequence of factional infighting (p. 208). A conclusion of a study based on interviews in 1961 with all candidates running for both houses of the Indiana state legislature: "Legislative candidates from urban districts perceived their party organizations as strong . . . ; rural districts were seen as having weak party organizations." See Henry Teune, "Legislative Attitudes Toward Interest Groups," ch. 6 in Kessler, pp. 107, 113-114, quotation at p. 114. A 1974 dissertation by James A. Thurber, based substantially on interviews in 1969 with members of the Indiana assembly, sets out some features of the state's politics evident in Munger's picture a decade and a half earlier: the rooting of the parties in patronage, pp. 5, 87, 90, 93-103, 107; organization recruitment of candidates for lower offices, pp. 107, 125, 219; organization slating in primaries, pp. 120-121, 234, 239. See Thurber, "Political Party Recruitment and Legislative Role Orientations" (Ph.D dissertation, Indiana University, 1974).

[60] Jonathan R. Laing, " 'The 2% Club': Kicking Back Pay Is Way of Life in Indiana for Employes of State," *Wall Street Journal*, April 8, 1971, pp. 1, 18. "Mrs. Mercer and some 40,000 other patronage workers with state, county and local jobs in Indiana are forced to kick back part of their salaries to the party in power, even in nonelection years. Known as the '2% club', the group includes everyone from low-paid city garbagemen to highly paid professionals" (p. 1). "Besides the $700,000 annually that goes to the governor, county and city political organizations also do well. In such populous counties as Republican-dominated Marion County and Lake County, a Democratic bastion, the annual take exceeds $100,000" (p. 18).

ing organizations, often factions. A 1966 headline: "Lake County (Ind.) Machine Takes Beating in a Key Race."[61] An Evansville headline in 1972: "Demo Factions Split 6 Races."[62] A 1966 headline about the defeat of a slate backed by Marion County's Republican chairman: "Action Slate Routs Brown."[63] On another Marion Republican chairman in 1972: "Bulen Rocked by Defeat of Five on Slate."[64]

Vanderburgh County (168,772), chief metropolitan center in southern Indiana and site of Evansville (138,764), offers a paradigm of evenly matched parties with factionalism nevertheless in both—what has been described, looking back from the mid-1950s, as "an unbroken succession of factional struggles within both parties." In Munger's account, a typical Vanderburgh primary season featured two factions in each party, each with its own campaign headquarters and precinct captains, slating against each other for a range of offices.[65] An Evansville newspaper account in 1972 again reports well-organized slating matches on both sides.[66] A 1962 study of Howard County (83,198), site of Kokomo (44,042), revealed one organization in the Republican party and three in the Democratic, all busily backing candidates in primaries.[67] A 1975 report on Terre Haute (70,335) and its parent unit, Vigo County (114,528), where "the quest for jobs is pervasive, and the merit system has made only the tiniest of inroads on the patronage pool," tells of competition in primaries between two Democratic factions apparently centered in the mayoralty and the county treasurer's office, and of a single Republican organization that maintained itself on income from the county auto license bureau—a small source provided according to party custom by the governor.[68]

---

[61] *Chicago Daily News*, May 4, 1966, p. 6.

[62] *Evansville Courier*, May 3, 1972, p. 1.

[63] *Indianapolis Star*, May 4, 1966, p. 1.

[64] *Ibid.*, May 3, 1972, p. 1.

[65] Munger, "Two-Party Politics," pp. 107, 142, 143, 158, 159; quotation at p. 142.

[66] *Evansville Courier*, May 3, 1972, pp. 1, 2. In the Democratic party a faction led by the county chairman fought against "an elected officeholders group" called Democrats United For Change. In the Republican party it was a mayor's organization against the Better Government League Committee.

[67] Thomas M. Watts, "Application of the Attribution Model to the Study of Political Recruitment: County Elective Offices," ch. 8 in William J. Crotty (ed.), *Approaches to the Study of Party Organization* (Boston: Allyn and Bacon, 1968), pp. 320-322, 331-336.

[68] David S. Broder, "Old-Style Politics: Patronage Rules in Ind. County," *Washington Post*, June 15, 1975, pp. A1, A4. "A Spectator reporter calculated in April that members of Treasurer Schoffstall's immediate family were receiving $110,384 a year in salaries and pensions from the city and county—including a wife, a daughter and a niece on Schoffstall's own payroll. The treasurer's only comment was that nepotism 'is not unu-

In Marion County (793,590), site of Indianapolis (745,739), the official organizations of both parties routinely slated candidates for county and state legislative offices in the 1950s and 1960s and usually got them nominated. Apparently neither party sustained an opposing faction over a long series of elections, but opposition slates often did materialize—a Democratic "Blue Ribbon" slate in 1968, for example, and Republican slates that displaced those in power and took over the formal party apparatus in 1954 and 1966.[69] The victors in 1966—the Republican Action Committee—generated the election of Richard Lugar as Indianapolis mayor in 1967 and the consolidation of city and county administration in a "Unigov" arrangement in 1969.[70] A 1973 report on city and county looked back over the 1960s: "Party organization has been important in both the city and the county, with strong and active county, ward, and precinct staffing. The county has probably been a more significant political party unit than the city, with the county chairman usually directing city campaigns as well as those in the county itself."[71] The report discussed parties under the new Unigov system: "Political clearance through the party machinery is expected for most appointments to city jobs, and city employees at all levels are encouraged (at the least) to participate actively in partisan campaigns. But there appears also to be more conscious attention to management improvement than ever before."[72] Party organizations still arranged

---

sual at all' in Vigo county" (p. A4). As of 1984 Indiana's state and county organizations were still getting a rake-off from fees for driver's licenses, car registrations, and license plates; the party out of the governorship was now also cut in on the proceeds through a recent share-the-wealth arrangement. See E. R. Shipp, "Political Use of Auto Fees Is Challenged in Indiana," *New York Times*, May 29, 1984, p. A12.

[69] On party organizations and candidate slates in Marion County in the 1950s and 1960s: Munger, "Two-Party Politics," pp. 98-99, 158-159, 162; Jewell, *Metropolitan Representation*, pp. 7-8, 19-20; Howard D. Hamilton, "Legislative Constituencies: Single-Member Districts, Multi-Member Districts, and Floterial Districts," *Western Political Quarterly* 20(1967), 323; *Indianapolis Star*, May 6, 1964, p. 10; May 4, 1966, p. 1; May 8, 1968, p. 1; May 6, 1970, p. 1; May 3, 1972, pp. 1, 11. In the Republican party, H. Dale Brown put up a slate of candidates for state legislative and county offices that defeated the incumbent organization's slate in 1954. Brown took over the county chairmanship and held it until 1966, when L. Keith Bulen put up a slate that defeated Brown's. Bulen thereupon took over the chairmanship and held it until at least 1972. See Munger, "Two-Party Politics," pp. 98-99; Jewell, *Metropolitan Representation*, pp. 7-8, 24.

[70] York Willbern, "Unigov: Local Government Reorganization in Indianapolis," ch. 2 in Advisory Commission on Intergovernmental Relations, *Regional Governance: Promise and Performance; Substate Regionalism and the Federal System*, vol. 2, *Case Studies* (Washington, D.C.: U.S. Government Printing Office, 1973), pp. 48-59.

[71] *Ibid.*, p. 49.

[72] *Ibid.*, pp. 67, 69. An earlier source on patronage dealings in Marion County: Munger, "Two-Party Politics," p. 146.

nominations for city council positions in the late 1970s: "Party control of nominations is so strong that any serious candidate pays a slating fee to the party in order to be considered for the slate. (The Republican fee was $400 in 1975 and the Democratic fee was $480.)"[73]

City politics in South Bend (125,580), analyzed in a good recent monograph, may be the best modern approximation of the Jacksonian turnover model of the mid-nineteenth century. From 1955 through 1971, control of the city government shifted back and forth between regular Democratic and Republican organizations built on patronage. The city had no civil service rules, all employees except policemen and firemen were supposed to do work for the party in power and to give it 1 percent of their salaries, and a change in party control of the mayor-alty ordinarily brought about a "massive turnover of city personnel."[74]

Finally Lake County (546,253), site of Gary (175,415) and other industrial suburbs near Chicago, turned from a Republican into a Democratic stronghold during the New Deal. Its post–World War II Democratic organization, however, according to an observer in the 1960s, "has no more awareness of the ideals of FDR than the man in the moon—it's strictly a commercial undertaking."[75] Ample evidence supports this judgment. When Munger wrote in the 1950s, no one had ever built an authoritative Democratic organization at the county level. The county's Democrats were a hodgepodge of patronage fiefdoms loosely joined for nominating purposes in two rival alliances called the "Mayors' group" (three mayors were involved) and the "Commissioners' group" (three of them too).[76] In the 1950s and 1960s Gary had a cluster of black precinct committeemen whose acquisitive activity on primary days inspired respect in at least three monographic accounts. "Some of these officials are credited locally with power and skill enough to pro-rate primary votes in exact proportion to the amount of 'campaign contributions' received. . . . Some candidates enter what is nearly an open auction, with majorities promised the higher bidder, or

---

[73] Howard D. Hamilton, *Electing the Cincinnati City Council: An Examination of Alternative Electoral Representation Systems* (Cincinnati: Stephen H. Wilder Foundation, 1978), pp. 35-41 ("Indianapolis"), at p. 37. The organizations carried all but four of fifty-eight nominations in 1975, fifty of them for positions in single-member districts.

[74] William P. Hojnacki, "Kalamazoo, Michigan and South Bend, Indiana: A Comparative Analysis of Policy Outcomes" (Ph.D. dissertation, University of Notre Dame, 1977), pp. 75-85, quotation at p. 79.

[75] A statement of a "seasoned party hand" quoted in Marshall Frady, "Gary, Indiana," *Harper's Magazine*, August 1969, p. 40.

[76] Munger, "Two-Party Politics," pp. 159-160. Munger's summary comment on the county: "Lake County is notorious throughout the state for its free-swinging politics, tumultuous elections, and subjection to influence by syndicate gambling" (p. 143).

the last one to make an offer before the polls actually open."[77] After 1952 an able white entrepreneur, George Chacharis, did manage to build a machine at the city level in Gary that controlled municipal appointments and council nominations, and in the late 1950s he reached for the county offices and became the "first unofficial boss of the Lake County Democratic organization."[78] But Chacharis drew an indictment for tax fraud in 1962, went to prison, and his organization declined in influence, paving the way for the election of Richard G. Hatcher as Gary's first black mayor in 1967.[79]

Hatcher's rise to power is an interesting case of a big-city mayoralty breaking loose from control by a traditional party organization. He began by mobilizing a following of largely civil-rights activists to carry his campaign. The Democratic primary contest, during which Hatcher supporters provoked a "wave of black nationalism," divided the city unprecedentedly along racial lines. Hatcher narrowly won. Leaders of the Democratic county organization offered to back him in the general election if he promised to keep up their supply of patronage once elected. He refused and they backed a Republican. The organization leadership called Hatcher a "communist" and "black racist"; he called them "crooks" and "racketeers." Once in office he took steps to professionalize the city administration, denied jobs to the old-line black committeemen, and refrained from building a traditional precinct apparatus himself. The regular organization fell back on its county offices and survived into the 1970s, strong enough to staff the city precincts and to win city primaries for lower offices but no longer capable of electing a mayor—a common Midwestern pattern.[80] The TPO score for Indiana: 5-PF.

[77] Thomas F. Thompson, "Public Administration in the Civil City of Gary, Indiana" (Ph.D. dissertation, Indiana University, 1960), pp. 31-38, quotations at pp. 33, 35. See also William E. Nelson, Jr., "Black Political Mobilization: The 1967 Mayoral Election in Gary, Indiana" (Ph.D. dissertation, University of Illinois, 1971), pp. 168-185; Peter H. Rossi and Phillips Cutright, "The Impact of Party Organization in an Industrial Setting," ch. 2 in Morris Janowitz (ed.), *Community Political Systems* (Glencoe, Ill.: Free Press, 1961), pp. 86-87. For broader treatments of Gary's precinct organization: Nelson, pp. 154-185; Rossi and Cutright, ch. 2 *passim*.

[78] On the Chacharis machine in general: Thompson, "Public Administration in Gary," pp. 73-81, ch. 5; Nelson, "Black Political Mobilization," ch. 3. On Chacharis's control of elective and appointive officials: Thompson, pp. 151, 154. On branching out into the county offices: Nelson, pp. 146, 153, quotation at p. 153.

[79] On the downslide: Nelson, "Black Political Mobilization," pp. 143, 162-168, 186-202.

[80] General sources on Hatcher's initial election and first term: Nelson, "Black Political Mobilization," pp. 555-561; Charles H. Levine, *Racial Conflict and the American Mayor: Power, Polarization, and Performance* (Lexington, Mass.: Heath, 1974), ch. 5;

MISSOURI (4,677,399)

Students of Missouri's party organization have confined their attention to the state's two metropolitan centers. In Jackson County (654,178), site of Kansas City (507,330), Thomas J. Pendergast's well-known Democratic machine dominated politics in the 1920s and 1930s. It operated with no trace of difficulty in a model nonpartisan council-manager system introduced in 1925, and reached out like Jersey City's Hague machine to take over the state government during the New Deal.[81] But a reform group won power in Kansas City in 1940, and from then through the 1960s the city's politics looked like a cross between Cincinnati's and Baltimore's. A slating organization of a good-government type, the Citizens' Association, controlled the council and city administration through 1967 except for one four-year interruption.[82] But a set of old-line Democratic organizations called "the factions" operated on the city's north

William E. Nelson, Jr., and Philip J. Meranto, *Electing Black Mayors: Political Action in the Black Community* (Columbus: Ohio State University Press, 1977), chs. 6-8. A discussion of what motivated people to work in Hatcher's 1967 campaign: Nelson and Meranto, pp. 215-222. Race issues and racial polarization: *ibid.*, pp. 230-268, quotations at pages 245-246. Offers, refusals, epithets: *ibid.*, pp. 272-276, 284-285; Levine, p. 74; Charles H. Levine and Clifford Kaufman, "Urban Conflict as a Constraint on Mayoral Leadership: Lessons from Gary and Cleveland," *American Politics Quarterly* 2(1974), 100. Hatcher in office: Nelson, p. 556; Levine, pp. 73, 79-80. The county organization in 1967-1971: Nelson, pp. 555-562; Levine, p. 73; Nelson and Meranto, pp. 367-368. From an account of the election of 1975, when Hatcher survived another challenge by an organization-backed candidate: "Hostile remnants of the Democratic machine still survive at the precinct level in Gary. Out of necessity, Hatcher had attracted a following based mainly on his personal appeal, allowing him to ignore his traditional lack of party support." Edmond J. Keller, "Electoral Politics in Gary: Mayoral Performance, Organization, and the Political Economy of the Black Vote," *Urban Affairs Quarterly* 15(1979), 52-56, quotation at p. 53.

[81] See Lyle W. Dorsett, *The Pendergast Machine* (New York: Oxford University Press, 1968). On the reform in city structure, ch. 6; on the takeover of the state, ch. 7.

[82] On the Citizens' Association: Kenneth E. Gray, *A Report on Politics in Kansas City, Mo.* (Cambridge: Joint Center for Urban Studies, M.I.T./Harvard, 1959), pp. II:13-17. The electoral history: Thomas P. Murphy, *Metropolitics and the Urban County* (Washington, D.C.: Washington National Press, 1970), pp. 80-83.

side, sustained by patronage from county offices. There were eight or nine of these "factions" in the late 1950s—Alex Presta's organization in the Italian wards, for example, and Henry McKessick's in a cluster of black wards—and after additions and subtractions about the same number in the late 1960s.[83] The "factions" fought each other for turf, most joined forces on occasion to try to put another out of business, and in general they failed to unite on city council slates, but they did ordinarily control Democratic nominations for county and state legislative offices.[84] Jackson County's second city, Independence (111,630), had its own lineup of "factions."[85] In the mid-1960s an ambitious new good-government group called the Committee for County Progress set out to professionalize the county government. To the old-line organizations this was a particularly menacing objective, and a series of lively slating matches ensued in county Democratic primaries. Most "factions" were on one side and the CCP, allied with a rising black organization, Freedom Incorporated, was on the other. Election returns need to be read with this Democratic division in mind. In November 1968, for example, Jackson County voters elected two "factional" Democrats to the state senate, and six Republicans, nine CCP Democrats, and eight "factional" Democrats to the state assembly.[86]

St. Louis (622,236) supported a dualistic politics in the 1950s and 1960s something like Kansas City's. Democratic mayors with business and newspaper support but no anchor in party organization presided over broad policy making. At the same time traditional Democratic or-

---

[83] On the city's "factions": Gray, *Report on Kansas City*, pp. ii:7-13, 20; Murphy, *Metropolitics*, pp. 117-119. Banfield and Wilson wrote that some of these "factions" were genuine patronage organizations and others just "personal followings" (*City Politics*, pp. 134-135).

[84] On wrangling among the "factions": Gray, *Report on Kansas City*, pp. ii:11-13; Murphy, *Metropolitics*, pp. 117-118. On slating against the Citizens' Association: Gray, pp. ii:22-32. On state legislators: "The Kansas City delegation is without leadership, and each legislator owes loyalty only to the faction locally responsible for his election" (David R. Derge, "Metropolitan and Outstate Alignments in Illinois and Missouri Legislative Delegations," *American Political Science Review* 52 [1958], 1064). On slating control see also Gray, p. iv:1; and for the 1960s, Murphy, pp. 244, 246. Until 1959, at least, the city's veteran Democratic congressman, Richard Bolling, had closer relations with the Citizens' Association than with the "factions" (Gray, p. iv:2). This puts Bolling in a class with Ohio's John J. Gilligan and Connecticut's Abraham Ribicoff, other liberal Democrats of national stature who had important ties at least early in their careers with local good-government slating organizations.

[85] Gray, *Report on Kansas City*, pp. ii:7, 8, 11; Murphy, *Metropolitics*, pp. 118, 128-129.

[86] On the CCP and the slating contests: Murphy, *Metropolitics*, pp. 112-117, 119-123, 153-168.

ganizations with little interest in policy operated in the wards—in some cases especially manipulable "delivery wards"—supported by patronage from a set of county offices, the police department, and the board of education.[87] The ward organizations ordinarily controlled the nominations of aldermen, county officials, and members of the state assembly and senate.[88] Ward committeemen were still in command of Democratic nominations in the late 1960s. A 1968 report discusses an organization victory in a primary for president of the board of aldermen, and a 1969 study tells of committeemen in the black wards capable of purging incumbent legislators in favor of their own nominees.[89] On balance it seems inappropriate to refer to St. Louis's ward organizations as "factions," and in fact the term is not used locally. They do have a record of autonomous dealing—no county leadership existed in the 1950s and 1960s to orchestrate them—but their normal practice was to manage affairs on their own territory without invading each other or running slates against each other.[90] In their pattern of in-

[87] The "county officials" here—sheriff, collector of revenue, license collector, recorder of deeds, some magistrates—were figures elected in the autonomous city of St. Louis. They had nothing to do with St. Louis County, a populous and separate suburban unit next door. The city's teachers and policemen were professionals, but their agencies had patronage jobs to offer. General references on St. Louis: Kenneth E. Gray, *A Report on Politics in Saint Louis* (Cambridge: Joint Center for Urban Studies, M.I.T./Harvard, 1961), pp. II:1-35, III:4-21; Robert H. Salisbury, "St. Louis Politics: Relationships Among Interests, Parties, and Governmental Structure," *Western Political Quarterly* 13(1960), 498-505. A 1966 rundown: Hessler, *29 Ways to Govern a City*, p. 13. According to Salisbury the "county office group"—that is, the set of ward and county-office politicians—was "not particularly concerned with broad social or economic policy as such. It is concerned rather with the immediate needs of effective ward organization, and these needs are not notably different today than they traditionally have been. Patronage remains the lifeblood of the organization" (p. 504).

[88] Slating control of aldermen: Gray, *Report on Saint Louis*, p. II:8; Hessler, *29 Ways to Govern a City*, p. 13; Salisbury, "St. Louis Politics," p. 504. State legislators: Gray, pp. II:7, IV:4; Salisbury, p. 505.

[89] The 1968 election: Dempster Holland, "Coalition of Liberals and Blacks Can Elect City Officials," *Focus Midwest* 7, no. 6(1969), 18-21, 25. On the vote in middle-class wards of South St. Louis: "The ward organization is good for at least one-third of the votes. This means that the fifty patronage workers per ward can each generate about twenty other votes, from spouses, friends, and neighbors" (p. 21). Nonetheless, the organizations' hold on the electorate was becoming precarious by 1968. The 1969 study: Robert T. Perry, *Black Legislators* (San Francisco: R & E Research Associates, 1976), pp. 38, 39, 46-47.

[90] Gray reports in his 1961 account that the ward committeemen had a practice of respecting the wishes of any of their number on matters within his own ward (*Report on Saint Louis*, p. II:8). Also: "No ward leader has much influence outside his own ward" (p. II:23). The term "faction" did have one local referent in the 1950s and 1960s: a loose alliance of Democratic ward committeemen in *all* the well-organized wards was sometimes called the "North Side Faction" (p. II:20).

teraction they look more like Cleveland's organization than Baltimore's.

The rest of Missouri is a blank save for an old, unelaborated assertion that "smaller machines which get less publicity exist in the more remote areas of the state."[91] In general the state's traditional organizations of the 1960s seem to have been about as prominent as Ohio's: vigorous and influential in large metropolitan counties though not in control of mayoralties. In the Kansas City area, at least, the pattern was factional. Score for the state: 4-PF.

[91] Carl A. McCandless, *Government, Politics and Administration in Missouri* (St. Louis: Educational Publishers, 1949), p. 111.

CHAPTER 4

States of the Confederate South

Material on the South is uneven—especially good on Louisiana and Texas but dated or scanty on several other states, and pretty good on larger cities but weak on rural areas and smaller cities. What evidence there is ratifies the familiar generalization that the region on balance has proved inhospitable to party organization, traditional or otherwise. But there are exceptions to the rule—two big-city machines used to thrive, for example, as well as an unknown number of consequential organizations scattered through the countryside. Rural counties are especially difficult to get reliable information on, which makes coding judgments precarious in predominantly rural states. Yet each state does have its own set of evidence for the 1960s, plentiful or not, and the only available course is to appraise it and use it. Because the election of governors is a favorite topic of writers on Southern politics, one good way to gain material on local organizations is to examine accounts of Democratic gubernatorial primaries. Accounts of pre-1970 primaries in, say, Illinois, New Jersey, Maryland, and Kentucky turn up information on the mobilizing activities of local organizations—some factional and some not—and accounts on Southern states ought to furnish such information too if appropriate organizations existed and were operating. In some places they did. A detailed comparative work that proved indirectly useful is Malcolm E. Jewell's *Legislative Representation in the Contemporary South*. It investigates, among other things, the incidence of slating tie-ins between candidates for governor and the state legislature running in Democratic primaries.[1] Alliances of this sort often occurred where local organizations existed to do the requisite dealing.

LOUISIANA (3,643,180)

Grouping the eleven former Confederate states together is conventional and useful, but in a study of party organization it can be misleading. Louisiana, for example, may have more in common with Mary-

---

[1] Malcolm E. Jewell, *Legislative Representation in the Contemporary South* (Durham: Duke University Press, 1967).

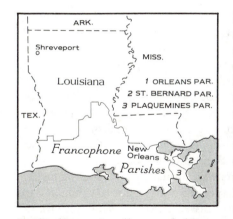

land than with any other secession state. Louisiana's similarities include an old big-city Democratic machine lapsed from monopoly into factionalism; a patchwork of traditional organizations in rural areas, many of them factional; a record of tie-ins between local organizations and candidates for governor in Democratic primaries; and a tradition (at about Maryland's level) of exceptionally crowded Democratic primaries for lower offices. Louisiana has generated many more candidates and much stiffer competition in primaries than any other ex-Confederate state.

New Orleans (593,471) has an organizational lineage worth reviewing.[2] From the mid-1890s through the mid-1940s the city supported one of the country's classic machines, a combine called the Old Regulars that ordinarily exercised considerable influence in statewide nominating and stood out in the 1930s as the last obstacle to Huey Long's consolidation of power in the state.[3] In 1934-1935 Long reached in and changed the machine's management. He put through laws taking away local prerogatives, triggered a vice investigation, sent in the national guard, drove the city near bankruptcy, and in general left the Old Regular ward leaders no choice but to accept an imposed city leader and join the Long team.[4] This was an extraordinary, probably unique use of muscle by an American state government against a city machine.[5] The reorganized Old Regulars ran the city until 1946, when a reform

[2] Louisiana has "parishes" rather than counties, and the city of New Orleans is coextensive with Orleans Parish.

[3] For a detailed monographic treatment see George M. Reynolds, *Machine Politics in New Orleans, 1897-1926* (New York: Columbia University Press, 1936).

[4] See T. Harry Williams, *Huey Long* (New York: Knopf, 1969), pp. 669-675, 717-744, 849-854.

[5] A number of governors have set out to destroy city machines, but Long (who in fact controlled the state at the time from his position in the U.S. Senate) had a quite different aim in the New Orleans case: to install a new and submissive management. The closest analogy that comes to mind is a Republican instance in New York: Thomas E. Dewey forced a managerial change in the Onondaga County (Syracuse) organization in the early 1940s by shutting off state patronage. But Dewey stopped short of sending in the national guard. See Warren Moscow, *Politics in the Empire State* (New York: Knopf, 1948), p. 80. In general American governors have left city machines alone, accepting them as givens of the political environment.

movement led by deLesseps S. Morrison took over the mayoralty.[6] From 1946 through 1961 Morrison ran what observers have called a "reform machine," an oxymoron that captures the uniqueness of his split-level organization.[7] On the one hand a business group called the Cold Water Committee supplied campaign funds and controlled the slating of candidates for district attorney and at-large council seats, and won from the regime such goods as "reform," "good government," urban planning, a favorable business climate, racial harmony, and low taxes.[8] On the other hand Morrison set up and presided over an organization called the Crescent City Democratic Association, a network of patronage-oriented ward leaders who dispensed favors in the fashion of a typical old-line machine and arranged the slating of candidates for state assembly and senate, sheriff, assessor, constable, city clerk, tax collector, and a number of other administrative posts. The CCDA taken alone was a run-of-the-mill traditional party organization with Morrison as its boss. "Morrison was able to hold the two elements [the CWC and CCDA] together because each faction was able to get what was most vital to its existence—the ward leaders got the major patronage offices and the financial supporters got the policy-making offices."[9] Meanwhile the Old Regulars stayed active, braced in part by patronage from the state government, and the city's Democratic primaries from 1946 through 1961 generated a series of slating matches between Morrison's CWC–CCDA coalition and the Old Regulars, both of which formed alliances every four years with rival candidates for governor.[10] When Morrison left office in 1961 his coalition collapsed, breaking for

[6] On the Old Regulars' last years of rule: Edward F. Haas, *DeLesseps S. Morrison and the Image of Reform: New Orleans Politics, 1946-1961* (Baton Rouge: Louisiana State University Press, 1974), ch. 1.

[7] For an excellent analysis of the organizational underpinnings of the Morrison regime see Joseph B. Parker, *The Morrison Era: Reform Politics in New Orleans* (Gretna, La.: Pelican Publishing Company, 1974), chs. 4 and 5. Also: Haas, *Morrison and the Image of Reform*, ch. 5.

[8] On the CWC: Parker, *The Morrison Era*, pp. 80-84, 92-96.

[9] *Ibid.*, p. 95. "It is accurate to say that the CCDA ward leaders were generally unconcerned about broad public policy and rarely injected themselves into the activity of the city council or the city's chief executive. Only very small scale administrative policy interested them. The Cold Water Committee, however, was almost exclusively concerned with high level policy-making offices" (p. 114).

[10] On New Orleans slating in these years see *ibid.*, pp. 76-78, 91-104; Haas, *Morrison and the Image of Reform*, pp. 122, 138, 152, 175-176, 229; Jewell, *Legislative Representation*, pp. 82-93. On electoral rivalry between Morrison and Earl Long, governor in 1948-1952 and 1956-1960 and patron of the city's Old Regulars: Michael L. Kurtz, "Earl Long's Political Relations with the City of New Orleans: 1948-1960," *Louisiana History* 10(1969), 241-254.

good the tie between electoral politics at the mayoral level and the ward organizations.[11] But remnants of the Old Regulars and CCDA continued as slating organizations in the wards, joined by a few patronage-oriented black organizations as blacks rose in politics after 1965. Spotty evidence suggests that New Orleans ward organizations in the middle and late 1960s were about as strong as Cleveland's.[12]

The rural Lower Delta has given rise to Louisiana's most conspicuous organizations outside New Orleans. The Perez family—the well-known Leander until 1969, then his sons—ruled Plaquemines Parish (25,225) from the 1920s through the early 1980s. Leander Perez's control of slating and patronage in Plaquemines was as close to absolute as one can imagine in a modern American constituency, and he used his secure (though small) home base to build personal influence in state-wide and even national politics.[13] The Perez influence spilled over into

[11] See Parker, *The Morrison Era*, ch. 6.

[12] "Whereas two factions [Morrison's and the Old Regulars] had dominated the political scene for sixteen years, after 1962 there were dozens of small organizations which sprang up and replaced the old bifactional cleavage. Many of the former CCDA ward leaders held on to their ward organizations and operated independently" (*ibid.*, p. 131). For a reference on the persistence of the Old Regulars—or rather their social arm, the Choctaw Club—see Neal R. Peirce, *The Deep South States of America: People, Politics, and Power in the Seven Deep South States* (New York: Norton, 1974), p. 112. On the rise of black ward organizations and their slating activities: Jack Bass and Walter De-Vries, *The Transformation of Southern Politics: Social Change and Political Consequence Since 1945* (New York: Basic Books, 1976), pp. 178-179. On electoral politics at the mayoral level in the 1970s, a pattern of competing candidate organizations: James Chubbuck, Edwin Renwick and Joe E. Walker, "The Emergence of Coalition Politics in New Orleans," *New South* 26(Winter 1971), 16-25; Bill Rushton, "New Orleans Elects Black Mayor (Dutch Morial)," *Southern Exposure* 6, no. 1(1978), 5-7; Alvin J. Schexnider, "Political Mobilization in the South: The Election of a Black Mayor in New Orleans," ch. 10 in Michael B. Preston et al. (eds.), *The New Black Politics: The Search for Political Power* (New York: Longman, 1982). When the city's first nonwhite mayor, Ernest N. "Dutch" Morial, took office in 1978, he crossed swords with the black ward organizations: "Some black political groups, fragmentary successors to the now-defunct New Orleans Democratic machine of the 1930s and '40s, complained hotly when he replaced their political appointees with blacks and whites from management and the professions" (James Ring Adams, "A Black Calvin Coolidge?" *Wall Street Journal*, May 1, 1979, p. 22).

[13] See Glen Jeansonne, *Leander Perez: Boss of the Delta* (Baton Rouge: Louisiana State University Press, 1977). On Leander Perez's control of Plaquemines Parish: ch. 7. On his influence in statewide and national politics: pp. 119-120, chs. 9-12, 15, 16. An account of what took place in Plaquemines nominating caucuses of the 1950s and 1960s: "Sometimes eight hundred people would show up. Frequently a brass band would play, and barbecue, beer, and soft drinks would be served. The Judge [Leander] would then make a speech, 'suggesting' nominees for parish posts. These recommendations would immediately be rubber-stamped by the compliant caucus, which would then break up into ward caucuses. Perez would speak before each of these smaller caucuses, which would

neighboring St. Bernard Parish (51,185), provoking a decades-long series of slating contests between a Perez faction and various home-grown St. Bernard factions—both sides ordinarily allying with Democratic governors or gubernatorial candidates.[14] In 1976 the Perez organization in Plaquemines and John F. "Jack" Rowley's organization dominant in St. Bernard backed opposing candidates in a Democratic primary for Congress; when the dust settled the apparent winner was serving a prison term for vote fraud and a Republican had the seat.[15]

In general, a considerable number of Louisiana's rural parishes have supported factional organizations of the sort typical of rural West Virginia and Kentucky: "In many parishes there are commonly two local factions, often distinguished only by the fact that one is in and one is out of power. Frequently in local primaries there are two slates, each headed by a candidate for sheriff."[16] The local factions also have a history of allying with candidates for governor in Democratic primaries.[17] A further generalization emerges concerning the state's cultural areas. Writers on Louisiana of the 1950s and 1960s report that "deliverable"

---

then approve his handpicked candidates" (p. 109). Most election-day votes came free, but some were bought. A Leander Perez statement on vote prices to a U.S. Senate committee in 1965: "As a matter of fact it was so well established that they knew each other, the $5 and $10 voters would not ride in the same automobile with the $2 voters when they are being brought to the polls. It was beneath their dignity. A $10 vote would not ride in the same car with a $2 vote" (p. 108). For treatments of the regime just after Leander's death see *ibid.*, pp. 365-370, and Roy Reed, "Insurgents Challenge Perez Dynasty in Louisiana Parish," *New York Times*, April 17, 1972, p. 38. The occasion for this Reed article was a local caucus in which "insurgents" took on the Perez forces and lost by a vote of 846 to 45.

[14] See, e.g., Jeansonne, *Perez*, ch. 6; pp. 158-161; ch. 11; pp. 350-351, 358.

[15] A telling comment on the disputed primary result: "Each side has claimed the other was responsible for most of the fraud" (*Congressional Quarterly Weekly*, April 30, 1977, p. 821). On the St. Bernard organization see John Huey, "In a Louisiana Parish, Sheriff Has Powers Out of the Ordinary," *Wall Street Journal*, May 9, 1978, pp. 1, 39. In 1979 the Perez sons, Chalin and Leander, Jr., had a public falling out that depleted the family inheritance. See Neil Maxwell, "Feud Between Judge Leander Perez's Sons Threatens Their Hold on Louisiana Parish," *Wall Street Journal*, April 22, 1980, p. 48; and Douglas Martin, "Attacks Mount Against Perez Political Empire in Louisiana," *New York Times*, May 11, 1981, p. A16. In 1983 over fifty candidates competed for seven seats in a free-swinging election for parish council, a sharp break with tradition: "In the 21 years since Judge Perez formed the commission council form of government, either he or his son, Chalin, anointed the other four members of the commission; since they faced no opposition, there were no elections" (Wendell Rawls, Jr., "Election Signals End of Delta Dynasty," *New York Times*, January 11, 1983, p. A16).

[16] Jewell, *Legislative Representation*, p. 82.

[17] General sources on Louisiana's local factions and their statewide tie-ins: *ibid.*, pp. 82-93; Allan P. Sindler, *Huey Long's Louisiana: State Politics, 1920-1952* (Baltimore: Johns Hopkins University Press, 1956), pp. 273-282.

votes, election fraud, publicizing of slates of candidates, and tie-ins between local and statewide candidates were particularly common, and
that electoral politics was especially highly organized, in the Catholic
and French-speaking parishes of roughly the southern half of the
state.[18] Northern Protestant parishes seem to have conducted their politics more in the typical rural Southern style of individual candidacies.

The Democratic "bifactionalism"—Longites versus anti-Longites—
that is often said to have characterized Louisiana politics from approximately 1928 through 1960 is not a direct concern here, since it disappeared after the last governor's term of Earl Long, Huey's brother, in
1956-1960.[19] It is worth stating, however, that nothing persisted in
Louisiana throughout the Long era that merits being called a statewide
organization—either a Long organization or an "anti-Long" organization.[20] Many politicians appealed to enduring "pro-Long" or "anti-
Long" sentiment in the electorate, but gubernatorial primaries were a
disjointed set of cutthroat contests among individuals (some allied on
"tickets" with candidates for lieutenant governor and other state offices). As Allan P. Sindler wrote in 1956: "Every four years there is a
wild, fresh scramble by state tickets for parish candidate and local
ticket support."[21] The Longs' electoral base shifted over time. Huey
started out by mobilizing rural areas against established interests, including the New Orleans machine.[22] But when Earl ran for statewide
office in 1940 and 1944, after the forced conversion of the city's Old
Regulars, he carried New Orleans with the machine's backing but lost
the rest of the state.[23] Earl won the governorship easily in 1948, but this
time New Orleans under Morrison fell into the bottom quartile of parishes in its Long support.[24] And so it went. Whatever "factional" continuity there was in the vote ended with the 1956 election; since then

[18] Jewell, *Legislative Representation*, pp. 45, 83-85, 91; Sindler, *Long's Louisiana*, pp.
32-33, 277-278. See also V. O. Key, Jr., *Southern Politics in State and Nation* (New
York: Vintage, 1949), pp. 172-173. Sindler on alliances between local and statewide candidates in primaries: "Public affiliations are confined largely to Catholic south Louisiana,
where high rates of illiteracy enhance the strategic role of poll commissioners and where
politics is so highly organized that running for parish and ward offices on local tickets is
traditional" (p. 277).

[19] The authoritative source on the state's "bifactionalism" and the source of most of
the material presented here on the subject is Sindler, *Long's Louisiana*.

[20] The formidable state organization run by Huey Long and his immediate inheritors
depended on control of the governorship and hence crumbled in 1940.

[21] Sindler, *Long's Louisiana*, p. 283.

[22] See Williams, *Huey Long*, pp. 203-204, 268; Sindler, *Long's Louisiana*, pp. 56, 72.

[23] Sindler, *Long's Louisiana*, pp. 150-151, 188-189.

[24] *Ibid.*, pp. 205-206. Shreveport seems to have stayed on the anti-Long side from start
to finish.

new candidates for governor have each built their own makeshift and unpredictable coalitions.[25] A Louisiana TPO score for the late 1960s: 3-PF.

TENNESSEE (3,924,164)

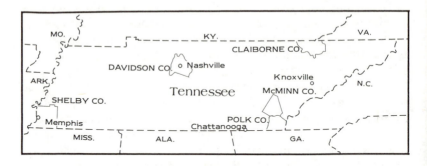

A few decades ago Tennessee had an impressive record as an organization state.[26] A 1954 report on local politics commented: "Nearly every county in Tennessee supports at least two permanent Democratic factions. . . . If one such faction supports a given candidate for governor in the August primary election, the other faction must of necessity support another candidate."[27] The state's power center in the 1930s and 1940s was the Edward H. Crump machine in Memphis (623,530) and more broadly Shelby County (722,111)—the second of the South's

[25] See for example William C. Havard, Rudolf Heberle, and Perry H. Howard, *The Louisiana Elections of 1960* (Baton Rouge: Louisiana State University Press, 1963); and on 1972, Charles E. Grenier and Perry H. Howard, "The Edwards Victory," ch. 29 in Mark T. Carleton, Perry H. Howard, and Joseph B. Parker (eds.), *Readings in Louisiana Politics* (Baton Rouge: Claitor's Publishing Division, 1975).

[26] A 1944 judgment: "From the benevolent dictatorship of Boss Ed Crump in Memphis, to the gunman-terrorized domain of Sheriff Birch Biggs in rural Polk County, 300 miles to the east, Tennessee has the unenviable distinction of being America's most bossed state in 1944" (Charles W. Van Devander, *The Big Bosses* [New York: Howell, Soskin, 1944], p. 167).

[27] William Goodman, *Inherited Domain: Political Parties in Tennessee* (Knoxville: Bureau of Public Administration, University of Tennessee, 1954), p. 32. A report by Key in 1949: "In most Democratic counties of Tennessee, according to old-time politicians, at least two factions compete for control of the county government. When state offices are at issue, one county faction is almost honor bound to support the state-wide candidate opposed by its local enemy. Consequently each of any two candidates for state-wide nomination with any prospect or hope of victory will poll a considerable vote" (*Southern Politics*, p. 61).

big-city machines.[28] The Crump organization mobilized both blacks and whites, took care of voters' poll taxes to increase turnout, and amassed enormous county majorities like those of New Jersey's Hague and Missouri's Pendergast organizations to swing outcomes in statewide Democratic primaries.[29] Weaker organizations used to operate in Nashville (population 170,874 in 1960) and its parent unit, Davidson County (447,877 in 1970, coterminous with Nashville after a consolidation in 1962). In the 1950s many Nashville area candidates reached office without organizational ties or support, but slating contests often took place between two patronage-based factional organizations centered in the mayoralty and in the county offices; the positions at stake were Nashville's mayoralty and nonpartisan city council and the county's public offices and Democratic executive committee.[30] In southeastern Tennessee, Sheriff Birch Biggs ran an eyecatching rural machine in the 1940s, dominating by a mix of patronage transactions, election fraud, and gunplay his home base, Polk County (11,669), and also three neighboring counties he referred to as "occupied countries." Biggs had an alliance with Crump and, like Louisiana's Leander Perez, exercised surprising influence in state affairs given his county's size.[31]

[28] On the Crump machine: William D. Miller, *Mr. Crump of Memphis* (Baton Rouge: Louisiana State University Press, 1964), especially ch. 8 ("The Organization"); Virginia E. Lewis, "Fifty Years of Politics in Memphis, 1900-1950" (Ph.D. dissertation, New York University, 1955), especially ch. 4 ("The Pinnacle of Power").

[29] Payment of poll taxes: Lewis, "Politics in Memphis," pp. 145-147; Miller, *Crump of Memphis*, pp. 294-295. On blacks as part of the machine's electoral base: David M. Tucker, *Memphis Since Crump: Bossism, Blacks, and Civic Reformers, 1948-1968* (Knoxville: University of Tennessee Press, 1980), pp. 16-20; Kenneth D. Wald, "The Electoral Base of Political Machines: A Deviant Case Analysis," *Urban Affairs Quarterly* 16(1980), 17-19. Machine influence in statewide primaries: Miller, chs. 7-13; Key, *Southern Politics*, pp. 59-69, 413-414. Tennessee nonetheless lacked a Democratic state-level organization of any importance in the 1930s and 1940s—Crump's operation was local—and a recent study concludes there was little consistency over time in Democratic statewide "factional" coalitions during these decades. See William R. Majors, "A Re-examination of V. O. Key's *Southern Politics in State and Nation*: The Case of Tennessee," *East Tennessee Historical Society's Publications*, no. 49 (1977), 117-135.

[30] See Bertil Hanson, *A Report on Politics in Nashville* (Cambridge: Joint Center for Urban Studies, M.I.T./Harvard, 1960), pp. ii:4-7, 9-18. A Nashville precinct organization drew notice in 1961: see David Halberstam, "Good Jelly's Last Stand," *Reporter*, January 19, 1961, pp. 40-41.

[31] See Van Devander's 1944 report in *The Big Bosses*, ch. 7 ("Mailed Fist in Tennessee") at pp. 167-168, 179-191. A report on events a few years later tells of an independent Paul Cantrell machine in McMinn County (35,462), one of the "occupied countries" in Van Devander's account. See Lee S. Greene, *Lead Me On: Frank Goad Clement and Tennessee Politics* (Knoxville: University of Tennessee Press, 1982), pp. 74-77.

Later reports, however, tell of decisive organizational decline. The Memphis machine, weakened by state primary setbacks in 1948 and leaderless after Crump died in 1954, faded away remarkably quickly and completely.[32] A remnant group called Citizens for Progress put up municipal and state legislative slates in the late 1950s, but this seems to have been the city's last important manifestation of traditional organization.[33] Newspapers and a series of reform coalitions exercised influence in city elections in the 1960s.[34] In Davidson County factional slating seemed to be dying out in the late 1950s, and a report on the 1960s said it was no longer significant: in state legislative primaries, at least, Nashville newspapers were the important endorsing organizations.[35] This one-sentence appraisal appeared after 1962: "In the reorganized Nashville-Davidson County, Mayor Beverly Briley has enjoyed substantial power, but he is a political leader of the newer stamp, not an old-fashioned 'boss.' "[36] A later report on party organization in Memphis, Nashville, and also Knoxville (174,587) said: "By 1970 none of the three cities had an active city-wide Democratic precinct organization."[37] A 1972 comment on Tennessee's rural organizations: "Local satrapies have existed in the rural areas and some still do. But they arouse little interest."[38] In the Appalachian region, organizations in the

[32] On the machine's decline: Tucker, *Memphis Since Crump*, chs. 4-6; William E. Wright, *Memphis Politics: A Study in Racial Bloc Voting* (New York: McGraw-Hill, Eagleton Case #27, 1962), pp. 2-3. The Hague machine is probably the closest analogue of Crump's: Hague and Crump rose in politics at about the same time, their machines' home-county pluralities in statewide primaries were as impressive as organizations have ever recorded anywhere, and their reigns both came to an end around 1950. But the Jersey City machine continued on for another generation under new management; the Memphis machine folded.

[33] On the late 1950s: Jewell, *Legislative Representation,* pp. 43-44, 55; Wright, *Memphis Politics,* p. 2; Tucker, *Memphis Since Crump,* pp. 86-89. Later: Jewell, *Metropolitan Representation,* p. 10; Tucker, chs. 6-10.

[34] Wright, *Memphis Politics, passim*; Tucker, *Memphis Since Crump*, chs. 6-10.

[35] On the late 1950s: Hanson, *Politics in Nashville*, pp. ii:13; iii:12-16, 21-24, 31-32; v:8. On state legislative primaries: Jewell, *Metropolitan Representation*, p. 10.

[36] Lee S. Greene and Robert S. Avery, *Government in Tennessee,* 2d ed. (Knoxville: University of Tennessee Press, 1966), p. 52.

[37] David E. Price and Michael Lupfer, "Volunteers for Gore: The Impact of a Precinct-Level Canvass in Three Tennessee Cities," *Journal of Politics* 35(1973), 424. This is a study of the Senate election of November 1970. Of course organizations of a factional type might come to life at other times but take little interest in a November Senate election. Still, it is hard to imagine a Democratic Senate candidate going into, say, Baltimore or Kansas City in 1970 and not finding organizations to deal with.

[38] Lee S. Greene and Jack E. Holmes, "Tennessee: A Politics of Peaceful Change," ch. 4 in William C. Havard (ed.), *The Changing Politics of the South* (Baton Rouge: Louisiana State University Press, 1972), p. 169.

Polk County area lost their salience and distinctiveness around 1950, though a recent study describes a more ordinary system of trifactional patronage politics going on undiminished in the 1960s in Claiborne County (19,420) on the Kentucky border—a regime like others in the impoverished West Virginia and Kentucky hill country.[39] A TPO score for Tennessee in the late 1960s: 2-PF. This is considerably lower than the score for neighboring Kentucky, a state similar politically to Tennessee in many ways, but it follows from the evidence.[40]

ARKANSAS (1,923,295) _____

In general Arkansas politics has centered on individual candidacies. Before television, for example, the state's Democrats used to compete in primaries for governor by traveling around the counties making speeches and doing whatever else they could think of to draw crowds and get their names across. There were fireworks displays, motorcades, hillbilly bands, gospel singers, performers from the Grand Ole Opry; one candidate made parachute jumps.[41] No evidence appears of slating alliances such as Kentucky's and Louisiana's between gubernatorial and state legislative candidates in Democratic primaries.[42] In a study of recruitment to the Arkansas state leg-

[39] On the Polk County area: Greene, *Lead Me On*, pp. 35, 44-45, 74-77, 127, 153. On Claiborne County: John Gaventa, *Power and Powerlessness: Quiescence and Rebellion in an Appalachian Valley* (Urbana: University of Illinois Press, 1980), pp. 141-150.

[40] An indirect confirmation of the Kentucky-Tennessee disparity appears in Jewell's comparative study of slating alliances between gubernatorial and state legislative candidates in Democratic primaries. Older reports notwithstanding, Jewell writes that these slating alliances were common in 1947-1964 in Kentucky and Louisiana but not in Tennessee. See *Legislative Representation*, pp. 55-56. It bears repeating that alliances of this sort are a good though not infallible indicator of the existence of traditional organizations of a factional kind at the county level.

[41] Boyce A. Drummond, Jr., "Arkansas Politics: A Study of a One-Party System" (Ph.D. dissertation, University of Chicago, 1957), ch. 7, especially p. 141. See also Richard E. Yates, "Arkansas: Independent and Unpredictable," ch. 6 in Havard (ed.), *Changing Politics of the South*, pp. 252-253.

[42] "Formal slates of candidates for state and district offices are unknown" (Drummond, "Arkansas Politics," p. 142).

islature in the 1960s, the most frequent response from legislators was that they recruited themselves.[43]

Even so, the state used to support one of the South's notable arrays of county machines in the 1940s.[44] These evidently operated in no more than about a quarter of the state's counties and counted for little in state politics by, say, New Jersey standards, but some exercised control over their counties' governments and electorates and turned in packaged pluralities in state primaries.[45] The McLaughlin machine, for example, in Garland County (54,131), site of Hot Springs (35,631), manipulated poll tax receipts, brought out black voters as well as whites, and circulated a "pink ticket" designating its candidates in primaries.[46] The C. H. "Sly Cy" Bond machine ran Crittenden County (48,106), a plantation area across the Mississippi River from Memphis, and produced unlikely majorities in statewide primaries until at least 1954.[47] What observers have called "machine counties" sprawled around the state, though some were clustered in the delta area along the Mississippi. In reality some of these may have amounted to control by plantation owners of the votes of their largely black tenant farmers rather than autonomous party regimes.[48] The sources here are old, but county organizations still drew notice in a work on Arkansas that covered the 1960s.[49] No evidence comes to light of a machine or other kind of organization in Pulaski County (287,189), the state's metropolitan core and site of Little Rock (132,483).[50] An overall TPO score for the late 1960s: 2.

[43] Donald T. Wells, "The Arkansas Legislature," in Alex B. Lacy, Jr., *Power in American State Legislatures: Case Studies of the Arkansas, Louisiana, Mississippi, and Oklahoma Legislatures*, Tulane Studies in Political Science, vol. II, (The Hague: Martinus Nijhoff, 1967), p. 12.

[44] See Drummond, "Arkansas Politics," pp. 75, 169-175, 218-220, 232; Key, *Southern Politics*, pp. 195-204.

[45] From a recent review of Southern politics just after World War II: "In Arkansas political informants spoke openly of 'the twenty-one controlled counties.' " (Numan V. Bartley and Hugh D. Graham, *Southern Politics and the Second Reconstruction* [Baltimore: Johns Hopkins University Press, 1975], p. 30). The authors point to four states with postwar county organizations said to have been important: Virginia, Arkansas, Georgia, and Texas.

[46] Drummond, "Arkansas Politics," pp. 75, 169-171, 219-220, 232; Key, *Southern Politics*, pp. 201-204.

[47] Drummond, "Arkansas Politics," p. 174; Key, *Southern Politics*, pp. 203-204.

[48] "The large majorities which certain delta counties have consistently produced for their favorites has been possible, in part at least, because of the large number of Negro farm tenant votes susceptible to the control of the planters" (Drummond, "Arkansas Politics," pp. 75-76). See also Key, *Southern Politics*, pp. 196-197.

[49] Yates, "Arkansas," pp. 244-247.

[50] The Little Rock newspaper's treatment of state legislative primaries in Pulaski

GEORGIA (4,589,575)

Georgia presents another tradition of individual candidacies, in which Eugene Talmadge, "adopting a rural 'Cracker' accent and snapping his gaudy suspenders for emphasis as he poured forth invective on his foes," dominated Democratic primaries for statewide office from 1926 through 1946.[51] At lower office levels, a 1970 study investigating how candidates enter politics concluded: "It appears that the recruitment of Democratic candidates is generally done either by the candidates themselves or by their friends. Key influentials, businessmen, and public officeholders sometimes suggest to social and business friends that they run for office, but they do not draft a broad slate of candidates."[52] No trace of traditional party organization comes to light in Fulton County (607,592), site of most of Atlanta (497,421). Atlanta mayors

County in the late 1960s was entirely a discussion of the fortunes of individuals; no mention was made of slates or organizations. See *Arkansas Gazette*, July 31, 1968, p. 1; August 26, 1970, p. 1.

[51] Reinhard H. Luthin, *American Demagogues: Twentieth Century* (Boston: Beacon, 1954), p. 182. See also Karl Rodabaugh, " 'Farmer Gene' Talmadge and the Rural Style in Georgia Politics," *Southern Studies* 21(1982), 83-96.

[52] John D. Parker, "Candidate Recruitment: A Model and a Multi-Office Study" (Ph.D. dissertation, University of Georgia, 1970), p. 169. The dissertation is based on interviews with 157 candidates for state legislative and county offices in twelve Georgia counties, four of them urban or suburban (including Fulton and De Kalb). The conclusion goes on: "There is no evidence among these [Democratic] candidates that other organized groups have replaced the party in the recruitment function. . . . It is the author's impression that the lack of organized group recruitment activity results primarily from the norm expressed by many candidates that group political activity is undesirable and undemocratic" (pp. 169-170). For a more detailed treatment see ch. 5, *passim* ("Political Structure"). A 1984 statement on the state's individualistic tradition: "Georgia is a state in which political parties play almost no role in recruitment; just about everyone can participate. Essentially, all one has to do to run for office is pick a primary (there is no registration by party) and pay a qualifying fee for the office one desires" (Lawrence R. Hepburn, "Georgia," ch. 8 in Rosenthal and Moakley [eds.], *The Political Life of the American States*, p. 186 and more generally pp. 186-190).

normally won election in the 1950s and 1960s by building or continuing coalitions of blacks, downtown businessmen, and the press; Maynard Jackson and Andrew Young in 1973 and afterward built coalitional bases mainly in the black community.[53] The city's nonpartisan aldermanic elections have evidently been individualistic affairs with no organizations of any kind engaging in decisive slating.[54]

Nonetheless, Atlanta aside, local slating organizations of various kinds do appear here and there in Georgia records. A machine run by Cracker party leader John B. "Big John" Kennedy dominated Augusta (59,864) and its parent unit Richmond County (162,437) in the mid-1940s; there is documentation on block captains, vote fraud, city and county patronage, salary kickbacks, particularistic tax assessments, and slating power.[55] A business and professional group called the Independent League for Good Government routed the Crackers in 1946, ushering in a decade or so of slating matches between the Crackers' traditional organization and the Independents' good-government organization (a dualism like Kansas City's), followed by a more diffuse politics without the Crackers as a component.[56] A business and professional group is said to have dominated Savannah (118,349) and its parent unit Chatham County (187,816) in the 1950s, and a slating group of this sort appears in Chatham state legislative primaries in 1965.[57] In De Kalb County (415,387), Atlanta's principal suburb, a

[53] On the 1950s and 1960s: Edward C. Banfield, *Big City Politics* (New York: Random House, 1965), pp. 24-28. On Jackson and Young: Duncan R. Jamieson, "Maynard Jackson's 1973 Election as Mayor of Atlanta," *Midwest Quarterly* 18(1976), 7-26; Mack H. Jones, "Black Political Empowerment in Atlanta: Myth and Reality," *Annals of the American Academy of Political and Social Science* 439(September 1978), 90-117, especially at pp. 105-108 ("Race and the 1973 Elections"); Reginald Stuart, "Young and 2 Others Emerging as Front-Runners in Atlanta Mayoral Race," *New York Times*, April 6, 1981, p. B15.

[54] See Banfield, *Big City Politics*, pp. 24-28; Iola O. Hessler, *29 Ways to Govern a City* (Cincinnati: Hamilton County Research Foundation, 1966), pp. 17-19; Jones, "Black Political Empowerment," pp. 105-108.

[55] See James C. Cobb, "Colonel Effingham Crushes the Crackers: Political Reform in Postwar Augusta," *South Atlantic Quarterly* 78(1979), 507-519; and *ibid.*, "Politics in a New South City: Augusta, Georgia, 1946-1971" (Ph.D. dissertation, University of Georgia, 1975), ch. 2.

[56] Cobb, "Politics in a New South City," chs. 2-4, 6.

[57] On the 1950s: Joseph L. Bernd, *Grass Roots Politics in Georgia: The County Unit System and the Importance of the Individual Voting Community in Bi-Factional Elections, 1942-1954* (Atlanta: Emory University Research Committee, 1960), p. 38. On 1965: *Savannah Morning News*, April 20, 1965, p. 10B; April 21, 1965, p. 1; May 4, 1965, p. 4A; May 6, 1965, p. 1. The April 20 report: "Eight of the 12 candidates qualified for the Democratic primary apparently are backed by a wide cross-section of business and political leaders, some of whom have been closely associated with county poli-

fresh Republican organization dependent on Manhattan-like "purposive" incentives was slating candidates for lower offices in the late 1960s.[58] Finally, in the 1950s and earlier there were some county organizations around the state that probably met the criteria of traditional organization—groups with enough local influence to tip their elections one way or another and profit from it in the state's pre-1962 "county-unit" system for counting votes in statewide Democratic primaries (a miniature electoral college).[59] Yet the author who reported on these organizations in 1960 wrote a later piece in 1972 telling of a "sharp decline in political bossism in Georgia. . . . The end of the county-unit system has diminished the economic utility of local county political machines and bosses. In Georgia few of them remain."[60] The TPO score chosen for the state is a 2, though a 1 could be defended.

MISSISSIPPI (2,216,912) ───────────────────────

When Key wrote on Mississippi in 1949, he mentioned in passing some local machines and also, separately, a dozen or so "money counties" said to be buyable in primaries.[61] But neither phenomenon seems to have drawn notice since. The predominant portrayal of Mississippi politics involves candidates seeking office on their own. Democrats running in primaries for Senator and governor have built their own personal coalitions since at least the early twentieth century.[62] At the county level, Democratic party officials have adhered to a Southern norm of neutrality in primaries.[63] A Democratic congressman's ac-

---

tics for many years." A May 4 editorial comment: "We question if it is a safe course for our community to select a slate pledged to speak as one." In the May 6 story the slate had grown by one and taken on the label "Nine for Chatham."

[58] Parker, "Candidate Recruitment," pp. 29-30, 139-142, 158. The author refrains from naming the suburban county he writes about, but a trail of clues leads to De Kalb.

[59] See Bernd, *Grass Roots Politics*, pp. 36-47. He mentions, for example, the Gillis organization in Treutlen County. See also Key, *Southern Politics*, pp. 122-123.

[60] Joseph L. Bernd, "Georgia: Static and Dynamic," ch. 7 in Havard (ed.), *Changing Politics of the South*, p. 362.

[61] Key, *Southern Politics*, p. 251.

[62] See, e.g., Albert D. Kirwan, *Revolt of the Rednecks: Mississippi Politics, 1876-1925* (New York: Harper and Row, 1965), chs. 11, 13, 17; Key, *Southern Politics*, p. 246; Raymond Tatalovich, " 'Friends and Neighbors' Voting: Mississippi, 1943-73," *Journal of Politics* 37(1975), 807-814; Ronn Hy and Richard T. Saeger, "The Nature and Role of Political Parties," ch. 3 in David M. Landry and Joseph B. Parker (eds.), *Mississippi Government and Politics in Transition* (Dubuque: Kendall/Hunt, 1976), pp. 38-39.

[63] Robert H. Elliott, "A Survey of County Party Organization and County Voting Patterns in a Southern State" (Ph.D. dissertation, University of Houston, 1975), pp. 70-76, 93-98.

count of winning his first nomination in the old Delta district in 1950 is a story of traveling around and meeting people without encountering anything that looked like an organization.[64] Newspaper coverage in the late 1960s in Hinds County (214,973), site of the state's metropolis, Jackson (153,968), says nothing about slating or organizational activity in Democratic primaries for the state legislature.[65] Finally, a description of electoral politics in Panola County (26,829) in the mid-1960s— one of the few detailed accounts of local electoral politics in the rural South—provides a picture of candidates maneuvering for office by themselves in a setting that was free of organization.[66] (See map below.) TPO score for Mississippi: 1.

ALABAMA (3,444,165) _____

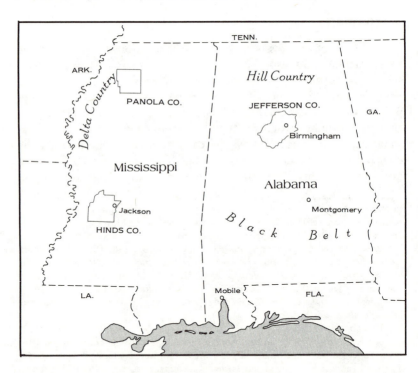

[64] Frank E. Smith, *Congressman from Mississippi* (New York: Random House, 1964), ch. 6.

[65] *Jackson Clarion-Ledger*, August 16, 1967, p. 1.

[66] Frederick M. Wirt, *Politics of Southern Equality: Law and Social Change in a Mississippi County* (Chicago: Aldine, 1970), pp. 42-47, 151-162.

Alabama Democrats running at the state level have had to build and tend personal coalitions; George C. Wallace's familiar career is a case in point.[67] Politics at lower levels has been individualistic too, as reported best in two excellent pieces by Karl A. Bosworth in the 1940s about (unidentified) counties typical of their sections of the state—one in the northern hill country and the other in the central Alabama Black Belt. Local Democratic primaries in the former generated hard-fought contests among a great many candidates unaccompanied by any trace of slating or organization: "Electioneering methods consist primarily of house-to-house canvassing, but campaign speeches are expected of all candidates. Farmer candidates for a place on the county commission who haven't faced an audience since school days are expected to take their turn on the rostrum at the neighborhood rallies."[68] The Black Belt county's elections were more sedate, but local officials all nursed their own personal coalitions.[69]

Birmingham (300,910), Alabama's metropolitan center, has evidently never been run by a machine.[70] The city's best-known official of the 1960s, public safety commissioner Theophilus Eugene "Bull" Connor, who came to national attention in a showdown with the Rev. Martin Luther King, Jr., got his start in politics as a radio sportscaster.[71] Birmingham campaigns for mayor and city council in the 1960s were personal enterprises of "ad hoc organizations assembled by the candidates themselves," with the leading newspaper the only important en-

---

[67] Key called it "a free-for-all, with every man looking out for himself" (*Southern Politics*, p. 37, and more generally pp. 37-52). For a brief treatment of Wallace's early campaigns for statewide office see Marshall Frady, *Wallace* (New York: World, 1968), pp. 91-92, 117-118, 122-127, 131-135. See also a treatment of an earlier master campaigner: Carl Grafton, "James E. Folsom's 1946 Campaign," *Alabama Review* 35(1982), 172-199.

[68] Karl A. Bosworth, *Tennessee Valley County: Rural Government in the Hill Country of Alabama* (University, Ala.: Bureau of Public Administration, University of Alabama, 1941), pp. 13-21, quotation at p. 19.

[69] Karl A. Bosworth, *Black Belt County: Rural Government in the Cotton Country of Alabama* (University, Ala.: Bureau of Public Administration, University of Alabama, 1941), pp. 10-16.

[70] For the early years see Carl V. Harris, *Political Power in Birmingham, 1871-1921* (Knoxville: University of Tennessee Press, 1977), especially ch. 4 ("Position and Politics"). The group operating most persistently in primaries in this period was an alliance of corporate interests that intervened to keep Jefferson County's state senate seat in friendly hands (see pp. 91-95). For more recent times up through the early 1970s the source is Charles H. Levine, *Racial Conflict and the American Mayor: Power, Polarization, and Performance* (Lexington, Mass.: Heath, 1974), ch. 6.

[71] Harris, *Political Power in Birmingham*, p. 88.

dorsing body.[72] Press coverage of Democratic state legislative primaries around 1970 in Jefferson County (644,991), Birmingham's parent unit, centered on individual candidacies, as in: "Incumbents hard hit in Jeffco solon races."[73] City commissioners ran for office on their own in nonpartisan Mobile (190,026) of the 1960s.[74] An element of organization, though not the conventional party variety, did intrude during the same decade in Montgomery (133,386), where a downtown establishment of business leaders and newspaper owners is said to have dominated city elections.[75] The TPO score for Alabama: 1.

FLORIDA (6,789,443)

Standard sources agree on the exceptional individualism of Florida politics: "Every man runs for himself, whether his office be a local, county, or state one."[76] "Party organizations are now, and have always been, too weak to deserve much notice."[77] Local evidence is best on Dade County (1,267,792), site of Miami (334,859), where indeed candi-

[72] See Levine, *Racial Conflict*, pp. 88-93, quotation at p. 90. In 1973 a council slate did materialize, a set of candidates backed by a businessmen's committee called Birmingham Action Group (p. 93). In 1981 Mayor Richard Arrington supported an all-black council slate, and the Fraternal Order of Police backed an all-white slate. See "Birmingham Vote: Whites vs. Blacks," *New York Times*, October 27, 1981, p. A27; Reginald Stuart, "Mayor of Birmingham Assailed for Runoff Role," *New York Times*, November 9, 1981, p. B15; Kelly Dowe, "Richard Arrington: Birmingham," *Southern Exposure* 12(February 1984), 78.

[73] *Birmingham News*, May 6, 1970, p. 18.

[74] "The political parties in the City of Mobile do not slate candidates per se; rather, any person interested in running for the position of city commissioner is able to do so. There has been little evidence to a 'party' supporting one candidate or another in the city races" (*Bolden v. City of Mobile*, 423 F. Supp. 399, 1976).

[75] "Before the 1970s, Montgomery was governed by a three-member commission, with one of the three positions designated as mayor. Mayors such as Earl James (1963-1970) were elected on the basis of solid 'establishment' support, following selection by business leaders and newspaper owners. The same caucuses usually produced the local state legislative delegation which then worked closely with the mayor and other commissioners" (Peggy Heilig and Robert J. Mundt, *Your Voice at City Hall: The Politics, Procedures and Policies of District Representation* [Albany: State University of New York Press, 1984], p. 40).

[76] William C. Havard and Loren P. Beth, *The Politics of Mis-Representation: Rural-Urban Conflict in the Florida Legislature* (Baton Rouge: Louisiana State University Press, 1962), p. 11, and more generally chs. 2, 4. See also Key, *Southern Politics*, ch. 5 ("Florida: Every Man for Himself"); Margaret T. Echols and Austin Ranney, "The Impact of Interparty Competition Reconsidered: The Case of Florida," *Journal of Politics* 38(1976), 142-152. The gist of this last piece is that Democratic gubernatorial primaries remain as free-wheeling as ever despite the Republican party's rise to parity in November elections for statewide offices.

[77] Douglas St. Angelo, "Florida," ch. 7 in Alan Rosenthal and Maureen Moakley

dates have won city and county offices mostly by building personal coalitions. Miami newspapers were the most important endorsing organizations in the area's patchwork of nonpartisan elections and Democratic primaries in the 1960s.[78] Tampa (277,767) grew as a center of Latin immigration and also generated a conspicuously corrupt politics in the 1940s, but traditional party organizations do not seem to have figured in city affairs then or since.[79] TPO score for Florida: an unproblematic 1.

SOUTH CAROLINA (2,590,516)

No scholarship deals directly and adequately with South Carolina's electoral politics at lower levels during recent times, and getting a good sense of it is difficult. But individual candidacies have unquestionably been the main route to office in the state's basic Democratic tradition.

(eds.), *The Political Life of the American States* (New York: Praeger, 1984), p. 162.

[78] See Edward Sofen, *A Report on Politics in Greater Miami* (Cambridge: Joint Center for Urban Studies, M.I.T./Harvard, 1961), pp. II:44-49, III:22-27; Thomas J. Wood, "Dade County: Unbossed, Erratically Led," *Annals of the American Academy of Political and Social Science* 353(1964), 64-71; Manning J. Dauer, "Multi-Member Districts in Dade County: Study of a Problem and a Delegation," *Journal of Politics* 28(1966), 625-626; Banfield, *Big City Politics*, p. 101. Sofen reports an instance of a candidate slate: a business and professional group called Independent Citizens for Better Metro backed a set of candidates in a nonpartisan county commissioner election in 1960 (pp. III:22-27).

[79] Gary R. Mormino, "Tampa: From Hell Hole to the Good Life," ch. 5 in Richard M. Bernard and Bradley R. Rice (eds.), *Sunbelt Cities: Politics and Growth since World War II* (Austin: University of Texas Press, 1983), pp. 142-147. "A traditionalistic social class colored Tampa's political environment from the Civil War until World War II. Rooted in the Old South's deference to elites and nurtured by the New South's embrace of the marketplace, politics in Tampa revolved around the strength of several old families and entrenched downtown business interests. Political parties exercised little control (still true today) and in such an environment groups not actively involved in governing, such as Afro-Americans, were not expected to participate, let alone vote. Cubans, Spaniards, and Italians displayed little interest in politics until the New Deal, in part because of their old-world backgrounds, in part because of the implacable opposition shown by the Anglo community" (pp. 142-143).

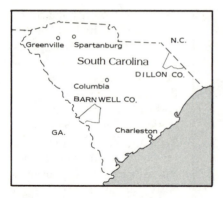

When Senator Strom Thur-
mond first ran for governor in
1946 (in a Democratic primary), he had to present himself along with ten other candidates in what we now call
cattle shows: "That 1946 campaign was a typical, although
somewhat intensified, example
of South Carolina's traditional
'county-to-county' Democratic
campaigning. The schedule of
stump speakings, worked out by the State Democratic Executive Committee, brought all candidates together successively at the same time
and place at every county seat in the state. Frequently, two stump
speakings were held each day, with occasional 'side meetings' arranged
individually by the candidates during evening or other 'off' hours. The
regular speakings, as in the case of the 1946 campaign with its numerous candidates, sometimes would last for three hours or more—providing a spectacle for the citizens and ordeal for the candidates."[80] Statewide Democratic primaries were less crowded, though still vigorous, in
the 1950s and 1960s, and Republicans also took to holding hard-
fought primaries in the 1970s.[81] To look backward again, a good treatment of a Democratic congressman's coalitional base in the 1920s and
1930s in the Piedmont area of Greenville (61,436) and Spartanburg
(44,546) outlines a setting free of party organization: the Democratic
party was "something of an impartial association" that "simply lacked
a design for allocating rewards." And "the important decisions came
with the primary contests," which the "nonpartisan quality of the regular party qualified it to supervise."[82]

At the county level, Key referred to "banker-planter-lawyer bourbon
rings" in 1949 as leadership structures in rural counties of the South

[80] William D. Workman, Jr., *The Bishop from Barnwell: The Political Life and Times
of Senator Edgar A. Brown* (Columbia, S.C.: R. L. Bryan Co., 1963), p. 105.

[81] On Democratic statewide nominating in the 1950s and 1960s see Chester W. Bain,
"South Carolina: Partisan Prelude," ch. 12 in Havard (ed.), *Changing Politics of the
South*, pp. 623-629. Republicans held close gubernatorial primaries in 1974 and 1978.
South Carolina has no record of Kentucky-style tie-ins on the Democratic side between
gubernatorial candidates and organizations or candidates at the county level. See Jewell,
Legislative Representation, p. 53.

[82] John C. Weaver, "Lawyers, Lodges, and Kinfolk: The Workings of a South Carolina
Political Organization, 1920-1936," *South Carolina Historical Magazine* 78(1977),
272-285, quotations at pp. 274-276.

Carolina coastal plain, which had large disfranchised black populations.[83] These "rings" were probably cozy, low-temperature arrangements among the dominant whites, with individual officials each attending to their own electoral coalitions. This was the case at least in
Barnwell County (17,176, mostly black in the 1940s), site of the most
prominent "ring": "There has been no party 'machine' in Barnwell, for
the reason that Brown and Blatt [the two leading politicians] simply do
not 'mesh' mechanically or politically. Under South Carolina's one-
party political system, which lasted from the days of Wade Hampton
[1876-1890] up to the 1960's, politicking on the local level as well as
statewide has been a matter of individual personality and appeal."[84] A
1961 work on the state related that "political activity and competition
in each county and in the General Assembly take place on a highly personal plane. Powerful politicians at any level are those who command
considerable numbers of followers loyal primarily to themselves and
not to the party."[85] A discrepant finding appeared very recently, however, one that is surprising and interesting. In 1982 prosecutors indicted thirty people in rural Dillon County (28,838) for flagrant election fraud, among them Democratic county chairman Alan Schafer,
who had run an organization since the mid-1960s that slated candidates and bought votes. It seems the county's tradition of "stump meetings" (local cattle shows) in Democratic primary campaigns had faded
away, a casualty of "school consolidations and the popularity of television." Schafer's organization grew and thrived in their absence; according to one local politician, "Alan didn't want any more stump
meetings because they threatened his candidates."[86] This is the only
clear instance anywhere in the country of what appears to be organization of the "traditional" sort coming into existence recently in a setting with no evident history of it.

And what of South Carolina's cities? Charleston (66,945) had a perhaps deserved reputation as a machine city before World War II, as discussed in monographic writing available.[87] Other than this, local news-

[83] Key, *Southern Politics*, p. 139.

[84] Workman, *The Bishop from Barnwell*, p. 126. The two Barnwell County politicians
exercised considerable influence in the state legislature in the 1940s and 1950s, arousing
others to detect and deplore a "Barnwell Ring." See *ibid.*, ch. 9; Key, *Southern Politics*,
pp. 152-155.

[85] Ralph Eisenberg, "The Logroll, South Carolina Style," ch. 13 in Richard T. Frost
(ed.), *Cases in State and Local Government* (Englewood Cliffs, N.J.: Prentice-Hall,
1961), p. 157.

[86] "Carolina Revives Its Stump Meeting," *New York Times*, May 23, 1982, p. 23.

[87] See Key, *Southern Politics*, pp. 133-134; Doyle W. Boggs, "Charleston Politics,
1900-1930: An Overview," *Proceedings of the South Carolina Historical Association*,

paper coverage is the only practical source, and it reveals that in Columbia (113,542) five candidates went after two nominations as individual petitioners in a 1970 Democratic primary for city council; during a ritual pre-election speaking session "all concluded their respective talks to the group with the general theme of 'vote for me and one other of these fine candidates.' "[88] Charleston's Democratic primary in 1971 produced a confrontation between two slates that each included a mayoral and sixteen at-large council candidates. Their joint appearance on the slates was apparently induced by an old "full slate law" requiring voters in primaries to choose a full sixteen council candidates to have any of their votes count. Both slates looked like Chamber-of-Commerce products: assortments of downtown businessmen, a pharmacist, a dentist, a physician, an architect, a director of the National Association of Real Estate Boards, a few black ministers in recognition of blacks just winning the vote. Nothing in these press accounts gives the flavor of traditional party organization.[89] The TPO score for South Carolina is a 1, though this could be a bit low.

NORTH CAROLINA (5,082,059)

Democrats in North Carolina of the 1960s maintained an array of county organizations that were active in general elections—a rarity in the South—but neither these nor party instruments at other levels had much of a role as slating organizations.[90] Democratic gubernatorial

---

1979, pp. 1-13; Marvin Cann, "Burnet Maybank and Charleston Politics in the New Deal Era," *Proceedings of the South Carolina Historical Association*, 1970, pp. 39-48. Neither article cited brings Charleston's prewar electoral politics into clear focus. A recent general piece on Greenville tells nothing about party organization but a great deal about textile firms, an understandable imbalance. See Cliff Sloan and Bob Hall, "It's Good to Be Home in Greenville . . . But it's Better If You Hate Unions," *Southern Exposure* 7, no. 1(1979), 82-93.

[88] *Columbia State*, February 24, 1970, pp. A1, B1 (site of quotation); February 25, 1970, p. 1; May 10, 1970, p. B1; May 13, 1970, p. 1. Democratic primaries have been the traditional route to power in Columbia, but in fact in 1970, when blacks were just entering the electorate in large numbers, a black minister won one of these council nominations and a Republican defeated him in the general election.

[89] *Charleston News and Courier*, June 6, 1971, p. 1; June 7, 1971, p. 10A; June 8, 1971, pp. 1, 2A, 8A; June 9, 1971, pp. 1, 8A. The "full slate law" was suspended in 1971, but it may have fostered slate-making habits among local politicians.

[90] On active county organizations: William J. Crotty, "The Party Organization and Its Activities," ch. 7 in William J. Crotty (ed.), *Approaches to the Study of Party Organization* (Boston: Allyn and Bacon, 1968), pp. 251-259, 269-277. General sources on lack of slating activity: *ibid.*, pp. 260-269; Jack D. Fleer, *North Carolina Politics: An Introduction* (Chapel Hill: University of North Carolina Press, 1968), pp. 99-120.

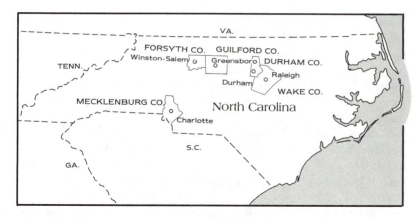

primaries in the 1950s and 1960s produced contests among candidate organizations.[91] Democratic county chairmen shied away from recruiting candidates: "Ordinarily, in his official capacity as county chairman, it is not his duty to seek out and actively support candidates of his choice. Rather, he is expected to remain relatively neutral in the selection of candidates and the primary battles that follow. His energy is concentrated on the general election."[92] Assembly and senate candidates evidently ran on their own in Democratic primaries: "State legislative politics in North Carolina is not based on slates."[93]

A closer inspection of urban areas does turn up a few slating organizations—in the Republican party, for example, which gained a competitive status in the 1960s. None appears in the Democratic party, however, and none in either party that has the attributes of a traditional organization.[94] Press reports on Wake County (229,006), site of Raleigh (123,793), say nothing about slating activity in county and state legislative primaries around 1970, and Raleigh's municipal politics came to light in a good 1962 study as a nonpartisan affair of businessmen and professionals apparently free of electoral organization.[95] A

[91] See Preston W. Edsall and J. Oliver Williams, "North Carolina: Bipartisan Paradox," ch. 8 in Havard (ed.), *Changing Politics of the South*, pp. 369-395; Fleer, *North Carolina Politics*, pp. 118-120.

[92] Crotty, "Party Organization," p. 266.

[93] Fleer, *North Carolina Politics*, p. 112. As in South Carolina, there is no record in North Carolina of Kentucky-like tie-ins in Democratic primaries between gubernatorial candidates and organizations or candidates at the county level. See Jewell, *Legislative Representation*, p. 53.

[94] The active role of the state's Republican county chairmen in enlisting candidates, which distinguishes them from Democratic chairmen, is discussed in Crotty, "Party Organization," pp. 262-266.

[95] Press reports: *Raleigh News and Observer*, May 5, 1968, p. 5; May 3, 1970, p. 1.

Republican organization did some slating in 1970 in Guilford County (288,645), site of Greensboro (144,076), although the city's party officials (of both parties), when interviewed in the mid-1960s, claimed to have next to nothing to do with nominating, and the city's nonpartisan council "has been dominated by professionals and businessmen from one geographical section of the city."[96] Charlotte (241,178) had a municipal politics through the 1960s "where neither political party nor slate of candidates is important in campaigns," although a Republican organization took up slating in parent unit Mecklenburg County (354,656) in 1968 and also in city elections in the early 1970s.[97] In the city of Durham (95,438), two endorsing organizations have exercised influence in nonpartisan municipal elections in recent times: the Voters for Better Government, a "liberal coalition of local labor, Negro, academic, and progressive business factions" from 1947 through 1958; and the Durham Committee on Negro Affairs (sometimes in alliance with the VBG) from around 1950 into the 1970s.[98] Two generaliza-

On municipal politics: Benjamin Walter, "Political Decision Making in Arcadia," ch. 6 in F. Stuart Chapin, Jr., and Shirley F. Weiss (eds.), *Urban Growth Dynamics in a Regional Cluster of Cities* (New York: Wiley, 1962), pp. 176-179, 186. The author conceals his city in this piece, but if his clues are honest it has to be Raleigh. See also Robert J. Mundt, "Referenda in Charlotte and Raleigh, and Court Action in Richmond: Comparative Studies on the Revival of District Representation," paper presented at the 1979 convention of the American Political Science Association, pp. 3, 20.

[96] On Republican slating: "Guilford County Republicans did what they were expected to do at the polls Saturday. They nominated the six candidates selected by party leaders for the state House of Representative" (*Greensboro Daily News*, May 3, 1970, p. D1). On party officials: Lewis Bowman and G. R. Boynton, "Activities and Role Definitions of Grassroots Party Officials," *Journal of Politics* 28(1966), 121-143. This is a study of party officials in three communities in Massachusetts as well as in Durham and Greensboro in North Carolina, so the conclusion holds for the locales in both states: "It is quite obvious that the local party officials interviewed in this study do not consider participation in nominations a basic part of their role. Not six per cent of the activities mentioned were oriented toward activities related to nominations, and less than four per cent of the party officials thought that their activity in the nominating process was the most important part of their job" (pp. 134-135). On the city council: James H. Svara, "Attitudes Toward City Government and Preference for District Elections," *South Atlantic Urban Studies* 3(1979), 75.

[97] On the 1960s: Theodore S. Arrington, "Partisan Campaigns, Ballots, and Voting Patterns: The Case of Charlotte," *Urban Affairs Quarterly* 14(1978), 254. On 1968: "The GOP, in an unprecedented move, had endorsed candidates for the primaries, asking members to nominate Martin, Peterson, Robinson, Bluford, and Ingram" (*Charlotte Observer*, May 5, 1968, p. 1C). Republicans first put up a municipal slate in Charlotte in 1973; by the next election in 1975 the state legislature had passed a bill changing the city's system of election from formally nonpartisan to formally partisan. See Arrington, pp. 253-254.

[98] See Lewis Bowman and G. R. Boynton, "Coalition as Party in a One-Party Southern Area: A Theoretical and Case Analysis," *Midwest Journal of Political Science* 8(1964),

tions seem in order about the cities of the industrial Piedmont Crescent (extending from Raleigh and Durham in the northeast to South Carolina's Greenville and Spartanburg in the southwest): business and professional communities have exercised a good deal of influence in electoral politics, and traditional party organizations are difficult to find.[99] TPO score for North Carolina: 1.[100]

VIRGINIA (4,648,494) _____

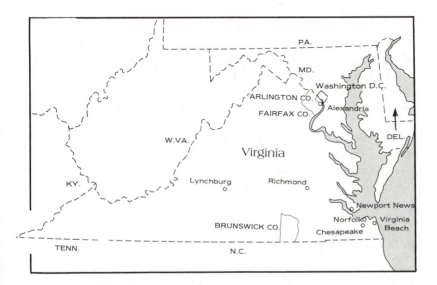

Virginia is a puzzling state. The Democratic organization of the late Senator Harry F. Byrd, Sr., unquestionably dominated the state's politics and government from the 1920s through the mid-1960s, but what kind of an organization was it?[101] This discussion will begin with city

---

277-286, quotation at p. 278; William R. Keech, *The Impact of Negro Voting: The Role of the Vote in the Quest for Equality* (Chicago: Rand McNally, 1968), pp. 15-16, 30-34, 43-46; David S. Broder, "Blacks Still 'on Fringe' Despite Political Gains," *Washington Post*, June 22, 1975, pp. A1, A6. The last is a feature story on Durham politics.

[99] On the Piedmont Crescent see Chapin and Weiss, *Urban Growth Dynamics, passim.*

[100] A volume edited by Thad L. Beyle and Merle Black, *Politics and Policy in North Carolina* (New York: MSS Information Corporation, 1975), is an equivalent of the 1975 volume edited by Alan Rosenthal and John Blydenburgh on New Jersey, *Politics in New Jersey* (New Brunswick, N.J.: Eagleton Institute of Politics, Rutgers University, 1975). Nowhere does Beyle and Black's work mention anything that has the properties of a traditional party organization.

[101] Harry F. Byrd, Sr., held a Senate seat from 1933 through 1965. His son Harry, Jr., more or less inherited it and held it until 1982.

and county electoral politics and then move up to organization at the state level.

Virginia's southeastern Tidewater section offers immediate evidence of traditional party organization. The city of Virginia Beach (172,106) was run in the 1950s and most of the 1960s by the Sidney S. Kellam organization, which operated hierarchically, had a reputation for sensitivity to voters' personal problems, and slated candidates effectively in municipal and district elections.[102] Kellam was the only local "boss" with baronial standing in the Byrd organization, a status that was clouded: "Kellam's Virginia Beach operations were often controversial, and many Byrd loyalists preferred to work with him at arm's length."[103] His organization's decisive setbacks in Democratic primaries in 1967 drew newspaper treatment ordinarily only accorded big-city machines. The *Richmond Times-Dispatch* recounted: "Political forces headed by Sidney S. Kellam, the long dominant chief of the Coastal precincts, suffered the loss of Kellam's brother, State Senator William P. Kellam, and one House candidate."[104] And the *Washington Post*'s page-one headline read: "Kellam Upset in Virginia Beach Contest," and its followup: "The powerful Kellam organization received staggering blows as it lost five of eight races. . . ."[105]

But Virginia Beach was exceptional.[106] Of local units documented

---

[102] See David G. Temple, *Merger Politics: Local Government Consolidation in Tidewater Virginia* (Charlottesville: University Press of Virginia, 1972), pp. 37-41, 150, 163-165. The city whose population reached 172,106 in 1970 was the result of a 1963 consolidation that joined Princess Anne County and an old tiny city called Virginia Beach. The Kellam organization dominated both units before 1963 and the single unit afterward.

[103] James W. Ely, Jr., *The Crisis of Conservative Virginia: The Byrd Organization and the Politics of Massive Resistance* (Knoxville: University of Tennessee Press, 1976), p. 13. Writers listing leaders of the old Byrd hierarchy have been careful to assign Kellam an appropriate title. Thus: "The nucleus of the oligarchy consisted of the senator himself, the chairman of the compensation board, the speaker of the house, Sidney S. Kellam (the boss of Virginia Beach) and four or five congressmen and state officials" (Francis Pickens Miller, *Man from the Valley: Memoirs of a 20th-Century Virginian* [Chapel Hill: University of North Carolina Press, 1971], p. 169). And: "The 'high command,' as the ruling oligarchy was called, included at mid-century E. R. Combs, Bill Tuck, 'Blackie' Moore, Congressman Howard Smith, Sidney Kellam, boss of Princess Anne County, and state Senators Garland Gray and Harry Byrd, Jr." (J. Harvie Wilkinson III, *Harry Byrd and the Changing Face of Virginia Politics, 1945-1966* [Charlottesville: University Press of Virginia, 1968], p. 60).

[104] *Richmond Times-Dispatch*, July 12, 1967, p. 1.

[105] *Washington Post*, July 12, 1967, p. 1.

[106] "Sidney Kellam and the operation of the Kellam organization attained near-legendary proportions in Virginia political circles" (Temple, *Merger Politics*, p. 40). "In most respects it [the Kellam organization] must be considered atypical, for in 1963 it was perhaps the strongest local organization in the Old Dominion" (*ibid.*, p. 41).

for the 1960s, the only other place supporting what appears to have been a traditional party organization was nearby Norfolk (307,951), where court clerk William L. "Billy" Prieur, Jr., tended an old system of particularism and backed "organization" slates in Democratic primaries until the mid-1960s.[107] But Prieur exercised considerably less influence in Norfolk's elections then Kellam did in Virginia Beach's. Prieur had to share power or contend for it with a business community that ventured into politics now and then (in the late 1940s and late 1950s), and he was dogged in the 1960s by electoral slates associated with Henry Howell, then rising to prominence in the state as a liberal activist.[108] Elsewhere in the Tidewater, the city of Chesapeake (89,580) conducted politics in the 1960s without any important slating organizations. Newport News (138,177) had a business and professional group and several lesser groups that endorsed candidates in municipal politics in the late 1950s, but had nothing approaching a traditional party organization.[109]

The politics of nominating in Virginia's Washington suburbs—Arlington County (174,284), Fairfax County (455,901), and the city of Alexandria (110,938)—seems to have been largely a matter of individual candidacies in the late 1960s, though slates of liberals or incumbents occasionally turned up, as did candidates who accused each other of connections with the Byrd organization.[110] The state's capital city of Richmond (249,430) shows no trace at all of traditional organization, though its elections from 1946 through at least 1970 hinged on slating activity. The city's business community generated a succession of slat-

[107] "For over forty years [1920s through mid-1960s] Prieur augmented his power in the Norfolk courthouse by doing small favors for constituents, getting people jobs, using to the full his influence on state patronage, and closely supervising the appointive powers of Norfolk's corporation court judge" (Wilkinson, *Harry Byrd*, p. 190).

[108] On Norfolk in general: Temple, *Merger Politics*, pp. 34, 101-102; Wilkinson, *Harry Byrd*, pp. 187-190; Carl Abbott, *The New Urban America: Growth and Politics in Sunbelt Cities* (Chapel Hill: University of North Carolina Press, 1981), pp. 126-132. On competition between Prieur's and other electoral slates in the 1960s: Temple, p. 102; Abbott, pp. 131-132; *Norfolk Virginian-Pilot*, July 14, 1965, pp. 1, 10.

[109] On Chesapeake: Temple, *Merger Politics*, pp. 83, 127, 163-170. The point applies to the city of Chesapeake after a 1963 consolidation, and to the two units combined in 1963 to make up Chesapeake—the county of Norfolk and the city of South Norfolk. On Newport News: *ibid.*, pp. 112-119.

[110] *Washington Post*, June 11, 1967, pp. G1, G4; July 12, 1967, pp. A1, A10, A11; July 16, 1969, p. A16; and *Alexandria Gazette*, July 12, 1967, p. 1. A *Post* report on Fairfax County's Democratic primaries in 1967 for the county's positions of district supervisor gives a sense of the texture: "In the five contested district races, a field of 14 candidates most of whom were political newcomers, found images rather than issues more useful in their bids for the Democratic nomination. Only C. Meade Stull, of Centreville, who was defeated, was an incumbent" (July 12, 1967, p. A10).

ing groups to win council elections—the Richmond Citizens' Association in the mid-1940s, Richmond Forward in the mid-1960s, and the Team of Progress in 1970. A black group called Crusade for Voters put up candidates for the state legislature and supplied the opposition in municipal elections in 1958 and after. Blacks won a majority of council seats in 1977.[111] On Virginia's rural counties the evidence is meager. A brief 1968 discussion of politics in Brunswick County (16,172), a Southside jurisdiction with thousands of nonvoting blacks, tells of a circumspect oligarchy probably something like South Carolina's "Barnwell ring"—a collection of officials who were elected over and over again by a small electorate and who cooperated with each other on state and local affairs.[112]

No one should doubt that Senator Byrd's statewide organization, the "Byrd machine," deserves its reputation. Its high command, in league with local affiliates, authoritatively slated statewide candidates for several decades through the mid-1960s, when Virginia's Democratic primaries were the elections that counted.[113] No contemporary organization in any other state compiled a more impressive record and none in the South even came close. Yet unlike, say, state Democratic organizations in Rhode Island and Connecticut in the 1950s, Byrd's organization lacked a solid local base in traditional party organizations: the Kellam and Prieur operations hardly added up to Connecticut's or Rhode Island's city machines. And the incentive structure of the Byrd appara-

[111] On Richmond see Virginius Dabney, *Richmond: The Story of a City* (Garden City, N.Y.: Doubleday, 1976), pp. 334-338; Christopher Silver, *Twentieth-Century Richmond: Planning, Politics, and Race* (Knoxville: University of Tennessee Press, 1984), pp. 280-286; Wilkinson, *Harry Byrd*, pp. 176-187; *Richmond Times-Dispatch*, July 12, 1967, p. 1; July 16, 1969, pp. A1, A5; June 5, 1970, p. B1; June 6, 1970, p. B1; June 7, 1970, pp. A1, A4; June 10, 1970, p. A1. The TOP council winners in 1970 were all businessmen—a retired Standard Oil executive, president of the Metropolitan National Bank, vice president of a real estate firm, vice president of a funeral establishment, stockbroker, and chairman of the board of a lumber company: not even any lawyers. On the 1977 election: B. Drummond Ayres, Jr., "With Richmond's Old Guard Watching, Blacks Take on Aging City's Problems," *New York Times*, July 30, 1977, p. 6.

[112] Wilkinson calls the Brunswick ruling set a "small, secure, hereditary aristocracy," in recognition that local office-holding was a tradition in a number of families (*Harry Byrd*, ch. 1, characterization at p. 15). The study is based on interviews conducted in 1966. On Virginia's local organizations in general see also Key, *Southern Politics*, pp. 21-22; Temple, *Merger Politics*, pp. 30-37.

[113] For general treatments of the Byrd organization see Key, *Southern Politics*, ch. 2; Wilkinson, *Harry Byrd*, ch. 2; Francis P. Miller, *Man from the Valley*, ch. 14. For an account of statewide slating in the 1950s and 1960s: Ralph Eisenberg, "Virginia: The Emergence of Two-Party Politics," ch. 2 in Havard (ed.), *Changing Politics of the South*, pp. 46-74.

tus seems to have violated standards of traditional party organization—not enough reliance on "individual material" incentives and too much reliance on "purposive" incentives. The former had a place in Virginia, to be sure. A unique state instrument called the Compensation Board allowed central party leaders to manipulate salaries and expense allowances of individual officials in cities and counties, a power that is understandably said to have fostered organizational loyalty at the bottom.[114] Virginia's state government also appointed an unusually large number of local officials, which allowed another sort of hold on personnel.[115] Yet low-salary patronage jobs counted for little in the Byrd regime, and officials steered remarkably clear of particularism in awarding contracts and enforcing laws. Virginia government in Byrd's time was honest, even ostentatiously honest; there was none of the rollicking corruption readily evident across the border in West Virginia and Maryland.[116]

On the side of "purposive" incentives, one author reflects that "courthouse support for the Byrd organization throughout the state caused observers to look for an arm-twisting device enabling the state hierarchy to keep its local lieutenants in line. What has been overlooked, however, was the remarkable similarity of viewpoint among organization members, which, in the long run, unified them far more effectively and fundamentally than any pressure or patronage tactics

[114] It seems not to have been used much, though the potential was there. See the accounts in Key, *Southern Politics*, p. 21; and Wilkinson, *Harry Byrd*, pp. 31-32. Apparently the Board threatened use of its compensation power to keep some local officials in line in 1949 when an organization candidate for governor faced a tough primary. See Wilkinson, pp. 95-97; and Peter R. Henriques, "The Organization Challenged: John S. Battle, Francis P. Miller, and Horace Edwards Run for Governor in 1949," *Virginia Magazine of History and Biography* 82(1974), 396.

[115] See Key, *Southern Politics*, pp. 21-22; Wilkinson, *Harry Byrd*, pp. 33-35.

[116] On the lack of corruption see Key, *Southern Politics*, p. 32; Wilkinson, *Harry Byrd*, pp. 36-37. A reporter's characterization of the Virginia legislature just after World War II: "A terribly decorous place. It was a place where the members tended to be the leading citizens of their towns and counties. They came there as a great honor. . . . They were extremely ethical people, and it stunned reporters from other states that saw it. It stunned lobbyists from other states. It stunned everybody. There was no man to see to get a highway contract. There was no man to see to get a bill through the committee. There was no money ever changing hands" (quoted in Bass and DeVries, *Transformation of Southern Politics*, p. 343). Key found the same thing: "In Virginia, we are assured, a state contractor does not have to make a pay-off; he has to make a low bid. Even distilleries selling to the state liquor board, the almost incredible report is, do not concede a percentage to the organization" (p. 32). A recent comparison: Karlyn Barker, "Different Strokes: Maryland, Virginia Legislatures Are a Study in Contrasts," *Washington Post*, February 4, 1979, pp. B1, B3.

ever could have."[117] The people who supported and made up the Byrd organization seem to have been powerfully animated by a shared set of policy aims—briefly, a program of keeping government honest, budgets balanced, the public sector small, unions weak, and blacks segregated.[118] The Senator himself is memorable not as a wheeler and dealer but as a man of principle—in his unending crusade for balanced budgets, for example, and his state program of "massive resistance" to school desegregation. He thought of his Virginia apparatus as "a loose organization of friends, who believe in the same principles of government" and, surprisingly, this more or less Burkean characterization seems to be an important part of the truth.[119] The Byrd organization was in fact an American anomaly, and the key to its nature is very likely the size of the Virginia electorate. Key reported in *Southern Politics* that at least 85 percent of adult *whites*—a Southern record—ordinarily took no part in the state's Democratic primaries.[120] Evidently, at this level of participation the Virginia incentive mix could sustain a cohesive apparatus capable of dominating elections, though it should be said on the conventional "material" side that state employees and officeholders constituted an unusually large proportion of the electorate.[121] When Virginia's voter turnout surged in the late 1960s, the Byrd organization promptly collapsed; its practitioners probably had no idea how to manage a mass public. "Whig ascendancy" or something of the kind seems a better label for the Byrd apparatus than "traditional party organization." The TPO score for Virginia is a 2; the Kellam and Prieur organizations raise it above a 1.

TEXAS (11,196,730)

In most of the rural areas of Texas in the 1960s, the dominant Democratic party had a typically Southern texture. A report on rural county chairmen noted: "They have an apolitical, nonparty, legal-duty orientation. They are neither campaign nor organization oriented. They have no concept of party as organization . . . [they] endeavor to remain acceptable to all candidates in the Democratic primary by confin-

[117] Wilkinson, *Harry Byrd*, p. 16.

[118] To get a sense of this programmatic commitment see *ibid.*, chs. 1-3, 5.

[119] Quoted in William B. Crawley, Jr., *Bill Tuck: A Political Life in Harry Byrd's Virginia* (Charlottesville: University Press of Virginia, 1978), p. 9.

[120] Key, *Southern Politics*, pp. 20, 492-496, 504-505.

[121] According to one report, about a third of voters in 1905 through 1948. See J. Morgan Kousser, *The Shaping of Southern Politics: Suffrage Restriction and the Establishment of the One-Party South, 1880-1910* (New Haven: Yale University Press, 1974), p. 181.

ing themselves to impartially administering the election code."[122] Of the metropolitan counties encompassing the state's seven largest cities and about half the state population, only one supported a structure in the 1960s with the properties of traditional party organization.

Harris County (1,741,912), site of Houston (1,232,802), supported two quite influential organizations of a different kind: an alliance of white liberals, unions, blacks, and Mexican-Americans called the Harris County Democrats (HCD), grounded organizationally in ideological zeal, ethnic solidarity, money from small contributors and liberal "angels," and the efforts of CIO blockworkers; and a conservative counteralliance, Democratic Precinct Organizations (DPO), composed of businessmen and right-wing ideologues.[123] Both of these groups had elaborate networks of precinct workers, and they slated against each other throughout the 1960s for

---

[122] David M. Olson, "Toward a Typology of County Party Organizations," *Southwestern Social Science Quarterly* 48 (1968), 564.

[123] On the HCD see Kenneth E. Gray, *A Report on the Politics of Houston* (Cambridge: Joint Center for Urban Studies, M.I.T./Harvard, 1960), pp. II:36-55, v:38-39; Clifton McCleskey, "Houston: Tripartite Politics," ch. 4 in Leonard E. Goodall (ed.), *Urban Politics in the Southwest* (Tempe: Institute of Public Administration, Arizona State University, 1967), pp. 74-77; Jewell, *Legislative Representation*, pp. 97-98; Chandler Davidson, *Biracial Politics: Conflict and Coalition in the Metropolitan South* (Baton Rouge: Louisiana State University Press, 1972), pp. 44-47, 186-187. On the nature of HCD appeal: "Harris County liberals are issue-oriented. Liberal faction candidates get votes because they say they want a liberal and programmatic Democratic party, not because they promise to give jobs to their supporters if elected" (Gray, p. II:16). In 1968 the HCD lost part of its union base after endorsing Eugene McCarthy for President; splintering of this sort over issues or people who symbolize them, a chronic problem in issue-oriented organizations, rarely happens in traditional organizations (see Davidson, p. 44). On the conservative counteralliance see Gray, pp. II:36-55; McCleskey, pp. 74-77; Jewell, *Legislative Representation*, pp. 97-98; James R. Soukup, Clifton McCleskey, and Harry Holloway, *Party and Factional Division in Texas* (Austin: University of Texas Press, 1964), pp. 3-4, 87. The businessmen got down into the trenches: "In the 1960 Democratic primary at least twelve of the conservative candidates for precinct chairmen were management employees of Sheffield Steel, another nine of Humble Oil, and several others from Gulf Oil, the Texas Company, A. O. Smith Corporation, Tennessee Gas, So-

Democratic party offices, nominations to the state legislature, and places in delegations to party conventions.[124] In general they avoided Houston's nonpartisan municipal politics, a rather formless scramble among individual candidates for mayor and city council.[125] And they also generally stayed out of primaries for offices at the county level. These were the preserves of individual Democratic politicians who built personal followings and distributed some patronage, but had neither inherited nor assembled a county organization important in its own right.[126] The HCD and DPO, with their ideological underpinnings, might have fit better into the politics of the northern Midwest rather than of the South in the 1960s, though the Harris County setting at the time was typically Southern in its low voter turnout and its constraints on suffrage. More recently a study in 1980 of precinct committees in the county revealed a universe of affluent and well-educated functionaries, the Republicans conservative and formidably organized, the Democrats split into liberals and conservatives still at war with each other. The activating inducements on all sides were "purposive" rather than "material."[127]

---

hio Petroleum, and Brown and Root. Many of these business-affiliated conservatives were successful in their bid for party office" (*ibid.*, p. 87).

[124] On precinct workers see Davidson, *Biracial Politics*, p. 47; Olson, "Toward a Typology of County Party Organizations," p. 568. On slating see Gray, *Report on Houston*, pp. II:13, 41-44; Davidson, pp. 186-187; Jewell, *Metropolitan Representation*, pp. 10-11.

[125] On Houston's municipal elections: Gray, *Report on Houston*, pp. II:3-4, 21-35; McCleskey, "Houston," pp. 74-80; Richard D. Feld and Donald S. Lutz, "Recruitment to the Houston City Council," *Journal of Politics* 34(1972), 930. On the HCD and DPO keeping out of them: Gray, pp. II:3, 17, 36, 44; McCleskey, p. 75. See Chandler Davidson and Douglas Longshore, "Houston Elects a Mayor," *New South* 27(Spring 1972), 55-57, 61, for an especially good account of a municipal election, in 1971. A considerable number of organizations made endorsements—notably a coalition of civic clubs, an Informed Citizens Committee, two black groups, a labor council, and for the first time the HCD—but none seems to have exercised much influence. Candidates and their own organizations were the important actors.

[126] On Harris County politics: Gray, *Report on Houston*, pp. II:9-10. On HCD avoidance of elections for county offices: "It usually leaves county office campaigns alone, for two reasons. First, it is interested in liberal ideas and programs, not jobs. Second, liberal faction leaders know that their voting strength, especially among organized labor, will split in county elections, which involve personal factions more than issues. They prefer to consolidate their strength for what they think are more important battles" (p. II:13).

[127] Richard Murray and Kent Tedin, "Party Activists in Houston: A Study of an Emerging Party System," paper presented at the 1981 convention of the American Political Science Association. "The non-patronage base of Texas party organizations is reflected in the absence of precinct leaders that have held appointive, non-civil service, government jobs. The great majority of the party workers have non-political occupations and volunteer their time to the parties, with most of the remainder being housewives or retirees" (p. 12).

Electoral politics in the 1960s in Travis County (295,516), site of Austin (251,808), was predominantly an affair of individual candidacies in both nonpartisan city elections and Democratic county primaries.[128] A new Republican club movement in the style of Manhattan's reform Democrats slated candidates for some city and county offices without much luck.[129] Fort Worth (393,476) ran a candidate-centered municipal politics in the 1960s: "The Democratic and Republican parties certainly do not offer tickets for the council or candidates for mayor; nor has the charter prescription of nonpartisan election been circumvented by any other organized effort."[130] In Dallas (844,401) a businessmen's slating group, the Citizens Charter Association (CCA), exercised extraordinary control over nonpartisan mayoral and council elections from the 1930s through the mid-1970s, and in parent unit Dallas County (1,327,321) another business formation called the Democratic Committee for Responsible Government backed Democratic candidates for the state legislature in the 1960s and ordinarily got them nominated and elected.[131] In San Antonio (654,153), run by a machine

[128] On city council elections: David M. Olson, *Nonpartisan Elections: A Case Analysis* (Austin: Institute of Public Affairs, University of Texas, 1965), chs. 2, 3. A summary statement: "The candidates did not constitute slates. They were neither recruited by nor were they the symbols of well-organized, cohesive, and consistent factions in the community" (p. 50). On Democratic primaries for state legislature: David M. Olson, *Legislative Primary Elections in Austin, Texas, 1962* (Austin: Institute of Public Affairs, University of Texas, 1963), chs. 2, 3. A summary statement: "Not only did the Democratic legislative candidates have little association with the official party; they had little or no cooperation with one another. They did not form slates or factions, presenting themselves as a ticket to the electorate" (pp. 32-33).

[129] Olson, *Nonpartisan Elections*, pp. 45-46; Olson, *Legislative Primary Elections*, pp. 16-18, 43-44. The author draws the Manhattan analogy, pp. 43-44. Liberals took over the Austin city council in the mid-1970s after the lowered voting age enfranchised college students. See Paul Burka, "Liberal Education," pp. 236-239 in *Texas Monthly's Political Reader* (Austin: Texas Monthly Press, 1978).

[130] August O. Spain, "Fort Worth: Great Expectations—Cowtown Hares and Tortoises," ch. 3 in Goodall (ed.), *Urban Politics in the Southwest*, p. 59, and more generally pp. 59-64. A business group had intermittently slated municipal candidates in earlier decades. Another author writes of a predominantly candidate-centered municipal politics in the 1960s and 1970s, though he reports that a businessmen's Good Government League ran a council slate not very successfully in 1967. See Tom Curtis, "Who Runs Cowtown?" pp. 240-243 in *Texas Monthly's Political Reader*. Also on Fort Worth: Martin V. Melosi, "Dallas-Fort Worth: Marketing the Metroplex," ch. 6 in Bernard and Rice (eds.), *Sunbelt Cities*, pp. 181-183. None of these authors says anything about Democratic primaries in Fort Worth's parent unit, Tarrant County (716,317).

[131] On Dallas city politics see Carol E. Thometz, *The Decision-Makers: The Power Structure of Dallas* (Dallas: Southern Methodist University Press, 1963), pp. 39, 79-84. Thometz writes of an organization called the "Municipal Association," but it is unmistakably the same group others call the CCA. Later reports: Hessler, *29 Ways to Govern a City*, pp. 45-46; Neal R. Peirce, *The Megastates of America: People, Politics, and*

before World War II, the Good Government League, a business and professional organization, dominated postwar municipal elections until its demise in the mid-1970s. It filled all but four of eighty-one nonpartisan council openings from 1955 through 1971.[132] Democratic pri-

---

Power in the Ten Great States (New York: Norton, 1972), pp. 541-542; "Is Dallas Falling Apart?" *Texas Observer*, February 14, 1975, pp. 1, 3-5. According to this last account only four or five mayoral or council candidates had defeated CCA designees over a thirty-year period, but the organization's grip loosened in the mid-1970s. A court-induced switch from at-large to district-based council elections undermined CCA influence: see Howard D. Hamilton, *Electing the Cincinnati City Council: An Examination of Alternative Electoral-Representation Systems* (Cincinnati: Stephen H. Wilder Foundation, 1978), pp. 22-32 (a section about Dallas). Recent analyses of the structure of Dallas politics: June Kronholz, "If Businessmen Find Dallas Friendly, That's Natural—They Run It," *Wall Street Journal*, September 24, 1979, p. 1; Peter Applebome, "Dallas Means Business and Vice Versa," *New York Times*, May 10, 1981, p. 4E. The CCA itself was an offshoot of another group of two hundred or so high-ranking businessmen named the Dallas Citizens Council. Probably any method of studying Dallas in the 1950s or 1960s would have produced the conclusion that it was run by a power elite. On Dallas County politics see Charles Deaton, *The Year They Threw the Rascals Out* (Austin: Shoal Creek Publishers, 1973), pp. 152-153. A newspaper report on the 1970 Democratic state legislative primaries in Dallas County: "All the winners except Ratcliff and Reed were backed by the powerful Dallas County Committee for Responsible Government (DCRG), the conservative Democratic party leadership" (*Dallas Morning News*, May 3, 1970, p. 45A).

[132] On San Antonio's pre–World War II machine past see Green Peyton, *San Antonio: City in the Sun* (New York: McGraw-Hill, 1946), chs. 16, 17; Abbott, *The New Urban America*, pp. 132-136. Surprisingly, the machine's base was a black vote. This was a politics of extremely low turnout. For general treatments of the GGL and San Antonio's post–World War II municipal elections see Bill Crane, "San Antonio: Pluralistic City and Monolithic Government," ch. 7 in Goodall (ed.), *Urban Politics in the Southwest*, pp. 134-142; Wayt T. Watterson and Roberta S. Watterson, *The Politics of New Communities: A Case Study of San Antonio Ranch* (New York: Praeger, 1975), pp. 54-60, 67; David R. Johnson, "San Antonio: The Vicissitudes of Boosterism," ch. 9 in Bernard and Rice (eds.), *Sunbelt Cities*, pp. 237-252; John A. Booth and David R. Johnson, "Power and Progress in San Antonio Politics," ch. 1 in Johnson, Booth, and Richard J. Harris (eds.), *The Politics of San Antonio: Community, Progress, and Power* (Lincoln: University of Nebraska Press, 1983), pp. 19-25. A comment by Crane in his 1967 treatment: "The community has come to equate GGL spokesmen with progress, respectability, stability, efficiency and economy. Opponents automatically endure the onus of being against the council-manager form of government and in favor of a return to the dirty politics of the spoils system" (p. 136). The GGL lost its cohesiveness in the early 1970s and the mayoralty in 1973, and folded in 1976. In 1977, just after San Antonio had shifted from at-large to district elections, a coalition of five Mexican-Americans and a black took over the eleven-member city council, and in 1981 Henry Cisneros won the mayoralty by a wide margin in an election reported without mention of any slating organizations. See William K. Stevens, "San Antonio, With Mexican-Americans in Power, Seen at Crossroad," *New York Times*, April 7, 1979, pp. A1, A16; James R. Adams, "The New Political Forces in San Antonio," *Wall Street Journal*, April 2, 1981, p. 26; "New Mayor-Elect of San Antonio Hails Transcendence of 'the Ethnic Factor,' " *New York Times*, April 6,

maries in the 1960s in San Antonio's parent unit, Bexar County (830,460), were largely a series of slating contests over county and state legislative offices between the Bexar County Liberal Coalition—a group like Harris County's HCD though not as securely grounded at the precinct level—and the GGL, operating in the formally partisan sphere without its title. Individual county officials distributed some patronage jobs, but without generating an overall county organization as a result.[133] Corpus Christi (204,525), metropolis of Nueces County (237,544), is said to have followed until 1973 "a long city tradition of electing a slate of councilmen backed by the downtown establishment [the business community]"; 1973 was an anomalous year because the establishment's "Now Party" elected only six of the seven candidates on its slate. Otherwise the actors in city and Nueces County elections in the 1970s were personalities and members of family clans who lacked any apparent base in party organization.[134]

Houston, Austin, Fort Worth, Dallas, San Antonio, Corpus Christi, to which can be added the smaller city of Abilene[135] (89,653), do not

1981, p. A12. In general on the breakdown of GGL hegemony and afterward: Robert Brischetto, Charles L. Cotrell, and R. Michael Stevens, "Conflict and Change in the Political Culture of San Antonio in the 1970s," ch. 4 in Johnson et al. (eds.), *Politics of San Antonio*, pp. 78-94; Thomas A. Baylis, "Leadership Change in Contemporary San Antonio," ch. 5 in *ibid.*; and Tucker Gibson, "Mayoralty Politics in San Antonio, 1955-79," ch. 6 in *ibid.*

[133] On slating in county Democratic primaries see Soukup et al., *Party and Factional Division in Texas*, pp. 3, 4, 52-53; Crane, "San Antonio," pp. 138-140; Jewell, *Legislative Representation*, p. 98; Watterson and Watterson, *The Politics of New Communities*, pp. 70-72. The Liberal Coalition resurfaced under a new name after taking a beating in the 1966 primaries. A newspaper reference to a state legislative slate in the 1968 Democratic primaries: "Speaker [of the Texas House Ben] Barnes gave a strong assist to the moderate-conservative legislative ticket two days before the campaign [ended], the six representatives supported by a San Antonio business-oriented group of leaders" (*San Antonio Express/News*, May 4, 1968, p. 16A). On county-office politics in Bexar: Crane, pp. 138-141; Watterson and Watterson, pp. 70-72.

[134] Kaye Northcott, "Corpus Delicti: Is Corpus Christi dying and is anyone trying to save it?" *Texas Monthly*, January 1978, pp. 110-122, quotation at p. 114. "The South Side Anglo business establishment controls the majority of the city council and the school board. The West Side Mexican Americans, themselves split into factions by two competing clans (the Garcias and the Bonillas), have elected the state senator, two of the three state legislators, a county commissioner, and a sheriff. Then there's a newer Anglo faction, hard to define but usually described (at least by members of the other two groups) as the 'rednecks.' Jason Luby is their man" (*ibid.*, p. 113). Luby was elected mayor in 1975. Evidence is leaner for Nueces than for the other six metropolitan counties.

[135] Abilene's municipal elections were dominated from 1966 through 1982 by the Citizens for Better Government, a slating organization said to be similar to the ones in control of Dallas and San Antonio. See Luis Ricardo Fraga, "Domination Through Democratic Means: Nonpartisan Slating Groups in City Electoral Politics," paper presented at the 1985 convention of the American Political Science Association, pp. 14-15, 16.

show any modern trace of traditional party organization: no city bosses, no ward organizations living on patronage, no groups of county officials coalesced into machines, no factional organizations of a Louisiana or Kentucky type. The career of Texas's most successful Mexican-American politician of the 1960s, Congressman Henry B. Gonzalez, tells something about the state's urban setting. There was no useful organization of any kind for him to build on or rise up through in San Antonio's large Hispanic section. He won a city council seat in 1953 on a "San Antonians" slate bankrolled by oilmen, won again on a Good Government League ticket two years later, then as a visible city figure occasionally cooperated with Bexar County liberals but mostly steered clear of alliances with others. He reached Congress and stayed there on his own.[136]

The exception among larger Texas cities in the 1960s was El Paso (322,261), once a thoroughgoing machine city around the turn of the century.[137] It was not a jarring exception, for self-starting individuals dominated the city's nonpartisan elections—"free-for-alls open to anyone willing to pay a $100 filing fee," the area's Democratic primaries for state legislative offices engendered no more effective slating activity than Austin's, and officials of El Paso County (359,291) showed no more inclination to build an overall organization than their counterparts in Bexar and Harris counties.[138] But a group known simply as "the organization" paid people's poll taxes and mobilized votes on the city's Mexican-American South Side and often exercised significant influence in Democratic primaries and nonpartisan elections. In most respects "the organization" was a typical instance of traditional party organization. A boss ran it, and its *pistoleros* (workers) gave out legal

[136] A good sketch of Gonzalez's career through the mid-1960s appears in Charles R. Chandler, "The Mexican-American Protest Movement in Texas" (Ph.D. dissertation, Tulane University, 1968), pp. 136-147. "Since running with the 'San Antonians' in 1953, Gonzalez has never worked closely with a 'ticket,' a coalition, or any sort of political group other than the Democratic Party" (p. 146). "No powerful political organization has been established by Gonzalez, nor is one likely to be. Gonzalez must be characterized as a charismatic leader" (p. 145).

[137] See Mario T. Garcia, *Desert Immigrants: The Mexicans of El Paso, 1880-1920* (New Haven: Yale University Press, 1981).

[138] On city politics: Mark Adams and Gertrude Adams, *A Report on Politics in El Paso* (Cambridge: Joint Center for Urban Studies, M.I.T./Harvard, 1963), pp. ii:29-66, quotation at p. ii:29. See also Banfield, *Big City Politics*, pp. 70-73. Some candidates for mayor and alderman joined together in "tickets," but these were evanescent affairs not rooted in continuing organization. Banfield's conclusion: "Tickets are usually drawn up a few months before the election and generally melt away as soon as the votes are counted" (p. 70). On Democratic state legislative primaries: Adams and Adams, pp. iv:9-13. On county politics: pp. iv:1-6.

advice, political favors, and "honest graft" in exchange for votes. It differed from most traditional organizations in that it ordinarily endorsed candidates already in the running—normally for a price—rather than slating them itself, but this was probably a consequence of operating in a setting where no city or county officials ran for election in ward-sized districts.[139] Reports on the legwork in El Paso's mayoral campaign of 1961 give a sense of the city's electoral structure: the only important door-to-door campaigners were "the organization's" workers on the South Side and an ad hoc network of conservative activists who canvassed in middle-class precincts.[140]

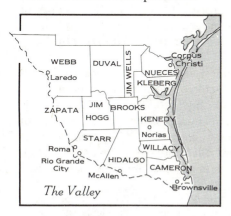

The Valley

This covers the metropolitan centers. In fact Texas's most interesting and durable local organizations have operated in "the Valley," an area of predominantly Mexican-American counties in the far south near the mouth of the Rio Grande.[141] Its politics has mid-nineteenth-century roots. Stephen Powers, a New York politician and army colonel, stayed on in the Valley after the

[139] The basic source on "the organization," said to be "the city's only permanent campaign group" (p. II:32), is Adams and Adams, *Politics in El Paso*, pp. I:14-22, 33; II:32, 41-43, 45, 51; v:5-6. Banfield gives a good thumbnail sketch in *Big City Politics*, pp. 70-71. See also Melvin P. Straus, "The Mexican-American in El Paso Politics," ch. 6 in Clyde J. Wingfield (ed.), *Urbanization in the Southwest: A Symposium* (El Paso: Texas Western Press, University of Texas–El Paso, 1968), pp. 63-66. Sometimes "the organization" backed candidates who ran as liberals, sometimes not. "Many Latin leaders and liberal Anglos deplore the 'organization's' tendency to support for state and county offices conservative candidates whose platforms don't offer much to poor *latinos*" (Adams and Adams, pp. I:14-15, and also p. I:19). Accounts are silent about where in government "the organization" got hold of goods and services to retail as "favors."

[140] Adams and Adams, *Politics in El Paso*, p. II:51.

[141] The authoritative sources on this area are Evan Anders, *Boss Rule in South Texas: The Progressive Era* (Austin: University of Texas Press, 1982), and two dissertations based on information gathered in the middle and late 1940s: Edgar G. Shelton, Jr., *Political Conditions Among Texas Mexicans along the Rio Grande* (thesis, University of Texas, 1946; repr. San Francisco: R and E Research Associates, 1974); and Ozzie G. Simmons, *Anglo Americans and Mexican Americans in South Texas: A Study in Dominant-Subordinate Group Relations* (Ph.D. dissertation, Harvard University, 1952; repr. New York: Arno, 1974), especially ch. 6 ("Social Organization: Politics"). Shelton gives a mid-1940s rundown of political organization in each of thirteen counties: Brooks, Cameron (site of Brownsville), Duval, Hidalgo (site of McAllen), Jim Hogg, Jim Wells,

war with Mexico to organize the indigenous Mexican-Americans: "In New York he had seen the uneducated and ignorant Irish immigrant being herded and voted by the Tammany machine. He saw great opportunities for the same thing here with the Mexicans."[142] Powers built and James B. Wells, Jr., after him consolidated and presided over a valleywide "empire of influence" that lasted until about 1920, based on Mexican-American voters organized on ranches or via county machines.[143] Texas disfranchised most of its blacks and (de facto) many of its whites around 1900 and local Democrats administered the new "white primary" to exclude Mexican-Americans in a number of counties north of Laredo and Corpus Christi, but politics in the Valley went on more or less unchanged. Vote mobilizers took up paying poll taxes and a good proportion of the area's Mexican-Americans continued to vote.[144]

The opening of the Rio Grande valley to agribusiness after 1900 brought in Anglo growers who generated reform movements and overthrew the machines in Cameron County (140,368), site of Brownsville (52,522), after World War I and in Hidalgo County (181,535), site of McAllen (37,636), in 1930.[145] But as late as the 1940s, heads of farms and commercial enterprises controlled blocs of Mexican-American voters in Hidalgo,[146] and ranchers in an older and more paternalistic

---

Kenedy, Kleberg, Nueces (site of Corpus Christi), Starr, Webb (site of Laredo), Willacy, and Zapata. Simmons in Chapter 6 gives a good picture of politics in the late 1940s in Hidalgo County.

[142] Shelton, *Political Conditions Among Texas Mexicans*, p. 22.

[143] See Anders, *Boss Rule in South Texas, passim*; and also Shelton, *Political Conditions Among Texas Mexicans*, pp. 10-11, 22-29 (quotation at p. 22); and Simmons, *Anglo Americans and Mexican Americans*, pp. 270-273.

[144] See Shelton, *Political Conditions Among Texas Mexicans*, pp. 11, 34; Simmons, *Anglo Americans and Mexican Americans*, p. 285.

[145] Anders, *Boss Rule in South Texas*, chs. 8, 11, 12, and Conclusion.

[146] Simmons, *Anglo Americans and Mexican Americans*, pp. 279-293 (a section entitled "The Controlled Vote and the Political Jefe"), 298-299. "The basis of the political power of the [Hidalgo County] *jefe* is of a different sort from that of the boss of the urban political machine in that he does not control strategic elective and appointive offices and through these many minor political jobs, nor does he have a formal political organization with a staff of workers capable of thoroughly canvassing the electorate. . . . The Valley *jefes* control votes through the personal influence and power which they exert in their capacity as employers and in other relations maintained through their business activities. Political leadership in McAllen is identified with top business status and has none of the stigma often found attached to it in the case of the machine boss or other type of professional politician. The controlled vote blocs are not considered machines, and the general consensus of opinion is that city politics are 'clean' and fair" (*ibid.*, pp. 283-284). On McAllen politics in recent years: Kenneth Bain and Paul Travis, "South Texas Politics," *Southern Exposure* 12(1984), 49-52.

relationship controlled Mexican-American cowhands' votes in settings such as Kenedy County (678) and Kleberg County (33,166).[147] Two enclaves of the Powers-Wells empire relatively unaffected by agribusiness continued into recent times as strongholds of traditional party organization: impoverished Starr County (17,707), still running a patronage politics in the mid-1970s; and Duval County (11,722), a machine holding of the Parr family from around 1910, when Archer Parr constructed an electoral base among Mexican-Americans, until his son George's conviction for income tax evasion in the mid-1970s.[148] The Parrs often dominated nearby Zapata (4,352) and Jim Wells (33,032) counties in addition to Duval, and it was in Jim Wells that George Parr achieved national notice by fabricating enough votes to tip Texas's 1948 Senate primary to Lyndon B. Johnson.[149] In general the

[147] Shelton, *Political Conditions Among Texas Mexicans*, pp. 84-86. Voting in Kenedy County as reported by Shelton in 1946: "Election day, which is usually once every two years, has always been a gala affair for all these Mexican cowboys in Kenedy County at Norias. The reason is this: that is the day when they are given heaping dishes of ice cream. Once every two years, on election day, the King Ranch people have several gallons of ice cream sent in for the cowboys. That, to the cowboys is what election day means—ice cream. The voting part is unimportant. All many of them know is that once every two years they go to Norias, mark some lines with a pencil on a piece of paper (where they are told to mark, of course) and are then rewarded by being given ice cream. Some have the idea that the more carefully they mark the line, that the straighter and heavier the line is, the more ice cream they will get. As a consequence, some of them take much time over their ballot to make sure that every detail is correct and that it is neat. . . . As for the voting itself, it is very simple. They are merely told which line to mark and that is that" (pp. 85-86).

[148] The background on Starr County: Anders, *Boss Rule in South Texas*, ch. 3, p. 283; Shelton, *Political Conditions Among Texas Mexicans*, pp. 60-74; Simmons, *Anglo Americans and Mexican Americans*, pp. 273, 548-551; Soukup et al., *Party and Factional Division in Texas*, pp. 127, 134. A reading in the mid-1970s: "Politics in Starr County over the decades have been notoriously corrupt and heavy-handed. Due to chronic economic depression, political favoritism and patronage are important sources of livelihood for many of the residents. For example, although teachers in Roma and Rio Grande City are reportedly no longer hired or fired on the basis of which faction (the Old Party, New Party, or New New Party) they support, political alignment is a major consideration for other school and public jobs and contracts. Chicano-style politics have made no inroads into this area" (Michael V. Miller, "Chicano Community Control in South Texas: Problems and Prospects," *Journal of Ethnic Studies* 3[Fall 1975], 85). On Duval County: Anders, ch. 9, p. 283; Shelton, pp. 47-60; "A Death in Duval," *Texas Observer*, April 25, 1975, pp. 1, 3-7; Dudley Lynch, *The Duke of Duval: The Life & Times of George B. Parr* (Waco: Texian Press, 1976).

[149] "Ex-official Says He Stole 1948 Election for Johnson," *New York Times*, July 31, 1977, pp. 1, 14. The story reports an admission by an oldtimer named Luis Salas that on Parr's instruction he added some 200 Johnson votes to a polling box in Jim Wells County after the state count was in. The last 202 names on the tally appeared alphabetically in the same handwriting in the same colored ink. Johnson carried the state by 87 votes. Sa-

Parr machine and others in South Texas, like Leander Perez's in Louisiana, exercised a good deal more influence in state affairs than their counties' sizes would seem to warrant.[150] The Valley's largest jurisdiction to support a traditional organization in recent times, if brief reports can be credited, is Webb County (72,859), site of Laredo (69,024), characterized as a machine preserve of the Martin family for ninety years. When it came to an end in 1978, Joseph C. "Pepe" Martin, Jr., had been on top the previous twenty-four years.[151] The TPO score for Texas: 2.

---

las's wistful recollection of Jim Wells politics in the 1940s: "We had the law to ourselves there. . . . We had iron control. If a man was opposed to us, we'd put him out of business. Parr was the Godfather. He had life or death control. We could tell any election judge: 'Give us 80 per cent of the vote, the other guy 20 per cent.' We had it made in every election" (p. 14). A detailed treatment of what happened in the 1948 primary appears in Mary Kahl, *Ballot Box 13: How Lyndon Johnson Won His 1948 Senate Race by 87 Contested Votes* (Jefferson, N.C.: McFarland and Co., 1983).

[150] See for example Key, *Southern Politics*, pp. 271-275.

[151] On Webb County: Shelton, *Political Conditions Among Texas Mexicans*, pp. 34-40; Simmons, *Anglo Americans and Mexican Americans*, pp. 284, 319-334; Soukup et al., *Party and Factional Division in Texas*, p. 137; George N. Green, *The Establishment in Texas Politics: The Primitive Years, 1938-1957* (Westport, Conn.: Greenwood, 1979), p. 5; James R. Adams, "A Sampler of Hispanic America's Diversity," *Wall Street Journal*, May 14, 1981, p. 26: "While he lasted, Pepe Martin was one of the most famous 'patrones' in South Texas, dispensing jobs and money to those who asked, provided they gave him their votes, and the votes of their sons, brothers and cousins." The aftermath: "Indicted and convicted of malfeasance in 1978, Mr. Martin, a millionaire, repaid some $500,000 to the city coffers and spent 30 weekends in the county jail" (Wayne King, "Laredo's Hopes Plunge Alongside Mexican Peso," *New York Times*, August 9, 1983, p. A19). None of these sources gives much detail. A magazine writer who went to Texas in 1945 to write an article on Webb County ran into a warning her life would be in danger if she did so. She gave up the project (see Shelton, p. 39).

The Northern Tier and Plains States

One reason for supplying the close documentation on traditional and other sorts of electoral organization in previous chapters is to show that it can be done. Good observers are capable of noticing organization, describing it, and telling what it does. This is important: it produces a suspicion that writers who give detailed accounts of nominating politics without discussing organization are dealing with places that do not have much organization to describe. This is the case in the twenty-six states still to be covered in this chapter and the next. There is little mention of organization (except candidate organization) in most accounts of these settings in the 1960s, and very likely there is not much worth mentioning. The rest of the country produces scarcely any traditional organizations or machines, little party hierarchy, only a few states with routines of publicized slating or endorsing, and none at all whose newspapers use New Jersey or Indiana terminology to tell what occurs in their primaries. Enough idiosyncrasy turns up to require alertness, but the overwhelming sense one gets in sifting through electoral politics at lower levels in the rest of the country—in nonpartisan elections as well as partisan primaries—is of individual candidates doing things on their own. Newspapers in most places have covered primaries by discussing the ups and downs of individual politicians ("Smith Edges Jones"), with special attention to incumbents ("Three Solons Bow to Challengers").

This is not a flat claim that party organizations have not existed in the rest of the country. In most states no doubt they have in one form or another, if only as statutory creations. But organizations "softer" in form than the traditional kind—or simply different from them—may take no part in nominating activity or else take a part in it that leaves little or no trace in accounts. "Parties" can take many forms. They may be organizations, of course, that take on a role of mobilizing voters in November elections but not a nominating role; groups of middle-class activists that hold discussions and pass resolutions; lists of elected officeholders who share a party label but little else; party officials in settings without a supply of material inducements who dabble in politics occasionally without much consequence; party leaders who manage to "recruit" candidates for worthless nominations but exercise little or no influence on nominations worth having; leaders who see it as their role to nudge "some good candidates" into primaries but not to choose among them; and occasionally groups of activists who do seek an important nominating role and set out to "build the party" but fight mostly losing battles in environments of aggressive individual politicians. We shall see conspicuous exceptions, in examining the remainder of the country in the late 1960s, in which real organizations of various kinds had records of regularly asserting undeniable authority in the selection of candidates who won elections, but these were rare.

MASSACHUSETTS (5,689,170) _____

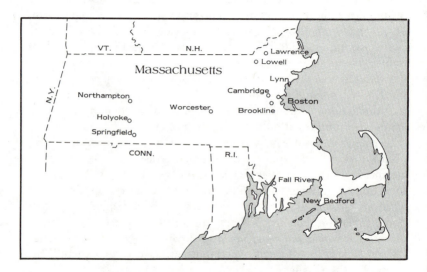

Twentieth-century Massachusetts has presented one of the country's best exhibits of individualistic politics. Making endorsements for statewide offices at conventions may have supplied some order in the dwindling Republican party in recent times, but for Democrats these gatherings have ordinarily amounted to tumultuous rehearsals for later competition in primaries.[1] Candidates for lower offices in nonpartisan

[1] Conventions were prescribed by law in 1954 through 1972 and again more recently. Some sources: V. O. Key, Jr., *American State Politics: An Introduction* (New York: Knopf, 1956), pp. 154-163; Murray B. Levin with George Blackwood, *The Compleat Politician: Political Strategy in Massachusetts* (Indianapolis: Bobbs-Merrill, 1962), pp. 41-46; Judith A. Center, "Reform's Labours Lost: Two Eras of Party Change in Connecticut and Massachusetts" (Ph.D. dissertation, Yale University, 1981), pp. 126-127.

municipal elections and partisan primaries have followed a tradition of running campaigns on their own.[2] A study of Democratic ward and town committees around 1970 found them to be weak structures unaccustomed to endorsing candidates in any kind of election.[3] The only notable exceptions were two committees newly taken over by liberal reformers in Cambridge and in Boston's partly gentrified Fourth Ward, which aggressively promoted candidates for a while in both partisan and nonpartisan processes but ran out of steam in the middle and late 1970s.[4]

Boston (641,071), of course, used to support some traditional organizations. Around 1900 a number of autonomous, patronage-based Democratic ward organizations—Martin Lomasney's in the West End, for example—exercised considerable influence in city nominating processes; they resembled Kansas City's "factions" of half a century later both in their level of influence and their pattern of making and breaking alliances from election to election as they competed with each other for power.[5] But they never controlled a mayoral administration and by the

---

[2] James MacGregor Burns gives an account of John F. Kennedy running in a congressional primary in 1946 in a district including Cambridge and parts of Somerville and Boston and lacking an incumbent candidate: "Primary elections are rather special affairs. Almost anyone who has a mind to can run for the party nomination, which means that a dozen or more politicians may join the race." Kennedy won nomination with 42% of the vote in a ten-candidate primary. "He had found that the Democratic party hardly existed as an organization in the Eleventh District; after he won office and consolidated his position, he could say, '*I* am the Democratic party in my district.' Thus he learned early that the key to winning politics—at least in Boston—was a personal organization, not the party committees." *John Kennedy: A Political Profile* (New York: Harcourt Brace, 1959), ch. 4, quotations at pp. 64, 69.

[3] Center, "Reform's Labours Lost," pp. 124-141. "Members of a ward and town committee usually belonged to one of several factions led by local Democratic officeholders that functioned as candidate organizations. . . . Divisions within the committee concerning candidates generally ran so deep as to render any official 'party' designation an empty prize at best. Although most Democratic committees formally endorsed Democratic nominees in general elections (typically by taking out a single newspaper advertisement praising the Democratic ticket), members participated in the campaign only if 'their' candidate was the nominee" (p. 125). See also Lewis Bowman and G. R. Boynton, "Activities and Role Definitions of Grassroots Party Officials," *Journal of Politics* 28(1966), 134-139, a 1966 study of Democratic and Republican officials in the western Massachusetts locales of Holyoke, Medfield, and Northampton, which suggests they stayed clear of nominating activity. Congressman Chester G. Atkins, Democratic state chairman in the late 1970s and a state representative and senator early in the decade, wrote a book in 1973 (with Barry Hock and Bob Martin) entitled *Getting Elected: A Guide to Winning State and Local Office* (Boston: Houghton Mifflin) in which he said nothing about having to deal with Democratic organizations of any sort; the advice was to aim for an office and build a good personal campaign organization.

[4] Center, "Reform's Labours Lost," pp. 134-138.

[5] Sources on Boston politics in the late nineteenth and early twentieth centuries: Geof-

1930s they no longer amounted to much. Reforms that rearranged the city's electoral and governmental structure in 1909 may have decisively weakened them.[6] In a survey of Boston politics in 1960, only one barely functioning ward organization, run by a black politician in Roxbury, had enough life in it to attract attention.[7] A multitude of politicians all running for office on their own is unquestionably the city's norm.[8]

Boston's twentieth-century mayoralty has had a place in electoral politics that recalls some of the South's governorships. Its two four-term occupants, James Michael Curley on and off between 1913 and 1949, and Kevin H. White from 1967 through 1983, put together impressive personal apparatuses made up of "personal followings" (especially in Curley's case), people in patronage jobs (both cases), and

---

frey Blodgett, "Yankee Leadership in a Divided City: Boston, 1860-1910," *Journal of Urban History* 8(1982), 371-396; John T. Galvin, "The Dark Ages of Boston City Politics," *Proceedings of the Massachusetts Historical Society* 89(1977), 88-111; Robert A. Silverman, "Nathan Matthews: Politics of Reform in Boston, 1890-1910," *New England Quarterly* 50(1977), 626-643; Geoffrey T. Blodgett, "Josiah Quincy, Brahmin Democrat," *New England Quarterly* 38(1965), 435-453; Center, "Reform's Labours Lost," pp. 189-201.

[6] A 1929 report: "Party machines, in the ordinary sense of the word, have broken down in Boston, except in three wards [of a total of 22] which are controlled by strong ward leaders" (Joseph P. Harris, *Registration of Voters in the United States* [Washington, D.C.: Brookings, 1929], p. 274). On the 1930s see Charles H. Trout, *Boston, the Great Depression, and the New Deal* (New York: Oxford University Press, 1977), pp. 41-42, 114, 275-279, 283. Trout's account strongly suggests that no leaders or organizations were slating candidates authoritatively in city council elections in the 1930s. A report in the 1940s: "The Boston ward leaders, on the whole, are of negligible importance in present-day politics. The Democratic City Committee, which they comprise, is equally impotent." Charles W. Van Devander, *The Big Bosses* (New York: Howell, Soskin, 1944), p. 123, and more generally ch. 5 ("Bay State, Streamlined"). On the 1909 reforms see Edward C. Banfield and Martha Derthick (eds.), *A Report on the Politics of Boston* (Cambridge: Joint Center for Urban Studies, M.I.T./Harvard, 1960), pp. ii:1-3 (adapted from a paper by Sam Speck).

[7] Ralph Otwell, "The Negro in Boston," in Banfield and Derthick, *Report on Boston*, pp. vi:56-57, 66, 73-79, 91.

[8] See Banfield and Derthick, *Report on Boston*, pp. ii:13-29 (adapted from a paper by Sam Speck). On nonpartisan city council elections: "Issues are not important in Council campaigns, and there is of course no party machine to help the candidate. He must, therefore, find some way to differentiate himself from the many other candidates. If he has a 'magic name' (like William Foley), the support of a city-wide pressure group (like ex-policeman McDonough), the attention of the press (like McDonough), or a long record of political activity (like ex-Acting Mayor Kerrigan), his name may mean something to the voters. Most candidates, however, do not have these advantages, and the ethnic ring of their names is especially important" (*ibid.*, p. ii:21). For an account of the mayoral election of 1959 see George Blackwood, "Boston Politics and Boston Politicians," ch. 1 in Murray B. Levin, *The Alienated Voter: Politics in Boston* (New York: Holt, Rinehart and Winston, 1960).

"policy professionals" (certainly in White's case). Both built electoral support through personal appeal, individual favors, and promise and production of general governmental programs.[9] Curley drew on "a gift for swaying masses of people into frenzied ecstasy or uncontrolled rage" to assault the ward bosses and the city's social and economic elite.[10] His character and image, the issues he raised, the corruption he generated around him, and his expensive programs (he is said to have "rivaled Caesar Augustus as a monumental builder, especially of projects which redounded to the benefit of lower-income voters") combined to bring about a striking class cleavage in city elections.[11] Kevin

[9] The authoritative source on White's mayoralty is Martha W. Weinberg, "Boston's Kevin White: A Mayor Who Survives," *Political Science Quarterly* 96(1981), 89-97. She writes of "three different subcultures of political participants" in the White administration: "policy professionals," " 'meal-ticket' seekers, who support White in return for salaried jobs and other material rewards," and " 'team-players,' who consider the game of Boston politics a way of life and who feel that they must be part of one organization or another to be able to play" (pp. 95-96). Sources on Curley: Joseph F. Dinneen, *The Purple Shamrock: The Hon. James Michael Curley of Boston* (New York: Norton, 1949); Francis Russell, "The Last of the Bosses," *American Heritage* 10(June 1959), 21-25, 85-91; Trout, *Boston, passim*; Martin J. Schiesl, *The Politics of Efficiency: Municipal Administration and Reform in America, 1800-1920* (Berkeley: University of California Press, 1977), pp. 158-160; Dennis Hale, "James Michael Curley: Leadership and the Uses of Legend," ch. 8 in Peter D. Bathory, *Leadership in America: Consensus, Corruption, and Charisma* (New York: Longman, 1978).

[10] Trout, *Boston*, quotation at p. 39. Edward C. Banfield and James Q. Wilson, in *City Politics* (Cambridge: Harvard University Press and M.I.T. Press, 1963), pp. 130 and 131 on Curley: "Few politicians have been able to create large, city-wide followings. James Michael Curley of Boston was one and Fiorello La Guardia of New York City was another. Both relied mainly on charm and charisma, the one basis for a personal attachment that extends beyond a small, relatively intimate circle." A follow-up point: "A politician who gets power by winning a city-wide following is almost certain to try to destroy an existing machine rather than to take control of it. This is what Curley and La Guardia did; and it is hard to imagine that any man who can win elections by the charm of his personality will see anything to be gained from the limiting business of maintaining an organization—limiting because the chief executive of an organization cannot be a *prima donna*. If he should succeed in maintaining the organization, there would always be a danger that someone would take it away from him and use it against him. So long as he relies upon his personal appeal to the voters, he runs no risk of that; the appeal is his and his alone."

[11] Trout, *Boston*, quotation at p. 40. Also on Curley's programmatic side: Russell, "Last of the Bosses," pp. 85-87. His first term: "By 1917 the administration had extended public transit systems, expanded hospital facilities, replaced slum sections with parks and playgrounds, and filled in swampy lowlands to provide beaches for lower-class groups" (Schiesl, *Politics of Efficiency*, p. 159). On the class cleavage in city elections see Jerome S. Bruner and Sheldon J. Korchin, "The Boss and the Vote: Case Study in City Politics," *Public Opinion Quarterly* 10(1946) 8-10. This is a study of Curley's last election as mayor in 1945. With voters divided into three socioeconomic brackets, Curley won 24% of the top stratum, 46% of the middle, 66% of the bottom.

White drifted during his sixteen years from "purposive" toward "material" incentives in sustaining his personal apparatus.[12] With one qualification, neither Curley nor White seems to have dealt with any slating organizations or to have shown more than a trace of interest in anybody's electoral fortunes but his own. The one exception was White's break with city tradition during his last term when he wheeled his personal organization rather furtively into Democratic state legislative primaries in 1980, where he assisted four candidates, all of whom lost, and into nonpartisan city council elections in 1981, where he helped a slate of seven candidates—the "Kevin Seven"—six of whom lost.[13]

Accounts of other Massachusetts cities report nothing approaching a traditional party organization. Cambridge (100,361) ran municipal elections in the 1960s that centered mostly on individual candidacies, though endorsees of a durable academic and professional group called the Cambridge Civic Association ordinarily won four out of nine council seats.[14] City politics in Lynn (90,294) hinged on individual candidacies from 1969 through 1979.[15] "Ad hoc personal followings" operated in New Bedford (101,777) in the mid-1970s: "There is no machine to centralize control over political resources and to be a focal point for bargaining with the ethnic community. As in most communities in Massachusetts, political organization of any kind is weak and quite fluid, even in partisan campaigns for the state legislature or Congress. Municipal elections are nonpartisan in fact as well as in form; there is no involvement by party organizations."[16]

[12] See Weinberg, "Boston's Kevin White," pp. 102-105; Kathryn Christensen, "Boston's Kevin White Is Talented, Impatient and Under Heavy Fire," *Wall Street Journal*, April 28, 1983, pp. 1, 23; Fox Butterfield, "Troubles of Boston's Mayor Are Tied to Political Machine," *New York Times*, December 26, 1982, pp. 1, 26.

[13] On Curley attending to just his own career see Trout, *Boston*, p. 280. He did once support a mayoral candidate (to succeed himself) who lost. See p. 144. Kevin White built a "tight, personal organization." "Historically, political loyalty has not been transferable from one person to another in Boston" (Weinberg, "Boston's Kevin White," pp. 97, 101). On White's ventures in 1980 and 1981 see *Boston Globe*, September 23, 1981, p. 22; November 4, 1981, pp. 22, 23. The candidate of the "Kevin Seven" who did win was a member of a well-known political family.

[14] See for example "6 Councilors, 3 Others Win In Cambridge," *Boston Globe*, November 9, 1969, p. 5: "For the first time since the early 1950s, a majority of candidates supported by the Cambridge Civic Association, a 'better government' organization, were elected to the council."

[15] Harvey Boulay, *The Twilight Cities: Political Conflict, Development, and Decay in Five Communities* (Port Washington, N.Y.: Associated Faculty Press, 1983), pp. 57-59, 65-66, 77-79.

[16] Arnold M. Howitt and Rita Moniz, "Ethnic Identity, Political Organization, and Political Structure," paper presented at the 1976 convention of the American Political Science Association, p. 13, and more generally pp. 13-16, 28. (Also available in Rita

A detailed 1960 report on Worcester (176,572), another Catholic industrial city, turned up a good-government group, the Citizens' Plan E Association, which made endorsements in the city council elections, but said nonetheless that "ethnicity, personality, and issue orientation provide the foundation for political appeal in Worcester. The requirement that municipal elections be non-partisan, the reluctance of the parties to participate informally in local affairs, and the weakness of party organization place the burden of political success upon the individual politician."[17] On ward organizations: "There are no ward machines in Worcester."[18] On the city's Democratic party: "The general state of the local party is one of weakness bordering on anarchy. The only time the party looks strong is when election returns are tabulated."[19] On state legislators: "Representatives to the state legislature are elected by wards, but they have not built strong ward organizations and cannot deliver votes to a candidate for the city council. There are no precinct or block captains and few party workers for a general campaign."[20]

The New Bedford and Worcester studies both describe local politicians resourcefully tending a working-class electoral base in environments evidently lacking both party structure and a supply of ad hoc governmental goods and favors. New Bedford's George Rogers created a "political and social club," Rogers Associates, whose thousand or so members did electoral chores on his behalf and got together to celebrate New Year's Eve and his birthday.[21] Worcester councillor George Wells, a practitioner of "crusading negativism" against downtown parking plans, an expressway, and fluoridation, built an organization called The George A. Wells Association, Incorporated, whose 680 or so members helped him in elections, staged an annual outing and country fair, celebrated St. Patrick's Day and Bastille Day, and according to Wells were "capable of producing 20,000 votes or signatures 'on any

Moniz, "The Portuguese of New Bedford, Massachusetts and Providence, Rhode Island: A Comparative Micro-Analysis of Political Attitudes and Behavior" [Ph.D. dissertation, Brown University, 1979], pp. 241-251). On New Bedford see also Elmer E. Cornwell, Jr., "Ethnic Group Representation: The Case of the Portuguese," *Polity* 13(1980), 5-20.

[17] The general reference on Worcester is Robert H. Binstock, *A Report on Politics in Worcester, Massachusetts* (Cambridge: Joint Center for Urban Studies, M.I.T./Harvard, 1960), pp. I:21; II:11-54; III:1-6; IV:2, quotation at p. II:39. On the CEA: pp. II:39-50. The flavor more recently: Terri Minsky, "Worcester mayor gets attention in a largely ceremonial post," *Boston Globe*, April 1, 1983, p. 2.

[18] Binstock, *Report on Worcester*, p. I:21.

[19] *Ibid.*, p. II:20, and more generally pp. II:18-21.

[20] *Ibid.*, p. II:21.

[21] Howitt and Moniz, "Ethnic Identity," pp. 14, 28.

issue at any moment.' "[22] Neither association branched out beyond its founder; the Rogers club worked only for Rogers and the Wells club only for Wells.

The abrupt organizational discontinuity of Massachusetts in comparison with its southern neighbors has attracted attention. Two recent dissertations build on it: a work by Judith A. Center on Connecticut's organization and Massachusetts's lack of it, and a study by Rita Moniz of ethnic politics in Providence's machine setting versus New Bedford's environment of candidate-centered elections and strict civil service rules.[23] Elmer E. Cornwell, Jr., concludes, "The party tradition in Rhode Island, and in its capital city in particular, has been one of strong, active organizations that have tended to dominate the electoral process. . . . In the Bay State [Massachusetts], by contrast, parties have long been weak and relatively ineffectual."[24] An overall TPO score for Massachusetts: 1.

NEW HAMPSHIRE (737,681)

If any important traditional organizations operated in New Hampshire, no doubt somebody would have written about them by now, given the volume of background material the national media have to supply every four years in tracking the state's presidential primaries. Manchester (87,754), the state's largest city, white, working-class, Democratic, and mostly French-Canadian, is made to order for stories about machines, bosses, and delivery wards if any existed there. But they have not. A good 1961 report tells of candidates running for office on their own, unencumbered by slating practices.[25] Neither local nor state party organizations figure in accounts of New Hampshire's primaries for

---

[22] Binstock, *Report on Worcester*, pp. II:22-26, quotation at p. II:22.

[23] Center, "Reform's Labours Lost," chs. 2, 3; Moniz, "The Portuguese," pp. 236-251.

[24] Cornwell, "Ethnic Group Representation," p. 8.

[25] Robert H. Binstock, *A Report on Politics in Manchester, New Hampshire* (Cambridge: Joint Center for Urban Studies, M.I.T./Harvard, 1961), pp. II:16-17, 29-38.

Senator and governor, in which candidates build their own campaign networks and personal followings and worry about the one organization that often does carry electoral weight—the late William Loeb's strident newspaper, the *Manchester Union Leader*.[26] TPO score for New Hampshire: 1.

MAINE (993,663) ———————————————————————

The few, mostly dated works on Maine's electoral politics reveal nothing that points persuasively to traditional party organization. A 1950 dissertation reports lower-level party organizations conferring some order in nominations for the state legislature, but does not supply evidence of hierarchical relations or material incentive structures.[27] Incumbent-free Republican congressional primaries, back before Democrats in the state had any chance, were "free-for-alls. Any politician of

[26] Some accounts of statewide nominating: Duane Lockard, *New England State Politics* (Princeton: Princeton University Press, 1959), ch. 3; Robert B. Dishman and Joseph P. Ford, "New Hampshire: Republican Schisms, Democratic Gains," ch. 6 in George Goodwin, Jr., and Victoria Schuck (eds.), *Party Politics in the New England States* (Durham, N.H.: New England Center For Continuing Education, 1968); Richard F. Winters, "New Hampshire," ch. 12 in Alan Rosenthal and Maureen Moakley (eds.), *The Political Life of the American States* (New York: Praeger, 1984), pp. 281-283; Robert E. Craig and Richard F. Winters, "Party Politics in New Hampshire," in Josephine F. Milburn and William Doyle (eds.), *New England Political Parties* (Cambridge, Mass.: Schenkman, 1983), pp. 146-153; Eric P. Veblen, *The* Manchester Union Leader *in New Hampshire Elections* (Hanover, N.H.: University Press of New England, 1975), ch. 2. A concern in much of the scholarship of recent decades is whether New Hampshire's Republican politicians have arrayed themselves in two persisting and competing statewide "factions." On the evidence they have not, though whether they have or not is irrelevant here. A good 1975 assessment of the New Hampshire parties at the statewide level: "Neither the Democrats nor the Republicans have powerful, cohesive party organizations. There is no strong party 'machine' able to discipline dissident members. Fragmentation among party leaders, not unity, is the common state of affairs. From time to time certain individuals are able to build strong personal organizations within a party. The most prominent example in recent decades was the late Senator Styles Bridges, several of whose protégés achieved political prominence in their own right (for example, former Governor [Wesley] Powell and Congressman [Louis] Wyman). But cohesive personal organizations like Bridges' have been rare and are obviously not the same thing as official party organizations. In both the Democratic and Republican parties, the institution of the primary election has worked against party unity. Candidates are able to succeed by appealing directly to the voters rather than by placing top priority on cooperation with party leaders" (Veblen, p. 18). On the *Union Leader*'s influence: Veblen, *passim*.

[27] Philip S. Wilder, Jr., "Maine Politics" (Ph.D. dissertation, Harvard University, 1950), pp. 179-199. Another source of the 1950s: "Discussions with many Maine politicians have brought evidence of the strength of many local organizations, even though they are not necessarily 'bossed' in the sense that only one man handles the helm" (Lockard, *New England State Politics*, pp. 92-93).

the district is free to seek the nomination, and a large proportion of them do."[28] Republican primaries for governor were "waged primarily on a personal basis. It is virtually unknown for one candidate to cooperate openly with anyone running for another office, and it is basically every man for himself."[29] "Friends and neighbors" voting patterns appeared (that is, candidates in primaries ran much better in their home areas than elsewhere).[30]

At the local level, brief discussions of politics in Portland (65,116) and Brunswick (10,867) in the 1960s contain nothing about party organizations. (See map under New Hampshire.) A group of "new liberals" is said to have exercised influence late in the decade in Portland, and disagreement between a "business-academic group" favoring a council-manager plan and the Citizens for Representative Government, loyal to town meetings, disrupted Brunswick.[31] The interesting area is Androscoggin County (91,279), site of Lewiston (41,779) a Democratic, French-Canadian industrial city similar to Manchester. One writer says of Androscoggin in the 1970s that "a classic political machine controls the political process in a way that Mayor Daley would recognize favorably."[32] Another says of Lewiston's veteran state assemblyman Louis Jalbert: "Many see him as the rough-tough political boss whose heavy-handed authority allows him to handpick candidates and government appointees."[33]

But no account of actual behavior bears any of this out.[34] A close study of a Maine Democrat's 1956 congressional compaign says nothing about any local organization activity in a hard-fought primary in which most of the votes were cast in Lewiston.[35] The city's Georgette Berube won a state assembly seat around 1970 by running "a family campaign" entirely independent of party.[36] Detailed press reports on

---

[28] Wilder, "Maine Politics," p. 257, and more generally pp. 253-260.

[29] *Ibid.*, p. 233, and more generally pp. 222-238.

[30] Lockard, *New England State Politics*, pp. 89-91.

[31] On Portland: John Lovell, "Rebirth of a City," *Down East* 25(February 1979), 57-66. On Brunswick: Lincoln Smith, "Another Charter Contest in Brunswick," *Social Science* 44(1969), 225-231.

[32] Louis Maisel, "Party Reform and Political Participation: The Democrats in Maine," ch. 6 in Louis Maisel and Paul M. Sacks (eds.), *The Future of Political Parties* (Beverly Hills, Calif.: Sage Publications, 1975), p. 195.

[33] Gloria Hutchinson, "New Vitality for Lewiston," *Down East* 27(February 1981), 66.

[34] Although Lewiston may have supported a machine in the 1930s. See *ibid.*, p. 70.

[35] John C. Donovan, *Congressional Campaign: Maine Elects a Democrat* (New York: McGraw-Hill, Eagleton Case #16, 1960), pp. 7-14.

[36] Hutchinson, "New Vitality for Lewiston," pp. 69-70.

Lewiston and Androscoggin County elections in 1969 and 1970 do not mention machines, bosses, organizations, or slating activity, dwelling instead on maneuvers by individual candidates. An item on the city's nonpartisan elections: "Some hard-hitting campaigning has been going on for a few weeks in Ward Five where veteran politician Frank J. Bussiere is trying to unseat Alderman George F. Richer."[37] On Democratic primaries for county office: "There are three Democrats who are going at each other for the six year term as Androscoggin County Commissioner. The outgoing member of the board, Chairman Lucien R. Fournier, decided to call it quits this year and some folks are surprised there aren't more candidates for the spot."[38] A Democratic primary for six at-large seats in the state legislature attracted eleven candidates: "The House race in Lewiston has always been an interesting one but this year the entry into the contest of some pros who haven't been heard from for some time and some fresh new candidates have made it even more challenging for politician and voter alike."[39] The *Portland Press Herald* has covered primaries around the state for Maine's assembly and senate by discussing the fortunes of individual candidates.[40] TPO score for Maine: 1.

VERMONT (444,330)

Party organization, traditional or otherwise, seems unimportant in Vermont. Parties at the state level are loose collections of politicians who share the same label.[41] Press coverage of state legislative primaries has documented wins and losses of individual candidates.[42] A former state senator's account of winning a 1972 nomination in rural Windsor County reveals a civil, low-temperature, individualistic politics in a race where three Republican senate nominations were available and seven candidates (including one incumbent) went after them.[43] (See map under New Hampshire.) TPO score for Vermont: 1.

[37] *Lewiston-Auburn Evening Journal*, November 22, 1969, p. 1. Other coverage: October 1, p. 1; November 8, pp. 1, 6.

[38] *Ibid.*, June 9, 1970, p. 1.

[39] *Ibid.*, June 11, 1970, p. 1.

[40] See, e.g., the issue of June 16, 1970, p. 11.

[41] The best source is Frank M. Bryan, *Yankee Politics in Rural Vermont* (Hanover, N.H.: University Press of New England, 1974), ch. 3 ("Party Politics in a Rural Setting").

[42] See for example *Burlington Free Press*, September 9, 1970, p. 17.

[43] Frank Smallwood, *Free and Independent* (Brattleboro, Vt.: Stephen Greene, 1976), chs. 1-4.

MICHIGAN (8,875,083)

Traditional party organizations make no appearance in the considerable literature on Michigan of the 1950s and 1960s, an absence attributable to, among other things, a meager patronage supply.[44] The state's elite party processes of the period involved a great deal of important maneuvering, since conventions at the congressional district level chose delegates to state conventions, which in turn chose party leaders and national convention delegates and nominated candidates for all statewide offices except Senator and governor. But industrial organizations (ordinarily allied with issue-oriented activists) were the most important organized entities doing this maneuvering. Representatives of the major automotive companies used to operate directly in Republican processes, Ford and General Motors, for example, fueling a 1955 showdown over the state chairmanship.[45] The CIO, dominated by the United Auto Workers and working through COPE (Committee on Political Education, the CIO's instrument for political activity), moved into Democratic processes in the late 1940s, where it encountered opposition chiefly from the Teamsters union. The UAW under one label or another exercised a great deal of influence in conventions of the 1950s and 1960s.[46] Labor organiza-

[44] On patronage in the state in general: J. David Greenstone, *Labor in American Politics* (New York: Vintage, 1969), pp. 114-115; Stephen B. Sarasohn and Vera H. Sarasohn, *Political Party Patterns in Michigan* (Detroit: Wayne State University Press, 1957), p. 26. On patronage in Wayne County and Detroit: "With the exception of a relatively few judicial appointees and the highest level of the county bureaucracy, such as the deputy county clerk, there is no patronage in either city or county government." "There is not enough patronage even to begin to build a precinct organization for elections." "There is no patronage-based political machine among Detroit Negroes." David Greenstone, *A Report on the Politics of Detroit* (Cambridge: Joint Center for Urban Studies, M.I.T./Harvard, 1961), quotations at pp. II:28, v:26.

[45] Sarasohn and Sarasohn, *Political Patterns in Michigan*, pp. 41-43, and in general on the Republicans up through 1956, pp. 26-45.

[46] *Ibid.*, pp. 45-68; Dudley W. Buffa, *Union Power and American Democracy: The*

tions have also endorsed and mobilized in Michigan's primaries for Senator and governor, arenas where candidate organizations are hard to defeat. In the 1966 Democratic Senate primary, for example, the UAW and "virtually all of the county and Congressional District party organizations" (well stocked with union workers) went all-out in support of popular former governor G. Mennen "Soapy" Williams in a 3-to-2 victory over the mayor of Detroit; but in 1976 Congressman James G. O'Hara, running with union support, finished third with 23.2 percent, losing to Congressman Donald W. Riegle, Jr., who staged an "intensive television campaign" dwelling on the alleged shady practices of the candidate who ran second.[47] Nominating for the Michigan state legislature seems to hinge ordinarily on individual candidacies; unions were a fairly important influence in the Democratic party in the 1950s and 1960s but official party organizations for the most part were not involved.[48]

Detroit (1,512,893) has evidently never been run by a machine, and both the city and its parent unit, Wayne County (2,669,604), have conducted politics at least in recent times without traditional organizations. A once powerful good-government association, the Detroit Citi-

---

UAW and the Democratic Party, 1935-72 (Ann Arbor: University of Michigan Press, 1984), chs. 1-3, 10, 11. On the Teamsters: Buffa, pp. 16-19, 30-34, 113-114.

[47] *Congressional Quarterly Weekly*, July 22, 1966, p. 1598; August 5, 1966, p. 1706; July 24, 1976, p. 2008; August 7, 1976, p. 2155. A 1984 reading: "The state's politics has gradually evolved into a strange admixture of relatively important political parties and individualistic candidates seeking to mount a strong personal appeal to an increasingly independent electorate" (Peter Kobrak, "Michigan," ch. 5 in Rosenthal and Moakley [eds.], *The Political Life of the American States*, p. 108).

[48] A 1957 statement referring to company- and union-centered alliances operating in convention processes in the 1950s: "It should be made clear at the outset that factions seeking power in Michigan parties have rarely attempted to influence nominations to the United States House of Representatives, to county offices, or to the state legislature. Congressmen have usually been divorced from state party matters. County officials and legislators in areas outside Wayne County are chosen largely on personality and for local reasons, with incumbents favored" (Sarasohn and Sarasohn, *Political Patterns in Michigan*, p. 4). A work based on a sample of Michigan state senators and representatives serving in 1971-1972 gives an individualistic flavor: "The vast majority of the Michigan legislators who were interviewed perceived themselves as self-starters—at least in their initial candidacy." "Of thirty-eight legislators consulted, only five were actively recruited by their party. Three were Republicans and two were Democrats." "Once the candidates make their decision to seek elective office, the majority of these individuals received little, if any, assistance from their political parties—neither in the primary elections nor in the general election." "The organization of the legislators is largely an independent and personal one." Gerald H. Stollman, *Michigan: State Legislators and Their Work* (Washington, D.C.: University Press of America, 1978), pp. 2-3, 42-46, quotations at pp. 42, 54, 43, 44.

zens' League, was still endorsing candidates in the city's nonpartisan elections in the 1950s but evidently had withdrawn by the early 1970s.[49] The organization most influential in Democratic primaries and city elections in the 1950s and 1960s was COPE, as noted, for example in this 1961 report: "In Detroit and Wayne County, the Wayne County AFL-CIO Council and its Committee on Political Education function as a political party. No labor party appears on the ballot, but the Council drafts a platform, endorses candidates and, in COPE, has the strongest precinct organization in the county."[50] Union members, motivated by issue concerns and by wages paid by the UAW for party work, supplied the principal organizational substance of the official Democratic party; Wayne County's Democratic organization by itself has not amounted to much.[51] A detailed 1956 study of the party concluded: "The frustration of the top-echelon leaders is itself eloquent

[49] Older works on Detroit politics which have to be read carefully: George B. Catlin, *The Story of Detroit* (Detroit: Detroit News, 1923), beginning at ch. 97; William P. Lovett, *Detroit Rules Itself* (Boston: Gorham, 1930). Good recent analyses of earlier times: Melvin G. Holli, *Reform in Detroit: Hazen S. Pingree and Urban Politics* (New York: Oxford University Press, 1969); Raymond R. Fragnoli, *The Transformation of Reform: Progressivism in Detroit—and After, 1912-1933* (New York: Garland, 1982); Sidney Fine, *Frank Murphy: The Detroit Years* (Ann Arbor: University of Michigan Press, 1975). An appraisal in the 1940s: "There is no 'machine' through which Detroit's politicians must be processed. For the most part, candidates are self-starters, with a neighborhood club and parochial praise feeding their ambition. They qualify because their name is Murphy, or Castator, or Oakman, or Webster, or Jeffries, or because they won popularity in baseball or football" (See Leo Donovan, "Detroit: City of Conflict," pp. 148-167 in Robert S. Allen [ed.], *Our Fair City* [New York: Vanguard, 1947], p. 165). On the Citizens' League see Fragnoli, *passim*; Greenstone, *Report on Detroit*, pp. v:56-58; Saadia R. Greenberg and Ronald Matheny, "The Effects of Endorsements in Non-Partisan Systems: A Study of Primary and General Elections in Two Michigan Cities," paper presented at the 1974 convention of the American Political Science Association, pp. 5-19.

[50] Greenstone, *Report on Detroit*, p. II:39.

[51] General reports on union and party: Greenstone, *Report on Detroit*, pp. II:36-47; Greenstone, *Labor in American Politics*, ch. 4. "The United Automobile Workers, who control the district Democratic organization" is the characterization given relations between union and party in 1970 in Detroit's East Side, the core of the city's black community (see Stanley B. Greenberg, *Politics and Poverty: Modernization and Response in Five Neighborhoods* [New York: Wiley, 1974], p. 57, and more generally pp. 53-59). For an excellent statement on the incentive structure of Wayne County's union-based Democratic party see James Q. Wilson, *Political Organizations* (New York: Basic Books, 1973), pp. 137-138. On union and party in the county's several congressional districts of the 1960s see Buffa, *Union Power*, pp. 148-153, 163-171, 174-178. Organized nonunion liberals supplied an important counter to labor in the predominantly white-collar 17th district.

testimony. To a man they decried the tenuousness of their control, the absence of sanctions, the absence of patronage, the virtually impossible task of maintaining harmony, their own recognized expendability."[52] COPE, however, for all its resources and lack of organizational rivals failed even in its peak years to exercise influence in city and county electoral processes as effectively as a well-grounded traditional party organization. Especially in Detroit's municipal elections, candidates have ordinarily put together campaigns and won and held office on their own. The name Murphy used to help a great deal, and no one could beat a former Tigers shortstop in council elections in the 1950s.[53] In the county's state legislative primaries, labor at top strength had a mixed record, ranging from a set of conspicuous defeats in 1960 (eight COPE endorsees took on incumbent Democratic assembly members and lost) to a conspicuous 2-to-1 UAW victory that purged the party's senate leader in 1970.[54]

Suburban Oakland County (907,871, predominantly Republican) and Macomb County (625,309, predominantly Democratic) supported Democratic parties in the 1960s that were made up, like Wayne County's, principally of labor organizations, individual politicians with followings, and in the Oakland case liberal activists.[55] At Michigan's municipal level, reports on seven cities other than Detroit (all but one formally nonpartisan) produce no evidence of traditional party organization in recent decades. A business and professional group called "the caucus" authoritatively slated candidates from 1955 through 1971 in Kalamazoo (85,555).[56] A similar group slated in the 1950s

[52] The statement refers to both Wayne County parties, Republican minority as well as Democratic majority. The source: Samuel J. Eldersveld, *Political Parties: A Behavioral Analysis* (Chicago: Rand McNally, 1964), p. 527. For an elaboration see especially ch. 13 ("The Party as a Task Group"). Only a few sentences of this 544-page work on Wayne County parties say anything about candidate selection, a revealing indication of its unimportance as an organization activity. Eldersveld uses the word "stratarchy"—something well short of hierarchy—to characterize the internal relations of the county's parties.

[53] Limits on COPE influence: Greenstone, *Labor in American Politics*, pp. 120-128. On candidates running and winning on their own: Greenstone, *Report on Detroit*, pp. II:1-7, 12-20. On the considerable value of surnames in elections: Maurice M. Ramsey, *Name Candidates in Detroit Elections* (Detroit: Detroit Bureau of Governmental Research, Report No. 158, 1941). On Detroit municipal elections in general from the late 1930s through the 1960s: Buffa, *Union Power*, chs. 6, 7.

[54] Greenstone, *Labor in American Politics*, pp. 125-126; Buffa, *Union Power*, pp. 123-126.

[55] Buffa, *Union Power*, ch. 9 (Oakland) and pp. 178-193 (Macomb).

[56] William P. Hojnacki, "Kalamazoo, Michigan and South Bend, Indiana: A Compar-

without such complete success in Jackson (45,484).[57] A powerful city employees union dominated council elections in the 1950s in Bay City (49,449).[58] Muskegon (44,631) of the 1950s "had no formal or continuous informal group performing an effective job of recruitment, endorsement, or promotion of city candidates."[59] Nor, according to a report on public endorsements, did Grand Rapids (197,649) from 1950 through 1973. In Flint (193,317), the UAW seems to have been the chief organized influence in electoral politics as of about 1950.[60] Formally partisan Ann Arbor (99,797) supported three parties in the early 1970s, Democratic, Republican, and Human Rights. Workers and candidates of all three are said to have been animated by issues as well as by a sense of sport: "The games are played every spring when local elections are held with great enthusiasm and expenditure of energy. In Ann Arbor, politics is an exhausting sport played by amateurs who, in the words of one council member, 'beat their heads against each other and burn themselves out.' "[61] TPO score for Michigan: 1.

---

ative Analysis of Policy Outcomes" (Ph.D. dissertation, University of Notre Dame, 1977), pp. 65-70, 84. On Kalamazoo parties: "The structure of both parties is weak. Party organization is decentralized, and many people are able to share what little power is available. The absence of patronage and other institutional forms of control means that party leadership positions are largely honorary" (p. 67). On Kalamazoo in the 1950s see also Oliver P. Williams and Charles R. Adrian, *Four Cities: A Study in Comparative Policy Making* (Philadelphia: University of Pennsylvania Press, 1963), pp. 58-65. The authors call their four cities Alpha, Beta, Gamma, and Delta, but their code is breakable and Alpha turns out to be Kalamazoo.

[57] Williams and Adrian, *Four Cities*, pp. 69-73. Jackson is Beta.

[58] *Ibid.*, pp. 73-76. Bay City is Delta.

[59] *Ibid.*, pp. 69-73, quotation at p. 72. Gamma is evidently Muskegon, though this is the one decoding of the four that is not certain.

[60] On Grand Rapids: Greenberg and Matheny, "Effects of Endorsements," pp. 20-27. In Grand Rapids's parent unit, Kent County (411,044), the Democratic party chairman in 1975 was a former supporter of Eugene J. McCarthy and the Republican chairman a political science professor. See David S. Broder, "New Political Wave Hits Grand Rapids," *Washington Post*, June 29, 1975, pp. A1, A8. On Flint: Ronald William Edsforth, "A Second Industrial Revolution: The Transformation of Class, Culture, and Society in Twentieth-Century Flint, Michigan" (Ph.D. dissertation, Michigan State University, 1982), pp. 228-231, 280. In 1948, "the U.A.W. strengthened its alliance with local Democrats by providing the Party with a precinct-by-precinct organization of campaign workers. In subsequent years, as this electoral 'machine' was perfected, the union won a permanent, powerful voice for its members in Flint politics" (p. 231).

[61] Jeffrey L. Davidson, *Political Partnerships: Neighborhood Residents and Their Council Members* (Beverly Hills, Calif.: Sage Publications, 1979), p. 44 and more generally ch. 2 ("The Ann Arbor Political System"). See also Agis Salpukas, "2 Radicals Elected to Ann Arbor Seats," *New York Times*, April 9, 1972, p. 37.

WISCONSIN (4,417, 933) ———————————————

As in Michigan, Wisconsin reveals negligible patronage and no sign of traditional organization.[62] Wisconsin party organizations that drew national attention two or three decades ago were sets of dues-paying volunteers, mostly urban, middle-class liberals in the Democratic party and conservatives in the Republican who took an interest in primarily state and national affairs.[63] Republicans at the state level, though not Democrats, have a custom (unrecognized by state law) of conferring convention endorsements for governor and Senator. The endorsees sometimes go on to win primaries, sometimes not. Notable setbacks occurred in 1956, when conservative party regulars tried to defeat incumbent Senator Alexander Wiley in a primary but lost, and in 1978 when a party endorsee for governor lost to Lee Sherman Dreyfus, a "surprisingly effective entertainer and orator" who invoked the La Follette tradition of progressivism and independence and won both primary and general elections.[64] Evidently neither party's dues-paying organizations have tried to bring much influence to bear in primaries for county and state legislative offices, for which candidacy seems largely an individual enterprise.[65]

Good reports on the state's five largest cities discuss self-propelled candidates and various organizations other than the patronage-based

[62] On lack of patronage in the state in general: Leon D. Epstein, *Politics in Wisconsin* (Madison: University of Wisconsin Press, 1958), pp. 29-30. In the city of Milwaukee: Bertil Hanson, *A Report on the Politics of Milwaukee* (Cambridge: Joint Center for Urban Studies, M.I.T./Harvard, 1961), pp. II:7-8, 14.

[63] See Frank J. Sorauf, "Extra-Legal Political Parties in Wisconsin," *American Political Science Review* 48(1954), 692-704; Epstein, *Politics in Wisconsin*, ch. 5; Hanson, *Report on Milwaukee*, pp. II:16-19. A report in the late 1960s: David Adamany, *Financing Politics: Recent Wisconsin Elections* (Madison: University of Wisconsin Press, 1969), pp. 24-25, 71.

[64] Epstein, *Politics in Wisconsin*, pp. 86, 92-96; *Congressional Quarterly Weekly*, August 26, 1978, p. 2270; September 16, 1978, p. 2473.

[65] Epstein, *Politics in Wisconsin*, pp. 31-32, 92-93, 138-144, 205.

sort operating in nonpartisan municipal elections in the 1960s. Democratic and Republican dues-paying units exercised some influence in Milwaukee (717,372), the earlier site of a considerable Socialist organization, but candidates seeking office on their own is the theme of an authoritative 1961 report: aldermanic campaigns, for example, were "largely based on personalities."[66] City elections in the 1950s and early 1960s in Madison (172,007), the state's capital and the center of the main branch of the state university, ordinarily produced contests between slates of candidates interested in issues and identifiable as Democratic and Republican partisans: "Issues have become highly charged with tension and conflict, sometimes for many years."[67] "Loosely defined liberal-Left coalitions" dominated both Madison and parent unit Dane County (290,272) in the mid-1970s.[68] In Kenosha (78,805) of the 1950s, "two quasi-party electoral organizations normally took a considerable part in local elections. One was the United Voters organization, made up mainly of Democrats and labor people; the other was known as the Independent Good Government committee, made up largely of Republicans and Chamber of Commerce people." These gave way to less structured election contests in the 1960s.[69] Working-class Racine (95,162) generated an instance of personal following in the 1960s that resembles ones in New Bedford and Worcester: "One prominent leader described his own following which he had been building for at least three years, and now included a list of 260 persons in all of the wards of the city who had actually worked in his campaign. According to him, 90 percent of the persons were not active for either party, but only on his behalf."[70] In Green Bay (87,809) of two decades

[66] Hanson, *Report on Milwaukee*, p. III:12. The conclusion of a passage on politicians powerful in the wards: "None of these men, however, derives his strength from control over patronage, law enforcement, or public contracts. They succeed because of personal characteristics (looks, speaking ability, ethnic background, and the like)" (p. II:24). Socialists held the Milwaukee mayoralty for thirty-eight years in the period from 1910 through 1960. On their organization in its peak years: "The Socialist Party, though it did not use patronage, did maintain an organization with help from idealistic volunteers and small contributors; it was able to conduct campaign rallies and distribute literature 'in 11 languages' " (p. II:12). The general reference on Milwaukee: Hanson, pp. II:11-25, III:5-14.

[67] Robert R. Alford and Harry M. Scoble, *Bureaucracy and Participation: Political Cultures in Four Wisconsin Cities* (Chicago: Rand McNally, 1969), pp. 108-109, quotation at p. 114.

[68] Philip G. Altbach and Dennis Carlson, "Militants in Politics," *Society* 13(July/August 1976), 54-57, quotation at p. 54.

[69] Alford and Scoble, *Bureaucracy and Participation*, pp. 68-71, quotation at p. 68.

[70] *Ibid.*, pp. 87-92, quotation at p. 88.

ago, one account said: "Not even quasi-party organizations exist, or if they have been tried, have not proven strong enough to elect a mayor or even an alderman, and have disappeared quickly."[71] TPO score for Wisconsin: 1.

MINNESOTA (3,805,069)

In one respect, at least, Minnesota resembles New Jersey. Primaries in Minnesota generate newspaper stories about party organizations. For example, state legislative primaries (then formally nonpartisan) in Hennepin County (960,080) in 1970 drew this report: "With one exception all candidates endorsed by either the Republican or DFL parties either won nomination or had fairly comfortable leads. In House races, two DFL-endorsed candidates—incumbent Dr. John Salchert and James Rice, former executive secretary to ex-Gov. Karl Rolvaag—won handily two of the four ballot spots in District 39 in the northwest corner of Minneapolis."[72] Minnesota law has not given standing to preprimary endorsements, but conventions of the Democratic-Farmer-Labor party (founded when Democrats merged with the Farmer-Labor party four decades ago) have regularly conferred them anyway for statewide, congressional, and state legislative

[71] *Ibid.*, pp. 47-48, quotation at p. 47. "As recently as World War II, organizations such as the Eagles and the American Legion played dominant roles in city election contests. While these organizations had declined since then, no other organizations had arisen to take their place. There was no party organization at the neighborhood, precinct, or ward level in Green Bay" (p. 48). Alford and Scoble give a summary on political parties in their four cities at pp. 128-133.

[72] *Minneapolis Tribune*, September 16, 1970, p. 14. A story of the same sort on the same page reports returns in neighboring Ramsey County, parent unit of St. Paul. See also *ibid.*, September 11, 1968, p. 13. Minnesota state legislators have been elected since 1974 on a conventional partisan ballot; before that they were elected for over a half a century on a nonpartisan ballot.

offices since the 1940s; less well reported Republican units have also endorsed at least much of the time.[73] As of the mid-1960s the DFL customarily sent out a preprimary "sample ballot" to every household in the state listing its endorsees.[74] Reports on St. Paul (309,828) and Minneapolis (434,400) in the late 1950s refer to DFL ward clubs and endorsing activity in nonpartisan mayor and council elections.[75]

Endorsements and ward clubs notwithstanding, the Minnesota DFL is far from a traditional party organization. Not supported by patronage, its units have depended to a large extent on liberal, middle-class members drawn into politics by the opportunity to discuss issues and pass resolutions, which makes for, by machine standards, weak Twin Cities precinct apparatuses that outsiders have sometimes found it easy to permeate or take over.[76] The party had a hard time exercising influ-

[73] On endorsements for statewide office: G. Theodore Mitau, *Politics in Minnesota* (Minneapolis: University of Minnesota Press, 1960), pp. 47-49; Robert Agranoff, "The Minnesota Democratic-Farmer-Labor Party Organization: A Study of the 'Character' of a Programmatic Party Organization" (Ph.D. dissertation, University of Pittsburgh, 1967), ch. 7; Frederick C. Klein, "Candidate Factory: Minnesota Produces Multitude of Runners for National Offices," *Wall Street Journal*, October 4, 1976, pp. 1, 17. For congressional office: Agranoff, p. 267. For state legislative office: Mitau, pp. 66-75; Agranoff, pp. 96, 256-259; David Lebedoff, *Ward Number Six* (New York: Scribner's, 1972), pp. 81-86, 106-114; Anne W. S. Walcott, "Accountability and Political Organization: A Comparative View of the Caucus-Convention and Primary Systems of Nomination and Endorsement" (Ph.D. dissertation, University of California at Santa Barbara, 1980). The dissertation builds on a contrast between the importance of Minnesota's DFL organizations and the unimportance of Wisconsin's Democratic organizations in recruiting candidates for the state legislature.

[74] Agranoff, "Democratic-Farmer-Labor Party Organization," pp. 340-341.

[75] Alan Altshuler, *A Report on Politics in St. Paul, Minnesota* (Cambridge: Joint Center for Urban Studies, M.I.T./Harvard, 1959), pp. II:5-8, 18-22; Alan Altshuler, *A Report on Politics in Minneapolis* (Cambridge: Joint Center for Urban Studies, M.I.T./Harvard, 1959), p. II:7-8, 10-12, 18-23. In the early 1970s municipal elections in Minneapolis, St. Paul, and Duluth switched from a nonpartisan to a partisan ballot.

[76] On lack of patronage in St. Paul: Altshuler, *Report on St. Paul*, p. II:2. In Minneapolis: Altshuler, *Report on Minneapolis*, p. II:2. For a good treatment of precinct caucuses as discussion groups, based on a study of units in both Minnesota parties around the state in 1972 and 1974, see Thomas R. Marshall, "Party Responsibility Revisited: A Case of Policy Discussion at the Grass Roots," *Western Political Quarterly* 32(1979), 70-78. Minneapolis DFL clubs of the 1950s are said to have been middle class and most were "essentially study groups" (Altshuler, *Report on Minneapolis*, p. II:8). Yet the St. Paul clubs were "distinctly working class in composition." They were "activist groups, not policy-making or discussion groups as in Minneapolis." "Having no material rewards to offer [in St. Paul], the DFL motivates its campaign workers in other ways. It concentrates on issues, 'blue-ribbon' candidates, and appeals to party loyalty. In general, it stands for New Deal 'liberalism.' For example, it favors increasing the state income tax rather than adding a new sales tax." Altshuler, *Report on St. Paul*, pp. II:7, 8. On Twin Cities precinct apparatuses: Altshuler, *Report on St. Paul*, p. II:8; Altshuler, *Report on Minneap-*

ence in Minneapolis's candidate-centered municipal politics of two or three decades ago, in which aldermen built personal followings, Scandinavian names carried weight, and a police detective won the mayoralty via a law-and-order appeal in 1969 and again in 1971 without either party's backing.[77] In addition, the DFL units in both Twin Cities had the problem of coexisting with unions, which were constituent elements of the party in one role but were also endorsing organizations in their own right at least as influential in city elections as the party.[78] Labor organizations probably had more electoral influence in St. Paul in the 1950s than in any other sizable American city—enough to elect a majority of the governing council.[79] In Minneapolis's parent unit, Hennepin County, the DFL broke into factions in the 1960s with "labor-oriented people" opposing the "university crowd" as the Vietnam War became the central issue in endorsements for offices as far down as the state legislature.[80]

---

olis, pp. II:7-8; Agranoff, "Democratic-Farmer-Labor Party Organization," pp. 87-88, 343-354; Lebedoff, *Ward Number Six*, chs. 1, 4.

[77] See Altshuler, *Report on Minneapolis*, pp. I:4, II:10-18; and a report first published in 1949: Robert L. Morlan, "The Unorganized Politics of Minneapolis," pp. 279-285 in Edward C. Banfield (ed.), *Urban Government: A Reader in Administration and Politics* (New York: Free Press, 1969). On the mayoralty of Charles Stenvig: Martin A. Levin, *Urban Politics and the Criminal Courts* (Chicago: University of Chicago Press, 1977), pp. 21, 46.

[78] On relations between the DFL and labor: Altshuler, *Report on Minneapolis*, pp. II:8-13; V:5-7; Altshuler, *Report on St. Paul*, pp. II:8-10; V:1-4; Agranoff, "Democratic-Farmer-Labor Party Organization," pp. 140-146. Elsewhere in the state: "In some areas where the party organization is weak and labor is strong, as in the case of certain iron range counties, labor *is* the DFL party organization. The local party organizations are almost completely controlled by the union people. Organizational finances often come directly from union treasuries. Party tasks are executed or ignored at their command" (Agranoff, pp. 140-141).

[79] Labor's place in the party: "If it were not for the cooperation of labor, the St. Paul DFL would probably be as weak as the Minneapolis DFL. Labor is heavily represented in the leadership of the party. In addition, a representative of the Labor Assembly attends DFL endorsing meetings at which candidates are questioned and discussed. The labor representative may veto a candidate who is unacceptable" (Altshuler, *Report on St. Paul*, p. II:8). On St. Paul politics in recent years: Richard J. Margolis, "Reaganomics Redux: A Municipal Report," *Working Papers*, May-June 1983, pp. 45-47.

[80] On the party split: Agranoff, "Democratic-Farmer-Labor Party Organization," pp. 150-151. As of 1967: "In the City of Minneapolis, there is present a dual organizational structure which reflects these factions. If one group controls the official ward caucus, the other tends to form a ward club which enables the losers to channel activities into some organization. About half of the wards in the city have this dual structure. For example, the first ward, which is heavily labor-Eastern European, has a 'red-neck' controlled caucus and a 'goo-goo' controlled ward club. The second ward, which contains the University of Minnesota, is controlled just as solidly by the 'goo-goos.' The minority labor and

Minnesota's other population center, St. Louis County (220,693), site of Duluth (100,578), had a record as a left-wing stronghold in the Farmer-Labor party in the 1930s and also briefly in the DFL after the Democrats and Farmer-Laborites merged: "By 1946, the Communists had . . . virtually taken over the Duluth-St. Louis County section of the party."[81] Duluth politics later in the 1960s featured "domination of the [two major] parties by issue-conscious persons, rather than by persons interested in politics as a business."[82] A DFL party of labor leaders, intellectuals, and small businessmen slated candidates for municipal, state legislative, and (according to one report) county offices, and evidently enjoyed considerable success. The opposition was a Republican slating apparatus said to be very conservative.[83] "In reality, the basic social cleavage in the community [Duluth in the 1960s] is carried directly over into politics. Each party is an adjunct of one of the two socio-economic coalitions that dominate the city and each commands the loyalty of the overwhelming majority of its voters on the basis of their class orientation."[84]

On balance the DFL seems to have endorsed more effectively for statewide, congressional, and state legislative offices, where its record is impressive, than in municipal races.[85] A newspaper story in 1976, for

party people in this ward have established a club" (p. 151). Lebedoff's *Ward Number Six* is an account of DFL nominating politics in Hennepin County at the time of Sen. Eugene McCarthy's antiwar campaign in 1968. On a McCarthy supporter seeking an endorsement of his candidacy for the state legislature: "When questioned about state issues on which every legislator could be expected to vote, he admitted knowing nothing whatsoever about them. He didn't have to. He was against the war and so he didn't have to talk about this local stuff. That's just what he intended to say as he went about waging his campaign." Lebedoff's characterization of the DFL's endorsees for state legislature in his home district: an "angry adolescent" and a "smiling defrocked priest" (pp. 85, 86, and more generally pp. 81-86, 106-118).

[81] Daniel J. Elazar, "Constitutional Change in a Long-Depressed Community: A Case Study of Duluth, Minnesota," ch. 10 in William L. Hathaway (ed.), *Minnesota Political Parties and Politics: Essays and Readings* (University of Minnesota, 1976), p. 176. (Study originally published in 1965.) See also Millard L. Gieske, *Minnesota Farmer-Laborism: The Third-Party Alternative* (Minneapolis: University of Minnesota Press, 1979), pp. 159, 215, 249-250, 265, 286; John E. Haynes, "Communists and Anti-Communists in the Northern Minnesota CIO, 1936-1949," *Upper Midwest History* 1(1981), 55-73.

[82] Elazar, "Constitutional Change," p. 175.

[83] *Ibid.*, pp. 169-177. On county offices, also formally nonpartisan: Agranoff, "Democratic-Farmer-Labor Party Organization," p. 97.

[84] Elazar, "Constitutional Change," p. 177.

[85] See, e.g., the assessment in Agranoff, "Democratic-Farmer-Labor Party Organization," pp. 266-276.

example, on state legislative endorsing by the DFL and also by the state's Republican party (now called Independent Republicans), reported striking accomplishments: "Earlier this month, all 150 persons backed by the DFL for state legislative posts won in the primary, as did all but two of 160 IR-backed candidates."[86] More recently, the DFL suffered alarming defeats in a primary for Senator in 1978 and one for governor in 1982,[87] and no doubt it misses now a vital resource it drew on from the origins of the party in the mid-1940s until 1978—Hubert Humphrey's leadership skills. But in the context of the fifty states the DFL record of the last three decades is unique. Minority parties aside (such as the Republicans in the South a generation ago), no other state-wide party without a local base in traditional organization or the assistance of endorsing powers conferred by law has managed to endorse for such a range of offices with such regularity and authority. The appropriate TPO score for Minnesota: 1.

IOWA (2,825,041)

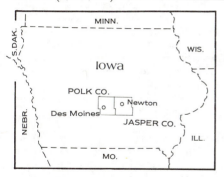

A New York politician from Nassau County who was helping George Bush's 1980 Presidential campaign in Iowa found an unfamiliar politics: " 'In Iowa I have never heard of the 1 percent,' Mr. [Rich] Bond said at the Bush headquarters in Des Moines. He spoke a term of political art, familiar back in Nassau, referring to the 1 percent of patronage workers' salaries that is taken as tribute to the party coffers. Accordingly, the visiting political technician from New York is grateful for undemanding Iowa veterans like Barbara Creagan, a recent Republican chairman here in Jasper County [35,425], who has worked hard for the Bush campaign since August. . . . She laughs at the idea of patronage ever serving as a motive for her kind of effort. 'In Iowa, it's people persuading people—that's what pol-

---

[86] Klein, "Candidate Factory," p. 17.

[87] In 1978 Congressman Donald M. Fraser, the DFL endorsee, lost to "millionaire businessman" Robert Short. See E. Lester Levine, "Is Minnesota a Two-Party State Again?" *Publius* 9, no. 1(1979), 197-204. In 1982 Warren Spannaus lost to Rudy Perpich. See *Congressional Quarterly Weekly*, September 18, 1982, p. 2323.

itics really is,' she explained to a doubting outsider at her home in this blue-collar, predominantly Democratic factory community [Newton, population 15,619]."[88]

The Creagan account rings true. Studies from the 1960s tell of widespread recruiting activity by the Iowa parties' county leaders, often efforts to "fill the ticket" by finding "capable candidates" to run for long lists of offices. But neither party had a tradition of making preprimary endorsements, and party leadership posts themselves were uninviting, high-turnover assignments short on resources needed to assert control over largely inert precinct workers.[89] The Farm Bureau, rather than any network of party organizations, is said to have ranked first in organization influence in Iowa's state legislative primaries of the 1940s and 1950s; the Bureau's grassroots units in all ninety-nine counties added up to something like a party.[90] Polk County (286,101), site of the state's metropolis, Des Moines (201,404), generated a fresh Demo-

[88] Francis X. Clines, "Iowa's Caucus Organizers Stress Persuasion Instead of Patronage," *New York Times*, January 12, 1980, p. 9.

[89] The sources are Harlan Hahn, *Urban-Rural Conflict: The Politics of Change* (Beverly Hills, Calif.: Sage Publications, 1971), pp. 179-193—a brief discussion of unpublished work by others on Iowa county leaders; and Robert J. Kulisheck, "Political Activism at the Grassroots: A Study of County Party Organizations in Iowa" (Ph.D. dissertation, University of Iowa, 1972), especially chs. 2, 3, 6—a work based partly on interviews with party leaders in five eastern Iowa counties in the late 1960s. On recruiting but not endorsing: Hahn, pp. 187-189; Kulisheck, ch. 6. On leaders' lack of resources: Kulisheck, pp. 55-56. On precinct workers: Kulisheck, pp. 47-48, 55. On turnover in and perceived value of party leadership positions: Hahn, pp. 180-184; Kulisheck, pp. 52, 55. "Party officeholders frequently are chosen by the officials who preceded them. In 1963, 68.6 percent of the Republican and 51.9 percent of the Democratic county chairmen and vice-chairmen were recruited by the previous party leaders. The prevalence of this system of co-option might suggest relatively rigid control of party activities by a self-perpetuating elite; but, perhaps more accurately, it reflects the willingness of party officials to accept new recruits and the relatively low prestige that normally is associated with partisan jobs. Since there usually are few potential candidates available for leadership roles, party officeholders must either draft their own replacements or remain in the position themselves" (Hahn, pp. 180-181). In a 1969 study of state legislative recruitment in Iowa, the parties' county leaders emerged as nudgers of consequence even though "party organization is generally not very highly developed in Iowa," and "the legislative recruitment function is by no means dominated by party leaders, and is, indeed, fairly widely diffused in the politically active subculture represented by the leadership groups analyzed here [legislators, lobbyists, 'attentive constituents,' and county party chairmen]." Samuel C. Patterson and G. R. Boynton, "Legislative Recruitment in a Civic Culture," *Social Science Quarterly* 50(1969), 250-263, quotations at p. 255.

[90] "One of the long recognized facts of life of Iowa politics is the screening process which the Farm Bureau Federation applies to state legislative candidates before the holding of the biennial primary elections. . . . Uncooperative or antagonistic state legislators are placed on a 'must go' list. The system operates to evoke a good deal of cooperation from rural state legislators" (John R. Schmidhauser, *Iowa's Campaign for a Constitutional Convention in 1960* [New York: McGraw-Hill, Eagleton Case #30, 1963], p. 15).

cratic organization after World War II that came to exercise considerable influence in partisan general elections and (by inference) in Democratic primaries of the 1950s and 1960s. It was the enthusiasm of its
leaders and members and an alliance with the United Auto Workers,
however, that kept it going; patronage had little importance.[91] A 1963
study suggests it stayed clear of Des Moines municipal elections: "In
Des Moines elections since the 1949 adoption of non-partisanship,
party organizations have played little or no active role in the campaigns
and candidates have not been perceived as Republican or Democratic.
In some elections rival slates have competed with backing from sharply
differentiated interest groups. In others the major groups have been relatively quiet. During the period we are examining it seems clear that
there was no well defined political structure, partisan or otherwise,
to the processes of recruitment and campaigning."[92] TPO score for
Iowa: 1.

NORTH DAKOTA (617,761) _____

Scholarship on North Dakota parties diminished a few decades ago as
a political tradition faded as well. This was a deep-seated conflict between the state's orthodox conservatives and its left-wing, farmer-ori-
ented Nonpartisan League. At an institutional level it took the form of
a long series of ritualized slating contests between the two sides, in Republican primaries, for the offices of governor down through the state
legislature.[93] In more recent times, North Dakota parties have regularly
held conventions prescribed by law to confer preprimary endorsements
for state and district offices, giving an endorsees-vs.-challengers cast to
press treatment of primaries.[94] But there is no reason to suppose that
traditional party organizations have operated in either the earlier or the

---

See also James C. Larew, *A Party Reborn: The Democrats of Iowa, 1950-1974* (Iowa
City: Iowa State Historical Society, 1980), pp. 16-19.

[91] Larew, *A Party Reborn*, ch. 3, pp. 89-90, 117-118.

[92] Robert H. Salisbury and Gordon Black, "Class and Party in Partisan and Non-Partisan Elections: The Case of Des Moines," *American Political Science Review* 57(1963),
587.

[93] See Ross B. Talbot, "The North Dakota Farmers Union and North Dakota Politics,"
Western Political Quarterly 10(1957), 875-901; Key, *American State Politics*, pp. 250-
254. On the League's peak years: Robert L. Morlan, *Political Prairie Fire: The Nonpartisan League, 1915-1922* (Minneapolis: University of Minnesota Press, 1955). On the
incentive structure of the NPL: Wilson, *Political Organizations*, pp. 103-104.

[94] For an account of the endorsing process see Lloyd B. Omdahl and Boyd L. Wright,
1977-79: Governing North Dakota (Grand Forks: Bureau of Governmental Affairs, University of North Dakota, 1977), pp. 98-99. On primaries see, e.g., *Bismarck Tribune*,
September 4, 1968, p. 2; September 3, 1970, p. 1; *Fargo Forum*, September 4, 1968, p.
1; September 3, 1970, p. 1.

more recent processes.[95] (See map under South Dakota.) Score for North Dakota: 1.

SOUTH DAKOTA (666,257)

Alan L. Clem comments, in his authoritative 1967 work on South Dakota parties and elections, *Prairie State Politics*: "The principle of popular control has taken away so much of the flexible, discretionary power of party leaders in South Dakota that they can seldom make important decisions, and many of the same leaders would shrink from making such crucial decisions if they had the opportunity. No power, no interest; no interest, no power."[96] On party activities: "Party organizations have had little impact on candidate selection for major offices. They do not play a prominent role in patronage, although even in South Dakota there are a few jobs available to be filled. They do not control candidates. They have little to do with developing issues."[97] At the state legislative level: "Party officials are generally unwilling (and perhaps unable) to exert control in the selection of their local legislative candidate, and this inevitably reinforces the legislator's impression that he is in fact a free agent."[98] TPO score for South Dakota: 1.

[95] On recent endorsing processes see, e.g., *Fargo Forum*, May 20, 1970, p. 1; May 21, 1970, p. 1; May 22, 1970, pp. 1, 9; May 27, 1970, pp. 1, 2; May 29, 1970, pp. 1, 2.

[96] Alan L. Clem, *Prairie State Politics: Popular Democracy in South Dakota* (Washington, D.C.: Public Affairs Press, 1967), p. 51, and more generally ch. 4 ("Party Politics: Agencies of Participation").

[97] *Ibid.*, p. 64.

[98] *Ibid.*, pp. 113-114.

NEBRASKA (1,483,791)

A 1968 dissertation by Bernard D. Kolasa characterizes electoral politics in Nebraska: "The political parties are quite rigidly controlled by law and the statutes provide little opportunity for independent action. The primary system leaves little room for party decision-making beyond appeal to the party rank and file in the voting booth. With a primary largely free of organizational influence, the party leadership is hampered in efforts to enforce its policy or to punish dissidents. Parties have been unable to circumvent the primary through informal means or by pre-primary slate-making to ensure the success of the candidates the party organization supports."[99] Nebraska, like Minnesota, elected its legislature in formally nonpartisan elections in the 1960s, but nothing approaching Minnesota's DFL had been organized to try to structure them.[100] Of state legislators answering Kolasa's questionnaire who recalled "non-personal influences" in deciding to run for office (half of them recalled none), "political party leaders" ranked fourth in mentions behind businessmen, farmers (and ranchers), and bankers.[101] In a probe for "groups most helpful in campaign," "political party groups" came in tenth after business groups, educational groups, "personal efforts (own, friends, relatives)," women's groups, civic and fraternal groups, professional groups (lawyers, doctors), agricultural groups, labor, and religious groups.[102] The conclusion was that "by any standard, party activity in Nebraska's legislative elections is indeed slight."[103]

In Omaha (346,929), a ward boss named Tom Dennison exercised considerable influence in municipal politics from the 1890s until the 1930s, but his organization died with him, leaving a formless politics during the last half century.[104] Recent mayors, including Edward Zo-

---

[99] Bernard D. Kolasa, "The Nebraska Political System: A Study in Apartisan Politics" (Ph.D. dissertation, University of Nebraska, 1968), p. 238, and more generally ch. 6.

[100] On lack of party activity in Nebraska state legislative elections: *ibid.*, pp. 256-275, 310-319. An abbreviated treatment appears in Bernard D. Kolasa, "Party Recruitment in Nonpartisan Nebraska," ch. 4 in John C. Comer and James B. Johnson (eds.), *Nonpartisanship in the Legislative Process: Essays on the Nebraska Legislature* (Washington, D.C.: University Press of America, 1978).

[101] Kolasa, "The Nebraska Political System," pp. 311-312, 568-569. The legislators were serving in 1967.

[102] *Ibid.*, pp. 312-313, 568-569.

[103] Kolasa, "Party Recruitment," p. 40.

[104] On Dennison: John Kyle Davis, "The Gray Wolf: Tom Dennison of Omaha," *Nebraska History* 58(1977), 25-52. On the last half century: Lawrence H. Larsen and Barbara J. Cottrell, *The Gate City: A History of Omaha* (Boulder, Colo.: Pruett, 1982), pp. 227-228, 237-239, 256-262.

rinsky (later Senator), have built and tended electoral bases through personal appeal. Eugene Leahy, elected in 1969, "rode elephants, read Sunday funnies on television, gave several hundred speeches in one four-month period, and delivered tirades against the city council. He gained a reputation as a 'people's mayor,' a 'City Hall jester,' and as 'Omaha's Harry Truman.' "[105] (See map under South Dakota.) A TPO score for Nebraska: 1.

KANSAS (2,249,071)

Nowhere in the slim literature on Kansas does traditional organization make an appearance.[106] Some conclusions about electoral politics at the state legislative level: "Neither party has been particularly well organized for recruiting purposes. . . . Principally because of the relatively rural nature of the state, Kansas parties have never developed the highly articulated precinct organizations that are more characteristic of urban politics. . . . Legislative candidates are pretty much on their own in running for office."[107] Press coverage of primaries has focused on wins and losses of individual candidates.[108] Wichita (276,554), the

[105] Larsen and Cottrell, *The Gate City*, p. 261. Other Omaha officials in the 1960s: "Members of the city council had small power bases, usually associated with neighborhood needs or a specific interest group. . . . Given the constraints, about all they could do was to concentrate on winning support for pet issues, serve the needs of constituents, and keep making an occasional headline to remain in the public eye" (p. 259).

[106] See for example Marvin A. Harder, "Some Aspects of Republican and Democratic Party Factionalism in Kansas" (Ph.D. dissertation, Columbia University, 1959); Ronald A. Averyt, "The Minority Party in a Non-Competitive State: The Case of Kansas" (Ph.D. dissertation, University of Kansas, 1970).

[107] John G. Grumm, "The Kansas Legislature: Republican Coalition," ch. 3 in Samuel C. Patterson (ed.), *Midwestern Legislative Politics* (Ames: Institute of Public Affairs, University of Iowa, 1967), pp. 50-52.

[108] See, for example, *Topeka Daily Capital*, August 5, 1970, p. 1; *Wichita Eagle*, August 5, 1970, p. 11A. It would be useful to know more about Wyandotte County (186,845), site of Kansas City (168,213), Kansas, adjoining Kansas City, Missouri. The *Kansas City* [Missouri] *Times*, which had no trouble recognizing slating organizations in the 1960s—Jackson County's "factions" drew front-page banner headlines in primary encounters with reformers late in the decade—told only of wins and losses of individual candidates in covering Wyandotte's Democratic primaries and municipal elections during the same years. See *Kansas City Times*, August 3, 1966, p. 7; March 14, 1967, pp. 1, 7; March 15, 1967, p. 1; August 7, 1968, p. 4A; August 2, 1970, pp. 4, 5; March 10, 1971, pp. 1A, 5A. But this report appeared in 1970: "Charles M. Sugar, who for years dominated Democratic politics in Wyandotte County, last night lost his bid to regain his party's nomination for county assessor. . . . Schoneman, a 27-year-old insurance manager, became the second man to beat Sugar. In 1968, after 14 years in the county assessor's office, Sugar was defeated in an upset by F. H. Banks, a Republican" (*ibid.*, August 5, 1970, p. 4A).

state's largest city, conducted candidate-centered elections for municipal offices in the 1950s and 1960s—seventeen candidates pursued two commissioner's posts in 1957, for example—though a business and professional group had a brief run of effective slating in 1959 and 1961.[109] Primaries for partisan offices in Wichita's parent unit, Sedgwick County (350,694), also hinged on individual candidacies.[110] (See map under South Dakota.) TPO score for Kansas: 1.

OKLAHOMA (2,559,253) _____

Seeking office in Oklahoma has evidently always been a personal enterprise, from the days of stump speaking and hillbilly bands through the television campaigns of the 1970s.[111] The state government used to support a lavish patronage system before a 1959 civil-service reform, but individual state legislators, rather than party leaders or organizations, used the jobs to build their own labor-intensive, year-round candidate organizations.[112] County commissioners (three per county) were doing the same in the early 1960s, as one explained: "I have 85 employees—garage men, road workers, janitors, elevator operators—and

[109] See Marvin A. Harder, *Nonpartisan Election: A Political Illusion?* (New York: McGraw-Hill, Eagleton Case #5, 1960); Dwight M. Carpenter, "Wichita: Cowboys, Crises and Tuesday Night Fights," ch. 11 in Leonard E. Goodall (ed.), *Urban Politics in the Southwest* (Tempe: Institute of Public Administration, Arizona State University, 1967), pp. 230-231, 235-240.

[110] Carpenter, "Wichita," pp. 230-231.

[111] See, e.g., Stephen Jones, *Oklahoma Politics in State and Nation*, vol. 1, *1907 to 1962* (Enid, Okla.: Haymaker Press, 1974), especially ch. 6. "Famous-name" candidacies hit a peak in the 1930s, though in 1954 a rancher changed his name to Cowboy Pink Williams, outfitted a sound truck, campaigned around the state, and defeated a twenty-year incumbent in a Democratic primary for lieutenant governor (p. 93). An account of an old-timer's campaign in the Democratic Senate primary of 1978 appears in Mark Singer, "A Reporter at Large: Prince," *The New Yorker*, April 2, 1979, pp. 41-92. A side note on a candidates' supper in rural Le Flore County, part of "Little Dixie" in southeastern Oklahoma: "Forty or so candidates for various local and statewide offices—including twelve contenders for a vacant seat on the Le Flore County Board of Commissioners—were permitted two minutes each to argue their cases. The county politicians outbragged one another in an innovative manner, each one claiming that he had been married longer, sired more children, and hunted deer more avidly than any of his opponents. Most of them also had harsh words for alcohol, gambling, big government, and giving away anything that rightfully belonged to Little Dixie" (p. 62). This brings to mind activity by local candidates in Alabama's hill country in the 1930s, and the custom of "stump meetings" in local South Carolina.

[112] Jean G. McDonald, "Oklahoma Patronage, the Political Parties, and State Elective Officials" (Ph.D. dissertation, Michigan State University, 1972), ch. 7. Whatever patronage was left in the 1960s was still going to legislators rather than to party organizations (pp. 104-116).

they work for me when I need them. This isn't the regular party organization, which isn't much. These people care if I stay in office. I can't expect them to work for other candidates, but they can if they want to. That is their business."[113] It is a pertinent consequence that "because these important local politicians withhold their resources, there is no firm foundation for a regular statewide (county by county) party organization, neither for Republicans nor Democrats."[114] Giving out patronage to individual officeholders is hardly peculiar to Oklahoma, but no other state seems to have done this so elaborately. The commissioners' system continued into the 1980s.[115]

Both of Oklahoma's major cities conducted electoral politics in the 1960s without either traditional party organizations or, evidently, significant patronage transactions. In nonpartisan Oklahoma City (368,856) the Association for Responsible Government, a good-government group equipped with impressive dues-paying ward organizations as well as some eighty elected officers (the honor of holding office may have provided an incentive to work), slated municipal candidates effectively in the mid-1960s but subsided soon afterward: "The last ARG councilmembers left office in 1971 at which time personality politics engulfed city elections."[116] Tulsa (330,350) ran a formally partisan municipal politics in the 1960s, where candidates nonetheless had to build their own organizations, financial bases, and public images to win primaries and general elections.[117] (See map under South Dakota.) TPO score for Oklahoma: 1.

[113] Bertil L. Hanson, "County Commissioners of Oklahoma," *Midwest Journal of Political Science* 9(1965), 396-398, quotation at p. 396.

[114] *Ibid.*, p. 397.

[115] For a good analysis see Phillip M. Simpson, "The County Government Scandals in Oklahoma: The Structure/Corruption Relationship," paper presented at the 1982 conference of the Southern Political Science Association. Also: "Oklahoma Inquiry: Effect Is Unclear," *New York Times*, October 12, 1981, p. A21; Adam Clymer, "Republicans Seize Initiative in Oklahoma Scandals," *New York Times*, October 29, 1981, p. A20.

[116] On the 1960s: George J. Mauer, "Oklahoma City: In Transition to Maturity and Professionalization," ch. 5 in Goodall (ed.), *Urban Politics in the Southwest*, pp. 96-99. On subsiding: Richard M. Bernard, "Oklahoma City: Booming Sooner," ch. 8 in Richard M. Bernard and Bradley R. Rice (eds.), *Sunbelt Cities: Politics and Growth since World War II* (Austin: University of Texas Press, 1983), quotation at p. 230 and more generally pp. 226-231.

[117] Bertil L. Hanson, "Tulsa: The Oil Folks at Home," ch. 10 in Goodall, *Urban Politics in the Southwest*, pp. 202-210.

CHAPTER 6

The Western States

Politics in the northern mountain states is largely rural. In the southwest and on the Pacific periphery it is largely urban. Neither setting has generated much in the way of party organization.

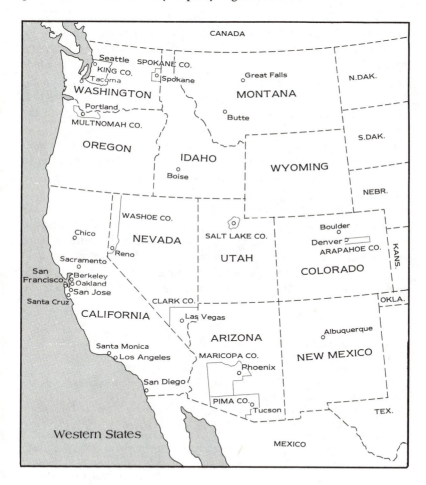

Western States

MONTANA (694,409) _____

A work on Democrat Leo Graybill's 1960 congressional campaign in Montana's eastern district paints a good picture of the state's electoral politics.[1] On entering the primary: "There was no seeking of influential individual or group blessing before his announcing his candidacy." Why not? "There are no individuals, with any significant resources, who require pre-primary bargaining by a candidate." Graybill could see "no 'deliverable vote' in the system."[2] Once past a five-candidate primary that generated a "friends-and-neighbors" voting pattern, he set out "to build a personal following among party people throughout the district. In doing so he was following the traditional pattern set by every successful Montana Democrat from [Senator Thomas H.] Walsh to Senator [Mike] Mansfield. He had to campaign personally in order to mobilize 'Graybill people' in the various communities. In Montana almost every person active in the party has a favorite candidate or office holder. That person, then, becomes known as a "[Senator James E.] Murray man,' a '[Senator Lee] Metcalf man,' et cetera. This means that any contribution, financial or otherwise, to an election will go to the person to whom the primary loyalty is felt."[3] In general, the district supported "a politics of personality, small groups, and cliques attempting to capture the party nominations," an understandable pattern in "a state, and district, in which party organizations are virtually non-existent."[4]

Western Montana's city of Butte (23,368), which used to be the state's mining center and metropolis, is said to have conducted a politics back in the 1940s in which "almost everyone runs for office at some time or another with the utmost enthusiasm. Public office pays as well, or better than, the mines; it's cleaner and much cooler. It is not unusual to find fifteen hopefuls vying for the lucrative post of Sheriff, or a dozen

---

[1] Joseph P. Kelly, "A Study of the 1960 Primary and General Election Campaigns for United States House of Representatives in Montana's Second Congressional District" (Ph.D. dissertation, Washington University, 1963).

[2] Quotations at *ibid.*, pp. 40-41.

[3] On the primary: *ibid.*, pp. 140-142, 146. Quotation at p. 191.

[4] Quotations at *ibid.*, pp. 14, 18. For a discussion of the weakness of Democratic precinct organizations in the Second District, in particular in Great Falls, see pp. 168-170. On Republicans: "It seems likely that any significant leadership control is also absent in the Republican party" (p. 42). For another treatment of Montana politics, which jibes with Kelly's, see Thomas Payne, "Under the Copper Dome: Politics in Montana," in Frank H. Jonas (ed.), *Western Politics* (Salt Lake City: University of Utah Press, 1961), especially pp. 194-197. "On the whole, Montana resembles a catch-as-can land in which personalities and personal followings are of more importance than traditional organization" (p. 194).

for the lowly job of constable. And personal popularity is about the only requirement, from Justice of the Peace to Chief Justice of the [state] Supreme Court." Evidently the only organization with influence in local elections (though it fell short of dominance) was the Anaconda copper company: " 'The Company' itself has never actually controlled more than about fifteen hundred votes in Butte—those of its managerial staff, its large battery of lawyers, their families, and friends. Only by persuasion of the business community and miners can it impose its will upon Butte at the polls, and it often fails." There is no mention of party organization.[5] TPO score for Montana: 1.

WYOMING (332,416)

"Political party organizations in Wyoming are weak. It is difficult to get people to run and to serve as precinct men and women. . . . Even the county chairmanships often eagerly sought after in other states, go to the persons willing to assume the responsibilities."[6] The state's politics is said to be "very personal," an emphasis that "tends to keep political party organization relatively weak and plays up the importance of candidates developing their own personal organizations in a campaign."[7] In the state's nonpartisan municipal elections, "since political parties are not formally involved, other groups such as chambers of commerce or service clubs have somewhat more influence. There is less campaigning and personal characteristics of the candidates seem to be emphasized."[8] In the election of state legislators, "neither party does a great deal to recruit candidates nor do the parties do much to aid the legislator's bid for election. To a very great extent, state legislators appear to be self-starters."[9] TPO score for Wyoming: 1.

COLORADO (2,207,259)

A typical newspaper story on Colorado's primaries of the late 1960s reported: "Two GOP contenders seeking the candidacy for the State

[5] Joseph Kinsey Howard, "Butte: The City with a 'Kick' in it," pp. 297-323 in Robert S. Allen (ed.), *Our Fair City* (New York: Vanguard, 1947), quotations at p. 314.

[6] Charles P. Beall, "Wyoming: The Equality State," in Jonas, *Western Politics*, p. 344, and more generally pp. 341-349.

[7] *Ibid.*, p. 336.

[8] John B. Richard, "Wyoming," ch. 9 in JeDon A. Emenhiser (ed.), *Rocky Mountain Urban Politics* (Logan: Utah State University, 1971), p. 152.

[9] B. Oliver Walter, Kendall L. Baker, and Kendall Stewart, *The Wyoming Legislature: Lawmakers, the Public, and the Press* (Laramie: Government Research Bureau, Department of Political Science, University of Wyoming, 1973), p. 32.

Senate and the House of Representatives overcame the bottom-line designation jinx to defeat favored candidates in the primary election held here Tuesday."[10] Colorado law provides for party "assemblies"—conventions, more or less—which regularly award preprimary "designations" to candidates for statewide, congressional, and state legislative offices. Two or more candidates may be designated by an assembly for the same office, and hence win entry into a subsequent primary as competitors, but the candidate who runs first in assembly voting wins a coveted "top-line designation" on the primary ballot.[11] The endorsement activity of assemblies in fact decides many nominations without primary contests (the also-rans tend to drop out), and also gives Colorado parties a tangibility that parties in most Western states lack, but there is no reason to suppose that traditional organizations have operated in the Colorado processes in modern times.[12] Patronage has been too scarce, "not available in large enough quantities nor in high enough quality for either party to use as an inducement for discipline."[13] Party workers are volunteers; "their only reward, ordinarily, is whatever satisfaction they get out of their activity and whatever sense of accom-

[10] The locale is Arapahoe County. *Denver Post*, September 11, 1968, p. 91. See also, e.g., *ibid.*, September 9, 1970, p. 80.

[11] For a detailed treatment of the assembly system, see R. John Eyre and Curtis Martin, *The Colorado Preprimary System* (Boulder: Bureau of Governmental Research and Service, University of Colorado, 1967), chs. 1-4. For a sense of what takes place in official meetings at various levels see Robert S. Lorch, *Colorado's Government* (Boulder: Colorado Associated University Press, 1976), pp. 91-99. The system begins at the grass roots with precinct caucuses: "Most precinct meetings are so small that the problem is to find people willing to spend a day at the county assembly. A precinct caucus, often composed only of nine or ten people sitting in someone's living room, will probably be conducted quite informally. Anyone who wants to go to the assembly simply says so. If there should happen to be more who want to go than the number allotted, then, while tea and cookies are served, it is decided who 'really' wants to go, who 'more or less' wants to go, and who 'doesn't care.' Finally, it's agreed that the 'really' want to go individuals will go, and if there are some seats left over, then a couple of the 'more or less' want to go people fill them. The 'don't cares' are invited and often drafted to attend the county convention as alternates" (*ibid.*, p. 91).

[12] On low level of primary contesting: Eyre and Martin, *Colorado Preprimary System*, pp. 56-62.

[13] Rudolf Gomez, "Colorado: The Colorful State," in Frank H. Jonas (ed.), *Politics in the American West* (Salt Lake City: University of Utah Press, 1969), p. 133, more generally pp. 133-134. On scarcity of patronage see also Eyre and Martin, *Colorado Preprimary System*, pp. 94-96; LeRoy W. Goodwin, "The Democratic and Republican County Chairman in Colorado: A Stabilizing Influence in an Unstable System" (Ph.D. dissertation, Columbia University, 1971), pp. 159-168; and on Denver, where "few city and county jobs are available as patronage," see Kenneth E. Gray, *A Report on Politics in Denver, Colorado* (Cambridge: Joint Center for Urban Studies, M.I.T./Harvard, 1959), pp. II:27-28, 30, quotation at p. II:27.

plishment and prestige they may feel."[14] And unsurprisingly, given the incentive structure, party organizations are not very hierarchical: "County and state officials must rely on salesmanship and persuasion to sell programs and candidates to the party rank and file."[15] When primary contests do occur, both parties' county chairmen ordinarily avoid interfering.[16]

The Democratic organization in Denver (514,678, city and county coterminous) was the most conspicuous Colorado organization of the 1950s and 1960s.[17] District captains and precinct workers existed and operated; Democratic assemblies slated candidates authoritatively for state legislative primaries, now and then purging an incumbent.[18]

[14] Curtis Martin, *Colorado Politics* (Denver: Big Mountain Press, 1960), p. 41.

[15] Eyre and Martin, *Colorado Preprimary System*, p. 93, more generally pp. 92-93. "Discipline is relatively unknown in most party organizations in Colorado. It is true that Democratic state legislators from Denver can be disciplined by the organization but this is the exception and not the rule, even in the Denver organization" (Gomez, "Colorado," p. 133).

[16] From a study based on interviews with nearly all of Colorado's county chairmen of both parties in 1967-1968: "*Only one Chairman of the ninety-three responding regularly intrudes in Primary contests for local offices in his party,* though two more say their behavior depends on several factors. An additional Chairman says he states his position as to who he thinks is better qualified, seven say they don't necessarily always stay out, and three declare they try to stay out." At higher levels: "When a District (State Legislative or U.S. Congressional) or statewide Primary is in the offing, the Chairmen don't feel so strongly about neutrality, though by a margin of nearly three to one they still stay out of the intraparty fight." Goodwin, "County Chairman in Colorado," p. 145. Emphasis in the original.

[17] From a study of Colorado party leaders at various levels: "Most of those interviewed thought the party organization that most nearly fitted the 'strong' classification is the Denver County Democratic party." The criterion: "If an organization is able to 'name' the candidate with a minimum of conflict and without alienating too many organization 'regulars' . . . it is considered to be strong." Gomez, "Colorado," pp. 131, 131-132. General sources on Denver: Gray, *Report on Denver,* pp. ii:1-3, 7-34; Eyre and Martin, *Colorado Preprimary System,* pp. 110-118; Alan Ware, *The Logic of Party Democracy* (London: Macmillan, 1979), ch. 6 ("Party Democracy and the Denver Democrats"), pp. 133-140, and ch. 9; Alan Ware, "The End of Party Politics? Activist-Officeseeker Relationships in the Colorado Democratic Party," *British Journal of Political Science* 9(1979), 237-250; Alan Ware, "Why Amateur Party Politics Has Withered Away: The Club Movement, Party Reform and the Decline of American Party Organizations," *European Journal of Political Research* 9(1981), 219-236.

[18] On party officials and workers: Gray, *Report on Denver,* pp. ii:26-27; Eyre and Martin, *Colorado Preprimary System,* pp. 112-114. On slating: William P. Irwin, "Colorado: A Matter of Balance," ch. 2 in Malcolm E. Jewell (ed.), *The Politics of Reapportionment* (New York: Atherton, 1962), pp. 72-75; *ibid., Metropolitan Representation: State Legislative Districting in Urban Counties* (New York: National Municipal League, 1969), pp. 9, 24; Eyre and Martin, pp. 55-56, 72; Ware, *Logic of Party Democracy,* pp. 106-129.

Workers of both parties backed candidates readily identifiable as Democrats and Republicans in the city's nonpartisan municipal elections.[19] Even so, according to a meticulous 1959 report that noted Denver's lack of a patronage supply, discussed the Democratic party's ward apparatus, and evidently used the hierarchical, patronage-based party organizations of some Eastern cities as a standard in choosing language: "There are no machines in Denver."[20] And of course other sorts of organizations are capable of slating candidates and staffing precincts. In fact an alliance of liberals took over the city's Democratic organization in the 1950s and dominated it in the 1960s. They were supplemented after 1965 by an infusion of feisty antiwar activists who engineered the defeat of a Democratic congressman in an assembly and follow-up primary in 1970.[21] When Denver's seventeen-member House delegation ceased being elected at-large in the mid-1960s, switching to election in single-member districts instead, liberal Democrats who controlled the party's nominating process feared their leading members could no longer get elected: the at-large, citywide Democratic delegations had accommodated "a large proportion of lawyers and other business and professional persons, mostly residents of the higher-income sections of the county."[22]

Elsewhere in Colorado, a study of nonpartisan city elections from 1949 through 1963 in Boulder (66,870) describes a "political environment of individual candidates who emphasize their 'free agent' qualities," and in which "formal organized political activity at the municipal level is almost nonexistent."[23] TPO score for Colorado: 1.

[19] Gray, *Report on Denver*, pp. ii:6, 22; Eyre and Martin, *Colorado Preprimary System*, pp. 115-116. Denver shifted to formally partisan elections in 1968.

[20] Gray, *Report on Denver*, pp. ii:2-3, 27, quotation at p. 27. No traditional organizations operated in black or Hispanic areas of the city. See pp. ii:31-33. Gray wrote similar reports at about the same time on Cincinnati, St. Louis, and Kansas City, and had no difficulty finding "machines" at the ward or county level in these other places.

[21] *Ibid.*, pp. ii:25-26; Eyre and Martin, *Colorado Preprimary System*, pp. 115-117; Ware, *Logic of Party Democracy*, ch. 6, pp. 133-140, in particular, pp. 94-99 on the 1970 congressional nomination; Ware, "Why Amateur Politics," pp. 226-229.

[22] Jewell, *Metropolitan Representation*, p. 20: "Some persons who were interviewed expressed concern that the result [of having single-member districts] would be a delegation many of whose members had lower levels of education and experience. Democratic leaders were particularly concerned because some of their ablest legislators who had been elected at-large lived in districts that were likely to choose Republicans in district elections. They felt that legislators who were most skillful and effective in working for liberal legislation were not necessarily those living in lower income districts."

[23] Leonard A. Stitelman, "Nonpartisan Municipal Elections in Boulder, Colorado—A Case Study" (Ph.D. dissertation, University of Colorado, 1965), chs. 5, 6, 8, 9, quotations at pp. 165, 197. Parties of some kind seem to have played an informal role in city

UTAH (1,059,273) _____

Utah, like Colorado (and Rhode Island, Connecticut, and North Dakota), has an official preprimary endorsing system for state and district offices. In each party a convention cuts down the number of contestants for an office to a maximum of two, permitting both to go on to a primary as in principle equals.[24] As in Colorado, no doubt because weak candidates are winnowed out and because a first-place finish in an endorsing convention carries at least unofficial authority, primary contests have been relatively rare. Except in their official endorsing role, however, Utah parties have been weak as structures. The state's party organizations, according to a 1969 report, play an "insignificant role . . . in finding prospective nominees and in aiding an individual campaign."[25] "The real incentive and the best results in campaign organization and activities, including fund-raising, have come from individual candidate campaigners. . . . Party organization in Utah simply is neither strong nor continuous."[26] A 1961 report on Salt Lake City (175,885) concluded: "There have been no stable, enduring machines in either the city or state."[27] Five more or less equal commissioners (one also the mayor) figured in the city's nonpartisan municipal elections, all building and attending to their own citywide electoral coalitions, which often included pertinent groups of city employees.[28] TPO score for Utah: 1.

IDAHO (713,008) _____

Students of Idaho's politics dwell on the state's unending search for a satisfactory way of choosing party nominees.[29] Several plans covering

---

elections, though they ranked well behind women's organizations, service clubs, and the Chamber of Commerce in influence. See ch. 8.

[24] The best treatment of Utah nominating procedures and party organizations is Frank H. Jonas, "Utah: The Different State," in Jonas (ed.), *Politics in the American West*, pp. 350-362.

[25] *Ibid.*, p. 351.   [26] *Ibid.*, p. 362.

[27] Dixie S. Huefner, *A Report on Politics in Salt Lake City* (Cambridge: Joint Center for Urban Studies, M.I.T./Harvard, 1961), p. 11:10.

[28] *Ibid.*, pp. 11:1-31. Salt Lake City shifted to a mayor-council system in 1979. See Molly Ivins, "G.O.P. Interest Stirs Mayor Race in Utah," *New York Times*, November 4, 1979, p. A20.

[29] Some sources: Boyd A. Martin, "Idaho: The Sectional State," in Jonas (ed.), *Politics in the American West*; R. John Eyre and Victor S. Hjelm, "Idaho Political Parties," ch. 4 in Glenn W. Nichols, Ray C. Jolly, and Boyd A. Martin (eds.), *State and Local Government in Idaho: A Reader* (Moscow: Bureau of Public Affairs Research, University of Idaho, 1970).

various offices have prevailed at one time or another: an ordinary primary system, a primary with runoffs, a primary with preferential voting, a straight convention system, and a convention system with preprimary endorsements. The reforms have addressed problems thought to be brought on by primaries: too many candidates, incompetent candidates, crackpot candidates, plurality victories, raids of one party's primaries by the other's voters, and invasion of primaries by special interests—ranging from the Nonpartisan League in 1918 to gambling advocates around 1960. No one suggests that the state's party organizations at any level have had sufficient clout to help ward off these troubles by forestalling or operating in primaries. Press reports on the Boise area's legislative primaries and nonpartisan city elections discuss the wins and losses of individuals. The lead on a 1973 mayoral election in Boise (74,990): "A close race was predicted, but a surprise landslide vote Tuesday night made longtime television newsman Dick Eardley Boise's mayor for the next four years." The runner-up's reflection: "The main reason I lost, I think, is because I ran against a name and a face that have been on TV the past 18 years."[30] Idaho seems to resemble its neighboring mountain states in organizational texture, though evidence is scanty. TPO score: 1.

NEW MEXICO (1,016,000)

The most diverse and interesting organizational forms in the mountain states are found in New Mexico. Three settings stand out. The first is a cluster of six southeastern counties referred to as Little Texas (total population 192,551) because of their inhabitants' origin and cultural background.[31] An excellent treatment of a typical (unidentified) Little Texas county in the 1950s tells of candidates running on their own, in the rural South's typical style, in organization-free Democratic primaries.[32] In the second setting, nonpartisan Albuquerque (243,751) in Bernalillo County (315,774), an organization called the Albuquerque Citizens Committee slated city candidates effectively from 1954

[30] *Idaho Statesman* (Boise City), November 7, 1973, p. 1. See also *ibid.*, November 4, 1969, pp. 1, 7, and for an account of state legislative primaries, August 5, 1970, p. 1.

[31] The counties: Chaves (43,335), Curry (39,517), De Baca (2,547), Eddy (41,119), Lea (49,554), and Roosevelt (16,479).

[32] Charles B. Judah, *Recruitment of Candidates from the Northern and Eastern Counties to the New Mexico House of Representatives—1956* (Albuquerque: Division of Research, Department of Government, University of New Mexico, 1961), pp. 13-20. See also Jack E. Holmes, *Politics in New Mexico* (Albuquerque: University of New Mexico Press, 1967), p. 59. Democrats in Little Texas used extralegal primaries to do their nominating for several decades before New Mexico enacted its first direct primary law in 1939 (*ibid.*, pp. 216-217).

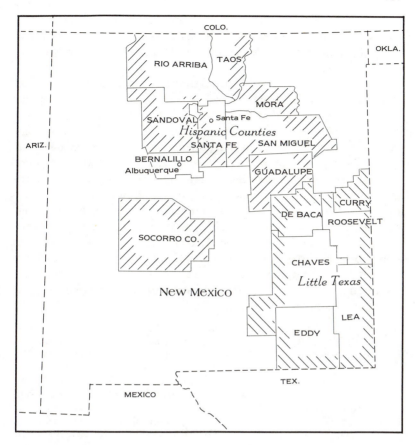

through 1963. It gave way in 1966, after displays of political incompetence, to an evidently similar good-government group, the People's Committee for Better Government.[33] No organization made much difference in an Albuquerque election in 1974 featuring 33 candidates for mayor and 122 for nine council seats; two frontrunners tied with 12.8% of the vote apiece reached the mayoral runoff. "Networks of acquaintances" are said to have paid off in producing votes.[34] A good re-

[33] Dorothy I. Cline and T. Phillip Wolf, "Albuquerque: The End of a Reform Era," ch. 1 in Leonard E. Goodall (ed.), *Urban Politics in the Southwest* (Tempe: Institute of Public Administration, Arizona State University, 1967), pp. 14-21. At its start the ACC built "an effective precinct organization manned by hundreds of volunteers" (p. 14).

[34] Paul L. Hain, "How an Endorsement Affected a Non-Partisan Mayoral Vote," *Journalism Quarterly* 52(1975), 337-340. The endorsement of two daily newspapers is said to have been worth 5 to 7% in the preliminary mayoral election, but the newspapers' candidate still won only 8.9% of the vote.

port on Bernalillo's Democratic primaries for the state legislature in 1956 (when Democrats were still the majority party) documents a free-for-all for nine countywide nominations that involved thirty-two candidates.[35]

The extraordinary New Mexico setting is the third, a cluster of eight rural counties in the Hispanic northern part of the state (total population 155,290)—the oldest European settlement in the United States.[36] This is unquestionably an environment of traditional party organizations—of county organizations in both parties built on patronage, routinized slating in primaries, strong leaders, elections run without issues, much sought-after county offices, and Appalachia-like school systems that have served as cornucopias of party-controlled jobs.[37] In 1978 Emilio Naranjo, said to be an exceptionally talented leader, had been running Rio Arriba County (25,170) as Democratic *jefe* for a quarter century.[38] San Miguel County (21,951) supported rival Democratic slating organizations in the early 1970s headed by Donald A. Martinez (the regulars) and Apolonio Duran (the gadflies). Each had backed factional candidate slates in county and state primaries for two decades; Martinez was still in business in 1978.[39]

[35] Charles B. Judah and Dorothy P. Goldberg, *The Recruitment of Candidates from Bernalillo County to the New Mexico House of Representatives, 1956* (Albuquerque: Division of Research, Department of Government, University of New Mexico, 1959).

[36] The counties: Guadalupe (4,969), Mora (4,673), Rio Arriba (25,170), Sandoval (17,492), San Miguel (21,951), Santa Fe (53,756), Socorro (9,763), and Taos (17,516). Two authors designate these the Hispanic counties as of about 1970. See T. Phillip Wolf, "The 1968 Elections in New Mexico," *Western Political Quarterly* 22(1969), 512; Maurilio Vigil, *Chicano Politics* (Washington, D.C.: University Press of America, 1977), p. 328. The list would have been longer fifty or a hundred years ago. Santa Fe County, site of the state capital, is not as rural as it used to be.

[37] The best source is Judah, *Recruitment from Northern and Eastern Counties*, pp. 1-12, an account of state legislative nominating in 1956 in a typical though unidentified Hispanic unit given the name Coronado County. "What, then, are the qualifications for a place on the ticket? As already indicated, ability to deliver votes not only for the candidate himself but for the ticket, particularly the county ticket, is important. Equally important is loyalty to the party, or more accurately to 'the organization,' for in Coronado County the party leadership equates the party with itself. So the candidate must be one who, when elected, will use the patronage and other advantages of office in the interest of perpetuating and strengthening the organization's power" (p. 5). See also Holmes, *Politics in New Mexico*, pp. 126-128.

[38] Molly Ivins, "For Rio Arriba, Cultures and Strife, Old and New," *New York Times*, November 12, 1978, p. E5. On Naranjo see also Vigil, *Chicano Politics*, pp. 294-295; Cal Clark and Janet Clark, "New Mexico," pp. 103-132 in B. Oliver Walter (ed.), *Politics in the West: The 1978 Elections* (Laramie: Institute for Policy Research, University of Wyoming, n.d.), pp. 126-127.

[39] On the early 1970s: Vigil, *Chicano Politics*, pp. 332-333, 337-338. Vigil reports San Miguel to be unique among the Hispanic counties in its "extreme factionalism." "The

New Mexico's traditional organizations counted for a great deal less in the 1960s than they did, say, in the 1920s, when Republicans using caucuses and conventions dominated the state's Hispanic counties in a largely pre-Anglo politics.[40] Surprisingly, New Mexico used to be one of the country's solid organization states, but the appropriate TPO score for the 1960s is a 2.[41]

ARIZONA (1,770,900)

Some Arizona officials still tended individual patronage networks in the 1960s, but there is no sign of traditional party organizations.[42] A good-government group, the Charter Government Committee (called the "country club set" by some), dominated nonpartisan city elections in the 1950s and 1960s in Phoenix (581,562). It furthered the early career of Barry Goldwater, among others, and turned back rival slating groups including a 1963 liberal-labor Action Citizens Ticket and a 1961 Stay American Committee, which advanced a connection between Phoenix's council-manager plan and an international Communist conspiracy. (Both liberals and Stay Americans ran especially well in poorer sections of the city.) No non-CGC candidate won the mayoralty or even a council post from 1949 through 1965.[43] A busi-

---

Democratic Party in the county has, since the mid-1950s, been characterized by extensive factionalism often characterized by splits in which the regular and gadfly organization hold separate county conventions, select separate county officers, send separate delegations to state party conventions, and endorse separate competing slates for county and state offices" (p. 333). On Martinez in 1978: Clark and Clark, "New Mexico," pp. 126-127.

[40] New Mexico adopted the direct primary in 1939 (only two states brought it in later), used it in unqualified form through 1948, then used preprimary nominating conventions (for statewide offices, at least) from 1950 through 1954, then went back to a straight primary in 1956-1962, shifted again to preprimary conventions in 1964-1966, straight primaries in 1968-1974, preprimary conventions yet again in 1976. See Paul L. Hain, "Voters, Elections, and Political Parties," ch. 9 in F. Chris Garcia and Paul L. Hain (eds.), *New Mexico Government* (Albuquerque: University of New Mexico Press, 1976), pp. 211-214.

[41] For treatments of New Mexico's pre–New Deal Republican regime rooted in powerful county organizations see Thomas C. Donnelly, "New Mexico: An Area of Conflicting Cultures," ch. 7 in Thomas C. Donnelly (ed.), *Rocky Mountain Politics* (Albuquerque: University of New Mexico Press, 1940), pp. 237-245; and Holmes, *Politics in New Mexico*, chs. 5, 6.

[42] On individual patronage networks: Ross R. Rice, "Arizona: Politics in Transition," in Jonas (ed.), *Politics in the American West*, pp. 52-57.

[43] The source on Phoenix: Leonard E. Goodall, "Phoenix: Reformers at Work," ch. 6 in Goodall (ed.), *Urban Politics in the Southwest*, pp. 117-122. Also on the Stay American Committee: "Arizona: 'Red' Victory," *Time*, November 24, 1961, p. 17. The CGC

ness-oriented Better Government Association, probably spun off from the CGC, slated effectively in the 1950s for county offices in Phoenix's parent unit, Maricopa County (968,487).[44] Tucson (262,933) held officially partisan city elections in the 1950s and 1960s, but candidates actually put together their own campaigns to win nominations.[45] A good case study of a spirited 1962 Democratic primary for state representative in a Tucson district of subaverage income near the center of the city turned up hardly a trace of party activity where it might have been expected.[46] Personalities and ideological factions crossing and muddling party lines caught a political reporter's attention in Tucson and its parent unit Pima County (351,667) in the mid-1970s.[47] TPO score for Arizona: 1.

NEVADA (488,738) _____

Though specifics are hard to pin down, Nevada seems typical of the urban Southwest in its organizational flavor. Politicians build personal followings, primaries take place without evident slating, and outsiders easily permeate official party organizations at the grass-roots level.[48]

---

lost its grip in the mid-1970s and seems to have disappeared by the early 1980s. See Bradford Luckingham, "Phoenix: The Desert Metropolis," ch. 12 in Richard M. Bernard and Bradley R. Rice (eds.), *Sunbelt Cities: Politics and Growth since World War II* (Austin: University of Texas Press, 1983), pp. 318-320; and *Arizona Republic*, November 4, 1981, p. A1.

[44] Ross R. Rice, "Amazing Arizona: Politics in Transition," in Jonas (ed.), *Western Politics*, p. 55.

[45] Conrad Joyner, "Tucson: The Eighth Year of the Seven-Year Itch," ch. 9 in Goodall (ed.), *Urban Politics in the Southwest*, pp. 176-185.

[46] Robert E. Riggs, "The District Five Primary: A Case Study in Practical Politics," *Arizona Review of Business and Public Administration* 12(1963), 1-14. One or more of the four Democratic candidates mentioned newspaper support, ethnic blocs, name renown, strength of candidate organizations, and the city's "big interests" when asked to talk about how they would do in the primary and why. None mentioned party organization.

[47] See David S. Broder, " 'Growth Backlash': A New Coalition," *Washington Post*, June 21, 1975, pp. A1, A8. This is a feature story on politics in Tucson and Pima County. One faction: "Asta and Mrs. Cauthorn are part of a group of liberal Democrats, many of them products of the McGovern movement, who scored a near-sweep of elections in city, county and legislative races from 1972 through 1974" (p. A8).

[48] Some sources: Albert C. Johns, *Nevada Politics* (Dubuque: Kendall/Hunt, 1973), ch. 4 ("Nevada Elections and Political Parties"); Elmer R. Rusco, *Voting Behavior in Nevada* (Reno: University of Nevada Press, 1966), ch. 4 ("Voting for Individual Candidates"); Eleanore Bushnell, "Nevada: The Tourist State," in Jonas (ed.), *Politics in the American West*; Joseph N. Crowley, *Democrats, Delegates, and Politics in Nevada: A Grassroots Chronicle of 1972* (Reno: Bureau of Governmental Research, University of Nevada, 1976), especially ch. 1.

Newspapers concentrate on individuals' wins and losses in covering county and state legislative primaries in Clark County (273,288) and Washoe County (121,068) and nonpartisan elections in their central cities, Las Vegas (125,787) and Reno (72,863).[49] TPO score for Nevada: 1.

CALIFORNIA (19,953,134) _____

There is no point in dwelling on California's well-known Progressive tradition, which is demonstrated in its hostility toward parties, lack of patronage, nonpartisan city elections in form and ordinarily in fact, weak or nonexistent precinct and ward organizations, and assertive individual candidacies prominent in primaries and general elections.[50] California is about the last place anybody would look to find traditional party organizations, and in fact none turns up in records of the last half century. Extralegal organizations of another sort operated with influence in statewide, congressional, and state legislative primaries during part of this time. The California Republican Assembly, which began as a group of progressive activists in the 1930s, endorsed in Republican primaries with considerable success in the 1940s and 1950s (Richard Nixon won his 1950 Senate primary as a CRA endorsee), but faded in the 1960s. The California Democratic Council, which was formed in 1953, asserted a liberal voice in Democratic primaries for a decade before it tore itself apart over Vietnam.[51] The CDC was an organization Democratic politicians had to reckon with, but even in its best years it probably exercised less influence than Minnesota's DFL.[52]

[49] See *Las Vegas Sun*, June 6, 1967, pp. 1, 4; June 7, 1967, pp. 1, 6; September 2, 1970, pp. 1-4; June 8, 1971, pp. 1, 4; June 9, 1971, pp. 1, 4. And *Nevada State Journal* (Reno), June 1, 1969, p. 1; June 4, 1969, pp. 1, 2; September 2, 1970, pp. 1, 2.

[50] Some standard treatments of California parties and elections: Dean R. Cresap, *Party Politics in the Golden State* (Los Angeles: Haynes Foundation, 1954); John R. Owens, Edmond Costantini, and Louis F. Weschler, *California Politics and Parties* (Toronto: Macmillan, 1970). For an especially good thumbnail sketch see James Q. Wilson, *The Amateur Democrat: Club Politics in Three Cities* (Chicago: University of Chicago Press, 1966), pp. 96-109.

[51] On the CRA and CDC in their early years: Leonard Rowe, *Preprimary Endorsements in California Politics* (Berkeley: Bureau of Public Administration, University of California, 1961). On the nature of the CDC: Wilson, *The Amateur Democrat*, chs. 4-11. Later treatments of CRA and CDC: Owens et al., *California Politics*, pp. 201-218; Bernard L. Hyink, Seyom Brown, and Ernest W. Thacker, *Politics and Government in California*, 9th ed. (New York: Crowell, 1975), pp. 95-98; John H. Culver and John C. Syer, *Power and Politics in California* (New York: Wiley, 1980), pp. 50-52.

[52] For an assessment of CDC influence in primaries see Wilson, *The Amateur Democrat*, pp. 320-330.

Activity by party organizations of any kind has been rare in California municipal elections.[53] From a 1967 report on San Diego (696,769):
"The organization backing a candidate for municipal office is typically
a committee made up of supporters, well-wishers and hangers-on. . . .
Slates of candidates are unknown."[54] A 1959 report on Los Angeles
(2,816,061): "The two major parties, the Democratic and the Republican, have not organized the city of Los Angeles for local elections."
"There is no organization vote which can be delivered in any of the [fif-
teen] Council districts." "There are no ward committeemen and no
ward organizations. . . . Councilmen are elected by creating large personal followings in their districts."[55] A 1975 treatment of Oakland
(361,561) reported a "noticeable absence of political party activity in
municipal elections," evidently the city norm, though a coalition of liberals organized to do some successful slating two years later.[56] Nothing
approaching party organization turns up in brief recent treatments of
San Jose (445,779) and Sacramento (254,413).[57] On San Jose in the

[53] Informants in 192 California cities answered the following question in a 1955 study:
"If someone wished to run for election to your city council, the support (public or behind
the scenes) of which of the following persons or groups would be most helpful to his success?" Respondents ranked "local newspaper" first among twenty-three specified options. "Political party organizations" ranked seventeenth in mentions, edged out by the
Masonic Lodge, "other lodges," bankers, and attorneys. See Eugene C. Lee, *The Politics
of Nonpartisanship: A Study of California City Elections* (Berkeley: University of California Press, 1960), pp. 76-77, and also ch. 7. From a study in the mid-1960s of 82 city
councils in the San Francisco Bay area: "Of the 435 councilmen who were interviewed,
only 17 reported having had the support of a party organization in the previous election"
(Heinz Eulau and Kenneth Prewitt, *Labyrinths of Democracy: Adaptations, Linkages,
Representation, and Policies in Urban Politics* [Indianapolis: Bobbs-Merrill, 1973], pp.
75-76). In both these studies party activity proved to be more common in large cities than
in small ones.

[54] Robert F. Wilcox, "San Diego: City in Motion," ch. 8 in Goodall (ed.), *Urban Politics in the Southwest*, p. 155, and more generally pp. 155-157, 162-163. See also David
Greenstone, *A Report on Politics in San Diego* (Cambridge: Joint Center for Urban Studies, M.I.T./Harvard, 1962), pp. II:2-14, 35-40, 55-70. More recently: Robert Lindsey,
"20 Vie to Become San Diego's Mayor," *New York Times*, March 6, 1983, p. 35.

[55] James Q. Wilson, *A Report on Politics in Los Angeles* (Cambridge: Joint Center for
Urban Studies, M.I.T./Harvard, 1959), pp. II:9, 8, 6, and more generally pp. II:1-14. For
a more recent study, centering on the personal organization of Mayor Tom Bradley, see
Raphael J. Sonenshein, "Bradley's People: Functions of the Candidate Organization"
(Ph.D. dissertation, Yale University, 1984).

[56] Jeffrey L. Pressman, *Federal Programs and City Politics: The Dynamics of the Aid
Process in Oakland* (Berkeley: University of California Press, 1975), p. 28, and more generally pp. 28-30. On the liberal coalition: John Mintz, "Victory at Last for the Liberals
of Oakland," *California Journal*, July 1977, p. 236.

[57] On San Jose: Stanley B. Greenberg, *Politics and Poverty: Modernization and Response in Five Poor Neighborhoods* (New York: Wiley, 1974), pp. 30-32, 43-48, a treat-

mid-1970s: "Candidates develop their own organizations, raise their own funds and run their own campaigns."[58]

Party structure in San Francisco (715,674, city and county coterminous), according to a 1974 study, is "only a thing of paper. There is no cadre of precinct workers except that provided by each candidate, and the candidate also does his own fund raising. There is a [Democratic] central committee, but no one seems to know why its control is important." The upshot: "In this context of invisible parties an election is much like the start of those long-distance races where everybody is on his own, eyes straight ahead, and there's a considerable amount of jostling in the pack. Candidates raise their own funds, rarely coalesce with other candidates in a slate, and strive earnestly to reach across party and ethnic lines. With a number of candidates for all offices, running at large with no runoffs (except for mayor, beginning in 1975), the process is symbolized by the local practice of slapping hundreds of election posters on buildings, fences, and poles all over the city. By election day the city is a kaleidoscope of jarring, confusing, and possibly self-defeating posters."[59]

The one California city where parties or partylike groups aggressively ordered municipal elections in the 1960s was academic Berkeley (116,716). A Stevensonian liberal group called the Berkeley Caucus took up slating city candidates in 1955 and settled into comfortable rule after a 1961 victory, but a spinoff antiwar, anti-establishment, and antiliberal opposition known as the April Coalition materialized in 1966. Subsequent liberals-vs.-radicals slating matches eventuated in radical (Berkeley Citizens Action) victories in 1979 and 1984.[60] New

ment of a poor inner-city section of San Jose around 1970; Robert Feinbaum, "The Politics of Growth in the 'Valley of Heart's Delight,' " *California Journal*, March 1976, pp. 95-97. On Sacramento: Culver and Syer, *Power and Politics*, pp. 156-157; Manuel Valencia, "The Unique 'Junkie Politics' of the State's Capital City," *California Journal*, November 1978, pp. 369-370.

[58] Feinbaum, "Politics of Growth," p. 96.

[59] Frederick M. Wirt, *Power in the City: Decision Making in San Francisco* (Berkeley: University of California Press, 1974), pp. 10-11, and more generally pp. 9-13 and ch. 4. In 1976 San Francisco switched to a district system for electing its board of supervisors, then went back to at-large elections in 1980.

[60] The general source on Berkeley is Harriet Nathan and Stanley Scott (eds.), *Experiment and Change in Berkeley: Essays on City Politics, 1950-1975* (Berkeley: Institute of Governmental Studies, University of California, 1978). Specific sources in Nathan and Scott: T. J. Kent, Jr., "Berkeley's First Liberal Democratic Regime, 1961-1970: The Postwar Awakening of Berkeley's Liberal Conscience," pp. 77-104; Thomas L. McLaren, "Berkeley's Political History, 1964 to 1974," pp. 254-262; Joel Rubenzahl, "Berkeley Politics, 1968-1974: A Left Perspective," pp. 338-353; Ilona Hancock, " 'New Politics' in Berkeley: A Personal View," pp. 401-405; Ed Kallgren, "Four Years on the Berkeley

Left slating organizations have won control of at least three other California locales in recent years: Santa Monica (88,314), where Santa Monicans for Renters' Rights (an offshoot of Tom Hayden's Campaign for Economic Democracy) took over the city council in 1981 but lost to a countermobilizing All Santa Monica Coalition in 1983; Chico (26,601); and Santa Cruz (41,483).[61] The pattern: "Most of the radicals' success so far has come in college towns like Santa Cruz and Chico that have large pools of youthful anti-establishment sentiment, but the successes have not been limited to college students."[62] The unquestionably appropriate TPO score for California: 1.

OREGON (2,091,385)

Oregon has some of the country's weakest party organizations. Each party is said to be "a loose and uncertain structure, providing principally a basis for grouping primary voters and a shadowy symbol to bind together diverse (and sometimes antagonistic) candidates who choose to run under it."[63] Grass-roots party units are "nonhierarchical, fragmented organizations staffed with sporadically active volunteers and some steadfast activists often elected to their precinct posts because they received a few write-in votes."[64] On emergence of candidates: "Oregon's parties and free-wheeling interest groups do not control recruitment. Each candidate must form his own campaign organization. In doing so, he may accept associational or party help, but he is apt to build the campaign organization around a nucleus of people he knows

---

City Council, 1971-1975," pp. 409-442. On the 1979 election: *San Francisco Chronicle*, April 16, 1979, p. 7; April 18, 1979, p. 1; April 19, 1979, p. 4; Robert Feinbaum, "Rebirth of the Radicals in the Politics of Berkeley," *California Journal*, July 1979, pp. 251-252. On BCA loss to the liberals' All Berkeley Coalition in 1981: "Berkeley Mayor Criticized on Travels," *New York Times*, January 3, 1982, p. 48. On BCA victory in 1984: Gerald C. Lubenow, "Berkeley: Matching Its Image," *Newsweek*, February 11, 1985, p. 11.

[61] On Santa Monica: James Ring Adams, "Santa Monica's Suburban Radicals," *Wall Street Journal*, July 1, 1981, p. 24; Robert Lindsey, "In 'People's Republic of Santa Monica,' Voters Turn to the Right," *New York Times*, April 17, 1983, p. 22; Derek Shearer, "How the Progressives Won in Santa Monica," *Social Policy* 12(Winter 1982), 7-14.

[62] Robert Lindsey, "Campus Radicals of 60's Are Reshaping Style of Local Government on Coast," *New York Times*, March 14, 1982, p. 22. Population figures for Santa Monica, Chico, and Santa Cruz are from the 1980 Census.

[63] John M. Swarthout and Kenneth R. Gervais, "Oregon: Political Experiment Station," in Jonas (ed.), *Politics in the American West*, p. 310, and more generally pp. 310-313.

[64] Lester G. Seligman et al., *Patterns of Recruitment: A State Chooses Its Lawmakers* (Chicago: Rand McNally, 1974), p. 185. The research was done in 1966.

and trusts, e.g. relatives, friends, colleagues, and the like."[65] Such individual candidacies evidently were the basis of municipal politics in Portland (380,620) around 1970.[66] A good study of a 1964 state senate primary in Portland's parent unit, Multnomah County (554,668), did reveal some loose candidate alliances on the Democratic (majority) side. In a field of fourteen candidates for five countywide nominations, three liberals (including one incumbent) joined forces as a slate; five candidates (including the three liberals, one other incumbent and one other nonincumbent) ran as endorsees of the Multnomah County Democratic Central Committee, which had broken precedent and raised hackles in the early 1960s by taking on the role of an endorsing body; and five conservatives (including two other incumbents) ran with the backing of a Democrats for Fair Taxation Committee rumored to be funded by insurance interests. All four incumbents and one other Fair Taxer (a former senator) won, a routine result in a setting where name familiarity counts for a great deal and incumbents seldom lose.[67] TPO score for Oregon: 1.

WASHINGTON (3,409,169) _____

Again a pattern of individual candidacies appears: "Washington's general elections are much like its primaries. Every candidate runs on his own all over again."[68] Several students of the state's politics tell of weak party organizations that are uninfluential in state and local nominating processes and easily permeated by activists mobilized for various

[65] *Ibid.*, p. 74, and more generally pp. 43-47, ch. 4, ch. 5, and pp. 171-187. "Among the variety of groups and individuals that sponsor legislative candidates (primary groups, interest groups, civic associations, political party leaders, factional leaders, and legislative leaders), political parties are neither the most important, nor are they even first among equals. To be sure, the direct primary prevents a political party from officially endorsing particular candidates. Yet, even sub rosa, party leaders do not exercise much influence in instigating candidates, except in the case of the minority party in the districts with one dominant party" (p. 185).

[66] A brief treatment appears in Carl Abbott, *Portland: Planning, Politics, and Growth in a Twentieth-Century City* (Lincoln: University of Nebraska Press, 1983), pp. 174-176, 180-181. On a future mayor's election to the (nonpartisan) city council in 1970: "Neil Goldschmidt finished first among sixteen candidates in the primary and coasted to an easy victory in the November runoff, even though he was a 'carpetbagger' who had lived in Portland less than three years" (p. 175).

[67] Donald G. Balmer, *Financing State Senate Campaigns: Multnomah County Oregon, 1964* (Princeton, N.J.: Citizens' Research Foundation, Study #8, 1966), pp. 10-21. On the county committee's new endorsing role: Donald G. Balmer, "The 1962 Election in Oregon," *Western Political Quarterly* 16(1963), 455.

[68] Willard Leavel, "The Election of Wes Uhlman," ch. 7 in Richard T. Frost (ed.), *Cases in State and Local Government* (Englewood Cliffs, N.J.: Prentice-Hall, 1961), p. 86, and

causes—notably Goldwater Republicans and antiwar Democrats who took over committee or convention processes in the 1960s in some of the larger counties.[69] Officially nonpartisan Seattle (530,831) has conducted municipal politics for several decades without patronage or party organizations: "There are no machines in Seattle which can deliver a bloc vote. . . . There has been no tradition of ward politics."[70] Candidates for mayor often run as partisans but they have to build their own campaign organizations.[71] Council candidates have also operated on their own, though around 1970 a group of energetic professionals— "lawyers who were under thirty-five and smacked of Harvard or Yale"—ran an endorsing organization called CHECC ("Choose an Effective City Council") that won some victories.[72] In 1974 a coalition of public employee groups ostentatiously brought its weight to bear in the Seattle area's primaries for the state legislature.[73] Officeholders in Se-

---

more generally pp. 79-94. This is an account of a Democrat's state legislative campaign (both primary and general elections) in a demographically heterogeneous Seattle district in 1958.

[69] General sources: Daniel M. Ogden, Jr., and Hugh A. Bone, *Washington Politics* (New York: New York University Press, 1960), chs. 1, 3-5; Hugh A. Bone, "Washington State: Free Style Politics," in Jonas (ed.), *Politics in the American West*, pp. 387-399, 404; William F. Mullen and John C. Pierce, "Political Parties," ch. 5 in Mullen, Pierce, Charles H. Sheldon, and Thor Swanson (eds.), *The Government and Politics of Washington State* (Pullman: Washington State University Press, 1978). On issue activists and party processes: Bone, pp. 398-399; Neal R. Peirce, *The Pacific States of America* (New York: Norton, 1972), p. 239. Washington has held conventions to choose delegates to national nominating conventions, but otherwise no official party bodies have had a significant role in nominating processes.

[70] Charles W. Bender, *A Report on Politics in Seattle* (Cambridge: Joint Center for Urban Studies, M.I.T./Harvard, 1961), p. ii:61. On patronage: pp. ii:21, 45. General source on the city's electoral politics: pp. ii:1-79.

[71] *Ibid.*, pp. ii:44-60. A television newsman won the mayoralty in 1977. See Terence Smith, "Big-City Machines Fared Poorly, As Did Blacks, in Local Elections," *New York Times*, November 10, 1977, p. A18.

[72] See Roger Sale, *Seattle: Past to Present* (Seattle: University of Washington Press, 1976), pp. 223-227, quotation at p. 224; Peirce, *Pacific States*, p. 255. The earlier pattern: "Success in a councilmanic election depends upon the familiarity of the candidate's name. Each councilman builds up a network of ties in his own residential district and extends his connections by joining community-wide organizations and making frequent public appearances" (Bender, *Report on Seattle*, p. ii:29, and more generally pp. ii:29-44.

[73] See David S. Broder, "Washington: New Political Generation," *Washington Post*, June 7, 1975, pp. A1, A8. The spokesman for the public employees groups: "We endorsed and elected four senators and seven representatives. . . . And what does a guy remember more? A $500 contribution or a caravan of 20 state employees doorbelling for an afternoon? With the politics of this state, the blanket primaries [in which any voter may switch back and forth between one party and the other in dealing with offices on the primary election ballot], political parties don't mean a thing. You move people into a district and you can really have an impact" (p. A8). And an earlier report on the manage-

attle's parent unit, King County (1,156,633), used to have some patronage to distribute, but they employed it to build their own personal networks rather than party organizations.[74]

Elsewhere, a 1961 study of Spokane County (287,487), site of Spokane (170,516), turned up a miniature version of King County and Seattle: city elections without party activity, no municipal patronage, county officials using patronage only to build their own followings, precinct committeemen doing little work and getting no material reward for what they did.[75] City elections in nonpartisan Tacoma (154,581) of the 1950s and 1960s ordinarily took the form of slating matches between a coalition supporting the city manager system (Republican, business-oriented and middle class) and a coalition opposing it (Democratic, union-oriented and working class). But there was room for creative maneuver: in 1967 a crusading Democratic loner, A. L. "Slim" Rasmussen, calling for lower taxes, won the mayoralty from an incumbent Republican who was tied to unions and had aggressively fostered a range of Great Society social programs.[76] TPO score for Washington: 1.

---

ment side: "The Boeing company also participates in candidate instigation and support. The company gives leaves of absence to employees elected to full-time public office. For many years the company protected these officeholders against financial loss and paid them while they served in the legislature. The company also makes provisions for time-off for people involved in campaigns or serving as election officials. In the 1964 election, over thirty Boeing employees ran for public office—many with the company's financial support" (Richard J. Tobin, "A Comparative Analysis of the Impact of Nominating Systems on State Legislative Recruitment and Behavior" [Ph.D. dissertation, Northwestern University, 1973], pp. 69-70).

[74] Bender, *Report on Seattle*, pp. II:21-25, 67-68, 76-78. In a study of 423 of King County's Republican precinct committeemen conducted in 1951, most turned out to be college educated, most had served in their positions no longer than two years, most "showed no evidence of any clear conception of the nature of the job of precinct leader," and only one displayed any interest in patronage. Some reasons they did give for getting into politics: to "save free enterprise," "preserve the American way," "work for good government," and "fight the traitorous machinations of the Franklin Roosevelt and Truman Administrations." The two parties were evenly balanced in King County at the time. See Hugh A. Bone, *Grass Roots Party Leadership: A Case Study of King County, Washington* (Seattle: Bureau of Governmental Research and Services, University of Washington, 1952), pp. 7-31, quotations at pp. 29, 26.

[75] Phillips Cutright, "Activities of Precinct Committeemen in Partisan and Nonpartisan Communities," *Western Political Quarterly* 17(1964), 93-108. (Cutright calls his second locale "Nonpartisan County," but its characteristics reveal it to be Spokane County.) In Spokane as in Seattle a TV newsman won the mayoralty in 1977: "[Ron] Bair's victory apparently reflected the familiarity he had gained with the Spokane citizens while performing anchorman duties for KXLY-TV news for 13 years" (*Spokane Spokesman-Review*, November 9, 1977, p. 1).

[76] William H. Baarsma, "A Study of Dissension and Conflict over Council-Manager Government in Tacoma, Washington and an Analysis of the Impact of that Dissension

ALASKA (300,382) _____

"Politics in Alaska," according to one account, "is uniquely individualistic, being determined primarily by local personalities and interests." The parties are "so loosely organized as to appear non-existent."[77] Treatments of statewide primary campaigns describe freewheeling contests among individuals without bringing up party organization.[78] Outsiders easily enter into the state's official convention processes (which are important in presidential though not in state and local nominating). The Moral Majority, for example, "seized control of Alaska's Republican Party" in 1980. "Delegations of Moral Majority members showed up unexpectedly at party district caucuses in February and elected a large majority of delegates to the state Republican convention, who made sure that Moral Majority's candidate, Ronald Reagan, won all 19 of the state's delegates to the party's national convention."[79] Party organization seems unimportant among Eskimos, Indians, and Aleuts, who made up approximately one-fifth of the Alaskan population in 1970. Their instruments of political mobilization in the 1960s showed "more than a passing resemblance to the national civil rights movement," and their new generation of officeholders elected after 1965 drew their "political identities . . . from activist regional Native organizations or from social action agencies connected with the anti-poverty programmes."[80] Newspapers in Anchorage (48,081) and Fairbanks (14,771) covered state legislative primaries and nonpartisan city

and Conflict on Governmental Decision-Making in Policy and Administrative Areas" (D.P.A. dissertation, George Washington University, 1973), chs. 8-10.

[77] Edwin W. Webking, Jr., "The 1968 Gruening Write-in Campaign" (Ph.D. dissertation, Claremont Graduate School, 1972), pp. 38, 45.

[78] See, for example, *ibid.*, ch. 3 ("Parties and Politics—1968"); Ronald E. Chinn, "The 1968 Election in Alaska," *Western Political Quarterly* 22(1969), 458-459; Ronald E. Chinn, "The 1970 Election in Alaska," *Western Political Quarterly* 24(1971), 235-236.

[79] Wallace Turner, "Group of Evangelical Protestants Takes Over the G.O.P. in Alaska," *New York Times*, June 9, 1980, p. B12.

[80] George W. Rogers, "Party Politics or Protest Politics: Current Political Trends in Alaska," *Polar Record* 14(1969), 445-458, first quotation at p. 457; Gordon Scott Harrison, "Notes on Alaskan Native Electoral Politics," *Polar Record* 16(1973), 691-700, second quotation at p. 695.

elections around 1970 by recording the wins and losses of individual candidates, incumbents in particular, though municipal employee unions and the Moral Majority have surfaced in recent commentary on Anchorage politics.[81] TPO score for Alaska: 1.

HAWAII (769,913)

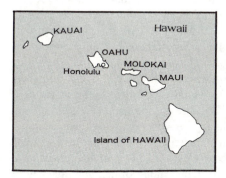

Hawaii's most interesting political settings are the "outer islands" of Maui (38,691), Kauai (29,761), and Hawaii (63,468), once holdings of the Republican business oligarchy that dominated territorial politics through World War II. Owners and managers of sugar and pineapple plantations and other enterprises tightly controlled the vote of their largely Oriental work force.[82] On Kauai, for example: "In the late 1920's, the plantation managers themselves became active in politics, many of them serving as campaign managers. They picked a number of key workers, gave them time off from their jobs, and taught them to recruit votes. In the 1930 election on Kauai, the manager of the McBryde plantation served as Republican campaign manager for the West Side. In East Kauai, a pineapple cannery executive ran the G.O.P. campaign. Frequently, managers called in *lunas* [overseers] shortly before election and explained which candidates

[81] See, for example, *Anchorage Daily News*, August 28, 1968, p. 1; October 6, 1970, pp. 1, 2; October 7, 1970, pp. 1, 2. And *Fairbanks Daily News-Miner*, August 28, 1968, p. 3; October 6, 1970, p. 1; October 8, 1970, pp. 1, 3. On the Anchorage mayoral election of 1981: "The general and runoff elections were marked by a campaign directed against [Mayor-elect Tony] Knowles by the Personal Liberties Committee, a political action committee aligned with the conservative Moral Majority group" ("Anchorage Mayoralty Is Won by Democrat," *Washington Post*, October 29, 1981, p. 4). The brief discussion of Anchorage politics in Evangeline Atwood, *Anchorage: Star of the North* (Tulsa: Continental Heritage Press, 1982), at pp. 126-130, 140, and 177, mentions public employee unions at p. 140.

[82] The main source for this paragraph is Lawrence H. Fuchs, *Hawaii Pono: A Social History* (New York: Harcourt, Brace and World, 1961). Politics in the "outer islands" during the last few decades of Hawaii's territorial status may be followed by consulting pp. 178-180, 198-205, 238-240, 311-315, 320, 328, 337, 340-342, 350-353, 356-359, 374, and 419. Another general source is Horace T. Day, Jr., "A Study of Political Opportunity Structure: Political Opportunity in Hawaii, 1926-1966" (Ph.D. dissertation, University of Hawaii, 1974), pp. 70-111.

were to be supported. *Lunas* were assigned to stand at the polls and hand copies of the approved slate to voters."[83] Every important "outer islands" political actor of the Republican era turns out to have been a business manager first and politician second.[84] But the system turned upside down in the late 1940s. The International Longshoremen's and Warehousemen's Union (ILWU) moved in and organized the plantation workers, converting Maui and Kauai into union and Democratic strongholds and establishing itself as the most influential slating organization in territorial elections. By the mid-1950s "the plantation vote was obviously no longer controlled by managers. In some cases, union leaders had replaced *lunas* as political bosses."[85]

By the 1960s, however, the influence of the ILWU had diminished, and in any case four out of five Hawaiians were then living on the metropolitan island of Oahu (629,176), site of Honolulu (324,871).[86] Oahu's political style is individualistic.[87] A good study delineates island-wide municipal politics in the early 1960s: mayor and council candidates ran in formally partisan elections, but patronage was meager, the grass-roots majority party (all nine council members were Democrats) had no tradition of slating in primaries, and Republican Mayor Neal S. Blaisdell (1954-1968) stayed in office by cultivating a

[83] Fuchs, *Hawaii Pono*, p. 179.

[84] The reality is muddled a bit on the eastern side of the island of Hawaii before and after World II, where some political entrepreneurship was not so obviously rooted in corporate policy. See *ibid.*, pp. 202-205, 351.

[85] *Ibid.*, p. 328. "On Maui and Kauai, where I.L.W.U. voting power could make or break the territorial legislature, [union leader Jack] Hall demanded strict obedience to union dictation. When a legislator became a little cocky, as did David Trask of Maui, during the 1955 session, the word was passed to cut him down at the next election" (pp. 340-341).

[86] Officially the "City and County of Honolulu" (city and county coterminous), ruled by mayor and council, took in the entire island of Oahu in the 1960s. Six council members were elected islandwide, three in rural districts. The unit conventionally known as Honolulu, the southeastern urban area with a 1970 population of 324,871, was formally a council district of the "City and County."

[87] Some sources: Norman Meller and Daniel W. Tuttle, Jr., "Hawaii: The Aloha State," in Jonas (ed.), *Politics in the American West*, pp. 162-169; Daniel W. Tuttle, Jr., "Hawaii's Two-Party System—1959," pp. 1-4 in *ibid.* (compiler), *Papers on Hawaiian Politics, 1952-1966* (Honolulu: Department of Political Science, University of Hawaii, 1966); Tom Coffman, *Catch a Wave: A Case Study of Hawaii's New Politics* (Honolulu: University Press of Hawaii, 1973). *Catch a Wave* is an account of primary and general elections for governor in 1970. Democrat John A. Burns, elected governor in 1962, 1966, and 1970, is said to have run a "machine," but this is local usage. See Paul C. Phillips, *Hawaii's Democrats: Chasing the American Dream* (Washington, D.C.: University Press of America, 1982), ch. 6 and footnote 2 on pp. 197-198.

personal following.[88] The place of the parties: "The major parties do not control the nomination of candidates for the City Council; they do not support the candidates for municipal elective office with financial contributions; and they are not organized to take a continuing interest in municipal affairs."[89] On council candidates: "They run for their respective council seats essentially as individuals without organized party backing."[90] Blaisdell's successor as mayor, Democrat Frank F. Fasi (1968-1980), has been characterized as "the gadfly, the untrusted spoiler, the bad penny who always turned up where he wasn't wanted." A resilient entrepreneur, he built a media image, took populist stances, and spent a great deal of energy attacking other local politicians, especially fellow Democrats.[91] Oahu politics supplies an excellent example of a formally partisan electoral system operating without party organizations. TPO score for Hawaii: 1.

[88] Joseph W. Maguire, "A Study of the Local Government Process in the City and County of Honolulu" (M.A. thesis, American University, 1965), pp. 102-105, 132-140, 166-174. On patronage: pp. 85, 104-105, 153-154, 227. On lack of a Democratic tradition of slating: pp. 104-105, 140. On Blaisdell: pp. 104-105, 166-170.

[89] *Ibid.*, p. 104.

[90] *Ibid.*, p. 140.

[91] Phillips, *Hawaii's Democrats*, ch. 9, quotation at p. 127. Fasi later turned Republican.

CHAPTER 7

Summary of State Sketches

The TPO scores for the fifty states (see Table 7.1) produce patterns that will be examined from several perspectives in Part II. A brief summary of Part I may aid this shift to a broader focus. The first eight "organization states"—Rhode Island out through Illinois—supported especially prominent traditional organizations of a monopolistic sort in the late 1960s. Strong, well-documented city machines operated in Providence, New Haven, Albany, Jersey City, Pittsburgh, Chicago, and East St. Louis (Illinois). Patronage-based organizations brought their weight to bear at least in nominating processes below the level of mayor in a number of other cities in Rhode Island, Connecticut, New York (including New York City's boroughs), New Jersey, eastern Pennsylvania (including Philadelphia), Delaware (in Wilmington), and Ohio. Especially influential county organizations operated in urban and suburban areas of New York, New Jersey, Pennsylvania, Delaware, and Ohio;

Table 7.1   State TPO Scores

Organization States		Southern States		Northern Tier and Plains States		Western States	
Connecticut	5	Alabama	1	Iowa	1	Alaska	1
Delaware	4	Arkansas	2	Kansas	1	Arizona	1
Illinois	5	Florida	1	Maine	1	California	1
Indiana	5-PF	Georgia	2	Massachusetts	1	Colorado	1
Kentucky	4-PF	Louisiana	3-PF	Michigan	1	Hawaii	1
Maryland	5-PF	Mississippi	1	Minnesota	1	Idaho	1
Missouri	4-PF	North Carolina	1	Nebraska	1	Montana	1
New Jersey	5	South Carolina	1	New Hampshire	1	Nevada	1
New York	5	Tennessee	2-PF	North Dakota	1	New Mexico	2
Ohio	4	Texas	2	Oklahoma	1	Oregon	1
Pennsylvania	5	Virginia	2	South Dakota	1	Utah	1
Rhode Island	5			Vermont	1	Washington	1
West Virginia	4-PF			Wisconsin	1	Wyoming	1

the Republican organizations of New York's Nassau County and Pennsylvania's Delaware County stood out as model suburban machines. Local organizations in seven of the eight states (Ohio Democrats supplying the clearest exception) had a record of exercising considerable influence in nominating processes at the statewide level.

The other five "organization states"—West Virginia, Maryland, Kentucky, Indiana, and Missouri—supported at least some local organizations of a "persistently factional" sort in the late 1960s. In the metropolitan areas patterns of enduring intraparty factional competition turn up in Charleston (West Virginia), Baltimore City, Baltimore and Prince George's counties in Maryland's suburbs, Louisville, Evansville, Kokomo, Terre Haute, and Kansas City (Missouri). St. Louis's ward organizations had a record of cooperating rather than competing, Indianapolis's parties seemed to proceed by factional succession (one faction now and then displacing another) rather than by stable factional competition, and Indiana's Lake County Democrats evolved in the 1950s from loose factional competition to a machine centered in Gary. Four of the five states (all but Missouri) also offer considerable evidence of local patronage-based organizations (many of them factional) operating in rural areas. These local groups profited, no doubt, from the same four states' traditions of alliances between the local organizations, who wanted state patronage in return for electoral support, and candidates for governor in statewide primaries (or in Indiana's old nominating conventions), who wanted support and promised state patronage. In areas of a number of factional as well as monopolistic states, well-organized oppositions of a nontraditional sort waged continual and consequential warfare against traditional party organizations in the 1960s—notably Democratic reform clubs in Manhattan and the Bronx (duplicating slightly earlier challenges in Maryland's Montgomery County) and municipal good-government parties in Cincinnati and Kansas City (and at least in the 1950s, in Hartford).

The ex-Confederate South displayed a familiar pattern of individualistic politics in the late 1960s. Local candidates in both urban and rural areas for the most part sought office on their own. Strong old machines in Memphis and New Orleans (the South's only cities with populations over 100,000 in 1900) had, respectively, withered away and decayed into ward organizations. Instances of influential nominating organizations (new Republican parties aside) were evident mostly at the region's fringes—there were patches of traditional party organization, for example, in Arkansas, the Virginia Tidewater, the Appalachian section of Tennessee, the Mexican-American areas of southern and western Texas, and francophone southern Louisiana. By 1967 traceable city machines operated only in Virginia Beach in the far northeast and in Laredo in the far southwest. Virginia's statewide Byrd organization closed out its idiosyncratic career in the mid-1960s. The Houston area's influential party organizations of the 1960s were notable for their ideological drive, bringing to mind counterparts in Michigan and California. The striking businessmen's or business-cum-professional parties that dominated municipal politics in Dallas and San Antonio in the 1960s seem more a southwestern than a southern phenomenon; other such signally successful organizations dominated elections in Oklahoma City, Albuquerque, and Phoenix.

The nominating politics of the rest of the country was overwhelmingly individualistic in the late 1960s. Party organizations that had unmistakable properties of the traditional variety operated only in the northern Hispanic section of New Mexico. Some anomalies deserve mention. Oklahoma continued an exceptionally well-developed patronage politics (at least outside its two big cities) that fueled candidate organizations rather than party organizations; patronage jobs were channeled through individual officeholders. The Boston mayoralty remained an interesting and unusual office that allowed under Kevin White, as earlier under James Michael Curley, an assembling of powerful personal organizations and followings rooted in a mix of patronage, programs, and rhetoric. Organizations of issue-oriented activists seem to have been especially influential in the 1960s in California (both parties), Wisconsin (both parties, though not in nominating processes in the Democratic), the Denver area (liberal Democrats), and the Des Moines area (liberal and labor Democrats). Slating activity flourished at the municipal level in the academic centers of Cambridge, Ann Arbor, Madison, and Berkeley. Michigan supported its unique UAW-based Democratic party, and Minnesota's Democratic-Farmer-Labor party continued as the country's most successful endorsing organization (covering state through local levels) that functioned without the assistance of state-prescribed endorsing procedures or an important patronage supply.

Comparison of American states or regions through the use of maps can of course be deceptive, since some areas are much more densely populated than others. This is a pertinent consideration in thinking about traditional party organizations. The thirteen organization states expand to absorb a considerably larger part of the country's space if all fifty states are weighted according to their populations (see map). In recent times, with the rise of the Sunbelt, the proportion of the American

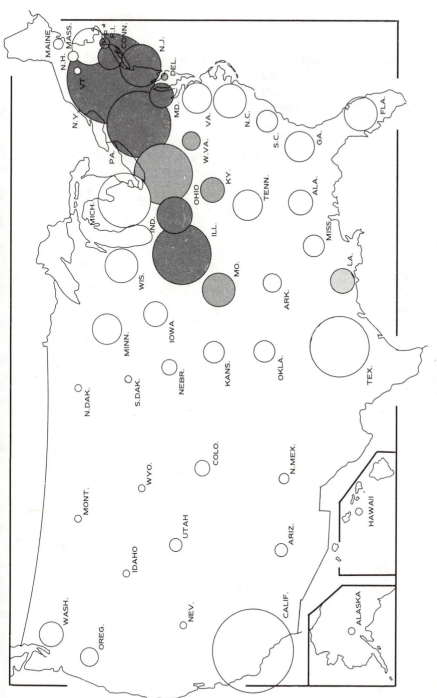

States Weighted by Population with TPO Score Indicated. Population based on 1970 census figures; TPO scores range from light (1) to dark (5).

public living in organization states has fallen to under 40 percent, though it was just under 50 percent during the first half of this century and over 50 percent during most of the nineteenth century (see Table 7.2). As Chapter 8 will argue, to compare the same geography over time is not a pointless exercise.

Table 7.2   Percentage of U.S. Population Living in "Organization States"

Census	% of Population	Census	% of Population
1790	44	1890	48
1800	45	1900	47
1810	50	1910	46
1820	51	1920	46
1830	53	1930	45
1840	55	1940	45
1850	55	1950	43
1860	53	1960	42
1870	52	1970	40
1880	50	1980	37

SOURCE: Decennial data from U.S. Bureau of the Census.

NOTE: "Organization states" are states with TPO scores of 4 or 5 (including 4-PF and 5-PF) in the late 1960s.

PART II

Background and Implications

The Historical Background

How does one explain the origin or existence of traditional party organization in the United States? Two styles of explanation can be called on from the social sciences, one sociological and the other economic. In the well-known functional argument of sociologist Robert K. Merton, American city machines (the strong subspecies of traditional organization), once they somehow come into existence, remain in operation because they fulfill functions: they supply particularistic goods or services to needy people, to politicians pursuing careers, and to legitimate and illegitimate businesses that formal governmental institutions do not or would not supply as easily or as agreeably or at all.[1] In the alternative logic of economics, a traditional organization might be regarded as a specifiable type of firm that can be expected to appear and operate wherever market conditions allow; its chief practitioners can use it to win money or power by dealing in votes and other private resources and in government goods and services. Max Weber, using an economist's formulation, characterized the American "boss" as "a political capitalist entrepreneur who on his own account and at his own risk provides votes."[2]

These functional and entrepreneurial interpretations are compatible and plausible, and indeed both in some measure are probably correct. Yet in practice neither is easy to make use of. In each case, evidence

[1] Robert K. Merton, *Social Theory and Social Structure* (New York: Free Press, 1968), pp. 125-136.

[2] Max Weber, "Politics as a Vocation," ch. 4 in H. H. Gerth and C. Wright Mills (eds.), *From Max Weber: Essays in Sociology* (New York: Galaxy, 1958), p. 109, and more generally pp. 107-111. Weber went on to draw a contrast between American and German party organizations of the nineteenth and early twentieth centuries, noting in particular that Germany's pre–World War I Social Democratic Party, a "guild of notables" that lacked access to governmental power and perquisites, drew its cohesion from a shared ideology, and operated in an environment where trained experts ran government institutions, had little in common with American parties except a mass following. One modern line of scholarship assumes that the study of American parties ought to begin with Robert Michels's 1911 work, *Political Parties*, a treatment of German and other European socialist parties of the turn of the century. This seems an idea of dubious value.

needed to show that a phenomenon originates, exists, or persists—here the phenomenon is traditional party organization or something like it—is ordinarily a great deal more vivid, concrete, and available than evidence that would be needed to show *why* it originates, exists, or persists. Is a function being fulfilled? Is it being fulfilled more or less than it used to be? What functions need to be fulfilled? How about market conditions? Do laws, as administered, permit or sustain the activity of organizational entrepreneurs? Does a political culture permit or sustain it? Is there a demand for products offered by traditional organization? Questions of this sort are difficult to answer without unusually sensitive inspection of political environments, and as a result they seldom are effectively addressed. In practice we have no problem accepting functional or entrepreneurial statements more or less as truisms that hover at an altitude somewhere above evidence. If we see, in particular, a city machine in action, we find it easy to account for it by imputing functions or by inferring a favorable marketplace; no additional evidence seems to be called for.

The course here will not be to explain the origin or existence of party organization in the manner of these covering theories but rather to look into historical antecedents of the *pattern* of traditional organization evident in the late 1960s. This is done to give a better sense of what an explanation (or set of explanations) must come to grips with and where in history answers might best be sought. The long run seems quite important; consider the evidence of Table 8.1, a cross-tabulation of states according to their TPO scores and dates of admission to the union. For a state to register a TPO score higher than 1 in the late 1960s, very nearly a necessary (though not a sufficient) condition is that it grew into a political entity early enough to achieve statehood by 1821.[3] This is a strikingly early date. The relation between admission date and organizational form crystallizes more usefully when one realizes that trans-Appalachian settlement and statehood took place earlier along the Gulf and in a central bulge out through Missouri than in the latitude of Michigan, Wisconsin, Iowa, and Minnesota. The only post-1821 states in Table 8.1 with TPO scores higher than 1 are Arkansas (admitted 1836), Texas (1845), and New Mexico (1912), and these achieve only a score of 2. In the latter two cases, the modern sites of traditional organization are Hispanic areas that were incorporated into American politics at about the time of the war with Mexico in the late 1840s.

---

[3] West Virginia is included in the 1791-1821 category of admission dates here. This placement among early noncoastal states such as Kentucky and Vermont probably does West Virginia better justice than its true admission date of 1863 after secession from Virginia.

Table 8.1   State TPO Scores by Date of Admission to Union

TPO Score	Original 13	1791-1821	1836-1867	1876-1896	20th Century
5	Connecticut Maryland New Jersey New York Pennsylvania Rhode Island	Illinois Indiana			
4	Delaware	Kentucky Missouri Ohio West Virginia			
3		Louisiana*			
2	Georgia Virginia	Tennessee	Arkansas Texas*		New Mexico*
1	Massachusetts New Hampshire North Carolina South Carolina	Alabama Maine Mississippi Vermont	California Florida Iowa Kansas Michigan Minnesota Nebraska Nevada Oregon Wisconsin	Colorado Idaho Montana North Dakota South Dakota Utah Washington Wyoming	Alaska Arizona Hawaii Oklahoma

* States with significant French or Hispanic settlements incorporated into U.S. electoral politics by the mid-nineteenth century.

New Mexico began a spirited electoral politics in the 1850s that lasted a full six decades of territorial government before statehood.[4] The annexed Hispanic sections of Texas and New Mexico may belong in a class with French Louisiana, another non-English-speaking settlement incorporated quite early and supporting traditional organization over a century later.

[4] On the origin of electoral politics in New Mexico see Howard R. Lamar, *The Far Southwest, 1846-1912: A Territorial History* (New York: Norton, 1970), ch. 4. This work gives the flavor of elections to the post of territorial delegate to Washington in the 1850s: "The Americans, hampered by numerical inferiority, did not hesitate to use meth-

The pattern of admission dates suggests that the origin of traditional organization, or its potential—conditions that might produce effects later—should be sought in colonial, territorial, or state political environments of the early nineteenth century or before. This is a suggestion easier to make than to follow up, since providing clear characterizations of party organization at the city or county level for any period of the nineteenth century has been a rare enterprise among historians (even Tammany Hall seems to lack a close account of its structure and activities until late in the century) and evidence on cultural or statutory settings that might have fostered, sustained, or inhibited organizational activity at one or another time or place is rare also.[5] There is nonetheless a literature to draw on, including Richard P. McCormick's valuable comparative analysis of early nineteenth-century politics at the state level in *The Second American Party System*, which contains among other things a set of sketches, based on whatever material was available in the mid-1960s (in several cases not much) of organization in states admitted to the union up through 1821.[6]

Does the early nineteenth century's pattern of organization prefigure the organizational map of the 1960s? In some essentials it does. An important McCormick conclusion is that the Middle Atlantic states stood out early in the century as builders of "extremely elaborate party machinery, operated by shrewd professionals" who dealt heavily in patronage: "More than in any other region, avidity for patronage and other spoils of office constituted a major theme of Middle States poli-

---

ods that would have ruined them politically in the states. In the early years each side vied to corral the support of anyone they could get. Pueblo Indians and Mexican citizens still living in the territory were invited to vote, and the federal soldiers there often voted repeatedly in a single election. The New Mexicans, unused to the American concept of the franchise, were willing to sell this new thing—the vote—for some economic advantage. Governor Lane learned to his amazement in 1853 that while many ballots had been cast in his favor at Taos, not a single one had been reported. The canvassers had been 'influenced' by the opposition. Then there was the case of the priest of San Juan, who, knowing that right was on his candidate's side in 1855, sat down with the ballot box and carefully removed all the votes unfavorable to his choice. A persistent pattern in elections had been established that was to continue until statehood" (pp. 105-106). On Texas: Edgar G. Shelton, Jr., *Political Conditions Among Texas Mexicans along the Rio Grande* (thesis, University of Texas, 1946; repr., San Francisco: R and E Research Associates, 1974), pp. 22-29.

[5] Henry Bain's recent treatment of electoral politics at the county level in Maryland of the 1870s shows what can in fact be done using imagination and readily available documents. (See ch. 3, note 17.)

[6] Richard P. McCormick, *The Second American Party System: Party Formation in the Jacksonian Era* (New York: Norton, 1973). All the states admitted through 1821, that is, except South Carolina, which held no statewide elections for any office before 1860.

tics"—an avidity that assumed importance "especially in New Jersey and Pennsylvania, and conspicuously in New York."[7] And New York, of course, was the setting of Martin Van Buren's innovative Albany Regency, the flagship of the American nineteenth-century spoils system, built at the state level at a time when many of New York's local officials—notably mayors of important cities—were appointed in the state capital. The Regency emerges in an analysis by Alvin Kass as the most successful of a considerable family of such organizations that appeared in New York in the first quarter of the nineteenth century. Run typically by "a clique grouped around an influential leader," each group sought to manage the careers of its politicians and to "impose discipline upon its membership through the distribution of patronage," producing a politics marked by the "inconsequential part played by doctrine, ideology, and principle" and "the idea that offices exist not as a necessary means of administering government but for the support of party leaders at public expense."[8] Another source on the Regency comments that "because their goal was the preservation of the party, the politicians lost interest in other, more ideological objectives. This is evident from their election appeals and campaign rhetoric. There were virtually no substantive planks in regency platforms—no programs of internal improvements, no plans for expanded education or agricultural improvements, no demands for expansion of the franchise, virtually no demands at all."[9] In other accounts Pennsylvania as well as New York appears as an organizational pioneer; both probably deserve credit as pattern states in the launching of traditional organization.[10] At the local level Tammany Hall evidently set up shop as a Manhattan slating

[7] *Ibid.*, pp. 104, 103, 168, and more generally part 4, "Party Formation in the Middle States." One should note, as McCormick does, the precariousness of the evidence. The full sentence containing the last phrases quoted above: "The relative importance of patronage in the Middle States, as compared with New England, can scarcely be evaluated on the basis of the available evidence, but it would appear that especially in New Jersey and Pennsylvania, and conspicuously in New York, avidity for the spoils of office exerted a powerful influence in politics" (p. 168).

[8] Alvin Kass, *Politics in New York State, 1800-1830* (Syracuse: Syracuse University Press, 1965), especially chs. 3, 4 and 7, quotations respectively at pp. 34, 28, 119, 29.

[9] Michael Wallace, "Changing Concepts of Party in the United States: New York, 1815-1828," *American Historical Review* 74(1968), 470, and more generally on the Regency, pp. 453-471. Also on the Regency: McCormick, *Second American Party System*, pp. 110-119; Robert V. Remini, *Martin Van Buren and the Making of the Democratic Party* (New York: Columbia University Press, 1959), pp. 8-11.

[10] Moisei Ostrogorski, *Democracy and the Organization of Political Parties*, vol. 2 (New York: Macmillan, 1902), pp. 41-44, 49-50, 53, 150-156; Roy F. Nichols, *The Invention of the American Political Parties* (New York: Macmillan, 1967), pp. 233-234, 281.

organization early in the century, and is said to have strengthened its position in the 1820s by taking advantage of suffrage expansion and reaching out to embrace immigrants.[11] It is reported that early organization in Pennsylvania centered in the counties, though organization in South Philadelphia began its long and influential life as a party base in the late 1820s, a Democratic holding until about 1900, then Republican until about 1950, then Democratic once again.[12] Farther south, McCormick treats Maryland as a Middle Atlantic rather than Southern state, partly on the basis of its elaborate organization from about 1800 on.[13]

But the Middle Atlantic area stands alone. New England's vigorous parties of the early nineteenth century seem in general to have lacked the incentive arrangements of the Albany Regency. Massachusetts in particular displayed no such propensity in an environment where "elections were relatively orderly affairs, conducted with decorum, and corruption was all but non-existent," though one's eyebrows may go up in reading about Rhode Island, where political tradition dating back a century accommodated "indigenous parties, which rarely concerned themselves with issues or ideologies" and "wholesale corruption" in elections—notably "the technique of bribing electors of the opposite persuasion to stay away from the polls."[14] Politics of the pre-Jacksonian South—Tennessee and Kentucky as well as Virginia, North Carolina, and Georgia in McCormick's classification—carried "a strong flavor of localism and personalism" and was conducted with "a minimum of formal machinery." "Candidates were self-nominated, negotiated

---

[11] On Tammany: Gustavus Myers, *The History of Tammany Hall* (New York: Boni and Liveright, 1917), chs. 1-9, pp. 73-74 on Tammany's strengthening its organizational base in the 1820s. The New York City election of 1827: "Cases of fraud and violence had hitherto been frequent; but nothing like the exhibition at the primaries and polls in November, 1827, had ever been known. Cart-loads of voters, many of whom had been in the country less than three years, were used as repeaters in the different wards" (p. 87).

[12] On early county organization: McCormick, *Second American Party System*, pp. 136-138, 146-147; Nichols, *Invention*, p. 233. On the odyssey of South Philadelphia: Sam Bass Warner, *The Private City: Philadelphia in Three Periods of Its Growth* (Philadelphia: University of Pennsylvania Press, 1968), pp. 86-91; Dennis Clark, *The Irish in Philadelphia: Ten Generations of Urban Experience* (Philadelphia: Temple University Press, 1973), pp. 117-118, 121; William S. Vare, *My Forty Years in Politics* (Philadelphia: Roland Swain, 1933), p. 79.

[13] McCormick, *Second American Party System*, pp. 154-166.

[14] On New England incentive arrangements: *ibid.*, part 3, "Party Formation in New England." Quotation on Massachusetts: p. 40. Nothing that resembles the Albany Regency turns up in Ronald P. Formisano, *The Transformation of Political Culture: Massachusetts Parties, 1790s-1840s* (New York: Oxford University Press, 1983). On Rhode Island: McCormick, *Second American Party System*, pp. 76-86, quotations at pp. 76, 78.

for support from men of influence, and conducted their own campaigns."[15] A familiar landed gentry ruled by informal arrangement in Virginia.[16] Nothing else in McCormick's accounts of Ohio Valley states points to a clear ancestry of later patterns of organization.

A leap forward to about 1900, over almost a century of industrialization, urbanization, and party evolution, permits an inspection of traditional organization (or at least structure approximating its properties) at about the height of its incidence. What was its location? Moisei Ostrogorski, using his term "the Machine" and an urgent style, supplied a geographic sketch in 1902 that no one seems to have improved on since:

> If on the map of the United States all the parts of the country where the Machine has developed were coloured red, the eye would at once be attracted to the right by a large blotch formed by the States of New York and Pennsylvania with a strip of the State of New Jersey on the east, with the State of Maryland on the south, and the State of Ohio on the west. This spot casts a faint shadow to the northeast over New England, while on the other side, to the west, the red will appear in more or less deep tints on the State of Illinois and will stain the neighboring States, marking with scarlet points most of the large cities, such as St. Louis in Missouri and others of less importance, like Louisville in Kentucky or Minneapolis in Minnesota, and other still smaller ones among the large ones; then, after making a brief pause in the States of the Far West and leaving some patches there, it will flow toward the Pacific slope and deposit a thick layer of carmine on San Francisco; and, finally, jumping right over to the Gulf of Mexico, it will cover New Orleans with a similar layer. A very considerable space will be left hardly coloured at all or will even exhibit the shot colour to be seen in certain fabrics: these are regions or cities where the Machine has no stable and regular existence; rings of mercenary politicians form in them, disappear after a short time and re-form under favourable circumstances. A good many points again on the map will appear almost white. . . . [T]he part of the map coloured red, while only a portion of the whole country, contains almost a third of the population of the United States and represents at least three-fifths of its economic interests. This domain of the Machine is daily growing larger. The machine is gaining ground, especially

---

[15] *Ibid.*, pp. 177, 178, 248, and more generally part 5, "Party Formation in the Old South."

[16] *Ibid.*, pp. 178-199.

in the West, where it is invading districts which appeared to be free from it.[17]

This proves to be a remarkably accurate organizational survey when matched against more recent evidence of geographic particulars at the turn of the century—if "the Machine" can be taken as more or less identical to traditional party organization—and it prefigures quite closely the organization map of the 1960s two-thirds of a century later. On specifics Ostrogorski was right (more or less) in reaching west to color in San Francisco around 1900,[18] though he probably should have

[17] Ostrogorski, *Democracy and the Organization of Political Parties*, vol. 2, pp. 422-423. Ostrogorski used a more general term, "the Organization," to refer to the top-to-bottom hierarchy of institutions of the post-1830s party system—national conventions extending down through state, county, township and ward committees. "The Machine," less common in incidence, was "Organization" given over to the "absolute power of the small cliques of managers, who settled everything behind the scenes," or in another reference "an aggregation of individuals stretching hierarchically from top to bottom, bound to one another by personal devotion, but mercenary, and bent solely on satisfying their appetites by exploiting the resources of a political party." The best clues to his usage, including the quoted material, are located at pp. 56-58, 128-129, 371, and 422-423.

[18] Ostrogorski may have been off by a decade. Christopher A. Buckley ran a strong Democratic organization of a traditional sort in San Francisco in the 1880s. He exercised considerable influence in the city and also the state, but his party's adoption of structural reforms in the early 1890s apparently undermined the influence of district leaders and precinct clubs. On Buckley see Alexander Callow, Jr., "San Francisco's Blind Boss," *Pacific Historical Review* 25(1956), 261-279; William A. Bullough, *The Blind Boss and His City: Christopher Augustine Buckley and Nineteenth-Century San Francisco* (Berkeley: University of California Press, 1979), especially pp. 92-93, 112-116, 131-133, 194-198; Curtis E. Grassman, "Prologue to California Reform: The Democratic Impulse, 1886-1898," *Pacific Historical Review* 42(1973), 519-521. On the structural reforms: Bullough, pp. 237, 266. Abe Ruef, a Republican district leader who masterminded the successes of the Union Labor Party in city elections just after the turn of the century, has been labeled a "boss," but in fact he looks more like an opportunistic fixer or campaign manager than the head of a traditional organization. No one has reported any durable organization he might have been heading. See Walton Bean, *Boss Ruef's San Francisco: The Story of the Union Labor Party, Big Business, and the Graft Prosecution* (Berkeley: University of California Press, 1952); James P. Walsh, "Abe Ruef Was No Boss: Machine Politics, Reform, and San Francisco," *California Historical Quarterly* 51(1972), 3-16. Walsh's conclusion, at pp. 7-8: "Ruef's powers were derived from his personal relationship with Mayor Eugene E. Schmitz, the attractive orchestra leader whose nomination Ruef finessed through the convention of the new and politically naive Union Labor Party. Ruef's temporary powers rested not on years of patient machine building, but upon his clear perception of San Francisco's shifting political tides and his ability to navigate their surges." San Francisco as of 1901: "The bipartisan political establishment was relatively weak and no dominant political machine or boss existed" (Jules Tygiel, ". . . where unionism holds undisputed sway: A Reappraisal of San Francisco's Union Labor Party," *California History* 62[1983], 199-200).

left the red off Minneapolis[19] and put some instead on Kansas City, Omaha, the Mexican-American areas of Texas, and Indiana in general and Indianapolis in particular.[20]

Another geographic survey, a recent sketch by Ernest S. Griffith judging which late nineteenth-century cities stood "in need of reform" and which did not, traces the familiar pattern of organization territory in the Middle Atlantic section but not to the north or south. He has good words for Portland, Maine; for Boston, though its council, he says, had deteriorated; for Springfield, Massachusetts, which despite some problems had "maintained the old New England tone"; for Brookline, Cambridge, Worcester, Lawrence, Lowell, and Fall River in Massachusetts and Hartford in Connecticut, though the last four "gave evidence of the strength of the old tradition" only "from time to time" and "not continuously." He has more good words for post-Reconstruction Lynchburg and Richmond in Virginia, and for Charlotte, Charleston, and Atlanta. Newark, he says, "seems to have maintained

---

[19] Lincoln Steffens gave notoriety to Minneapolis in 1902 in writing about its mayor, Albert A. "Doc" Ames. See *The Shame of the Cities* (New York: Hill and Wang, 1957), pp. 42-68 ("The Shame of Minneapolis"). Harold Zink later included Ames in a gallery of "bosses" in *City Bosses in the United States: A Study of Twenty Municipal Bosses* (Durham: Duke University Press, 1930), ch. 19, though he seemed uneasy about Ames's lack of fit. See pp. 47, 52-54, 342. In fact Ames was a genial rascal and former mayor who won the mayoralty again in 1900 via a write-in vote in the Republican primary, summoning a personal following made up substantially of Civil War veterans. Once in office he and his appointees engaged in imaginative looting that produced a round of indictments. But the case for a "machine" or traditional organization is no better than the inference of a national Republican "machine" in the 1920s from Teapot Dome. Studies of Minnesota politics around the turn of the century give no evidence of traditional organization in Minneapolis. For an instructive contrast see Carl H. Chrislock, *The Progressive Era in Minnesota, 1899-1918* (St. Paul: Minnesota Historical Society, 1971), esp. ch. 3 ("The Dynamics of Minnesota Progressive Politics"), and a book about Illinois politics of the same period that leaves no doubt about the important role of Chicago's Democratic and Republican ward organizations: Joel A. Tarr, *A Study in Boss Politics: William Lorimer of Chicago* (Urbana: University of Illinois Press, 1971). A recent treatment of "Doc" Ames's mayoralty: Richard B. Kielbowicz, "The Limits of the Press as an Agent of Reform: Minneapolis, 1900-1905," *Journalism Quarterly* 59(1982), 21-27 and 170.

[20] Scattered references to Indianapolis, all very brief, suggest the presence of traditional organization back at least as far as the 1880s. See John Bartlow Martin, *Indiana: An Interpretation* (New York: Knopf, 1947), pp. 101-102; Clifton J. Phillips, *Indiana in Transition: The Emergence of an Industrial Commonwealth 1880-1920* (Indianapolis: Indiana Historical Bureau and Indiana Historical Society, 1968), p. 36; Richard J. Del Vecchio, "Indiana Politics During the Progressive Era, 1912-1916" (Ph.D. dissertation, Notre Dame, 1973), pp. 144-145; John A. Davis, "The Ku Klux Klan in Indiana, 1920-1930: An Historical Study" (Ph.D. dissertation, Northwestern University, 1966), pp. 209-211.

an honest government with reasonable consistency" from 1870 through 1900, but elsewhere between New England and Virginia the large cities needed reform and of the middle-sized "not one stood out in the Middle States as consistently well governed."[21]

What of party organizations at the state level? In general these reached their peak of influence around 1900, and a study of traditional party organization should be alert to their geographic pattern, sources of support, and relationship, if any, with local structures. Hence a brief survey is presented here of state organizations that displayed hierarchy and operated with reasonable success for a decade or more around 1900 in nominating governors and state legislators, choosing Senators, and guiding activity in state legislatures.[22] Some states had organizations of this caliber but not very many. Senators, of course, appear in the thick of most such structures, induced into building or tending them because of their need for state legislative majorities in order to reach and hold office in Washington (before the Seventeenth Amendment switched the power to elect Senators from legislatures to popular electorates). Senators were supplied, especially on the Republican side, with federal patronage (notably in post offices and customs houses) that was helpful in supporting organizations back home. Information on turn-of-the-century state organization is spotty, unfortunately, and on a number of no doubt interesting states—notably Connecticut, New Jersey, Kentucky, Indiana, and Minnesota—silence is probably better than teasing conclusions out of a thin literature.[23] Twenty-three states come into focus pretty well. Private corporations as well as party organizations were dealing directly in nominating processes at the turn of the century, and it will be advisable to distinguish between the two and also to keep a lookout for hybrid forms.

Ostrogorski referred in passing to New York, Maryland, and Penn-

[21] Ernest S. Griffith, *A History of American City Government: The Conspicuous Failure, 1870-1900* (New York: Praeger, 1974), pp. 69, 98-99.

[22] The evidence requirement here is reasonably rigorous: state organizations are judged to satisfy the criteria specified in the text only if scholarship on them gives persuasive testimony on appropriate structure and activity. Vague or unelaborated references to "bosses," "machines," or such are not good enough. The criteria nonetheless pick up less than one would like to know—for instance, because information is sparse, organizational density at the county level is ignored. Turn-of-the-century Ohio and Illinois, to give two examples, very likely supported relatively strong county organizations that were well integrated into state-level party factions, though lack of stable state leadership keeps both states out of the "strong state organization" category. The criteria stipulated here are probably the most useful, for the purposes at hand, that the available evidence will bear.

[23] Indiana seems in particular need of some monographic work—for example, on the state Democratic organization headed by Thomas Taggart from the 1890s into the 1920s, apparently anchored in Indianapolis.

sylvania as having especially strong state organizations, and he was certainly correct.[24] In New York of the late 1890s, Republican Senator Thomas C. Platt presided over an informal ruling council of fifteen or so party influentials known as the 'Sunday school class," an assortment of local leaders (including Albany and Rochester bosses), newspapermen, old party pros, corporate lawyers, and businessmen—notably Chauncey M. Depew, president of the New York Central Railroad. Platt and his council ordinarily exercised control over selection of candidates in state nominating conventions, choice of state legislative officials, enactment of state laws, federal and state patronage jobs, and the state legislature's choice of Senators—notably Platt himself, who as Senator was said to be "unique and remarkable for having never, by spoken or written word, declared the shadow of an opinion concerning any of the vital issues of the time." The organization's key resources, aside from the harvest of state government itself, were votes supplied in elections by local leaders, the persuasive powers of affiliated newspapers, a diminishing federal patronage channeled through Platt, and money supplied by private corporations in exchange for favorable treatment in the legislature. Such corporate money had been given formerly to individual state legislators, but Platt, copying an innovation by the state's Democrats, substituted the party organization as recipient.[25] Democrat David B. Hill ran a comparable New York organization a decade earlier; his principal local barons were the party leaders of Buffalo, Brooklyn, and Tammany.[26]

In Maryland, a Democratic partnership of Senator Arthur P. Gorman and I. Freeman Rasin, head of the Baltimore machine, dominated politics during most of the last quarter of the nineteenth century. "Their organization nominated governors and other state officers at Democratic state conventions, was influential in Congressional and judicial conventions in the several districts, and elected United States Senators in the General Assembly. The organization was sustained by the usual resources—state, county and (at times) Federal patronage; contributions from economic interests desiring governmental favor; control of the party organization and the electoral machinery; and occasional fraud and violence at the polls."[27]

[24] Ostrogorski, *Democracy and the Organization of Political Parties*, vol. 2, p. 193.

[25] The source on Platt is Harold F. Gosnell's excellent monograph, *Boss Platt and His New York Machine* (Chicago: University of Chicago Press, 1924), chs. 4, 5, 7, 9, 10, 13, 14, quotation at p. 177. A recent discussion of Platt: Richard L. McCormick, "Prelude to Progressivism: The Transformation of New York State Politics, 1890-1910," *New York History* 59(1978), 253-276.

[26] Gosnell, *Boss Platt*, ch. 3.

[27] See Henry Bain, "Five Kinds of Politics: A Historical and Comparative Study of the

Pennsylvania's Republican organization was an especially elaborate structure, said in a 1904 study to be "the strongest, the most enduring, the most efficient of any similar organization for an entire State in the whole Union."[28] A sequence of three talented leaders, Senators Simon Cameron, Matthew S. Quay, and Boies Penrose, presided over nominating and legislating in the state's predominantly Republican environment from the mid-1860s through 1921. County organizations in rural areas supplied their loyal ranks; the Republican machines in Philadelphia and Pittsburgh constantly caused trouble by joining insurgent alliances.[29] In Cameron's day the organization depended substantially on federal patronage, but three innovations in the 1880s gave it a solid home base: a 2 percent salary assessment on state employees; Quay's centralization (a decade before this was done by the New York parties) of exchange relations with private corporations, which brought in money directly to the organization rather than to individual legislators; and, most important, Quay's inspired chicanery in the state treasurer's office, which generated vast funds from banks. His arrangement was to deposit state funds in banks without requiring interest payments; half the money then came back in collateral-free or interest-free loans he could channel to politicians of his choice.[30] Fortified by all this, Quay was able to withstand a challenge in the 1890s from an alliance of the Pittsburgh and Philadelphia machines, the railroads, and most of the

Making of Legislators in Five Maryland Constituencies" (Ph.D. dissertation, Harvard University, 1970), p. 143, and more generally pp. 142-149, 808-812. Another authoritative source is John R. Lambert, *Arthur Pue Gorman* (Baton Rouge: Louisiana State University Press, 1953).

[28] Jesse Macy, *Party Organization and Machinery* (New York: The Century Co., 1904), p. 112, and more generally ch. 9. The authoritative source on the organization in the 1880s and 1890s is now James A. Kehl, *Boss Rule in the Gilded Age: Matt Quay of Pennsylvania* (Pittsburgh: University of Pittsburgh Press, 1981). See also Philip S. Klein and Ari Hoogenboom, *A History of Pennsylvania* (University Park: Pennsylvania State University Press, 1980), chs. 21, 23.

[29] See Kehl, *Boss Rule*, pp. 74-81, 187-195.

[30] The salary assessment was in place by 1882, according to Kehl in *ibid.*, p. 29. Klein and Hoogenboom write of a 3% assessment in *History of Pennsylvania*, p. 362. On centralizing of exchange relations: "Businessmen . . . paid in dollars for Quay's services. They were actually relieved that there was an efficient and effective broker to receive their money, distribute it judiciously, and assure the desired results. In previous years there had been no such middleman, and the railroad interests had disbursed funds to legislators through their own agents only to be embarrassed by both legislative failure and public disclosure" (Kehl, p. 63 and more generally pp. 62-63). On the banks: Kehl, pp. 64-67. Quay is said to have remarked, "I don't mind losing a governorship or a legislature now and then, but I always need the state treasuryship" (p. 66). Kehl's treatment of the strengthening of the organization and its resources in the 1880s (still available in the 1890s) appears at pp. 24-30, 59-67.

state's newspapers, and also a later assault by Republican reformers.[31]

Impressive organizations, all peculiar in one way or another, operated in three other Eastern states around 1900. In Rhode Island, General Charles R. Brayton ran a Republican organization dealing in nominations, legislation, and patronage from the mid-1870s past the turn of the century, working in alliance with Senator Nelson W. Aldrich after 1880. The base of support of Brayton's apparatus seems to have shifted from federal patronage to corporate money as time went on, but important throughout was the systematic practice (now some two centuries old) of buying up votes in small towns—particularly from voters characterized at the time as "degenerate native stock" in inland areas near the Connecticut line.[32] In Virginia, the Democratic organization of Senator Thomas S. Martin kept on top of the relatively volatile politics of the 1890s by liberal resort to racism, railroad money, and election fraud, but settled into calmer invincibility after a constitutional settlement in 1901 drastically shrank the electorate. In all essentials except one—its lack of interest in issues—the post-1901 Martin regime resembled the Byrd regime a generation later; a canon of high integrity is said to have prevailed in governmental affairs except in the far southwest and Norfolk-Virginia Beach area.[33] In West Virginia, a hybrid apparatus led by Senator Stephen B. Elkins dominated state government and politics around the turn of the century. The state's Republican organization down to the precinct level was yoked with family coal and railroad holdings in the Senator's interest. The result was formidable: federal patronage, state patronage, a generous "barrel" of corporate money in elections, use of high-priced corporate officials in electoral politics, and a practice of putting ambitious local talent on the company payroll. In addition Elkins had a working alliance with the "Hog Combine," the Republican organization of Kanawha County (Charleston). The head of the Democrats' state organization around 1900 was

[31] *Ibid.*, pp. 187-195 and ch. 12.

[32] On the Brayton organization: Mary C. Nelson, "The Influence of Immigration on Rhode Island Politics, 1865-1910" (Ph.D. dissertation, Radcliffe College, 1955), especially chs. 2, 5-9; John D. Buenker, "The Politics of Resistance: The Rural-Based Yankee Republican Machines of Connecticut and Rhode Island," *New England Quarterly* 47(1974), 212-237. On vote buying: Nelson, pp. 27, 43-44, 278; Lincoln Steffens, *The Struggle for Self-Government* (New York: McClure, Phillips and Co., 1906), pp. 120-135; and "A Corrupt State: Analysis of Conditions in Rhode Island: Review of the Venal Towns," *New York Evening Post*, May 7, 1903, pp. 1, 8. This last is an interesting town-by-town review of electoral environments in Rhode Island.

[33] Allen W. Moger, *Virginia: Bourbonism to Byrd, 1870-1925* (Charlottesville: University Press of Virginia, 1968), chs. 5, 7-10, 15. On the Norfolk-Virginia Beach area: pp. 194-195, 354.

former Senator Henry G. Davis, Elkins's father-in-law and business partner. In the 1880s, a time of Democratic ascendancy, Davis had nudged Elkins into Republican affairs as a reaction to his own party's factionalism and the menace posed by tariff reform to family holdings. Turn-of-the-century election contests between these West Virginia parties were expensive and excitingly close.[34]

Three more organizations operated in the upper Midwest. In Michigan and Wisconsin, similar in pattern, Republican Senators James McMillan and Philetus Sawyer put together combinations that dominated legislative and nominating politics in the 1880s and exercised considerable influence in the 1890s—the "McMillan Alliance" in Michigan and a troika of politicians headed by Sawyer in Wisconsin.[35] Both men were business tycoons who drew on personal fortunes and corporate connections to fuel their organizations, though federal patronage supplied important post office bases in Madison and Milwaukee, and in Wisconsin a treasury scheme something like Matt Quay's came to light in a scandal around 1890.[36] But neither group seems to have assessed the salaries of public employees; no report of this appears in the standard accounts. Nor was either anchored in traditional party organizations in Milwaukee or Detroit, where such structures were weak or nonexistent, though McMillan depended on a mining vote apparently under corporate control in Michigan's Upper Peninsula.[37] In

[34] The excellent source on West Virginia is John Alexander Williams, *West Virginia and the Captains of Industry* (Morgantown: West Virginia University Library, 1976), especially ch. 4.

[35] The basic source on Michigan: Marie Heyda, "Senator James McMillan and the Flowering of the Spoils System," *Michigan History* 54(1970), 183-200. On Wisconsin: Richard N. Current, *Pine Logs and Politics: A Life of Philetus Sawyer, 1816-1900* (Madison: State Historical Society of Wisconsin, 1950), chs. 4-7; Robert S. Maxwell, *La Follette and the Rise of the Progressives in Wisconsin* (Madison: State Historical Society of Wisconsin, 1956), chs. 1, 2. McMillan first went to the Senate in 1889, Sawyer in 1881.

[36] On the Wisconsin treasury see Current, *Pine Logs and Politics*, pp. 255-269.

[37] For a sense of Milwaukee's electoral environment around the turn of the century see Joseph A. Ranney, "The Political Campaigns of Mayor David S. Rose," *Milwaukee History* 4(1981), 2-19. "Positions of power in city politics changed hands regularly before 1898 and no recognized 'ring' or other political leadership group existed" (p. 17). When Robert La Follette went after the Republican gubernatorial nomination in 1900, "it appears that he was the only candidate who had any real organization in the city" (Maxwell, *La Follette*, p. 19). Organizations other than the traditional party sort operated in Detroit's electoral politics of the 1880s. Rival electric lighting companies in search of contracts "entered actively into politics, each having its pledged candidates for aldermen and each spending money freely for the purchase of aldermanic votes." Also: "The saloon, liquor, and beer interests were thoroughly organized in a compact secret organization which enabled the several thousand men concerned to act as a unit in every political undertaking from the caucus to the convention and the election." See George B.

each state an extraordinary nemesis appeared around 1890 who assaulted the reigning organization relentlessly for a decade. In Michigan this was Hazen S. Pingree, Republican mayor of Detroit (and later governor), who became the national model of one type of Progressive mayor. He undertook social as well as structural reform, sought municipal ownership of public service corporations, and built a lower-rather than upper-income electoral coalition. The result was a cleavage of unusual clarity in Michigan politics; McMillan was not only Republican state leader, but also part-owner of virtually every important corporation in the Detroit area.[38] Sawyer's energetic foe in Wisconsin was Robert M. La Follette, later the country's pace-setter among Progressive reformers at the state level.[39] Both the McMillan and Sawyer organizations crumbled and vanished around 1900, partly as a consequence of these assaults.[40] La Follette won his first gubernatorial nomination by acclamation in Wisconsin's Republican convention of 1900.

The upper Midwest's most interesting and surprising structure at the

---

Catlin, *The Story of Detroit* (Detroit: Detroit News, 1923), pp. 561, 594. A Democratic ward boss figured in city politics around 1890, but he seemed to be dependent on federal patronage, a poor source, and he had probably dropped from the picture by 1895. See Melvin G. Holli, *Reform in Detroit: Hazen S. Pingree and Urban Politics* (New York: Oxford University Press, 1969), pp. 15-16, 125-126, 153. From about 1901 until World War I "a loose, bipartisan aggregation of petty precinct bosses popularly known as the Voteswappers League" exercised some influence in Detroit's elections (though no one writes of a VSL role in mayoral elections) through voter mobilization and election fraud. The VSL had no record of generating governmental favors, its practitioners ordinarily worked out of saloons, and on close inspection it turns out to have been mostly an instrument of the Royal Ark, the Detroit area's association of (heavily regulated) liquor dealers, which appointed ward captains and endorsed candidates. The best source on the VSL is Raymond R. Fragnoli, *The Transformation of Detroit: Progressivism in Detroit— and After, 1912-1933* (New York: Garland, 1982), pp. 11-15; see also William P. Lovett, *Detroit Rules Itself* (Boston: Gorham, 1930), ch. 2, and Arthur C. Millspaugh, *Party Organization and Machinery in Michigan Since 1890* (Baltimore: Johns Hopkins University Press, 1917), pp. 106-107, 117-120, 159-163. On the Upper Peninsula: Heyda, "Senator James McMillan," pp. 190-191; Millspaugh, p. 160.

[38] On Pingree see Holli, *Reform in Detroit*: "Pingree appeared to have the bad luck of trenching upon Senator McMillan's economic interests almost every time he attempted some municipal reform" (pp. 88-89).

[39] On La Follette: Maxwell, *La Follette, passim*; Current, *Pine Logs and Politics*, ch. 6, 7; Kenneth Acrea, "The Wisconsin Reform Coalition, 1892-1900," *Wisconsin Magazine of History* 52(1968-69), 132-157. La Follette broke with Sawyer in 1891 in the wake of the treasury scandal.

[40] Though not all nemeses end up winners. In Pennsylvania John Wanamaker conducted a crusade against Matt Quay at the same time that was of approximately the same intensity as La Follette's in Wisconsin against Sawyer. Wanamaker came close but could not dislodge Quay. See Kehl, *Boss Rule*, ch. 12.

turn of the century was Alexander McKenzie's authoritative organization in North Dakota.[41] McKenzie, an agent of railroad, banking, and grain elevator interests who often worked out of a suite in St. Paul, Minnesota, presided over Republican nominations for Congress and governor, activity in the North Dakota state legislature, and selection of Senators. This was made possible in part by the malleability of German farmers transplanted from Russia—one element in a state immigrant population that was proportionately the country's largest. The result was an organization supported not only by federal patronage and railroad money but by machines in Bismarck and Fargo and a controlled vote in at least some of the rural German counties.[42] A Progressive uprising aided by a Democratic governor destroyed McKenzie's elaborate system between 1906 and 1912, which left immigrant farmers free for mobilization by the quasi-socialist Nonpartisan League from 1915 on. The League employed techniques "not that different from those used so effectively by the McKenzie machine for years."[43] This was a unique organizational evolution.

A few other states had influential local organizations at the turn of the century that for various reasons failed to become building blocks of a stable state organization. In Ohio the problem was the heterogeneity of the state. In the mid-1890s a dominant alliance composed of Repub-

[41] There is good documentation on the McKenzie organization from start to finish: Howard R. Lamar, *Dakota Territory, 1861-1889: A Study of Frontier Politics* (New Haven: Yale University Press, 1956), pp. 215-216, 242; Robert P. Wilkins, "Alexander McKenzie and the Politics of Bossism," pp. 3-39 in Thomas W. Howard (ed.), *The North Dakota Political Tradition* (Ames: Iowa State University Press, 1981); Elwyn B. Robinson, *History of North Dakota* (Lincoln: University of Nebraska Press, 1966), pp. 215-216, 218, 230-231, 256-257, 264-268, 327; Edward C. Blackorby, "George B. Winship: Progressive Journalist of the Middle Border," *North Dakota Quarterly* 39(1971), 5-17; Charles N. Glaab, "The Revolution of 1906—N.D. vs. McKenzie," *North Dakota Quarterly* 24(1956), 101-109; Charles N. Glaab, "John Burke and the Progressive Revolt," pp. 40-65 in Howard (ed.), *North Dakota Political Tradition*.

[42] "The Burleigh County [site of Bismarck] machine was headed by E. G. 'Ed' Patterson. . . . It was Patterson's duty . . . to roll up large majorities in the city's Fourth Ward whose voters were blacks, Russian-Germans, and . . . the 'riff-raff and underworld of the town, [which were] chiefly carried by the free use of booze and money.' " Wilkins, "McKenzie and the Politics of Bossism," pp. 30-31. See also Lamar, *Dakota Territory*, p. 216. On Fargo: Glaab, "John Burke," p. 59. On the rural German vote see Robinson, *History of North Dakota*, pp. 230, 256, 257, 265; Glaab, "Revolution of 1906," pp. 102, 105; Glaab, "John Burke," pp. 60-61: "During the Burke Years [1907-1912], the McKenzie organization, in many respects a rural version of the better known, big-city machines of the era, had its greatest strength among Russian-German voters. Within the tightly knit, ethnically insulated communities, the machine techniques of personal politics proved highly effective."

[43] Glaab, "John Burke," p. 64.

lican leader Joseph B. Foraker (governor and then Senator) and Cincinnati's Cox machine briefly approximated the Maryland model of Senator Gorman and Baltimore boss Rasin. However, Foraker's persisting rivalry with a Mark Hanna faction based in Cleveland's business community supplied the more general pattern, Hanna assuming a party role in Cleveland something like McMillan's in Detroit.[44] In Illinois a Republican Senatorial regime under John Logan and then Shelby Cullom dominated politics in the 1870s and 1880s—it was probably the equivalent of Cameron's regime in Pennsylvania—but in the 1890s, the rising importance of Chicago and its ward organizations brought disorder.[45] At the turn of the century neither of Illinois's parties supported an authoritative state-level organization: each was an arena of shifting coalitions whose major figures included stockpilers of Chicago ward influence—William Lorimer in the Republican party and a partnership of Roger C. Sullivan and John P. Hopkins in the Democratic.[46] In Louisiana the Martin Behrman machine, in control of New Orleans from 1900, had too small a population base to dominate the city's unorganized and also rather hostile hinterland. Its strategy in Democratic gubernatorial primaries was to watch the campaigns, then to "endorse

[44] On the mid-1890s alliance: Everett Walters, *Joseph Benson Foraker: An Uncompromising Republican* (Columbus: Ohio History Press, 1948), chs. 7-9. On the factional rivalry: chs. 3-12; and Herbert Croly, *Marcus Alonzo Hanna: His Life and Work* (New York: Macmillan, 1923), chs. 11, 12. Cleveland supported a number of traditional organizations at ward, district, or neighborhood levels around the turn of the century, but by Cincinnati standards they seem to have played a minor role in city politics. Thomas L. Johnson, mayor in 1901-1909 in the Pingree mold, seems not to have encountered much trouble from organization politicians either in winning office or in governing; his main opposition came from elements of the business community. This gave Cleveland's politics of the time much of the texture of Detroit's. On the organizations: James B. Whipple, "Municipal Government in the Average City: Cleveland, 1876-1900," *Ohio State Archaeological and Historical Quarterly* 62(1953), 3-5, 17-19, 22-24. On Johnson: Eugene C. Murdock, "Cleveland's Johnson: Elected Mayor," *Ohio Historical Quarterly* 65(1956), 28-43; Eugene C. Murdock, "Cleveland's Johnson: First Term," *Ohio Historical Quarterly* 67(1958), 35-49; Carl Lorenz, *Tom L. Johnson: Mayor of Cleveland* (New York: A. S. Barnes Company, 1911), chs. 3, 4, 7, 9. Traditional organizations operated in both parties in Cleveland later in the 1920s and 1930s, and it is possible though well short of certain that at some points there was enough organization control of central administration to rank Cleveland a machine city. See Richard L. Maher, "Cleveland: Study in Political Paradoxes," pp. 123-147 in Robert S. Allen (ed.), *Our Fair City* (New York: Vanguard, 1947).

[45] On Logan and Cullom: James W. Fullinwinder, "The Governor and the Senator: Executive Power and the Structure of the Illinois Republican Party, 1880-1917" (Ph.D. dissertation, Washington University, 1974), ch. 1.

[46] On the Republicans: *ibid.*, chs. 1-3; Tarr, *A Study in Boss Politics*, chs. 1-6. The generalization probably holds for the Democrats, though no one seems to have done a close study. See *ibid.*, pp. 74-87, 119, 201-202.

and deliver New Orleans to the candidate who seemed to have the best chance of winning in the country and who did not propose war on the Machine."[47]

To recapitulate, the prime specimens of turn-of-the-century state organization were Platt's in New York, Quay's in Pennsylvania, the Gorman-Rasin combine in Maryland, Brayton's in Rhode Island, Martin's in Virginia, Elkins's in West Virginia, McKenzie's in North Dakota, and, perhaps in an asterisked category because they were fading away rather than thriving, McMillan's in Michigan and Sawyer's in Wisconsin. With further information (on Indiana, for example) a few others might join the list. But well-studied states that do *not* contribute to the list, besides the ones already discussed, include Massachusetts and New Hampshire in New England, Oregon and California on the West Coast, and Iowa, Missouri, Nebraska, Kansas, and Texas.[48]

Massachusetts drew notice in a shrewd comparative study in 1904 by Jesse Macy, who found it a polar opposite of Pennsylvania—a state just as safely Republican—in having a majority party that had "never

[47] George M. Reynolds, *Machine Politics in New Orleans, 1897-1926* (New York: Columbia University Press, 1936), p. 177, and more generally pp. 39-41, 175-187, 197-198. See also T. Harry Williams, *Huey Long* (New York: Knopf, 1969), pp. 129-131. There was a scheme in 1904 to join New Orleans with sugar parishes in a combination that would dominate the state, but it fell through. See Reynolds, pp. 197-198. William R. Majors draws an analogy between the Behrman machine's place in Louisiana's statewide Democratic primaries and the Crump machine's (later on in the 1930s) in Tennessee's statewide primaries. See Majors, "A Re-examination of V. O. Key's *Southern Politics in State and Nation:* The Case of Tennessee," *East Tennessee Historical Society's Publications,* no. 49 (1977), pp. 133-134.

[48] On Missouri: Jack D. Muraskin, "Missouri Politics during the Progressive Era, 1896-1916" (Ph.D. dissertation, University of California–Berkeley, 1969), ch. 1. On St. Louis in particular: "Ed Butler, the local Irish ward boss . . . had no desire to create an overall St. Louis Democratic organization. Aside from the difficulty of this task, Butler's own economic advancement and his son's political career could best be served by using his control of a few wards to make deals with the Republican party" (*ibid.*, p. 50). On St. Louis see also Jon C. Teaford, *The Unheralded Triumph: City Government in America, 1870-1900* (Baltimore: Johns Hopkins University Press, 1984), pp. 177-181. On Nebraska: Robert W. Cherny, *Populism, Progressivism, and the Transformation of Nebraska Politics, 1885-1915* (Lincoln: University of Nebraska Press, 1981). On Texas: Lewis L. Gould, *Progressives and Prohibitionists: Texas Democrats in the Wilson Era* (Austin: University of Texas Press, 1973), ch. 1 and pp. 35-39. Colonel Edward M. House, later associated with Woodrow Wilson, exercised influence in Texas electoral politics for a decade or so around 1900, with James B. Wells, Jr., of the "Valley" empire as one of his allies. House was a resourceful confidant and fixer who operated in an unstructured politics, however, rather than head of an organization. See *ibid.*, pp. 11-16, and Evan Anders, *Boss Rule in South Texas: The Progressive Era* (Austin: University of Texas Press, 1982), ch. 4.

been particularly strong" and was "much less effective and counts for much less in the government of the State [than Pennsylvania's]." It displayed what he took to be a New England trait, an "exaltation of the office-holder and the candidate for office, rather than that of the party machine which puts him into his place."[49] Massachusetts Republicans had a system of understandings, customs, and deals that ordinarily generated authoritative decisions on who had a right to move up to what office when, but their largely Brahmin leaders seem to have lacked the kind and level of authority that organization rooted in material inducements can confer.[50]

In a number of other states lacking strong party hierarchies, however, private corporations took up the slack—though in a more direct and differentiated fashion than the Michigan, Wisconsin, West Virginia, or North Dakota models, where party leaders more or less embodied corporate interests or wove party and corporate organizations together.[51] The state with the best documentation is New Hampshire, where the Boston & Maine Railroad used money, a "central board of strategy" headed by Lucius Tuttle in Boston, and an elaborate statewide network to dominate an otherwise loosely structured politics from 1895 through 1906. The B&M asserted its influence in state appointments, the legislative process, selection of Senators and the speaker of the state assembly, and Republican nominations for governor on down. "It was evident to all persons ambitious for political office that the way to power could be cleared only by the favor of the Boston & Maine." A special interest was taken in the governor's council (which could block appointments) and the state senate: "Nominations for both Council and Senate were carefully considered by the chief rail-

[49] Macy, *Party Organization*, chs. 11, 12, quotations at pp. 140, 141.

[50] See Richard M. Abrams, *Conservatism in a Progressive Era: Massachusetts Politics, 1900-1912* (Cambridge: Harvard University Press, 1964), especially pp. 30-43, 117-119, 183, 239. On the minority side, Massachusetts Democrats of the turn of the century were no better organized at the state level than the Democratic majority of recent times. See Judith A. Center, "Reform's Labours Lost: Two Eras of Party Change in Connecticut and Massachusetts" (Ph.D. dissertation, Yale University, 1981), pp. 25-31.

[51] Macy, writing in 1904, had a good eye for differences in organizational form: "There are certain States in which the owners of valuable franchises or leaders in some form of capitalistic organization hold the place of supreme power. These organizations are stronger than the legislature, the executive, and the state judiciary; stronger than any state party organization. In other States, of which Pennsylvania is an example, the dominant party organization shows a marked tendency toward gaining and holding supreme power. Still others, like Massachusetts, are pervaded by a sentiment in favor of maintaining the several departments of the regular state government in the position of supremacy" (*Party Organization*, p. 162).

road leaders; as a result of their deliberations a 'slate' was drawn up which was sent to the local politicians in the districts."[52]

In California, the Southern Pacific Railroad's Political Bureau, headed by William F. Herrin from 1893 through 1910, was the most influential organization operating in state politics around the turn of the century. Sometimes it worked in alliance with a traditional party organization in San Francisco.[53] Herrin's organization hardly had supreme control of the state, but it exercised influence "in almost every party convention [of both parties] during the period and in practically every election," took a particular interest in choosing judges, wheeled and dealed in the legislature, and maintained "a railroad political manager in every county in the state. This manager might be the Republican boss in a Republican county, or the Democratic boss in a Democratic county; in important or doubtful counties he was merely the railroad boss, with whom both Republican and Democratic bosses had to deal."[54] The Southern Pacific also operated with considerable success in the 1890s in Nevada's politics.[55]

In Iowa, which seems like New Hampshire in texture, the agents of two railroads—the Burlington and the Northwestern—managed networks of representatives in the counties, colonized Republican nominating processes, and "were generally considered the strongest influences in state politics during the nineties."[56] There are hints of such a

[52] See Leon B. Richardson, *William E. Chandler: Republican* (New York: Dodd, Mead, 1940), especially the excellent characterization of New Hampshire's railroad regime at pp. 616-625, quotations at pp. 619, 621. See also Thomas Agan, "The New Hampshire Progressives: Who and What Were They?" *Historical New Hampshire* 34(1979), 32-35.

[53] The sources are Walton Bean, *California: An Interpretive History* (New York: McGraw-Hill, 1978), chs. 21, 22; George E. Mowry, *The California Progressives* (Berkeley: University of California Press, 1951), ch. 1; Spencer C. Olin, Jr., *California's Prodigal Sons: Hiram Johnson and the Progressives* (Berkeley: University of California Press, 1968), ch. 1; W. H. Hutchinson, "Southern Pacific: Myth and Reality," *California Historical Society Quarterly* 48(1969), 325-334. On the San Francisco connection: *ibid.*, p. 331. For a statement that the political influence of the Southern Pacific has been exaggerated, see R. Hal Williams, *The Democratic Party and California Politics, 1880-1896* (Stanford: Stanford University Press, 1973), ch. 9.

[54] On party conventions: Mowry, *California Progressives*, p. 16. On judges: Bean, *California*, p. 259. On legislative influence (which peaked in 1905-1907): Hutchinson, "Southern Pacific," p. 333. On railroad county agents: Bean, p. 258.

[55] Gilman M. Ostrander: *Nevada: The Great Rotten Borough, 1859-1964* (New York: Knopf, 1966), ch. 4. See also Sally S. Zanjami, "Losing Battles: The Revolt of the Nevada Progressives, 1910-1914," *Nevada Historical Society Quarterly* 24(1981), 19-22.

[56] See Ralph M. Sayre, "Albert Baird Cummins and the Progressive Movement in Iowa" (Ph.D. dissertation, Columbia University, 1958), chs. 3, 4.

railroad role in two other Republican states with dispersed party authority, Oregon and Kansas.[57] In Montana indigenous copper tycoons deployed economic empires in battles with each other over Senate seats in the 1890s, but by 1903 the Amalgamated Copper Company (the familiar Anaconda functioning then as a Standard Oil affiliate) had risen to dominate the state's economy and exercise singular influence in its electoral politics.[58] There was a curious Downsian effect in which corporate interests assumed a role ordinarily associated with political parties: copper kings competing for votes around 1900 accommodated a miners' union and bid up worker benefits, but the Amalgamated, once secure, took to undercutting the union and in a decade destroyed it.[59]

A good way to generalize about the foregoing is to see the last quarter of the nineteenth century as a time between the high watermarks of two rather different party organizational forms—a nationally centered system at the start and a collection of state-centered systems at the close. Patronage from the national government supplied a vital ingredient in the Republicans' organizational mix of the 1870s; it was certainly a necessary underpinning of the party's authoritative state organizations in Rhode Island, Pennsylvania, and Wisconsin, and no doubt elsewhere. Accounts of post office and customs house jobs regularly come to light.[60] But civil service reform, occasional Democratic victories in state or national elections, and erratic support by Republican Presidents after Grant seem to have diminished the regimes of the 1870s as time went on—as evidenced in Quay's need to beef up the

[57] On Oregon's electoral environment at the turn of the century: Tony H. Evans, "Oregon Progressive Reform, 1902-1914" (Ph.D. dissertation, University of California–Berkeley, 1966), pp. 35-53. On Oregon railroads: pp. 38, 46-53. On Kansas's electoral environment around the turn of the century: Robert S. La Forte, "The Republican Party of Kansas During the Progressive Era, 1900-1916" (Ph.D. dissertation, University of Kansas, 1966), ch. 2. On Kansas railroads: pp. 39-41; and William Allen White, *The Autobiography of William Allen White* (New York: Macmillan, 1946), pp. 177-178, 232-233.

[58] The authoritative source is Michael P. Malone and Richard B. Roeder, *Montana: A History of Two Centuries* (Seattle: University of Washington Press, 1976), ch. 9. See also K. Ross Toole, *Montana: An Uncommon Land* (Norman: University of Oklahoma Press, 1959), pp. 176-210.

[59] See Malone and Roeder, *Montana*, pp. 168, 176-177, 209-211; Arnon Gutfield, "The Speculator Disaster in 1917: Labor Resurgence at Butte, Montana," *Arizona and the West* 11(1969), 30.

[60] A recent account, for example, points to the importance of federal patronage in Cameron's Pennsylvania regime: Robert Harrison, "Blaine and the Camerons: A Study in the Limits of Machine Power," *Pennsylvania History* 49(1982), 157-175. No effort is made here to provide a comprehensive treatment of the Republicans' national organizational system of the 1870s. None seems to exist.

Pennsylvania organization in the 1880s, the inability of Illinois's Cullom to deal with Chicago ward organizations, and the late-century sag of the McMillan and Sawyer organizations in Michigan and Wisconsin. The increasing flow of corporate money into politics, which considerably expanded the stock of resources in circulation, probably also depreciated the older patronage resource. At any rate state party organizations that were healthy and authoritative toward the end of the century seem to have depended a good deal less on federal patronage than had their counterparts of the 1870s.[61] Three points can be made about these turn-of-the-century state organizations, which were an interesting and time-specific brand of apparatus. First, in all cases enterprising leaders had developed sometimes ingenious ways of keeping an organization going without relying much on Washington. Second, all depended significantly on money or other support from private corporations—to a greater extent than the state regimes of the 1870s had and probably more than most county- or city-level organizations of a traditional sort did around 1900 or have since.[62] Third, apart from North Dakota's exceptional regime, they operated in the familiar geography of traditional party organization at the local level, though in some cases (Pennsylvania and Rhode Island) their local connections were more rural than urban. Rhode Island, New York, Pennsylvania, Maryland, West Virginia, Virginia appearing as an unusual southern appendage—this comprises the more-or-less Middle Atlantic territory of patronage-based organization at the local level, both then and since. Direct corporate colonization of nominating processes, on the other hand, took place, if at all, in states relatively free of traditional local organization—New Hampshire and California at opposite ends of the country provide paradigmatic instances.

Again, the time around 1900 was a high-water mark for state organization. Reform movements that gathered momentum soon afterward sought to overhaul parties and electoral processes at all levels of government, yet scored their greatest successes at the state level. The rail-

[61] Maryland's Democratic organization ran into trouble in the mid-1890s by losing elections to Republicans. But with its grounding in Rasin's Baltimore machine, it probably had never depended much on episodic Democratic patronage from Washington.

[62] A New York contrast between Platt's Republican regime and Roscoe Conkling's a generation earlier: "Platt differed from his predecessor in a more significant way. In his day Conkling had relied chiefly on federal patronage to control the party organization, but as civil service reform began to undermine the spoils system, Platt cast about for a better means of political management. He discovered it in party financing by powerful corporations anxious for political protection and privilege" (G. Wallace Chessman, *Governor Theodore Roosevelt: The Albany Apprenticeship, 1898-1900* [Cambridge: Harvard University Press, 1965], p. 10).

roads' political networks and almost all the stronger state party organizations were brought down by about 1912 (Pennsylvania's held on a bit longer until Penrose died in 1921).[63] Only in low-turnout Virginia and primary-free Connecticut (where all nominating was done by caucus and convention until 1955) did party hierarchies of an unambiguous late nineteenth-century character function effectively in later times.[64] In Virginia the Byrd organization succeeded Senator Martin's; in Connecticut J. Henry Roraback's Republican organization operated between 1912 and the mid-1930s and John M. Bailey's Democratic apparatus functioned after World War II. Roraback, doubling during part of his career as head of the Connecticut Light and Power Company, dominated Republican conventions and the state legislature by drawing on corporate money, state patronage, the advantage of rural overrepresentation in state and party assemblies, and, evidently, a loose alliance based on patronage with the Hartford organization of Democrat Thomas J. Spellacy, Bailey's predecessor as local leader.[65] Insurance kickbacks provided a moderately important organizational glue in both the Roraback and Bailey apparatuses.[66]

Virginia's and Connecticut's organizations were nonetheless exceptions, stray survivors of a class of state-level structures that largely disappeared before World War I. Traditional organization at the local level has followed a quite different trajectory. It too rose to prominence in the nineteenth century and diminished in the twentieth, but its decline came much later. Indeed it is not even decisively clear that local organizations counted for less in, say, the late 1940s than in 1900, though in general they sloped downward between 1950 and the late 1960s and have fallen off precipitously since. Centralized city machines

[63] On the demise of the authoritative Pennsylvania organization see Richard C. Keller, "Pennsylvania's Little New Deal," pp. 45-76 in John Braeman, Robert H. Bremner, and David Brody (eds.), *The New Deal*, vol. 2: *The State and Local Levels* (Columbus: Ohio State University Press, 1975), at pp. 45-48.

[64] A requirement for inclusion here was that a state's party leaders had to have good enough stocks of resources independent of the twentieth century's generally stronger governors to be able to transcend the incumbencies of particular governors.

[65] The sources on Roraback: Buenker, "The Politics of Resistance"; Duane Lockard, *New England State Politics* (Princeton: Princeton University Press, 1959), pp. 245-251; Joseph I. Lieberman, *The Power Broker: A Biography of John M. Bailey, Modern Political Boss* (Boston: Houghton Mifflin, 1966), pp. 27-32, 39, 52, 57-58. On Spellacy: Lieberman, pp. 31, 33, 52-53; Lockard, pp. 259-260; Buenker, p. 228. Bailey became a municipal judge in the early 1930s as a consequence of a deal between Roraback and Spellacy (see Lieberman, p. 52). There are hints of dealings between the Roraback organization and Democratic leaders in New Haven (Lieberman, p. 31) and Waterbury (Buenker, p. 228).

[66] Lieberman, *Power Broker: John M. Bailey*, ch. 14.

in particular are a surprisingly late phenomenon; their golden age seems to have been from about 1890 through 1950. With a few exceptions, urban party organizations of the last decades of the nineteenth century seem to have been relatively autonomous factional or ward organizations, even in New York City and Philadelphia. A central Tammany organization gained authoritative control over Democratic nominations, ward units, and legislative delegations in New York only around 1890 (evidently by building a network of district clubs), and Philadelphia's Republican party seems to have held off going through a similar consolidation until roughly 1900.[67]

In many places local party organizations, whether urban or not, fared strikingly well in the early years of the twentieth century. Students of New Jersey and Pennsylvania, for example, speculate that newly introduced direct primaries may have been more help than hindrance to county organizations. Primaries may have been "easier to control than numerous local primary meetings and conventions that had featured the old system."[68] Tammany Hall stayed at peak influence until the mid-1920s; the New Orleans and Kansas City machines had their classic eras in the first few decades of the twentieth century rather than earlier; Jersey City's Hague and Memphis's Crump got their machines off the ground only after World War I; Cleveland's variety of

[67] The best summary treatment of late nineteenth-century urban organizations appears in Teaford, *The Unheralded Triumph* (1984), pp. 51-52, 175-187. Teaford's list of leaders between 1870 and 1900 who did achieve citywide control of their parties and also sometimes of their municipal governments: Tammany's Richard Croker in the late 1880s and 1890s, George B. Cox in Cincinnati in the 1890s, Christopher A. Buckley in San Francisco in the 1880s, and Hugh McLaughlin much of the time in Brooklyn (pp. 181-186). On the 1890 Tammany consolidation see Martin Shefter, "The Electoral Foundations of the Political Machine: New York City, 1884-1897," ch. 7 in Joel H. Silbey, Allan G. Bogue, and William H. Flanigan (eds.), *The History of American Electoral Behavior* (Princeton: Princeton University Press, 1978), pp. 263-267, 290-296. "Honest John" Kelly is said to have augmented the authority of Tammany leadership over followers in the late 1870s and 1880s, but Tammany under Kelly was one faction among two or more competing for power within the Democratic party. See Alfred Connable and Edward Silberfarb, *Tigers of Tammany: Nine Men Who Ran New York* (New York: Holt, Rinehart and Winston, 1967), pp. 175, 179-188. On the Philadelphia consolidation see the recollections of William S. Vare in *My Forty Years in Politics*, pp. 45-46, 70-72, 78-81, 84. The account here is scanty and does not dwell on clubs, but after one reads Shefter on New York it has a familiar ring.

[68] Richard P. McCormick, "An Historical Overview," ch. 1 in Alan Rosenthal and John Blydenburgh (eds.), *Politics in New Jersey* (New Brunswick, N.J.: Eagleton Institute of Politics, Rutgers University, 1975), quotation at p. 15. On Pennsylvania see Charles E. Gilbert, *Governing the Suburbs* (Bloomington: Indiana University Press, 1967), p. 67; Frank J. Sorauf, *Party and Representation: Legislative Politics in Pennsylvania* (New York: Atherton, 1963), p. 119.

traditional organization probably had a more important role in the 1920s and 1930s than earlier; the powerful Democratic machines of Pittsburgh (succeeding a Republican machine), Chicago (uniting the ward organizations), and Providence (no record of an earlier machine) took form in the 1930s; and Gary's conspicuous machine coalesced only in the 1950s.[69] Of course the casualty list began early in the century as well. Traditional organization disappeared from San Francisco somewhere around 1900 and from the wards of Omaha and Boston by the 1930s. North Dakota wiped its slate clean. Tammany Hall began its long decline upon the death of its most effective leader, Charles F. Murphy, in 1924. It went on through a crisis of resources and an entanglement with organized crime in the 1930s and 1940s to its last stand in the 1960s. A list of well-documented instances in which central administrations of cities shifted away from control by traditional organizations runs from El Paso during World War I through Cincinnati and Rochester in the 1920s, Kansas City in 1940, Philadelphia, New Orleans, Memphis, and San Antonio at about midcentury (World War II and its aftermath seem to have shaken up local leadership structures), Pittsburgh and Gary in the late 1960s, Providence and New Haven in the 1970s (though with complicated and confusing politics in ensuing years) to, on the evidence so far, Chicago in the 1980s.

Changes over time have been given suitable attention in this examination of party history, yet of greater pertinence here is a pattern over space persisting through time. Enduring cross-sectional differences in forms of party structure show through the long rise and decline of patronage-based organization. It appears that in the nineteenth century the basic territory of traditional party organization expanded beyond the Middle Atlantic region to encompass states settled early in the Ohio and Mississippi valleys. The enlarged area amounted to something of a homeland of traditional organization around 1900, and was still evident a good deal later, on the map of the 1960s. Some expansion took place beyond this basic territory in the late nineteenth century but it seems to have been limited and temporary; areas west of the Mississippi River proved inhospitable and older areas to the north and south remained so.

This pattern of geographic differentiation casts some doubt on two

---

[69] Features of Providence's electoral politics around 1930: "an absence of discipline within the political parties and ever-present ethnic rivalries" (David L. Davies, "Impoverished Politics: The New Deal's Impact on City Government in Providence, Rhode Island," *Rhode Island History* 42[1983], 87). See also Norma L. Daoust, "The Perils of Providence: Rhode Island's Capital City during the Depression and New Deal" (Ph.D. dissertation, University of Connecticut, 1982), pp. 299-300, 461-463.

commonplace generalizations about American politics. The first might
be called a stages theory of machines. This is the view that the normal
developmental course of American cities (except perhaps very new
ones) has been to evolve into a machine phase and then out of it. In ac-
tuality the classic machines arose in sea, river, and lake ports of older
states in the Middle Atlantic region and the Ohio and Mississippi valleys, and in addition in some newer industrial cities of these same
states—East St. Louis and Gary, for example. If the standard is relaxed
to cover all forms of traditional organization and not just certifiable
machines, South Bend and some industrial centers in northern Ohio
can be included. Outside this broad area, unambiguous instances of
machines are hard to find.[70] There are instances, of course, in Rhode
Island, Connecticut, and southern Texas, and the case of San Francisco,
and there may be others in small and middle-sized cities of the South,
but where else?[71] Probably not with appreciable frequency in the many
newer industrial cities of the Carolina Piedmont, Michigan, or Wisconsin, and almost certainly not in Birmingham (Alabama) or in Grand
Rapids, which are both well covered in recent studies.[72] After ransack-
ing through political histories for some time, one takes account of what
does *not* turn up—a machine in Worcester? Lowell? Manchester, New
Hampshire? Portland, Maine? Kenosha? Seattle? Richmond? The least
that should be said against an undiscriminating stages theory is that it
misconstrues the record of urban evolution in Massachusetts, Michigan, Wisconsin, and Minnesota. A prize should go to anyone who can
locate a convincing machine at any time in the history of Detroit, Milwaukee, or Minneapolis; the instances if any are well concealed.

[70] Denver may belong in a category with San Francisco at the turn of the century, but
its electoral environment needs fuller characterization. See J. Paul Mitchell, "Municipal
Reform in Denver: The Defeat of Mayor Speer," *Colorado Magazine* 45(1968), 42-60;
and Paul Mitchell, "Boss Speer and the City Functional: Boosters and Businessmen versus Commission Government in Denver," *Pacific Northwest Quarterly* 63(October
1972), 155-164. One sentence in each of two books refers to a "machine" in St. Paul at
the turn of the century. See Millard L. Gieske, *Minnesota Farmer-Laborism: The Third-
Party Alternative* (Minneapolis: University of Minnesota Press, 1979), p. 17; and Chrislock, *Progressive Era in Minnesota*, p. 34. But it is hard to know what to make of this,
given the general practice of using the term promiscuously.

[71] On the South, Key in 1949 mentioned Jacksonville and Chattanooga without elaboration (besides a few other cities already treated here in the text of Part I). See *Southern
Politics in State and Nation* (New York: Vintage, 1949), pp. 397-398.

[72] On Birmingham see Carl V. Harris, *Political Power in Birmingham 1871-1921*
(Knoxville: University of Tennessee Press, 1977). No trace of traditional party organization turns up in a good treatment of electoral politics in Grand Rapids from 1906
through 1916. See Anthony R. Travis, "Mayor George Ellis: Grand Rapids Political Boss
and Progressive Reformer," *Michigan History* 58(1974), 101-130.

The second generalization alleges a link between machines and immigrant groups. There is no doubt that immigrants served as raw material for machines in a good many places, but they were hardly unique in this respect, and they settled into politics in many other places without encountering machines or becoming their clienteles. New York, Chicago, and Pittsburgh aside, the large American cities with certifiable machines lasting over decades—Baltimore, Philadelphia, Cincinnati, New Orleans, Memphis, and Kansas City—are hardly the urban areas most affected by the sizable wave of European immigration around 1900. Among exceptionally large cities, Philadelphia used to rank lowest in foreign-born population and highest, at least by reputation, in corruption; and the histories of Kansas City and Memphis (to which might be added the less well documented traditions of Louisville and Indianapolis) are sufficient testimony that native whites and blacks can supply a perfectly good organization base.[73] Of the fifteen states with the highest percentage of immigrant population in 1900, only four— Rhode Island, Connecticut, New York and New Jersey—appear on the list of thirteen "organization states" (TPO scores of 4 or 5) established in Part I.[74]

Nor should it easily be assumed that immigrants came from Europe with fixed political traits waiting to be displayed. The importance of the receiving environments emerges nicely in a recent collection of essays on Polish communities entering politics from the 1890s on in four American cities. The Chicago essay deals with political careers in ward organizations and the difficulties of building them otherwise; the Buffalo essay with the community's persisting efforts to work somehow through or around the dominant Democratic organization; the Milwaukee essay with immersion in an issue-based politics setting off controversy within the community between Catholics and Socialists; the Detroit essay with enthusiastic support for Republican reform mayor Hazen Pingree in the 1890s, the hopelessness of trying to win public office after a 1918 charter switched city council elections to an at-large basis, and successful mobilization in the 1930s by the United Auto Workers—"To be Polish was to be a worker, a union member, and a

---

[73] On Philadelphia see Delos F. Wilcox, *Great Cities in America: Their Problems and Their Government* (New York: Macmillan, 1910), pp. 9, 244; and Clifford W. Patton, *The Battle for Municipal Reform: Mobilization and Attack, 1875-1900* (Washington, D.C.: American Council on Public Affairs, 1940), p. 13.

[74] The states ranking 1 through 15, respectively: North Dakota, Rhode Island, Massachusetts, Minnesota, Montana, Connecticut, New York, Wisconsin, California, Nevada, New Jersey, Michigan, South Dakota, Washington, and New Hampshire. North Dakota, of course, went through an organization phase around the turn of the century.

labor Democrat."[75] Even in the case of the Irish, the classic instance of stereotyping, different environments seem to have selected out different sorts of political leaders. From roughly 1930 through 1950, for example, Irish "bosses" operated in appropriate profusion in the expected places—among them Edward J. Flynn in the Bronx, Frank V. Kelly in Brooklyn, Daniel P. O'Connell in Albany, Frank Hague in Jersey City, William Curran in Baltimore (leader of a district-based factional organization), Edward J. Kelly in Chicago, and Thomas J. Pendergast in Kansas City.[76] The list is impressive. But farther north one runs into Irish leaders not of the "boss" variety: the master of rhetoric, James Michael Curley; Senator Joseph R. McCarthy of Wisconsin, another showman; James E. Murray, the labor Senator from Montana; Eugene J. McCarthy, product of the Irish-dominated politics of St. Paul; and the interesting Frank Murphy of Detroit, mayor in 1930-1933, then governor-general of the Philippines, governor of Michigan (where he

[75] On Chicago: Edward R. Kantowicz, "The Limitations of Ethnic Politics: Polish Americans in Chicago," pp. 92-105 in Angela T. Pienkos (ed.), *Ethnic Politics in Urban America: The Polish Experience in Four Cities* (Chicago: Polish American Historical Association, 1978). Of the two outstanding leaders of Chicago's Polish community before World War I one was a ward boss and the other "eminently respectable, a banker, businessman, and attorney; but he was so respectable as to find politics distasteful, and thus he soon abandoned office-seeking" (p. 94). On Buffalo: Walter A. Borowiec, "Politics and Buffalo's Polish Americans," pp. 16-39 in Angela T. Pienkos. On Milwaukee: Donald E. Pienkos, "The Polish Americans in Milwaukee Politics," pp. 66-91 in Angela T. Pienkos. "Indicative, perhaps, of the political divisions within Polonia is the fact that between 1918 and 1932, five of the twelve Poles who were elected to the state assembly from Milwaukee were socialists, four others were Republicans and three were Democrats" (p. 86). See also Donald Pienkos, "Politics, Religion and Change in Polish Milwaukee, 1900-1930," *Wisconsin Magazine of History* 61(1978), 179-209. Later the New Deal settled Milwaukee's Poles into a routine Democratic affiliation. On Detroit: Thaddeus C. Radzialowski with Donald Binkowski, "Polish Americans in Detroit Politics," pp. 40-65 in Angela T. Pienkos, quotation at p. 58. "The union local became an extension of the community and especially of its political and economic aspirations" (p. 56).

[76] On Flynn and Kelly see Charles W. Van Devander, *The Big Bosses* (New York: Howell, Soskin, 1944), pp. 40-52. On Curran see Edwin Rothman, "Factional Machine-Politics: William Curran and the Baltimore City Democratic Party Organization, 1929-1946" (Ph.D. dissertation, Johns Hopkins University, 1949), *passim*; Bain, "Five Kinds of Politics," pp. 820-822. Curran was something of a philosopher: "I never pick up a book on United States Government but what I find a condemnation of organization in our cities. But what the staid and conservative citizen never seems to realize is that the organization stands between the demagoguery and conservatism. The organization is always tied in with conservatism because the solid side will always prevail in the long run. Let a mountebank break forth with promises to every voter, and you must have some real power somewhere to combat him. The time will come when organization politics will be found to be the only anchor against radicalism" (E. Rothman, p. 48).

put through a tight civil service law and served as chief mediator in the auto industry's sitdown strikes of 1936-1937), Roosevelt's attorney general, and finally Supreme Court justice.[77] Murphy, the important link in Michigan's progressive/liberal tradition that ran from Pingree through G. Mennen Williams and the UAW-based coalition of the 1950s, won his first citywide office by displaying, among other things, "forensic abilities and charismatic appeal" and attracting the key backing of a Hearst newspaper. He went on in the early 1930s to build what may have been the first New Deal electoral coalition anywhere—blacks and Eastern European Catholics as one side of a class cleavage—in the organization-free environment of Detroit's nonpartisan municipal elections.[78]

The opening exhibit on historical background in this chapter was a table showing a relation, in the full set of fifty states, between date of statehood and incidence of traditional organization in the late 1960s. Expressing the relation in the form of an equation allows the addition of another independent variable, how urban the states are or, more specifically, the percentage of each state's population living in urban areas in 1970. See Table 8.2.[79] Being admitted in any cohort of states after

[77] On St. Paul: "To a party without patronage personalities are very important. DFL organizations throughout Minnesota consciously develop and promote party candidates. In Minneapolis, the party has focused on Senator Humphrey and Governor Freeman. In St. Paul, its idol is Eugene McCarthy. These names rally workers." (Alan Altshuler, *A Report on Politics in St. Paul, Minnesota* [Cambridge: Joint Center for Urban Studies, M.I.T./Harvard, 1959], p. II:12).

[78] On Murphy see the excellent two-volume biography by Sidney Fine, *Frank Murphy: The Detroit Years* (Ann Arbor: University of Michigan Press, 1975), and *Frank Murphy: The New Deal Years* (Chicago: University of Chicago Press, 1979). On civil service reform and the sitdown strikes: Fine, *New Deal Years*, chs. 8-10. On Murphy as link in tradition: Fine, *Detroit Years*, p. 455; Fine, *New Deal Years*, pp. 280-281. On Murphy's first victory: Fine, *Detroit Years*, pp. 102-118, quotation at pp. 104-105. On the New Deal coalition: *ibid.*, pp. 215-233, 432-440.

[79] A few words may be in order on how to read tables that report the results of equations. A regression coefficient tells how much a difference of one unit in any independent variable makes in the dependent variable, measured in its own units (the dependent variable in Table 8.2 is state TPO score.) Thus, in the case of the percent urban variable in Table 8.2, the difference between 0 and 1 percent urban makes a difference of .045 in the TPO variable: multiplying .045 by 60 produces the 2.7 TPO difference reported in the text. (In fact the urban variable was employed here with the decimal point in an odd place, but that has no importance.) In the cases of the set of five "dummy" variables in Table 8.2 that stand for spans of years, the coefficient for each tells how much the difference between being admitted as a state in a reported span (e.g. 1836-1867) and being admitted in the only *unreported* span (i.e. in 1787-1790 when the original thirteen states ratified the Constitution) makes in the TPO variable. Thus, the − 2.04 coefficient for the 1836-1867 variable means that being admitted as a state during that period as opposed to 1787-1790 causes (or at least indexes in some complicated fashion) a negative differ-

Table 8.2   State TPO Scores as a Function of Admission Date
and Percent Urban

Independent Variable	Regression Coefficient	Standard Error	t Ratio
1791-1821	.25	.48	.51
1836-1867	− 2.04	.46	− 4.47***
1876-1896	− 1.81	.53	− 3.44***
1907-1912	− 1.99	.73	− 2.71***
1959	− 2.02	.87	− 2.32**
% urban 1970	.0045	.0012	3.66***
Constant	.081		
N = 50			
Adj. R^2 = .478			

NOTE: No distinction was made between "regular" and "persistently factional" states in coding for TPO score (the dependent variable). That is, both New Jersey and Maryland have scores of 5. Two asterisks indicate a .01 level of significance; three indicate a .001 level.

1821 yields a modern TPO score significantly and substantially lower than the scores of the original thirteen; the twelve states admitted from 1791 through 1821 score about the same as the original thirteen. And not surprisingly, given the obvious affinity between cities and machines, being an urban state generates a significantly higher TPO score: a difference between being 30% and 90% urban (roughly the full actual range among states in 1970) is worth about 2.7 points on the 1-to-5 TPO scale.

Beyond this little is certain about origins or causes. Has traditional party organization figured more prominently in "competitive" states— that is, Democrats and Republicans about evenly balanced—than in

ence of just over 2 in the TPO variable (on its 1 to 5 scale). To put some factual flesh on the relation, consider Arkansas (admitted 1836, TPO score of 2) and Delaware (ratified the Constitution in 1787, TPO score of 4). The size of a relationship between an independent variable and a dependent variable is one thing (as discussed above); the level of certainty that it really exists is another. The latter can be ascertained by reading across in a table (disregarding minus signs). A regression coefficient roughly twice or more as large as its standard error produces a *t* value large enough to be worth taking cognizance of (more or less). One asterisk beside a *t* value points to a relation between an independent and a dependent variable that satisfies a .05 test of significance; there is only one chance in twenty that the relation is a statistical fluke rather than real. Satisfying a .01 significance test reduces the fluke possibility to one in a hundred, and satisfying a .001 test reduces it to one in a thousand. In Table 8.2 all the relationships reported in the coefficients of the independent variables are quite solid except the one for the 1791-1821 variable.

"safe" states? The logic of this, which gets tortuous, is that parties that have had to fight close elections at the state level might have organized themselves especially well at some time in the past, producing strong organizations at the local level even where local elections were one-sided. This is a slippery idea to deal with, requiring as it does some difficult judgments on what "competitive" means, which offices to examine election returns for, and which times in the past to look at. But it seems an unpromising line of inquiry. The fit is not convincingly good even from 1876 through 1892, in principle a reasonable period to investigate and one in which a number of modern "organization states" did indeed stand out as competitive in presidential elections—in particular New York, Indiana, and Connecticut. But there was a lot of non-accommodating behavior: New Hampshire and California also ranked among the exceptionally competitive states, in general the border states (Maryland, West Virginia, Kentucky, and Missouri) were not very close, Rhode Island voted safe Republican along with Massachusetts, and Pennsylvania was no more competitive than Michigan, Oregon or Wisconsin. In addition, outside the South at any rate, the late nineteenth century's authoritative state-level organizations hardly clustered in states standing out as especially competitive.

Is there a relation between structural reform and party organization? In particular, has the movement making some cities but not others officially nonpartisan shaped the modern map of party organization? Probably not, or not very much. It is true that a disproportionate share of cities in several "organization states" of the 1960s were formally partisan—all or nearly all in Connecticut, New York, Pennsylvania, and Indiana, and almost half in Illinois, New Jersey, and Ohio.[80] But in general the causation on this more likely ran the other way. States or cities well endowed with traditional organization seem to have held out relatively successfully against the nonpartisan movement, which did especially well in states or cities where traditional organization was weak, insecurely rooted, or nonexistent. Nonpartisan reform in some cases had a prophylactic quality—in Boston, for example, where the objective was to keep a citywide machine from taking hold rather than to destroy one, and evidently in Minnesota (in switching the legislature to nonpartisan elections in 1913) where "rural legislators worried that Minneapolis and St. Paul would turn into bastions of party corruption."[81] At any rate the relation between incidences of official partisan-

[80] Source of data on partisan and nonpartisan cities is *Municipal Year Book* 30(1963), 168-183.

[81] Steven T. Seitz and L. Earl Shaw, "Partisanship in a Nonpartisan Legislature," ch. 11 in Millard L. Gieske and Edward R. Brandt (eds.), *Perspectives on Minnesota Government and Politics* (Dubuque: Kendall/Hunt, 1977), p. 178.

ship and traditional organization is poor enough to foreclose any simple model relating legal form to actual structure. Formally partisan cities have included Honolulu, Rockford, Tucson, Manchester (New Hampshire), and Tulsa, and the nonpartisan have improbably included Virginia Beach, East St. Louis, Atlantic City, Trenton, Chicago (the board of aldermen though not the mayor), Memphis under Crump, Kansas City under Pendergast, and Jersey City under half a century of Hague and Kenny.

Perhaps "political culture," somehow construed, is responsible for or associated with some important differences among states in organizational traditions.[82] There are patterns suggesting it or something like it. A heritage of individualism appears in much of the South's electoral politics, for example, and an inhospitality toward traditional party organization appears in much of the territory originally settled by New Englanders and perhaps infused with their reputed communitarian, antiparticularistic ethos—Massachusetts, northern New England, also Michigan, and possibly other states to the northwest and west.[83] To give another sort of example at the city level, a particular difference between Boston on the one hand and New York City and Philadelphia on the other seems to have produced decisive differences in the texture of electoral politics: Boston's social and intellectual elite continued to participate in local and state affairs through the end of the nineteenth century, long after New York and Philadelphia elites had opted out.[84]

But what is "political culture"? The subject is vexed and cloudy.[85] It

[82] For one prominent assignment of geographic location to a set of political cultures, see Daniel J. Elazar, "The American Cultural Matrix," ch. 1 in Daniel J. Elazar and Joseph Zikmund II (eds.), *The Ecology of American Political Culture: Readings* (New York: Crowell, 1975).

[83] Ronald P. Formisano on hostility toward the idea of having parties at all in mid-nineteenth-century Michigan: "The origin of evangelical antipartyism in New England Protestantism seems fairly clear. Long after the Massachusetts Bay Christian Commonwealth disintegrated, a puritan-derived compulsion continued to propel drives for cultural and moral homogeneity in the community. Antiparty probably was more intense among evangelicals imbued with a 'sense of solidarity,' the belief that 'the good of each is bound up with the good of all,' the outlook that the community was a moral whole, and the desire to work for the moral integration and regulation of society" (*The Birth of Mass Political Parties: Michigan, 1827-1861* [Princeton: Princeton University Press, 1971], p. 78, and more generally ch. 4).

[84] See E. Digby Baltzell, *Puritan Boston and Quaker Philadelphia: Two Protestant Ethics and the Spirit of Class Authority and Leadership* (New York: Free Press, 1979), ch. 18; and Frederic C. Jaher, "Nineteenth-Century Elites in Boston and New York," *Journal of Social History* 6(1972), 65-66.

[85] One common tendency in pertinent literature is to limit the components of "political culture" to ideational matters (values, beliefs, attitudes, etc.). This seems an unhelpful constraint. Why not include some political practices?

may help to identify some kinds of illumination that "political culture" might in principle be expected to offer in studying electoral politics. Three come to mind, the first two though perhaps not the third geared to generating statements of causation. The first might be called a theory of *ethnocultural imprinting*. Specifiable ethnocultural groups might be expected to impart distinctive traditions of conducting electoral politics wherever they lay the foundations of political communities (or perhaps affect them decisively at early junctures)—traditions that endure in the geographic jurisdiction even if new ethnocultural groups move in and old ones thin out. There is probably some basic truth to this idea; New Englanders moving west and setting up states, for example, perhaps gave a certain cast to Michigan and more particularly Detroit politics that is still evident today. A second, quite familiar line of theorizing deals with what might be called *ethnocultural bearers*. This posits an empirical, invariant (at the limit) connection between specifiable ethnocultural groups and their characteristic modes of engaging in electoral politics wherever and whenever they engage in it. This has some obvious truth to it too. Banfield and Wilson's distinction between "public-regarding" and "private-regarding" politics (associated roughly with middle-class WASPs and immigrant ethnics, respectively) builds on something like this idea, and the Irish did after all produce a lot of good ward bosses.[86] "Bearers" turn up nicely in some of the details on twentieth-century migration set out in Part I. Anglo agrobusinessmen destroyed machines (imposing "reform") once they settled the lower Rio Grande, for example; blue-collar Baltimoreans transported their stylized factionalism out to suburban Baltimore County in the 1940s; and Southerners packed along their nominating practices in moving to New Mexico's Little Texas.

There are good insights in these varieties of theorizing, but unfortunately trying to carry analysis further runs into nightmarish problems of specification, ethnocultural mix and flux, and just plain contrary realities. On the matter of "imprinting," for example, how many certifiably distinctive ethnocultural groups can be said to have founded American states (or proto-states)? Three? Twelve? Thirty? Do Rhode Island's colonial brand of New Englanders qualify by themselves? Are Virginians unique both in founding and tradition? Are Louisianians? How, precisely, do we think about patronage-based factionalism evolving in Ohio Valley states settled largely by Southerners from the East Coast? And what of the complexities of the West?[87] A "bearer" theory,

---

[86] See James Q. Wilson and Edward C. Banfield, "Public Regardingness as a Value Premise in Voting Behavior," *American Political Science Review* 58(1964), 876-887.

[87] An entirely different "nationwide wave" idea might be introduced to help account

as argued earlier, at a minimum runs into the problem of widespread behavioral puzzles: in particular, why the rather poor relation between incidence of immigrants and incidence of machines? Some of the most interesting records of political behavior seem to defeat both the "imprinting" and the "bearer" lines of thinking. Neither an overall New Englander "imprint" nor a "bearer" model does much good, for example, in accounting for striking differences between Massachusetts and Rhode Island electoral heritages—in one case a strait-laced and antiorganization tradition handed down by Yankees to Irish politicians well short of strait-laced though no less individualistic in behavior, in the other a Yankee tradition of organizational hierarchy and two centuries of election fraud handed down to Irish and Italian politicians who run machines. What here is explaining what?

In the circumstances—which, it should be added, include conspicuous shortages of evidence about many times, places, and heritages—a fallback to a third, less ambitious construction of "political culture" may be a good provisional move. This is an assertion that *there exist geographically rooted traditions* of conducting electoral politics, however and whenever they came about and whoever their bearers have been. The claim in turn is separable into the assertions (a) that institutional arrangements and politicians' practices specific to American state and local electoral politics have tended to persist rather stubbornly and, beyond this, (b) that arrangements and practices thus persisting may usefully be characterized and perhaps typologized. The treatment here pointing to lineages of "traditional party organization" (with factional and nonfactional variants) is obviously one such effort at characterization—or part-characterization, since a fullblown version of "political culture" no doubt would need some mass attitudinal components (a bit more on this later). No effort will be made here to present other (nonorganization state) lineages and flesh out a full national typology. Given the diversity of even the South alone, any such enterprise would have its problems.[88]

---

for the political traditions of Oklahoma (statehood 1907) and Arizona (1912), both much influenced by Progressivism at their foundings. This is a suggestion that has little to do with "political culture" except insofar as the whole country can be said to have been going through a Progressive phase, perhaps a culture phenomenon, at the time.

[88] Key wrote at midcentury: "The political distance from Virginia to Alabama must be measured in light years. Virginian deference to the upper orders and the Byrd machine's restraint of popular aberrations give Virginia politics a tone and a reality radically different from the tumult of Alabama." (*Southern Politics*, p. 36). It would take considerable imagination to develop an overall category of Southern "political culture" that is attuned to electoral politics and covers both pre-1960s Virginia (honesty, deference, low turnout, quiet nominating processes) and Louisiana (the New Orleans machine tradition, populism, buffoonery, corruption, hypercompetitive nominating processes).

But beyond the specifics of characterizing and typologizing, it seems finally worthwhile in the American case to assert the sheer fact of geographically rooted traditions (whatever their content), of temporal connectedness, of durable ways of conducting electoral politics that once somehow initiated have seemed capable of surviving national changes in mass attitudes about political practices—and even sweeping ethnic overhauls of the population of a kind common in the country's northeastern quadrant in the last century. In many Southern states a candidate-centered politics survived intact through the transition from plantation society to the twentieth century's metropolitan business society. Bain offered the following reflection after tracking his five Maryland electoral environments from the 1870s through the mid-1950s: "The most important conclusion to be drawn from the data on these localities is that local political organization has displayed a long-term continuity, as remarkable as the continuity of partisan loyalties, during nearly a century of rapid change in American social and economic life."[89]

[89] Bain, "Five Kinds of Politics," p. 979.

CHAPTER 9

Environments and Processes

What are the implications of having traditional party organizations or not having them? One way to probe for answers, the preoccupation of this chapter and the next, is to do some comparative analysis across American space, setting the incidence of traditional organization (in the late 1960s though also earlier, by reasonable extrapolation) against the incidence of other pertinent twentieth-century phenomena. This way of proceeding can raise problems of spurious inference. The thirteen "organization states" (TPO scores of 4 or 5) are uniformly old and form a contiguous geographic bloc; consequently they have more in common than organizational type. But they also vary a great deal in important respects—in per capita income, religion, population density, immigrant versus native population, urban versus rural environment, occupational structure (manufacturing, services, agriculture, and mining are all represented), and source of original settlers (from New England through the South in the cases of the trans-Appalachian states). The analysis undertaken here ranges from impressionistic to statistical and will be presented under three headings, the first two in this chapter: *autonomy*, a consideration of different sorts of states' susceptibilities to "pressure politics," then briefly—taking up the matter of studying "community power"—a look at the place of corporations in two specified sorts of electoral environments, then the dealings of unions in various sorts of electoral settings; and *issues and cleavages*, a discussion first of what might be called "issue density" in organization and nonorganization electoral environments, then of geographic incidences of demagoguery, ideological movements anchored in organization, and social-class cleavages in voting.

The first thing to say about traditional party organization is that it amounts to something rather than nothing. It is something real and tangible that has operated with considerable *autonomy* in electoral and governmental sectors and has required a reckoning by other actors trying to operate in these sectors. This must be seen against a larger American background in which parties have figured more as arenas than as organizations, and in which in general other actors (either individuals or groups) have as a consequence probably operated more freely. Belle Zeller seems to have picked up the contrast three decades ago in a study investigating, among other things, the prominence of "pressure politics" in state legislatures.[1] See Table 9.1. A clear, if short of perfect, relationship appears between traditional organization and

Table 9.1   State Prominence of "Pressure Politics"

Pressure Politics	Organization States	Confederate States	Northern Tier and Plains States	Western States
STRONG	Kentucky	Alabama	Iowa	Arizona
		Arkansas	Maine	California
		Florida	Michigan	Montana
		Georgia	Minnesota	New Mexico
		Louisiana	Nebraska	Oregon
		Mississippi	Oklahoma	Washington
		North Carolina	Wisconsin	
		South Carolina		
		Tennessee		
		Texas		
MODERATE	Delaware	Virginia	Kansas	Nevada
	Illinois		Massachusetts	Utah
	Maryland		South Dakota	
	New York		Vermont	
	Ohio			
	Pennsylvania			
	West Virginia			
WEAK	Connecticut			Colorado
	Indiana			Wyoming
	Missouri			
	New Jersey			
	Rhode Island			

SOURCE: Belle Zeller (ed.), *American State Legislatures: Report of the Committee on American Legislatures, American Political Science Association* (New York: Crowell, 1954), pp. 190-191. Data not reported for Idaho, New Hampshire, or North Dakota (or Alaska or Hawaii).

[1] Belle Zeller (ed.), *American State Legislatures: Report of the Committee on American Legislatures, American Political Science Association* (New York: Crowell, 1954), pp. 190-191, and more generally pp. 189-194 and ch. 13. This dated measure of "pressure politics" was based on lean information and probably incorporated considerable error, yet nothing has superseded it. Two or more expert informants in each state were asked by questionnaire about pressure politics and a range of other matters; at least one answer, and in most cases two or three, were returned from each state.

"pressure politics": the more prominent the former, the less prominent the latter. "Pressure politics" is not clearly defined in the Zeller study, but its paradigmatic "strongest" form was no doubt one in which organizations other than parties (interest groups, unions, or corporations) could bring to bear resources that dwarfed those of individual legislators in state capitals and also legislative candidates in primary and general elections; "pressure" was made possible by the asymmetry in resources.[2] Good instances would be Farm Bureau activities of the 1940s and 1950s in Iowa politics, and California politics of the 1930s and 1940s, in which Arthur H. Samish, a notable entrepreneur in the art of influence peddling, worked for liquor, horse-racing, theater, banking, gambling, railroad, tobacco, and other interests as a lobbyist in the state capital and also as a supplier of electoral resources, earning himself the title "secret boss of California."[3]

There are at least two ways a political environment with strong traditional organizations might be expected to differ from these Iowa and California settings. First, a greater centralization of influence might occur on the politicians' side, with party leaders rather than individual politicians doing much of the dealing. Second, politicians might have more resources (especially to ensure nomination or election), which would reduce or reverse their asymmetrical position vis-à-vis outside organizations and thus would decrease their susceptibility to these groups' influence. Raymond E. Wolfinger states the second argument: "Where it is available, patronage provides politicians with a good share of the resources used in the political arena. . . . Thus wherever there are political machines—in a ward, city, county, or state—the party in that jurisdiction *can* be less dependent on constituent interest groups because the availability of patronage relieves somewhat the party's need to rely on those groups for money and manpower."[4] Whether beyond this outside organizations, or perhaps some kinds of outside organizations, do in fact get less of what they want in a politics of traditional party organization is more difficult to say. They might get what they want, after all, in a symmetric relationship of reciprocity, exchange, or other kind of mutual adjustment that does not carry a suggestion of "pressure," or simply because party leaders, for whatever reasons, wish to confer it.

---

[2] The electoral connection is a reasonable inference, though Zeller does not discuss it.

[3] See William Buchanan, *Legislative Partisanship: The Deviant Case of California* (Berkeley: University of California Press, 1963), pp. 19-48.

[4] Raymond E. Wolfinger, *The Politics of Progress* (Englewood Cliffs, N.J.: Prentice-Hall, 1974), p. 119.

The significance of autonomy will be taken up again later on, but some points may be worth making here on the place of private corporations in local politics and on the relationship between party organizations and unions. There is no reason to suppose that private corporations have ever had much trouble satisfying their needs in an environment of traditional party organization; there is no logically inherent conflict and little evidence of actual conflict. A basic relationship of exchange or reciprocity seems a natural and stable accommodation (though the price can occasionally get high, as in the case of Jersey City's business shakedowns). One of the most interesting accounts of relations between business and party, Edward C. Banfield's on Chicago in *Political Influence*, presents a picture of Mayor Daley dealing with corporate claims in an authoritative though scarcely hostile fashion. But a distinction needs to be made. This is a set of arrangements quite different from the situation in which a local "business community," often in league with professionals, organizes itself to seek goals beyond immediate corporate interests, generate candidates for office, win elections, staff the government, set its agenda, and impose a corporate ethos on public affairs. The clearest such assertions in the 1960s were Dallas's and Kalamazoo's hegemonic businessmen's parties—the Citizens Charter Association in Dallas was probably as close as anything can get to an executive committee of a ruling class—and perhaps Phoenix's and San Antonio's dominant parties composed of businessmen and professionals, though in many other places less formal groups of business leaders supplied coalitional bases at the mayoral level—in Atlanta, for example.

The contrast between Chicago and Dallas suggests a point about the study of city politics. Sociologists and political scientists investigating cities in recent times have differed in methodology. Sociologists have used a "reputational" technique, in which asking people for names of local leaders results in lists of leaders then designated as elites. Political scientists have examined the actual exercise of influence. But the two sets of investigators differ also in geography. Political scientists, probably because of an interest in distinctively political phenomena, have given a great deal of attention to cities with strong party organizations; studying cities has meant to a surprising degree studying New York and Chicago over and over again. Both Banfield's *Political Influence* and Robert A. Dahl's *Who Governs?*, classic statements on the subject of influence, were written about machine cities (Chicago and New Haven around 1960) whose mayors owed much of their considerable autonomy to their party organizations' control of council majorities and nominating processes.[5] On the other hand, sociologists in the "community power" tradition have largely steered clear of cities with traditional organizations, concentrating instead on cities whose business communities are active in politics—Atlanta and Dallas, for example. They seem to have dwelt in particular on small and middle-sized cities in North Carolina and Michigan with the persistence of political scientists studying New York and Chicago.[6] To a remarkable degree the scholars of the two disciplines have studied cities in quite different kinds of political settings.

The basic and unsurprising generalization about labor unions and parties is that unions have had a difficult time influencing nominating processes in environments supporting traditional party organizations.[7] The relationship has predictably been one of conflict to the degree that unions have sought on their own to mobilize and politicize large numbers of lower-income voters. Accordingly the CIO, when it was in its militant phase a generation ago, had worse relations with the regular organizations in many places than the AFL had at the time. Extreme examples are the no-holds-barred efforts by Hague and Crump to keep the CIO out of Jersey City and Memphis in the 1930s and 1940s.[8] In

[5] On organization control see Edward C. Banfield, *Political Influence: A New Theory of Urban Politics* (New York: Free Press, 1961), ch. 8; and Robert A. Dahl, *Who Governs? Democracy and Power in an American City* (New Haven: Yale University Press, 1961), ch. 9 and pp. 251-253.

[6] On Atlanta: Floyd Hunter, *Community Power Structure: A Study of Decision Makers* (Chapel Hill: University of North Carolina Press, 1953). On Dallas: Carol E. Thometz, *The Decision-Makers: The Power Structure of Dallas* (Dallas: Southern Methodist University Press, 1963). The methodology Dahl used in studying New Haven was very likely sensitive enough to have uncovered a power elite in Dallas if applied there in the 1950s or 1960s. For a geographic breakdown of community power studies see Willis D. Hawley and James H. Svara, *The Study of Community Power: A Bibliographic Review* (Santa Barbara, Calif.: ABC-Clio, 1972), ch. 2.

[7] Specifically on Chicago: J. David Greenstone, *Labor in American Politics* (New York: Vintage, 1969), ch. 3; Fay Calkins, *The CIO and the Democratic Party* (Chicago: University of Chicago Press, 1952), ch. 4. On New Haven: Wolfinger, *Politics of Progress*, p. 119. On Pennsylvania in general, where party organizations were able to "fend off intruding nonparty groups" in the 1950s: Frank J. Sorauf, *Party and Representation: Legislative Politics in Pennsylvania* (New York: Atherton, 1963), p. 57. On Wilkes-Barre: Jeffrey Kampelman, "Democratic Politics in Luzerne County" (Yale course paper, 1977), p. 2. On Steubenville: Calkins, ch. 3. A general treatment of unions operating in city politics: Edward C. Banfield and James Q. Wilson, "Organized Labor in City Politics," pp. 487-500 in Edward C. Banfield (ed.), *Urban Government: A Reader in Administration and Politics* (New York: Free Press, 1969).

[8] "When the CIO sent organizers into Memphis to unionize Ford and Fisher Body, an enraged Crump declared war. He had Mayor Overton call the CIO 'un-American' and Police Commissioner Cliff Davis declare that he would not 'tolerate them.' Crump chose

general, however, unions from the New Deal through the 1950s accepted roles as junior partners in organization-centered Democratic coalitions. There are reports that they settled for a share of the patronage pool in Pendergast's Kansas City apparatus, solicitude on policy matters in a relation of "co-optation" in Lawrence's Pittsburgh regime, a role "narrowly circumscribed by . . . bondage to the Democratic party" in Philadelphia of the 1950s, and a place as one minority interest among several in Connecticut's Democratic party of the 1950s.[9] In Rhode Island the AFL, said to be "oriented toward patronage" and "sympathetic with the small-business interests of the Democratic legislators," had a comfortable and influential role in the party in the 1950s, but conflict broke out after union leadership passed to a merged AFL-CIO in 1958.[10] In a unique adjustment to an environment of or-

---

more than verbal opposition, for police brutality against the CIO organizers was the order of the day with the worst beating being administered to Norman Smith, the head CIO organizer" (Alfred Steinberg, *The Bosses* [New York: Macmillan, 1972], pp. 113-114). See also David M. Tucker, *Memphis Since Crump: Bossism, Blacks, and Civic Reformers, 1948-1968* (Knoxville: University of Tennessee Press, 1980), pp. 54-56. On Jersey City: Dayton D. McKean, *The Boss: The Hague Machine in Action* (Boston: Houghton Mifflin, 1940), ch. 11; Leo Troy, *Organized Labor in New Jersey* (Princeton, N.J.: Van Nostrand, 1965), pp. 176-177, 183.

[9] On Kansas City: "Labor's fidelity to the Kansas City organization cannot be explained in terms of policy. . . . Labor's loyalty to the Kansas City machine continued predominately because many labor leaders in the western half of the state were themselves integral members of the Democratic organization. Their loyalty to the organization had been secured through patronage" (Gary M. Fink, *Labor's Search for Political Order: The Political Behavior of the Missouri Labor Movement, 1890-1940* [Columbia: University of Missouri Press, 1973], pp. 155-156, and more generally pp. 120-127 and ch. 9). On Pittsburgh: Martin A. Levin, *Urban Politics and the Criminal Courts* (Chicago: University of Chicago Press, 1977), p. 42. On Philadelphia: James Reichley, *The Art of Government: Reform and Organization Politics in Philadelphia* (New York: Fund for the Republic, 1959), p. 65, and more generally pp. 64-68. Robert L. Freedman in 1963 on the Philadelphia labor movement: "It lacks bargaining power. . . . The reason for this state of affairs is that the unions control no votes. They have no precinct organization. Their members do not often vote on the basis of their union leaders' recommendations" (*A Report on Politics in Philadelphia* [Cambridge: Joint Center for Urban Studies, M.I.T./Harvard, 1963], p. v:14 and more generally pp. v:12-16). On Connecticut: Duane Lockard, *New England State Politics* (Princeton: Princeton University Press, 1959), pp. 263-264.

[10] Jay S. Goodman, *The Democrats and Labor in Rhode Island, 1952-62: Changes in the Old Alliance* (Providence: Brown University Press, 1967), p. 108. "After the merger of the AFL and CIO in 1958, however, labor was dominated by CIO leaders who were concerned primarily with social reform. This interest carried labor in a direction that could lead only to a collision with the party" (pp. 108-109). In 1962 the AFL-CIO presented a report that accused the Democrats of placing "the interests of race tracks, insurance companies, medical lobbies, liquor dealers, and self-seeking political hacks ahead of the welfare of the general public" (p. 36).

ganization, the Tammany setting, New York City's garment unions generated their own American Labor party in the 1930s and the Liberal party in the 1940s as third-party vehicles.[11] Populous settings where American unions have at any time played a dominant or nearly dominant role in electoral politics seem few in number, and all are outside the belt of organization states. In Minneapolis the Central Labor Union was "the most important single force" in electoral politics from 1941 through 1957; in St. Paul the Labor Temple carried decisive weight in elections in the 1950s; in Seattle Dave Beck's Teamsters rose to the top in a volatile municipal politics in the 1930s; in San Francisco the Union Labor party held office at the beginning of the century and labor was also especially strong in the 1960s; and at the state level Hawaii had its phase of ILWU influence in the 1950s and Michigan had its UAW phase in the 1950s and 1960s.[12]

On the subject of *issues and cleavages*, it seems a plausible hypothesis that American environments supporting traditional party organization have ranked relatively low in issue content in their electoral processes—taking as a whole their mixes of primary and general election processes for state, local, and district offices, both nonpartisan and partisan. This may be impossible to prove (or even to state with airtight

[11] For a treatment of relations between unions and Tammany Hall early in the century see Irwin Yellowitz, *Labor and the Progressive Movement in New York State, 1897-1916* (Ithaca: Cornell University Press, 1965). "There is no doubt that organized labor, dabbling in politics as a subsidiary function, could not contend with the effective methods of the professional political machines; and nowhere is this clearer than in Tammany Hall's command of the working-class vote in New York City" (p. 181).

[12] On Minneapolis: Alan Altshuler, *A Report on Politics in Minneapolis* (Cambridge: Joint Center for Urban Studies, M.I.T./Harvard, 1959), p. v:6, and more generally pp. ii:8-9, v:5-7. On St. Paul: Alan Altshuler, *A Report on Politics in St. Paul, Minnesota* (Cambridge: Joint Center for Urban Studies, M.I.T./Harvard, 1959), pp. ii:3-10, v:1-4. On Seattle: Charles W. Bender, *A Report on Politics in Seattle* (Cambridge: Joint Center for Urban Studies, M.I.T./Harvard, 1961), pp. ii:1-6. On San Francisco: Ralph V. Giannini, "San Francisco: Labor's City: 1900-1911" (Ph.D. dissertation, University of Florida, 1975); Jules Tygiel, ". . . where unionism holds undisputed sway: A Reappraisal of San Francisco's Union Labor Party," *California History* 62(1983). On San Francisco in the 1960s see Frederick M. Wirt, *Power in the City: Decision Making in San Francisco* (Berkeley: University of California Press, 1974), pp. 173-176. On Hawaii: Lawrence H. Fuchs, *Hawaii Pono: A Social History* (New York: Harcourt, Brace and World, 1961), ch. 14; Horace T. Day, Jr., "A Study of Political Opportunity Structure: Political Opportunity in Hawaii, 1926-1966" (Ph.D. dissertation, University of Hawaii, 1974), pp. 90-111. On Michigan: Stephen B. Sarasohn and Vera H. Sarasohn, *Political Party Patterns in Michigan* (Detroit: Wayne State University Press, 1957), pp. 45-68; Dudley W. Buffa, *Union Power and American Democracy: The UAW and the Democratic Party, 1935-72* (Ann Arbor: University of Michigan Press, 1984); Calkins, *CIO and Democratic Party*, ch. 6; Greenstone, *Labor in American Politics*, ch. 4.

precision), and it puts organization territory in relief against a quite miscellaneous American background of nonorganization territory, but some arguments and evidence back it up. The arguments: (a) By definition "material" incentives dominate "purposive" incentives in the upkeep of traditional organizations, generating workers and supporters unlikely by nature to want to raise, dwell on, or direct attention to issues. (b) Nominations for public office, insofar as they comprise part of a traditional organization's reward structure, are likely to go to the same sorts of people with the same tastes. (c) Politicians who build issue followings, or "personal followings" mixed with issue followings, are natural enemies of traditional organization and hence unlikely to be given nominations (though occasionally for reasons of electoral appeal they are indeed given them).[13] (d) To the degree that the resources of traditional organizations grease the way to nomination and election, they relieve favored candidates of the need to deal in issues, and on balance probably lower the incidence of dealing in them. From an opposite perspective, taking positions on issues is an obvious electoral tactic for lone operators in politics (though not all use it), even in nonorganization environments where they can build personal patronage networks once in office: they have to reach office on their own somehow in the first place.

Roundabout corroboration of the idea of differential resort to issues appears in a surprising source, a study by Warren E. Miller and Donald E. Stokes of the 85th Congress (1957-1958). It coded most of a sample of members as "self-starters" or "party recruits" on the basis of their reports on how they initially reached office. Reports of initial party backing were especially common among Northern Democrats, whose ranks in the late 1950s of course included a large number of organization regulars—nearly all the New York City delegation, for example. One interview question went as follows: "In seeking renomination [this evidently means in 1958], how would you compare the importance of your stands on issues with the importance of other factors—such as services to your constituents, your standing in the party, and so forth?" Among "self-starters" 61 percent said issues were "of equal or greater importance than all other factors"; among "party recruits" the figure was 25 percent—a disparity especially striking once it becomes clear that "self-starters' " districts ranked no higher in well-educated or high-income voters than "party recruits' " districts.[14]

---

[13] Edward C. Banfield and James Q. Wilson, *City Politics* (Cambridge: Harvard University Press and M.I.T. Press, 1963), pp. 130-131.

[14] The source is Warren E. Miller and Donald E. Stokes, "Representation in Congress," unpublished manuscript, pp. 2001-2006 and Tables 2.1, 2.2, and 2.6 of ch. 2 ("Recruit-

Specific evidence on the matter comes to light in direct testimony by many careful observers, some of which was summarized in the state sketches of Part I, that issue content has indeed been lean in organization territory. There are exceptions—in Plaquemines Parish, for example, Leander Perez used his political autonomy as a platform to campaign for decades against civil rights—but reports of low issue content appear routinely from Suffolk County on Long Island through the Hispanic counties of northern New Mexico.[15] Frank Sorauf's especially

---

ment of Candidates"). "Self-starters,"comprising 42% of a sample of about a hundred House members, were members coded *no* under the heading "Congressman was supported by his party in his first candidacy," and *yes* under the heading "Congressman actively sought office in his first candidacy." "Party recruits," comprising 29 percent of the sample, were members coded *yes* under the former label and *no* under the latter. On an interview question slightly different from the one on renomination: "In response to a subsequent question, 64 percent of the Self-Starters reported placing great emphasis on issues in their last campaigns, while only 38 percent of the Party Recruits did so."

[15] On Perez: Glen Jeansonne, *Leander Perez: Boss of the Delta* (Baton Rouge: Louisiana State University Press, 1977), chs. 10, 12-15. On New Haven in the machine proper: Wolfinger, *Politics of Progress*, p. 104. On the Bailey organization in Hartford: Everett C. Ladd, Jr., *Ideology in America: Change and Response in a City, a Suburb, and a Small Town* (Ithaca: Cornell University Press, 1969), p. 130. On Suffolk County: Richard F. Koubek, "The Intra-Party Uses and Influences of Personal Resources Distributed by Suburban Party Elites" (Ph.D. dissertation, City University of New York, 1980), pp. 74-77, 141-143, and ch. 4. On Pennsylvania in general: Sorauf, *Party and Representation*, pp. 14-15, 110. On Schuylkill County, Pa.: Richard L. Kolbe, "Culture, Political Parties and Voting Behavior: Schuylkill County," *Polity* 8(1975), p. 266. On Baltimore: Henry Bain, "Five Kinds of Politics: A Historical and Comparative Study of the Making of Legislators in Five Maryland Constituencies" (Ph.D. dissertation, Harvard University, 1970), p. 876; Edwin Rothman, "Factional Machine-Politics: William Curran and the Baltimore City Democratic Party Organization, 1929-1946" (Ph.D. dissertation, Johns Hopkins University, 1949), pp. 259-260. On Kanawha County, W.Va.: Rod Harless, *The West Virginia Establishment* (Huntington, W.Va.: Appalachian Movement Press, 1971), p. 33. On relatively low issue content in Ohio: Thomas A. Flinn, "American County Political Parties: Purposes and Other Purposes," paper presented at the 1982 convention of the American Political Science Association, pp. 19-27; and in Cuyahoga County in particular: Thomas A. Flinn and Ronald J. Busch, "Is Party Dead? A Study of Political Party Organization in a Large Urban County," paper presented at the 1982 conference of the Midwest Political Science Association, pp. 6-7, 38. On Indiana: Frank J. Munger, "Two-Party Politics in the State of Indiana" (Ph.D. dissertation, Harvard University, 1955), pp. 5-6, 177, 228-229. On Chicago: Leo M. Snowiss, "Congressional Recruitment and Representation," *American Political Science Review* 60(1966), 629; James Q. Wilson, "Two Negro Politicians: An Interpretation," *Midwest Journal of Political Science* 4(1960), 347-349, 355-363. On the regular organization in St. Louis: Robert H. Salisbury, "St. Louis Politics: Relationships Among Interests, Parties, and Governmental Structure," *Western Political Quarterly* 13(1960), 504. On "the organization" in El Paso: Mark Adams and Gertrude Adams, *A Report on Politics in El Paso* (Cambridge: Joint Center for Urban Studies, M.I.T./Harvard, 1963), pp. 14-16. On northern New Mexico: Charles B. Judah, *Recruitment of Candidates from the Northern and Eastern Counties to the New*

good statement on Pennsylvania in the 1950s is worth repeating: "The tradition of politics as personal gain perforce means that Pennsylvania politics are nonideological and often issueless. One can talk to hundreds of local political leaders in the state without hearing the words 'liberal' or 'conservative' spoken. In the local political barony in Pennsylvania, the reward system becomes, instead of a means to election success or policy enactment, the political end in itself."[16] The same evidently held true earlier under Cameron, Quay, and Penrose: "There was no place in the Republican machine or even in machine-dominated Pennsylvania for either popular or issue-oriented political leaders."[17]

The opposite of this Pennsylvania style, if states could somehow be ranked according to the issue content of their politics, is probably California's, which has featured among other things episodic issue eruptions: Kearneyism, for example, which generated a Workingmen's Party, "forced the adoption of a new constitution," and "upset the balance of power within the state" in the 1880s; the Union Labor party, victorious in San Francisco in 1901; Hiram Johnson's Progressivism, which swept the state in 1910; Upton Sinclair's End Poverty in California movement, which successfully colonized the Democratic party in 1934; the Townsend movement for old-age pensions in the 1930s, and a spin-off Ham and Eggs movement that produced a Senator in 1938; the wave of anti-Communism that helped Richard Nixon reach the House in 1946 and the Senate in 1950; the Democratic club movement of the 1950s and 1960s; and the aggressive conservatism that took hold in the state's southern metropolitan counties in the 1960s.[18]

More generally, there are two interesting and important patterns of issue expression that evidently have been more common over the years in American environments lacking traditional organization than in en-

---

Mexico House of Representatives—1956 (Albuquerque: Division of Research, Department of Government, University of New Mexico, 1961), p. 4.

[16] Sorauf, *Party and Representation*, pp. 14-15.

[17] Philip S. Klein and Ari Hoogenboom, *A History of Pennsylvania* (University Park: Pennsylvania State University Press, 1980), p. 362.

[18] On Kearneyism: Carey McWilliams, *California: The Great Exception* (New York: A. A. Wyn, 1949), p. 176, and more generally pp. 171-176. "There was nothing to break or check the rise of the movement and, by the same token, there was nothing to hold it together once its initial objects had been achieved" (p. 176). On the Union Labor party: Giannini, "San Francisco." On Hiram Johnson: George E. Mowry, *The California Progressives* (Berkeley: University of California Press, 1968). On Upton Sinclair: Walt Anderson, *Campaigns: Cases in Political Conflict* (Pacific Palisades, Calif.: Goodyear, 1970), ch. 7 ("California: Frank F. Merriam vs. Upton Sinclair"). On the pensions cause: Jackson K. Putnam, *Old-Age Politics in California: From Richardson to Reagan* (Stanford: Stanford University Press, 1970).

vironments having it. The first is demagoguery, more or less. This is a difficult concept to pin down, though it has been one of the twentieth century's major options, and has had importance in the United States at least to the degree that Huey Long was important in fact and potential.[19] Let us say that a demagogue is a politician who (a) operates as a lone wolf or with only a personal organization, (b) seeks the favor of a mass public substantially through (c) sensationalism and (d) vigorous, continual attacks on other people or groups of people (e) in a style geared to the poorly educated (although demagogic activity need not be all or even mostly meretricious), and (f) inspires distrust among other political actors and part of the public yet attracts intense support from another part of the public by ostentatiously flouting norms of interpersonal dealing among political actors.[20] These traits seem true to American usage and experience. The largely organization-free South has of course specialized in demagogues. All the states of the deep South plus Texas and Oklahoma have supplied twentieth-century instances, including Louisiana's Huey Long, Mississippi's James K. Vardaman and Theodore G. Bilbo, Arkansas's Jeff Davis, South Carolina's Cole Blease, and Georgia's Eugene Talmadge.[21] But a number of Northerners have also approximated the type, including James Michael Curley of Massachusetts (called "the Boston Brahmin-Baiter" in one account), Wisconsin's Joseph R. McCarthy, California's Samuel W. Yorty, who

---

[19] Helpful discussions of the concept "demagogue" or related matters appear in Dahl, *Who Governs?*, ch. 28; Reinhard H. Luthin, *American Demagogues: Twentieth Century* (Boston: Beacon, 1954), ch. 12; James W. Ceaser, *Presidential Selection: Theory and Development* (Princeton: Princeton University Press, 1979), pp. 318-327; and Cal M. Logue and Howard Dorgan, "The Demagogue," pp. 1-11 in Logue and Dorgan (eds.), *The Oratory of Southern Demagogues* (Baton Rouge: Louisiana State University Press, 1981).

[20] The last trait is quite important, since it can be read to prefigure unscrupulousness in a position of executive power. A reflection on a number of pertinent early twentieth-century Southern politicians: "A central characteristic of their message was their insolent methods of persuasion. Indeed, much of their personal appeal to white workers derived from their public contempt of social, economic, and political conventions—factors the average person was made to believe held him or her captive in poverty and powerlessness. Critics perceived the 'demagogues' as being dangerously authoritarian, whereas supporters felt pride in their belligerency and identified experientially with their intrepid discourse. . . . Persons caught in a cycle of poverty concluded that they could do better by the dictations of the 'demagogue' than they had done under the policies of politicians whose public behavior was usually judged as being more civil and 'gentlemanly' " (Logue and Dorgan, "The Demagogue," pp. 9-10).

[21] Even given the great resourcefulness of American politicians at all times, demagogues operating in the Deep South at the turn of the century seem to have brought something new to the country's electoral politics. Examining many American state and local electoral environments over time and space produces the surprising impression that both machines and demagogues are largely twentieth-century phenomena.

drew resourcefully on Red-baiting and other "anti-" formulations in a long career capped by twelve years as mayor of Los Angeles, and, to give a minor-league instance, Hawaii's Frank Fasi.[22] The case of Curley is especially interesting; it shows that an early twentieth-century urban, working-class environment uncontrolled by party organization could generate the type as effectively as the rural South.

The alleged relation between organization and demagoguery needs qualification, however, for this is one matter on which organization environments of "persistent factionalism" seem to have differed from environments of intraparty monopoly. The logic is that local factions in an environment such as Maryland's have regularly needed to choose up sides in close statewide primaries, which has allowed maneuvering room at the top (even if not the bottom) for candidates of a rhetorical bent who could move in and promise help in carrying the factional ticket.[23] This was the role of George "Your Home Is Your Castle" Mahoney in Maryland, and a hint of the same logic appears in a statement attributed to Huey Long about running for governor of Louisiana in the 1920s: "In every parish there is a boss, usually the sheriff. He has forty per cent of the votes, forty per cent are opposed to him, and twenty per cent are in-betweens. I'm going into every parish and cuss out the boss. That gives me forty per cent of the votes to begin with, and I'll hoss trade 'em out of the in-betweens."[24] There is in addition the complicated case of Indiana (and Indianapolis in particular) in the mid-

---

[22] On Curley: Luthin, *American Demagogues*, ch. 2. Worcester's George A. Wells, discussed earlier (see Robert H. Binstock, *A Report on Politics in Worcester, Massachusetts* [Cambridge: Joint Center for Urban Studies, M.I.T./Harvard, 1960], pp. II:22-26), seems a minor-league Massachusetts example. On Joseph McCarthy: Luthin, ch. 11 ("Joseph R. McCarthy: Wisconsin's Briefcase Demagogue"). On Yorty: John C. Bollens and Grant B. Geyer, *Yorty: Politics of a Constant Candidate* (Pacific Palisades, Calif.: Palisades Publishers, 1973). On Fasi: Paul C. Phillips, *Hawaii's Democrats: Chasing the American Dream* (Washington, D.C.: University Press of America, 1982), ch. 9 ("The Outsider—Frank Fasi").

[23] By contrast, almost all parties in the eight organization states with monopolistic (that is, nonfactional) parties used to nominate gubernatorial and Senatorial candidates either by convention or by assertions of one or a combination of local organizations that ordinarily warded off open primary competition. The party conforming least well to this standard was Ohio's Democratic, though even Ohio Democrats lacked a dynamic of factional competition of the Kentucky or Maryland sort engendering close statewide primary contests in nearly every election.

[24] The material on Mahoney is too scanty to allow a judgment that he certainly met all the conditions set out above in the text. See Bain, "Five Kinds of Politics," pp. 158-159, 396-397, 434, 823, 870, 876, 911, 918; John H. Fenton, *Politics in the Border States: A Study of the Patterns of Political Organization, and Political Change, Common to the Border States—Maryland, West Virginia, Kentucky and Missouri* (New Orleans: Hauser, 1957), pp. 184-187. On Long: T. Harry Williams, *Huey Long* (New York: Knopf, 1969), p. 181.

1920s, where the surging Ku Klux Klan used and also mimicked the indigenous party factionalism. It successfully penetrated both parties' primaries by playing faction against faction and then itself subsided into factional warfare, wrangling over patronage and a list of indictable practices.[25] The main point here is that the Indiana Klan's leader, David C. Stephenson, who worked the primary system to elect a governor (though not himself), was a charismatic sort said "to descend in his personal plane, covered with red paint and gold crosses, into a cleared portion of the field, to emerge clothed in his official robes of purple and gold, to harangue the hooded faithful of the Klan, and to fly away once more."[26] This seems to have been powerful stuff for a short time. Indiana abolished its primaries for governor and Senator just after the Klan's successes—the ban lasted several decades—and Frank J. Munger encountered a much more sedate politics in the 1950s: "The Indiana system rewards a talent for organization, and many of the state's governors and Senators have been former party state chairman. . . . [It] rewards personal warmth, and most of its products are friendly men. But the system provides little reward for demagoguery, and the vocal charlatans that have afflicted so many wide-open primary states have few counterparts in Indiana."[27]

So much for factional states. The heartland of nonfactional organization and also of generations of mobilizable immigrants, the strip of states on the East Coast from Rhode Island through Delaware, has had twentieth-century political traditions virtually devoid of important demagoguery.[28] This may be one of the more important sets of non-

---

[25] The basic source is John A. Davis, "The Ku Klux Klan in Indiana, 1920-1930: An Historical Study" (Ph.D. dissertation, Northwestern University, 1966), ch. 4. See also Norman F. Weaver, "The Knights of the Ku Klux Klan in Wisconsin, Indiana, Ohio and Michigan" (Ph.D. dissertation, University of Wisconsin, 1954), ch. 4.

[26] Munger, "Two-Party Politics," p. 301. See also Harold Zink, "A Case Study of a Political Boss," *Psychiatry* 1(1938), 527-533. In 1925 Stephenson was arrested, tried, and convicted for a "sex-orgy-murder of a most sordid nature" (see Davis, "Ku Klux Klan in Indiana," pp. 95-96). "At the critical moment when he might have gone on to become a real dictator of the Huey Long stripe, he . . . got careless in what he did" (Weaver, "Knights of the Ku Klux Klan," p. 170).

[27] Munger, "Two-Party Politics," p. 301. Memphis of the 1920s, with its white native population, was a natural target of the Klan movement, but Ed Crump's organization kept it from taking over. See Kenneth T. Jackson, *The Ku Klux Klan in the City, 1915-1930* (New York: Oxford University Press, 1967), ch. 4; and Kenneth D. Wald, "The Visible Empire: The Ku Klux Klan as an Electoral Movement," *Journal of Interdisciplinary History* 11(1980), 217-234.

[28] An exception who comes to mind (before the time of Frank Rizzo) is Adam Clayton Powell in loosely organized Harlem around 1950, whose political base was the Abyssinian Baptist Church, and whose appeals were "centered around Powell as the personal

events. The closest thing to a Middle Atlantic Huey Long was very likely William Randolph Hearst—*Citizen Kane* reworked to incorporate the political victories of *All the King's Men* suggests the possibilities. But Hearst, despite his newspaper empire and personal fortune, his "outstanding talents" in "the allied fields of promotion, propaganda, advertising and showmanship," his political influence considerable enough to affect events in California and Illinois, to win himself 263 votes for President at the Democratic national convention of 1904 (mostly from Iowa and points west), and to figure in national Democratic nominating as late as 1932, came out a loser in the organizational politics of New York.[29] He set his eye on the Presidency in about 1900 but needed a major New York office as a stepping-stone. Charles F. Murphy of Tammany, fancying press support, slated him in 1902 for Congress, where he did little but introduce bills and publicize them in his newspapers, furthering his campaigns against "the interests," "the trusts," the "robber barons of gold," and the "money power." Murphy, who "had developed a strong aversion to the publisher who seemed to think that Tammany should dance to his tune," ignored him in the national convention of 1904, whereupon Hearst undertook a third-party mayoral campaign of extraordinary power in 1905: "Thoughtful anti-Hearst men realized that this test was crucial. If Hearst should win despite the enormous obstacles he faced, it would stamp him as a popular hero and put him on the highroad to the governorship and the Presidency—something that made conservatives shudder. The fear of Hearst was even more pervasive than the fear of Bryan in 1896."[30]

---

embodiment, the projective personality, of the Negroes in his congregation." "Powell frequently makes public charges of racial discrimination and injustice in Manhattan and he is not slow to attack the Mayor, the Police Commissioner, Carmine DeSapio, and other officials. Harlem is not simply a constituency which elects Powell to Congress; it is also a source of political issues. Powell's political style in part depends on the existence of an 'enemy'—a source of alleged injustice against which Powell can direct his fire." And: "The interesting point thus far is that . . . Powell has not had to 'deliver' beyond winning successive challenges to his position. . . . The explanation in Powell's case seems to be that the need for 'delivering' in terms of substantive ends and benefits has been in good part obviated by his success in finding and defeating political enemies" (Wilson, "Two Negro Politicians," pp. 350, 351-352, 355).

[29] The sources are W. A. Swanberg, *Citizen Hearst: A Biography of William Randolph Hearst* (New York: Bantam, 1963), book 4, quotation at p. 222; John K. Winkler, *W. R. Hearst: An American Phenomenon* (London: Jonathan Cape, 1928), pp. 187-218; Yellowitz, *Labor and the Progressive Movement*, ch. 9; Thomas M. Henderson, *Tammany Hall and the New Immigrants: The Progressive Years* (New York: Arno, 1976), pp. 103-114.

[30] On Hearst's Congressional career: Swanberg, *Citizen Hearst*, pp. 236-242, 248-250, 252-253, 264-276. "He was the House pariah. Even the regular Democrats dis-

Hearst lost to the 1905 Democratic mayoral candidate by an official 3,471 votes, but in fact he was almost certainly counted out: credible tales circulated of "repeaters" and of ballot boxes dumped in the East River.[31] He reacted by publishing a picture of Murphy in prison stripes. Murphy, however, pondering the returns, reacted by slating Hearst for governor in 1906, setting off much discussed charges of a "deal" and another close and intense campaign in which the entire state Democratic ticket won except Hearst. Accounts disagree on whether Tammany knifed Hearst in Manhattan—the returns suggest not, or not much—but the Brooklyn Democratic organization certainly did, and this was an important ingredient in the loss.[32] Following the election, the *New York Herald* wrote: "Mr. Murphy thinks he is entitled to some credit. He thinks that but for his farsightedness and sagacity in nominating Hearst and reaping the fruit of his socialistic sowing the Democratic organization in the State would have been demolished. . . . He forgives himself for his dealings with Hearst, says the end justifies the means, and chuckles when he thinks that after all Hearst was not elected and the Tammany judiciary and legislative tickets were."[33] There was an aftermath lasting two decades—another losing third-party mayoral campaign by Hearst in 1909; organization denials of a Senate nomination in 1914, a mayoral nomination in 1917, and a gubernatorial or Senate nomination in 1922; Hearst's bizarre enchantment of organization mayor John F. Hylan in 1917-1925, more or less capturing him; and the sop of a Senate seat to a Hearst protégé in 1922.[34] But the critical events occurred in 1905 and 1906. This is a complicated story that lacks consistency of motive or action on the part of organization politicians, and chance played a prominent role, but the important point is that Hearst deployed his formidable resources in

---

owned him. Inherently incapable of cooperating with others, he ran his own show regardless of how many party-line Democratic toes he stepped on" (p. 253). Quotation on Murphy: pp. 264-265. Quotation on 1905: p. 280.

[31] On the 1905 campaign: *ibid.*, pp. 267, 273-283; Yellowitz, *Labor and the Progressive Movement*, pp. 190-202. Hearst cut into Tammany's normal working-class vote in lower Manhattan, though the three "Sullivan districts" (tightly controlled by "Big Tim" Sullivan) and Murphy's home district held firm. See Henderson, *Tammany Hall*, p. 106.

[32] On the 1906 campaign: Swanberg, *Citizen Hearst*, pp. 283-292, 296-300; Yellowitz, *Labor and the Progressive Movement*, pp. 202-215; Winkler, *Hearst*, pp. 210-218.

[33] *New York Herald*, November 8, 1906, p. 5.

[34] On the losses: Swanberg, *Citizen Hearst*, pp. 314-318, 345, 364-366, 403, 410-412. On Hylan and sending Royal S. Copeland to the Senate: pp. 365-371, 376-377, 400, 410, 411, 448-451. After 1906: "The peak of Hearst's popularity had passed and, while Murphy's fear of his influence would frequently help determine Tammany's strategy, his name never again appeared on the ballot" (Henderson, *Tammany Hall*), pp. 113-114.

New York politics for two and a half decades without being able to win a major office.

The other pattern of issue expression worth discussing is quite different from demagoguery, though it has also flourished in the United States outside organization territory. This is an electoral politics featuring (a) a prominent left-right ideological dimension, (b) a rhetoric of zero-sum conflict, (c) intellectuals in an important programmatic role, and (d) organizations on the left mobilizing a mass membership. This is a European formula, but there are times in the twentieth century when one or more American states would have fit fairly comfortably into a European party system—or at least a system like Australia's or New Zealand's that has an assertive Labor party. In North Dakota the rise to power of the Nonpartisan League in 1916, largely a triumph of farmers mobilized by socialists, generated a range of ambitious governmental programs—including some state-owned industries—and an ideological cleavage still evident in the 1950s.[35] In Minnesota the sometimes victorious Farmer-Labor party gave politics a distinctive structural and ideological cast in the 1920s and 1930s, partly by drawing attention to its own internal controversies between pragmatic and militant factions (Communists were influential in the 1930s) and over the role of the Farmer-Labor Association, an umbrella organization of farmers and workers.[36] The state of Washington had something of Minnesota's flavor in the 1930s, with politicized unions, ideological polarization, and showdown elections between left and right. The

---

[35] See Robert L. Morlan, *Political Prairie Fire: The Nonpartisan League, 1915-1922* (Minneapolis: University of Minnesota Press, 1955). A good summary appears at pp. 348-361.

[36] See Millard L. Gieske, *Minnesota Farmer-Laborism: The Third-Party Alternative* (Minneapolis: University of Minnesota Press, 1979). Farmer-Laborites in the 1930s built a considerable state-level patronage organization also, creating an extraordinary dissonance between ideological and material incentives in their ranks. Organizations in Hennepin, Ramsey, and St. Louis counties (the three urban areas) seem to have stayed in the hands of ideologues. The underpinnings of the Progressive tradition in Wisconsin differed in some interesting respects from the Farmer-Labor movement's in Minnesota. Philip La Follette, in presiding over the launching of a new Wisconsin party in 1934, reflected a majority view in arguing for the label "Progressive" rather than "Farmer-Labor," one ground being that "progressives had always worked for common, not class, objectives." And, a firm supporter of the Wisconsin tradition of open primaries, he fought successfully against giving any important role in the party to the left wing's Farmer Labor Progressive League, "modeled on the Minnesota Farmer-Labor Association and designed as a permanent dues-paying organization, which would write platforms, endorse candidates, and impose party discipline on elected officials." See John E. Miller, *Governor Philip F. La Follette, the Wisconsin Progressives, and the New Deal* (Columbia: University of Missouri Press, 1982), pp. 51-55, quotations at pp. 52, 53.

Washington Commonwealth Federation grouped together pertinent membership organizations and increasingly voiced Communist party doctrines as the decade progressed.[37] Finally Michigan, with its aggressive and programmatic UAW, supported a distinctively conflict-ridden and ideological politics in the 1950s, notably on tax and labor matters. The state's opposing sides were said to participate in politics not for "the traditional prizes" but with the aim of "controlling the social and economic policy of the state government."[38] This was an arresting spectacle to observers of the time, including political scientists who drew contrasts with more conventional organization states to the south.[39]

Robert R. Alford's breakdown of American "class voting" by region around the middle of the twentieth century meshes in some interesting particulars with the material presented in this chapter on organization and issue expression. A measure of "class voting" can be calculated for any geographic unit in any election in a two-party system by subtracting the percentage of nonmanual workers voting for the party of the Left (here the Democratic) from the percentage of manual workers voting for the same party of the Left (farmers are ignored). The sharper the class cleavage, the higher the index reading. Drawing on Alford's data from a number of national surveys, average class voting indexes can be calculated by region for the presidential elections from 1944 through 1956, a period when unions had become fully active in electoral politics but race had not arisen yet as a national issue. See Table 9.2.[40] The

[37] See Albert A. Acena, "The Washington Commonwealth Confederation: Reform Politics and the Popular Front" (Ph.D. dissertation, University of Washington, 1975). It was the WCF, though it hardly was running the state, that inspired Jim Farley's remark of the late 1930s: "There are forty-seven states in the Union, and the Soviet of Washington" (p. 280). See also David J. Saposs, *Communism in American Politics* (Washington, D.C.: Public Affairs Press, 1960), pp. 29-39.

[38] On Michigan see Sarasohn and Sarasohn, *Political Party Patterns in Michigan*, pp. 26-68, quotation at p. 69; Fenton, *Midwest Politics*, ch. 2; Buffa, *Union Power*.

[39] Michigan was contrasted with Connecticut in Fred I. Greenstein, *The American Party System and the American People* (Englewood Cliffs, N.J.: Prentice-Hall, 1970), pp. 78-83; and with Missouri and Illinois in Nicholas A. Masters, Robert H. Salisbury, and Thomas H. Eliot, *State Politics and the Public Schools: An Exploratory Analysis* (New York: Knopf, 1964), pp. 179-180, 210-215.

[40] Robert R. Alford, *Party and Society: The Anglo-American Democracies* (Chicago: Rand McNally, 1963), pp. 232-241, 358-361. Alford drew on seven national surveys done by four polling organizations in 1944 through 1960. The material presented here skips 1960, with its religious cross-current, leaving five surveys done by three organizations in 1944 through 1956 (including two in 1952). The regions are not all consistently defined. *New England* is always the customary six states, and *Mountain* (with the fewest respondents) the customary eight. *Pacific* is always California, Oregon, and Washington. *Middle Atlantic* always includes New York, New Jersey, and Pennsylvania, and sometimes Maryland, Delaware, West Virginia, and the District of Columbia. *East Central*

Table 9.2   Class Voting in Presidential Elections by Region, 1944-1956

	Mean Index of Class Voting	Median Index of Class Voting
West Central	29	30
New England	25	25
Mountain	24	25
Pacific	23	19
East Central	19	24
Middle Atlantic	16	16
South	10	16

SOURCE: Robert R. Alford, *Party and Society: The Anglo-American Democracies* (Chicago: Rand McNally, 1963), pp. 232-241, 358-361. For definition of regions, see footnote 40 above.

South's values are of course low. For all their open conflict at the state level, white Democrats still solidified across class lines in presidential elections at this time.[41] But readings for the Middle Atlantic states are hardly much higher. The clearest class division appears in the West Central region, which includes Minnesota and North Dakota; its class index is about halfway between American and British national indexes for roughly the 1950s.[42]

There is not much to go on here, but it is possible that the differences among regions in American "class voting" (the South aside) reflect to some appreciable degree the different experiences that individual states have had over many decades in conducting politics. Conflict between classes (as in the upper Midwest, or at important junctures in the municipal politics of Boston and Detroit), or directly between labor and management (as in Michigan, Hawaii, and the Seattle area), or between "the people" and corporations (as in California, Wisconsin, and New Hampshire during the Progressive period) may have helped to give sa-

always includes Ohio, Indiana, Illinois, and Michigan, and sometimes Wisconsin. *West Central* always includes Minnesota, Iowa, Missouri, the Dakotas, Nebraska, and Kansas, and sometimes Wisconsin. *South* always includes the eleven secession states, Oklahoma, and Kentucky, and sometimes Delaware, Maryland, West Virginia, and the District of Columbia.

[41] On the weak relation between social class and Democratic identification in the South see George Robert Boynton, "Southern Conservatism: Constituency Opinion and Congressional Voting," *Public Opinion Quarterly* 29(1965), 259-269.

[42] Alford, *Party and Society*, p. 102. Alford's mean national values for class voting in presidential or parliamentary elections from 1952 through 1962: Great Britain 40, Australia 33, United States 16, Canada 8.

lience to class cleavages that the functioning of party organizations in "organization states" on the whole helped to blur or muffle. At any rate Alford's data on the Middle Atlantic area in particular are intriguing.

American settings that have supported traditional party organizations, the evidence of this chapter suggests, have scored high in the autonomy of their party organizations. But on balance they seem to have scored relatively low in "pressure politics," in issue density, in class cleavage, in successful demagoguery, in ideological movements anchored in organization, in union influence of a Michigan sort, and in business community influence of a Dallas sort. These evident relationships may suggest what to expect in the way of a relationship between having traditional organizations and generating government activity. The next chapter explores that relationship as it considers a particular range or indicator of government activity.

Government Activity

What, again, are the implications of having or not having traditional party organizations? The subject of *government activity* allows some additional cross-sectional analysis, though arguments developed in Chapter 9 about *autonomy* and *issues and cleavages* will be adduced in the discussion as well. One summary way to match government activity against party organizational form is to calculate levels of overall government expenditure or revenue-raising for individual states, and then compare cross-state money patterns with cross-state organizational patterns.[1] Such relationships are tracked here over the last three decades.[2] In each figure and corresponding table the dependent variable is

[1] This is in the spirit of David R. Cameron, "The Expansion of the Public Economy: A Comparative Analysis," *American Political Science Review* 72(1978), 1243-1261, an investigation of determinants of the rise in size of the "public economy" in eighteen relatively developed capitalist nations in recent times. There are two traditions of comparative analysis dealing with revenue or spending patterns in the American states. One, in political science, was inspired by V. O. Key, Jr., in Chapter 14 of *Southern Politics in State and Nation* (New York: Vintage, 1949) and has been continued by, among others, Thomas R. Dye, *Politics, Economics, and the Public: Policy Outcomes in the American States* (Chicago: Rand McNally, 1966). The other, in economics, was given form by Solomon Fabricant in *The Trend of Government Activity in the United States since 1900* (New York: National Bureau of Economic Research, 1952).

[2] Data are from publications of the U.S. Bureau of the Census, which has been using the same decision rules since 1951 in collecting and coding state and local information on revenue and expenditure. Data for earlier periods are sparse and not easily comparable with recent material, except for good figures that exist for 1942, the basis of the Fabricant study, which are treated here in Appendix B. The Census Bureau publications: *State and Local Government Revenue in 1953*, State and Local Government Special Studies, no. 37 (release date October 27, 1954); *Census of Governments: 1962*, vol. 6, no. 4, *Historical Statistics on Governmental Finances and Employment* (Washington, D.C.: U.S. Government Printing Office [hereafter GPO], 1964); four reports, each entitled *Compendium of Government Finances*, part of the *Census of Governments* as follows: *Census of Governments: 1962*, vol. 4, no. 4 (Washington, D.C.: GPO, 1964); *Census of Governments: 1967*, vol. 4, no. 5 (Washington, D.C.: GPO, 1969); *Census of Governments: 1972*, vol. 4, no. 5 (Washington, D.C.: GPO, 1974); and *Census of Governments: 1977*, vol. 4, no. 5 (Washington, D.C.: GPO, 1979); and pertinent copies of the annual publication entitled *Governmental Finances in 19XX* for 1958 through 1963 and *Governmental Finances in 19XX-XX* from 1963-64 on (Washington, D.C.: GPO).

itself a relation—a ratio relation of a sort commonly thought (at least on the revenue side) to index fiscal "effort" or "burden": the higher the ratio, the greater the burden. The numerator in each instance records per capita government revenue or expenditure (multiplied by 1000) in a specified state in a specified year, and the denominator records per capita personal income in the same state in the same year.[3] Thus in Figure 10.1 the value of 129 for New York means that government revenue amounted to $129 for each $1000 of residents' personal income in 1953, and the Connecticut value of 82 suggests an accordingly lesser burden—more income stayed in people's pockets and less ended up in government hands.[4]

The logic of "burden" needs an immediate qualification here,

Three reports of the Advisory Commission on Intergovernmental Relations are important reading for anyone studying state and local finance: *Measures of State and Local Fiscal Capacity and Tax Effort* (M-16, 1962), *Measuring the Fiscal Capacity and Effort of State and Local Areas* (M-58, 1971), and *Tax Capacity of the Fifty States: Methodology and Estimates* (M-134, 1982). These will be cited hereafter as ACIR 1962, ACIR 1971, and ACIR 1982.

[3] Up through 1963 data are for state and local fiscal years ending in the specified calendar years. For 1964 and after, data are for state and local fiscal years closing during the twelve months ending in June 30 of the specified calendar year. On measuring "revenue effort" see, e.g., James A. Maxwell and J. Richard Aronson, *Financing State and Local Governments* (Washington, D.C.: Brookings, 1977), pp. 38-40. The Advisory Commission on Intergovernmental Relations has generated measures of state tax or revenue "capacity" using standards other than per capita personal income. See ACIR 1982, chs. 3-5; ACIR 1971, chs. 1, 2, 5; ACIR 1982, chs. 1-4, 7. The gist of the 1971 version: "The revenue capacity of any particular area is defined as the total amount of revenue that would result by applying, within the area, the national average rate of each of the numerous kinds of State-local revenue sources" (ACIR 1971, p. 7). The signal value of this work is to sensitize anyone examining taxes to the fact of tax exporting, about which more below. But the ACIR calculations of "capacity" have their problems: the standards used, even if immanent rather than transcendental, give considerable weight to regressive taxes because some important typical taxes are regressive; moreover, since sales taxes (a major source of revenue) pick up a higher proportion of the incomes of low-income people than of high-income people, a particular embarrassment is that states with poor populations (and therefore the potential of especially productive sales taxes relative to income) gain capacity points, so to speak, for being poor (see ACIR 1962, pp. 67-71); and there is difficulty in dealing with taxable property equal in value but variant in production of income (as evidenced in ACIR 1962, pp. 56-67, and ACIR 1971, pp. 11-14). At any rate the ACIR does not claim to be measuring the "burden" or "severity" of revenue patterns (see ACIR, 1962, pp. 74, 76). Whenever the federal government has taken into account states' fiscal "capacity" in devising allocation formulas for grant programs, for example in Medicaid, it has done so by using (up through 1981 anyway) the standard of states' per capita personal income (see ACIR 1971, pp. 34-37; ACIR 1982, pp. 2-3).

[4] All fifty states are included in the analysis here (Hawaii since statehood) except Alaska, whose fiscal patterns are very different from other states'.

though, since a few states have managed to "export" a significant share of their revenue bases—that is, more precisely, to gather significantly more revenue from residents of other states than their own residents pay out somehow to governments of other states. The important instances are Nevada, with its profitable amusement tax (paid by visiting gamblers and other tourists) and Louisiana, Oklahoma, Texas, New Mexico and Wyoming, with their royalties, rental charges and severance taxes on minerals, mostly oil and gas (businesses pass on the charges to outstate consumers). Louisiana seems to have raised some 20 to 25 percent of its revenue by such means in recent decades and the other five states on the order of 10 to 15 percent, though these and other states with energy resources evidently achieved higher percentages—giving tax exporting a precedent-setting workout—after the onset of the energy crisis in the mid-1970s.[5] It follows that ratio relations of the sort introduced above are a dubious guide to real in-state revenue "burden" in the cases of at least these six tax exporting states—their arrived-at ratios may be misleadingly high. One way to deal with the problem (others are taken up below) is to stay aware of it: all six states are marked with asterisks in the ensuing figures. This qualification registered, the ratio figures for states in general may reasonably be treated as guides to "burden" or "effort" or governmental "extractive" activity if calculated from revenue data, and as guides to the size or scale of states' public economies if calculated from either revenue or expenditure data. To be more precise, the public economies given attention are all jointly state and local, since all revenue and expenditure figures used here for any state pick up and add together money raised or spent by all its governmental jurisdictions at both state and local levels.[6]

[5] Precise figures on these matters are very difficult to pin down. Useful material on the logic and particulars of tax exporting appears in ACIR 1962, pp. 6-7, 32, 37-38, 42-43, 50, 69-70; ACIR 1971, pp. 54, 57; ACIR 1982, pp. 3, 8-10, 17-18, 22-23, 30-32. Pertinent data appear in U.S. Bureau of the Census, *Census of Governments* for 1962, 1967, 1972, and 1977, vol. 4, no. 4 in 1962 and no. 5 thereafter, *Compendium of Government Finances*.

[6] "The fact is that interstate comparisons of state government finances (or of local government finances) are treacherous, and may be quite misleading about the relative levels of services provided by the states. More revealing comparisons can be made, state by state, of aggregates or subaggregates of state plus local expenditure and revenue. Such figures, when expressed per capita or per $1,000 of personal income, provide a more useful measure of state-by-state differences in governmental provision of services and collection of revenues" (Maxwell and Aronson, *Financing State and Local Governments*, p. 32). The main reason for aggregating state and local data is that "one state government may perform functions that in another state are left to localities" (p. 3). See also ACIR 1962, p. 11.

The ratio relations dealt with here (in nineteen separate figures and tables) break down as follows in numerator, denominator, and year of coverage:[7]

Figure 10.1 and Table 10.1	all revenue	personal income	1953
Figures 10.2– 10.10 and Table 10.2	general revenue	personal income	1953, 1957, 1959, 1962, 1967, 1969, 1972, 1977, and 1980
Figure 10.11 and Table 10.3	general revenue	income produced	1959
Figures 10.12– 10.19 and Table 10.4	general expenditure	personal income	1957, 1959, 1962, 1967, 1970, 1972, 1977, and 1980

Figure 10.1, covering 1953, picks up in "all revenue" an especially comprehensive category of revenue—for each state virtually all money coming into its state and local government units from their own sources (that is, subventions from the federal government not included).[8] Figure 10.2, based also on 1953 data, and Figures 10.3 through 10.11 for later years shift down to a more conventional Census Bureau category, "general revenue," keeping about four-fifths of "all revenue" but omitting nongovernmental contributions to insurance and retirement programs (less important at state and local levels than at the federal), income of publicly owned utilities (especially important in Nebraska, Tennessee, and Washington), and proceeds of government-owned liquor stores (especially important in New Hampshire).[9] "General revenue" is about four-fifths taxes (of all sorts) and one-fifth "charges and miscellaneous general revenue"—for example, licenses, fees, and the

[7] The numerator categories abide by standard Census Bureau definitions. The decision rules for choosing years were as follows: (a) use all years covered by Census of Governments data (that is, 1957, 1962, 1967, 1972, and 1977), which are the most comprehensive data on state and local finances; (b) use also one other year at the end of each decade, taking data (derived partly from a sample) from annual Census Bureau publications; (c) use 1953 because of its available revenue data.

[8] The Census Bureau calls this "revenue from own sources," which includes just about everything except receipts from issuance of debt, recoupment of previous loans, and sale of securities.

[9] Utilities are water, gas, electric power, and transit systems.

income of government-owned concerns other than utilities and liquor stores.

"General expenditure," in Figures 10.12 through 10.19, is a counterpart of "general revenue," encompassing all money paid out by state and local government units, including capital outlays, except expenses associated with insurance and retirement systems, utilities, and liquor stores.[10] "General expenditure" is one-fifth to one-fourth more sizable than "general income," however, since it draws on federal subventions to lower governments as well as on indigenous state and local revenue. Treatments of "general revenue" and "general expenditure" for an earlier year, 1942, appear in Appendix B. The anomalous figure of the nineteen in this chapter is Figure 10.11, which uses a conventional numerator, "general revenue," but a special denominator, "income produced," a measure attributing income to states where it is produced (in mining, manufacturing, agriculture, etc.) rather than, following convention, to states whose residents come to receive it as "personal income."[11] (Profits from oil drilling might be identified with Louisiana by the first standard, but with shareholders in Connecticut by the second.) Some income does obviously get taxed at its source—notably oil and gas earnings through severance taxes—and the objective here is to see what happens to states' "burden" readings given a switch of assumption about what and where the taxable income pools are—a matter on which there are no certain answers.

The dependent variables thus established, the independent variables brought to bear to explain cross-state variation in them (separately in each of the nineteen data sets) are as follows: (a) State TPO score, appearing as a 1-to-5 interval-scale variable in the tables (which report the results of regression equations), but more simply as a set of thirteen "organization states" (scores 4 or 5) in the figures. (b) Confederate, a dummy variable assigning a 1 to each of the eleven secession states of the 1860s. The reasoning here is that a collection of particular sectional factors might have worked to make the Southern states' twentieth-century public economies relatively small—disfranchisement of much of their lower-income population at the turn of the century, their record of supplying meager public services to blacks, and perhaps until recently a not wholly exhausted hostility toward active government caused by Reconstruction (a hostility built into institutions as well as attitudes). (c) State per capita income, a variable inserted to allow for the possibility that state revenue or spending ratios vary with level of

[10] And it analogously excludes payments for debt retirement, extension of loans, and purchase of securities.

[11] Data on "income produced" are from ACIR 1962, pp. 23-30.

income. Spending ratios in particular may vary in an inverse relation with income because federal subventions go disproportionately to poorer states. (d) State population density and (e) proportion of state population living in urban areas, variables introduced in recognition of their appearance in other studies as modestly important explainers of variation in state and local expenditure patterns.[12]

The basic finding of the series of tables and figures is that having traditional party organizations is associated with having relatively small public economies—a relationship of statistical significance and considerable magnitude, apparently not reducible to anything else, and especially impressive in the 1950s, though it has tailed off since and conspicuously mispredicts New York (about which more later).[13] Consider the first exhibits, Figure 10.1 and its counterpart Table 10.1, the 1953 "all revenue" exercises based on the earliest good Census Bureau collection of state and local revenue data.[14] The range of the readings in the figure goes from Delaware, with $71 of revenue for each $1000 personal income, to North Dakota with $173. The thirteen organization states in general rank low and under-rank their nonorganization neighbors. The contrast in New England is especially sharp: Connecticut 82, Rhode Island 85, Massachusetts 121, Maine 131, Vermont 135, and New Hampshire 143.[15] The low placement of organization states in the figure corresponds to a stable negative coefficient for the TPO variable (-9.29) in the first equation of Table 10.1. This value, if quadrupled, gives a value of about -37 (roughly the real 1953 distance between

[12] With percent urban producing a positive coefficient and density a negative coefficient. See, e.g., Fabricant, *Trend of Government Activity*, ch. 6 and pp. 258-262; Glenn W. Fisher, "Determinants of State and Local Government Expenditures: A Preliminary Analysis," *National Tax Journal* 14(1961), 349-355; and Maxwell and Aronson, *Financing State and Local Governments*, p. 36. Frank M. Bryan, in "Toward a Theory of Rural Politics," paper presented at the 1978 convention of the American Political Science Association, finds an inverse relation between state population density and number of government employees per capita, which suggests economies of scale in densely settled environments.

[13] Table 10.1 reports, respectively, the results of two separate equations that address the same dependent variable (i.e., state variation in all revenue per $1,000 personal income, 1953). See footnote 79 in Chapter 8 for some general statements about reading such tables.

[14] The data on fiscal 1942 are technically good but 1942, just after Pearl Harbor, had highly atypical patterns of government activity.

[15] Midwestern data in this and other figures bring to mind John H. Fenton's distinction, in *Midwest Politics* (New York: Holt, Rinehart and Winston, 1966), between job-oriented states (Ohio, Indiana, and Illinois) and issue-oriented states (Michigan, Wisconsin, and Minnesota).

Massachusetts and Connecticut) as an estimate of what difference a four-step move (from 1 to 5) on the TPO scale makes in the dependent variable.[16] The Confederate and per capita income variables perform well enough and consistently enough in the full set of equations for 1953 through 1980 to merit inspection of their coefficients. In the 1953 "all revenue" equation reported in the top half of Table 10.1, being a Confederate state predicts an effect in the dependent variable of about − 16, and the full actual range in per capita income between the poorest state (Mississippi) and richest (Nevada) predicts an effect of about − 17. Density and urban variables perform poorly, however, in almost all data sets, as a perusal of the various figures will suggest they would (see the bottom half of Table 10.1 for the 1953 coefficients), and may consequently be ignored.[17] States with the worst fit in the "all revenue" 1953 equation are Louisiana, New York, and North Dakota; in all three cases large positive residuals point to actual state absorption of much more revenue than the relations of the equation would predict.[18]

The series of tables and figures on "general revenue" and "general expenditure" allow an examination of detail over time as well as space. In general the TPO variable works somewhat better throughout with revenue than with spending patterns. Given the real decline of traditional party organization in the last quarter century, which has made organization states less distinctive, the TPO variable might be expected to diminish over time in explanatory power, and it does. Of course many other things contributed to the homogenization of American politics and government during this period, and it should be noted that an unusual nationwide surge of state and local spending in the 1960s and early 1970s, accompanied by widespread adoption of new state and local taxes, gave a considerable shakeup in particular to traditional fiscal

[16] That is, a difference of one unit in the TPO independent variable produces a difference of − 9.29 in the dependent variable (state variation in all revenue per $1,000 personal income, 1953). Multiplying this result by four, to see what corresponds to the full 1-to-5 difference between minimal and maximal possible TPO scores, yields a value of − 37.16, or a drop of about $37. The TPO variable generates a standard error of 1.47 (in the top set of results reported in Table 10) and an accordingly high t statistic of − 6.32 (disregarding the minus sign). These results point to a relation easily strong enough to satisfy a significance test at the .001 level.

[17] The poor performance is not an artifactual consequence of high correlation between the urban and density variables.

[18] One way to deal with the problem of the six tax exporting states is to run equations for each of the nineteen data sets without them. What usually happens when they are dropped is that the coefficients and t ratios of the TPO and Confederate variables rise, as do the R-squared values. The deletion of Louisiana (Confederate and TPO score of 3) contributes to the improvement.

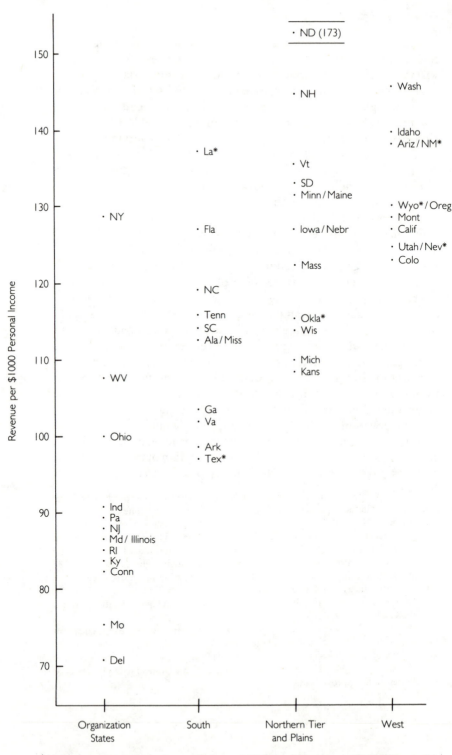

Fig. 10.1 Traditional Party Organization and All State Revenue per $1,000 Personal Income, 1953. Asterisks in figures refer to tax-exporting states; see p. 259.

Table 10.1   Determinants of State Variation in All Revenue per $1,000 Personal
Income, 1953

Independent Variable	Regression Coefficient	Standard Error	t Ratio
TPO score	−9.29	1.47	−6.32***
Confederate	−15.6	6.3	−2.49**
Per capita income	−.011	.008	−1.45
Constant	157.0		
N = 48			
Adj. R² = .533			
TPO score	−9.17	1.73	−5.30***
Confederate	−16.7	6.5	−2.56**
Per capita income	−.019	.012	−1.56
Population density	−.012	.020	−.59
% urban	26.1	29.3	.89
Constant	156.5		
N = 48			
Adj. R² = .520			

NOTE: Two asterisks indicate a .01 level of significance; three indicate a .001 level.

patterns.[19] In the revenue series here (Figures 10.2-10.10) the organization states appear conspicuously as something of a ghetto of low-revenue regimes in the 1950s, then decline in distinctiveness in the 1960s, though the TPO variable still registers an appreciable negative coefficient as late as 1977 (see Table 10.2). Its value of − 5.74, if quadrupled, yields roughly the actual 1977 distance between Michigan and Connecticut in Figure 10.9.

Calculations for the anomalous "income produced" variable are worth brief examination (see Figure 10.11 and Table 10.3). The chief effect of (unconventionally) attributing income to states producing rather than to states receiving it (compare Figure 10.11 with Figure 10.4, both based on 1959 revenue) is to lower the "burden" ratios of Western states relative to other states; the tapping of their abundant natural resources no doubt gives them the relatively larger denominators that lower the ratios. Otherwise little changes. In particular the or-

[19] See, e.g., Leon Rothenberg, "A New Look in State Finances: Tax Reduction and Restructured Tax Systems," *National Tax Journal* 27(1974), 175-181; Thomas F. Fleming, Jr., "State and Local Government Spending in 1975," *Monthly Labor Review* 94(August 1971), 19-28.

**Table 10.2   Determinants of State Variation in General Revenue
per $1,000 Personal Income, 1953-1980**

Year	Independent Variable	Regression Coefficient	Standard Error	t Ratio
1953	TPO score	−7.43	1.24	−5.99***
	Confederate	−10.2	5.3	−1.93*
	Per capita income	−.014	.006	−2.12**
	Constant	138.3		
	N = 48			
	Adj. R^2 = .536			
1957	TPO score	−6.38	1.38	−4.64***
	Confederate	−7.05	5.9	−1.19
	Per capita income	−.013	.007	−1.89*
	Constant	144.7		
	N = 48			
	Adj. R^2 = .436			
1959	TPO score	−6.23	1.51	−4.14***
	Confederate	−13.8	6.3	−2.21**
	Per capita income	−.016	.007	−2.32**
	Constant	157.5		
	N = 48			
	Adj. R^2 = .410			
1962	TPO score	−4.92	1.17	−4.22***
	Confederate	−8.70	5.36	−1.62
	Per capita income	−.007	.006	−1.27
	Constant	146.3		
	N = 49			
	Adj. R^2 = .315			
1967	TPO score	−6.21	1.60	−3.89***
	Confederate	−17.4	6.5	−2.66**
	Per capita income	−.009	.006	−1.34
	Constant	178.8		
	N = 49			
	Adj. R^2 = .338			
1969	TPO score	−6.00	1.54	−3.90***
	Confederate	−20.9	6.2	−3.35***
	Per capita income	−.003	.005	−.63
	Constant	159.3		

Table 10.2   (cont.)

Year	Independent Variable	Regression Coefficient	Standard Error	t Ratio
	$N = 49$			
	Adj. R^2 = .342			
1972	TPO score	−5.10	1.50	−3.39***
	Confederate	−17.7	6.0	−2.96***
	Per capita income	−.001	.005	−.12
	Constant	177.1		
	$N = 49$			
	Adj. R^2 = .270			
1977	TPO score	−5.74	1.71	−3.36***
	Confederate	−16.2	7.0	−2.30***
	Per capita income	.005	.004	1.29
	Constant	143.1		
	$N = 49$			
	Adj. R^2 = .254			
1980	TPO score	−3.90	1.92	−2.03**
	Confederate	−15.0	8.0	−1.87*
	Per capita income	.0002	.0034	.05
	Constant	166.3		
	$N = 49$			
	Adj. R^2 = .086			

NOTE: One asterisk indicates a .05 level of significance; two indicate a .01 level; three, a .001 level.

ganization states remain low-revenue regimes; the TPO variable generates a negative coefficient regardless of which assumption is made about what and where the taxable income pools are.[20]

It should be emphasized that the series of figures on revenue (Figures 10.2-10.10) and expenditure (Figures 10.12-10.19) presented below can

[20] In September 1985, the Reagan administration was considering two new formulas for distributing federal funds among the states. Both would calculate state fiscal "capacity" differently than the conventional formula of state income received per capita. One would hinge on state output of goods and services in something like the fashion of the "income produced" measure used here in Figure 10.11. The other would combine elements of "income received" with elements of "income produced." See Robert Pear, "Treasury Calls For New Formulas on Aid to States," *New York Times*, September 5, 1985, p. B15.

be read for particulars as well as generalizations. In a number of cases the distinctive fiscal standings of states, or their changes in standing during the last three decades, are marks produced by some of the more interesting performances in American politics (including some discussed here in earlier chapters). North Dakota's exceptionally large public economy, for example, is substantially a deposit left by A. C. Townley's Nonpartisan League during and after World War I. The NPL's corps of ideologically committed activists mobilized farmers in a door-to-door sales campaign that collected dues via postdated checks and then colonized Republican primaries, won elections, and undertook an experiment in state socialism generating, among other things, publicly owned flour-mill, terminal-elevator, and banking concerns that were still operating in recent years.[21] The high standing of Minnesota probably owes much to the programmatic drive of the Farmer-Labor movement and later the Democratic-Farmer-Labor party. Minnesota's income tax, for example, was introduced by victorious Farmer-Laborites just after the 1932 election.[22] The outlier status of Louisiana is certainly attributable to the Longs, as the analysis by Edward T. Jennings, Jr., has shown. The leadership of Huey Long, his immediate inheritors, and later Earl Long as governor in 1948-1952 and 1956-1960 catapulted up expenditures (notably for social services) and also evidently taxes; the data beginning with Figure 10.5 (revenue) and Figure 10.14 (expenditure) show Louisiana's extraordinarily high fiscal rank at the end of Earl Long's last term (extraordinary even after allowing for some tax exporting) and its subsequent decline toward the American average.[23] The instrument of fiscal surge in Louisiana was

[21] On organizing activity of the NPL see Robert L. Morlan, *Political Prairie Fire: The Nonpartisan League, 1915-1922* (Minneapolis: University of Minnesota Press, 1955), ch. 2. On electoral activity: Samuel P. Huntington, "The Election Tactics of the Nonpartisan League," *Mississippi Valley Historical Review* 36(1950), 613-632. In 1957, revenue of the North Dakota Mill and Elevator Association and the Bank of North Dakota supplied about 10% of North Dakota's "general revenue." (These are not public utilities in the Census Bureau's classification and their income and outgo hence appear in "general revenue" and "general expenditure.") See U.S. Bureau of the Census, *Census of Governments: 1957*, vol. 6, *State Bulletins*, no. 32, *Government in North Dakota* (Washington, D.C.: GPO, 1959), p. 11.

[22] See Gladys C. Blakey, *A History of Taxation in Minnesota* (Minneapolis: University of Minnesota Press, 1934), pp. 61-64.

[23] See Edward T. Jennings, Jr., "Some Policy Consequences of the Long Revolution and Bifactional Rivalry in Louisiana," *American Journal of Political Science* 21(1977), 225-246. Jennings investigates expenditures. Taxes are not easy to track, but there was a surge at least in Earl Long's first term. See Allan P. Sindler, *Huey Long's Louisiana: State Politics, 1920-1952* (Baltimore: Johns Hopkins University Press, 1956), pp. 79-80, 88-90, 200, 208-214.

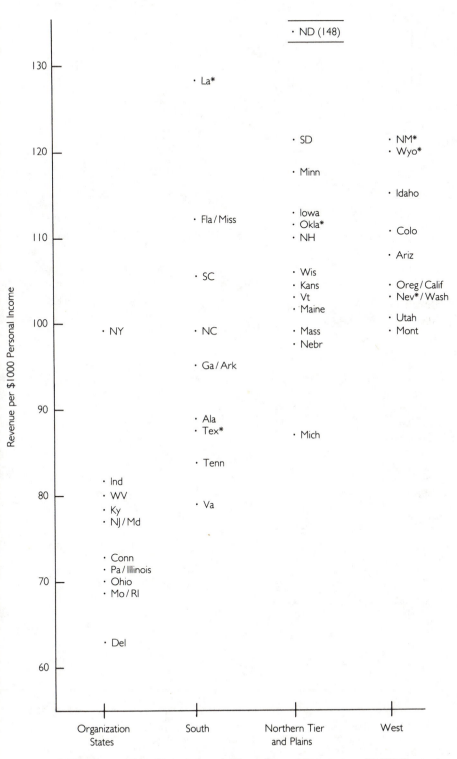

Fig. 10.2　Traditional Party Organization and State General Revenue per $1,000 Personal Income, 1953

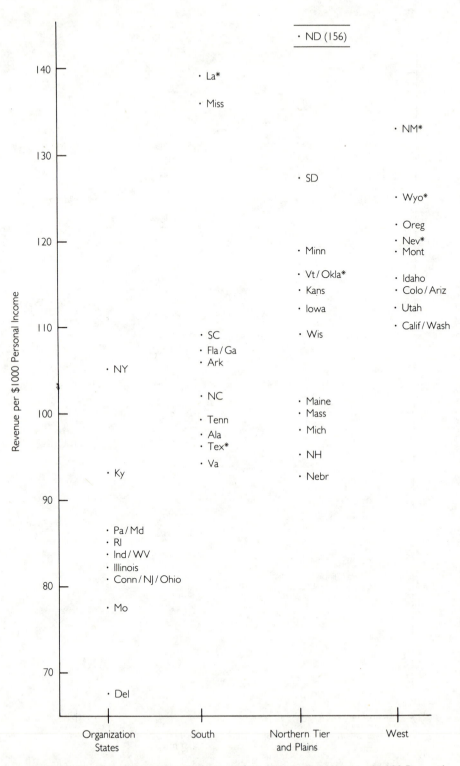

Fig. 10.3 Traditional Party Organization and State General Revenue per $1,000 Personal Income, 1957

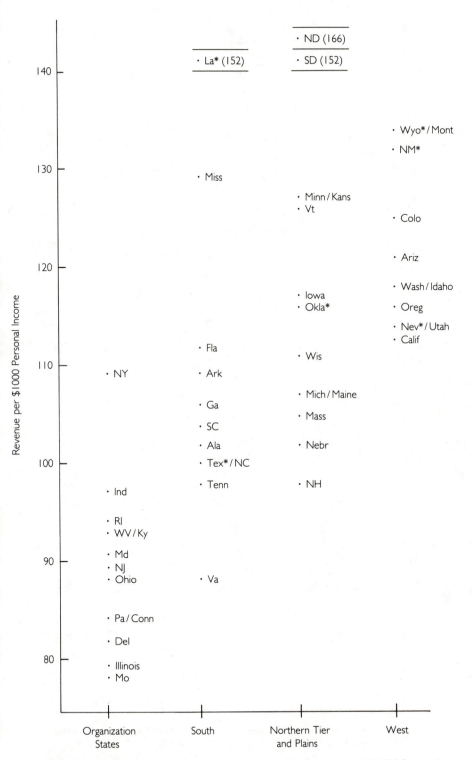

Fig. 10.4 Traditional Party Organization and State General Revenue per $1,000 Personal Income, 1959

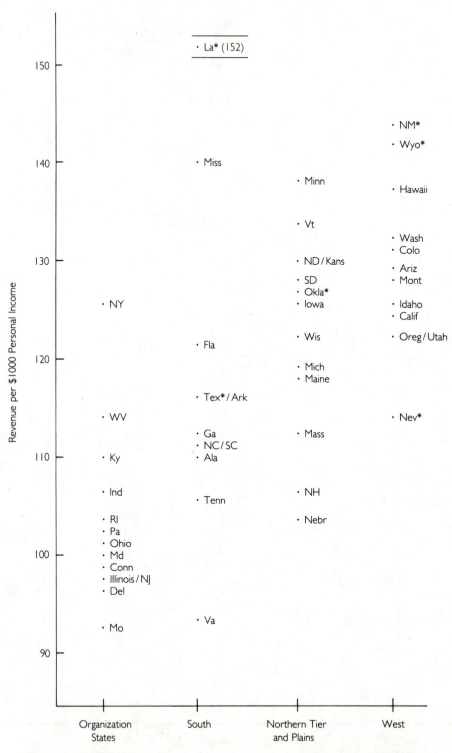

Fig. 10.5 Traditional Party Organization and State General Revenue per $1,000 Personal Income, 1962

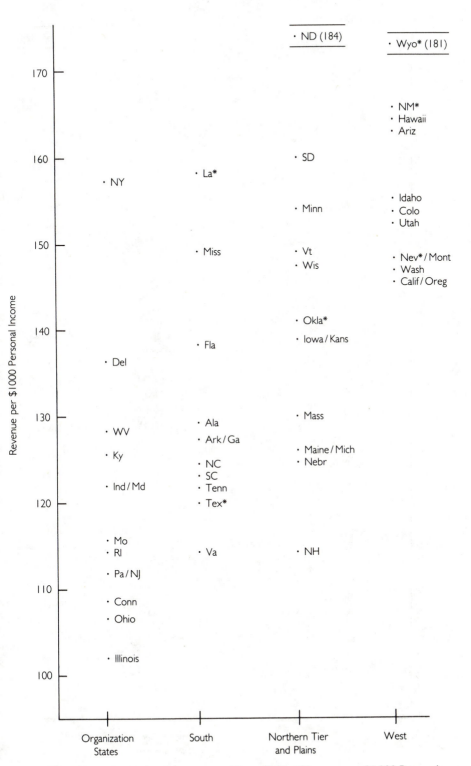

Fig. 10.6 Traditional Party Organization and State General Revenue per $1,000 Personal Income, 1967

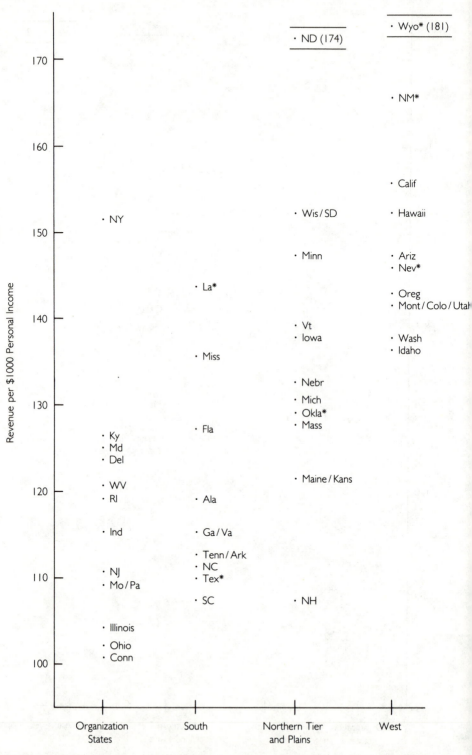

Fig. 10.7   Traditional Party Organization and State General Revenue per $1,000 Personal Income, 1969

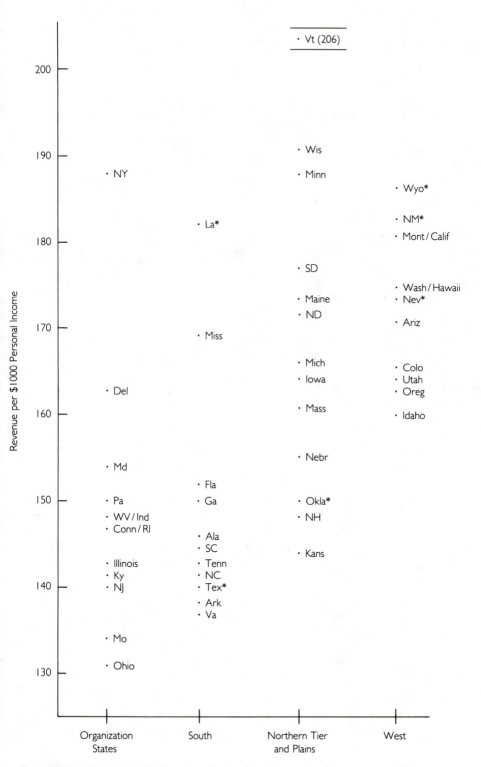

Fig. 10.8   Traditional Party Organization and State General Revenue per $1,000 Personal Income, 1972

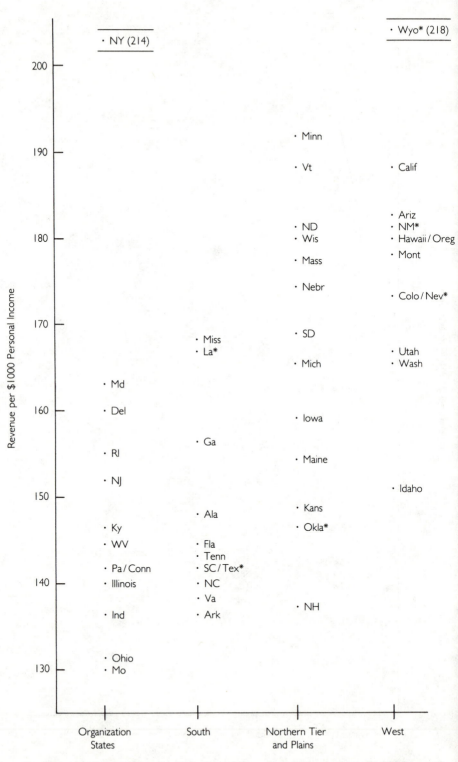

Fig. 10.9 Traditional Party Organization and State General Revenue per $1,000 Personal Income, 1977

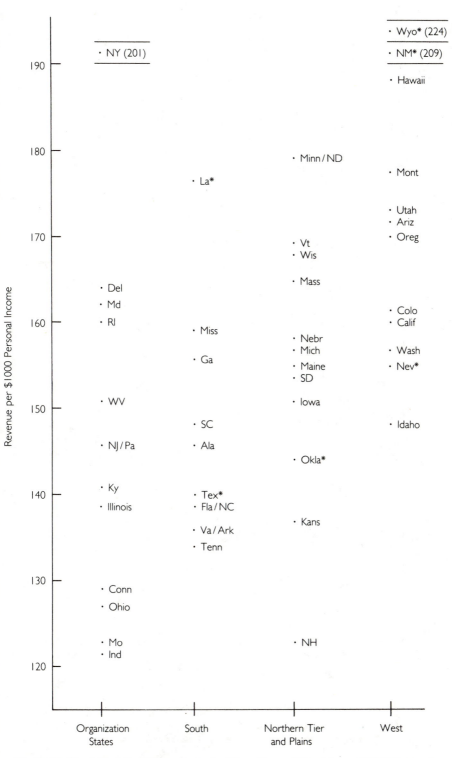

Fig. 10.10   Traditional Party Organization and State General Revenue per $1,000 Personal Income, 1980

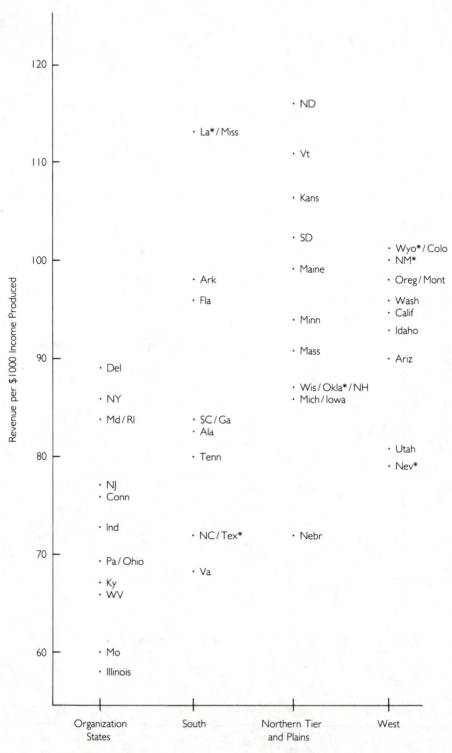

Fig. 10.11 Traditional Party Organization and State General Revenue per $1,000 Income Produced, 1959

Table 10.3   Determinants of State Variation in General Revenue per $1,000 Income Produced, 1959

Independent Variable	Regression Coefficient	Standard Error	t Ratio
TPO score	− 4.57	1.23	− 3.71***
Confederate	− 4.69	5.14	− .91
Per capita income	− .004	.006	.74
Constant	106.0		
N = 48			
Adj. R² = .260			

NOTE: Three asterisks indicate a .001 level of significance.

the Long family and its personal and issue-based following.[24] "Bifactional competition" between Longs and anti-Longs is customarily held by political scientists to have been the cause of Louisiana's unusual spending policies, but this seems a mistake: it wasn't bifactional competition, it was the Longs. The only Southern state close to Louisiana in the revenue and expenditure series is Mississippi. This raises the possibility that Theodore G. Bilbo, who came to power a decade before Huey Long with the help of a comparable anti-establishment appeal, personal following, and ambitious program (though Bilbo was an outspoken racist), and who refashioned the state's revenue and spending policies as governor, may have left a mark like the Longs' on Mississippi finances. Bilbo seems to have been the only Southern politician during the three decades before World War II who approximated Huey Long in style and programmatic thrust and also approached him in talent.[25]

The instances of North Dakota and Louisiana (and also Mississippi and Minnesota if the speculation above is correct) suggest that mobili-

[24] Huey Long, to be sure, built a formidable state machine while governor and Senator (he died in 1935), which his successors made use of until 1940. But it evidently crumbled once the governorship was lost in that year. Later Earl Long had to maneuver for office as Huey had done in the 1920s, by appealing to a mass audience.

[25] This is speculation. The sources on Bilbo's policy activities as governor are Albert D. Kirwan, Revolt of the Rednecks: Mississippi Politics, 1876-1925 (New York: Harper and Row, 1965), pp. 259-266, 270-272; Reinhard H. Luthin, American Demagogues: Twentieth Century (Boston: Beacon, 1954), p. 53; Vincent A. Giroux, Jr., "The Rise of Theodore G. Bilbo (1908-1932)," Journal of Mississippi History 43(1981), 198-199. Mississippi's low level of income and lack of taxable resources put a low ceiling on what even an ambitious welfare politics could achieve. See Key, Southern Politics, p. 230.

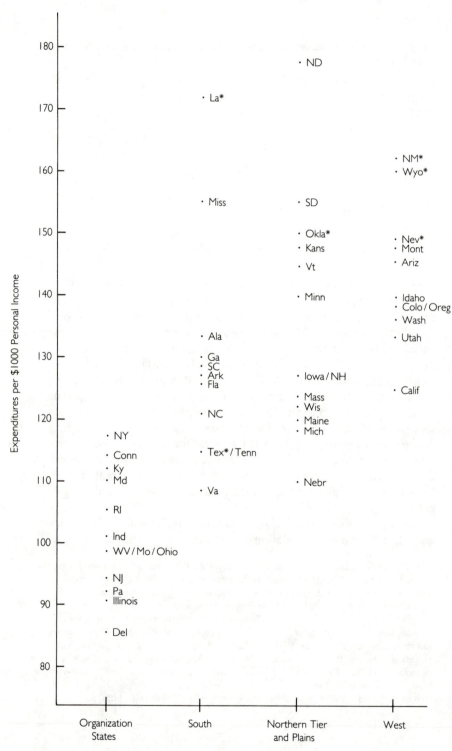

Fig. 10.12   Traditional Party Organization and State General Expenditures per $1,000 Personal Income, 1957

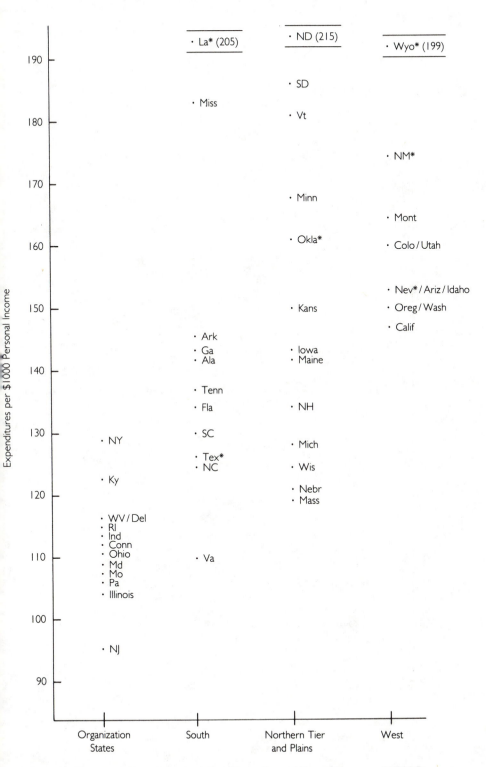

Fig. 10.13 Traditional Party Organization and State General Expenditures per $1,000 Personal Income, 1959

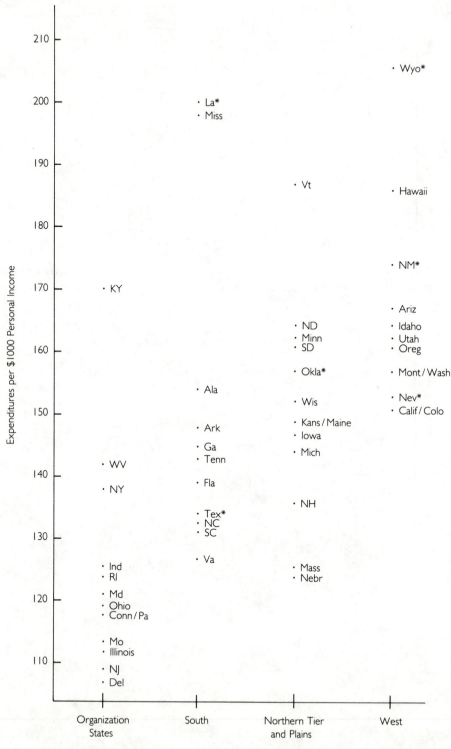

Fig. 10.14   Traditional Party Organization and State General Expenditures per $1,000 Personal Income, 1962

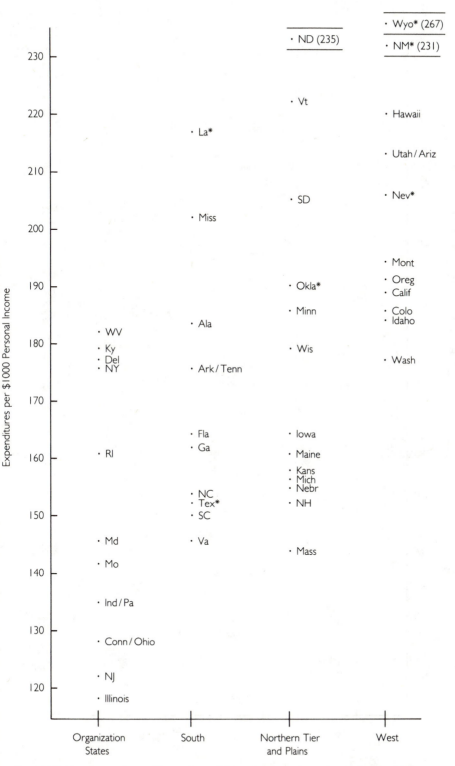

Fig. 10.15   Traditional Party Organization and State General Expenditures per $1,000 Personal Income, 1967

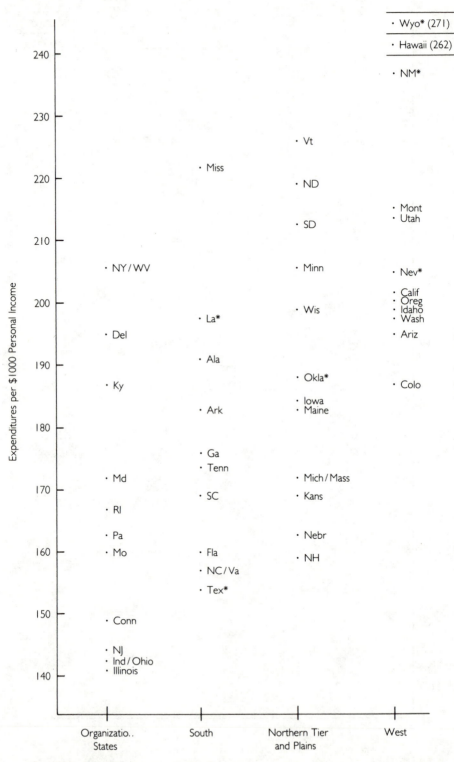

Fig. 10.16 Traditional Party Organization and State General Expenditures per $1,000 Personal Income, 1970

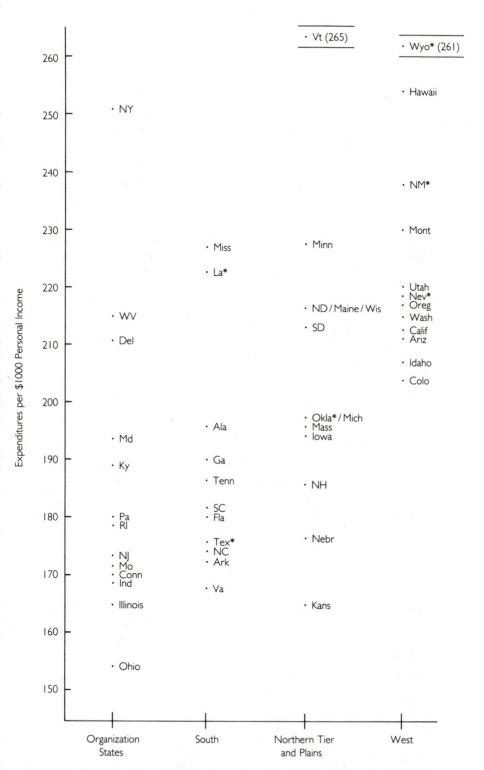

Fig. 10.17   Traditional Party Organization and State General Expenditures per $1,000 Personal Income, 1972

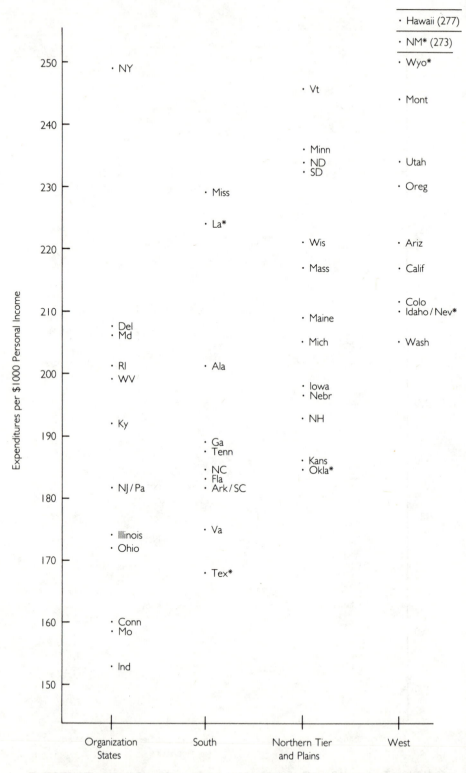

Fig. 10.18 Traditional Party Organization and State General Expenditures per $1,000 Personal Income, 1977

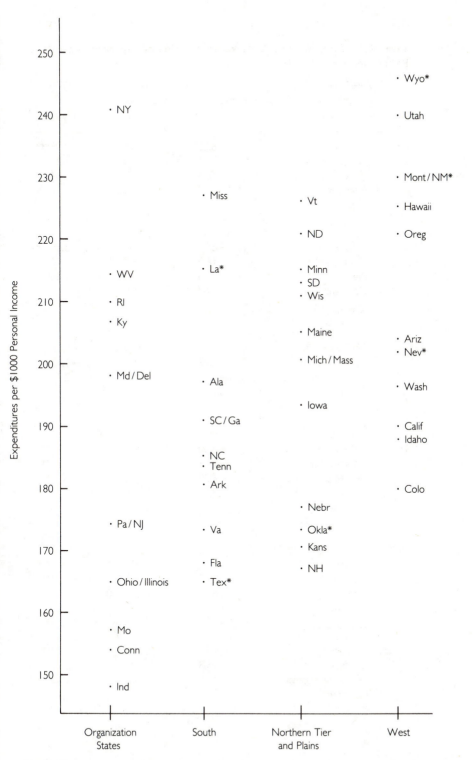

Fig. 10.19 Traditional Party Organization and State General Expenditures per $1,000 Personal Income, 1980

Table 10.4   Determinants of State Variation in General Expenditures per $1,000 Personal Income, 1957-1980

Year	Independent Variable	Regression Coefficient	Standard Error	t Ratio
1957	TPO score	−8.25	1.66	−4.98***
	Confederate	−8.91	7.11	−1.25
	Per capita income	−.014	.008	−1.64
	Constant	172.4		
	N = 48			
	Adj. R^2 = .449			
1959	TPO score	−8.55	2.20	−3.88***
	Confederate	−16.2	9.2	−1.76*
	Per capita income	−.024	.010	−2.44**
	Constant	211.4		
	N = 48			
	Adj. R^2 = .397			
1962	TPO score	−7.00	1.87	−3.75***
	Confederate	−14.8	8.6	−1.72*
	Per capita income	−.022	.009	−2.46**
	Constant	214.8		
	N = 49			
	Adj. R^2 = .348			
1967	TPO score	−8.00	2.62	−3.05***
	Confederate	−27.8	10.7	−2.59**
	Per capita income	−.028	.010	−2.71***
	Constant	282.2		
	N = 49			
	Adj. R^2 = .344			
1970	TPO score	−7.28	2.41	−3.02***
	Confederate	−30.5	10.1	−3.03***
	Per capita income	−.017	.008	−2.20**
	Constant	268.2		
	N = 49			
	Adj. R^2 = .295			
1972	TPO score	−6.17	2.38	−2.60**
	Confederate	−25.3	9.4	−2.68**
	Per capita income	−.008	.007	−1.05
	Constant	252.4		

Table 10.4   *(cont.)*

Year	Independent Variable	Regression Coefficient	Standard Error	t Ratio
	N = 49			
	Adj. R² = .201			
1977	TPO score	−7.76	2.21	−3.51***
	Confederate	−25.0	9.1	−2.74***
	Per capita income	−.003	.005	−.61
	Constant	247.7		
	N = 49			
	Adj. R² = .258			
1980	TPO score	−4.29	2.08	−2.06**
	Confederate	−21.9	8.7	−2.51**
	Per capita income	.009	.004	−2.31**
	Constant	282.4		
	N = 49			
	Adj. R² = .172			

NOTE: One asterisk indicates a .05 level of significance; two indicate a .01 level; three, a .001 level.

zation of lower-income voters through a class-based appeal has been an especially effective way to build a state's public economy.[26] Both demagoguery and ideology-based organization—two non-TPO electoral forms given special attention in Chapter 9—have evidently done the trick. The idea that class cleavage can take on a role as the occasion—though not the cause, strictly speaking—of fiscal surge conjures up some interesting counterfactual replays of American twentieth-century history. But there are other routes to taxing and spending. Scattered statements on Boston's finances suggest that the relatively high fiscal standing of Massachusetts is substantially the legacy of a Yankee hegemony that was relatively supportive of government in the nineteenth and early twentieth centuries. The state's mandated public welfare system, for example, equipped Boston with more generous relief funding than any other large city in the early 1930s.[27] Vermont has achieved a

[26] See the analogous argument in Edward T. Jennings, Jr., "Competition, Constituencies, and Welfare Policies in American States," *American Political Science Review* 73(1979), 414-429.

[27] On the mid-nineteenth century: Edward K. Spann, *The New Metropolis: New York City, 1840-1857* (New York: Columbia University Press, 1981), pp. 48, 322, 447, 496.

high fiscal rank (see especially the expenditure series) without the assistance of any notable electoral cleavage or structure (the "bifactionalism" once thought to operate within the dominant Republican party was a myth). In the last quarter century the state's spending rate is said to have been helped along by enterprising bureaucrats working in the climate of a high-yield income tax.[28] New York will be treated more fully later, but its striking budgetary surge of recent times (see Figures 10.4-10.10 and 10.13-10.19)—from an average fiscal rank in the late 1950s to a state and local revenue burden that probably broke all American records in the late 1970s—seems to have been largely the accomplishment of Nelson A. Rockefeller in his governorship lasting from 1958 hrough 1973.[29] The state government, rather than New York City, set the pace during these years in promoting expenditures

---

At about 1900: Robert A. Silverman, "Nathan Matthews: Politics of Reform in Boston, 1890-1910," *New England Quarterly* 50(1977), 631-632; Delos F. Wilcox, *Great Cities in America: Their Problems and Their Government* (New York: Macmillan, 1910), pp. 347, 379. At about 1930: Charles H. Trout, *Boston, the Great Depression, and the New Deal* (New York: Oxford University Press, 1977), pp. 30, 32-33, 59, 71, 86, 176-178, 284, 286, 328, 331-332, 347.

[28] On Vermont's electoral environment see Frank M. Bryan, *Yankee Politics in Rural Vermont* (Hanover, N.H.: University Press of New England, 1974), pp. 81-94, 106, 123. On 1926 through 1950: "To summarize, one-party politics in Vermont were dominated by a coalition of elected officials in the Republican party. . . . The only patterns evident in electoral statistics were friends-and-neighbors gravitational centers that usually defined the nature of the opposition. . . . When new forces confronted the system, they won quite easily—there was no powerfully organized machine to resist them. There was nothing in Vermont to approximate what we generally consider to be a bifactional system" (p. 93). And an implication: "Knocking down the bifactional view of Vermont's one-party system weakens the underpinning of an important thesis concerning the relationship between input mechanisms and policy outputs in political systems. Put briefly, the location of a one-party system lacking clear factional political camps within a political system that habitually produces benevolent policies concerning the 'have nots' in society plays havoc with Key's hypothesis that bifactional and/or two-party systems are necessary to ensure that the underprivileged classes get their share of the political pie. In his study of Vermont elections, sociologist Frederick Maher underscores Vermont's traditionally liberal tax policies and her strong commitment to spend large amounts of public money to serve the needy portions of the public sector" (p. 92). (The reference is to Frederick J. Maher, Jr., "Vermont Elections," Ph.D. dissertation, Columbia University, 1969, pp. 44, 94.) On the enterprising bureaucrats: Richard Winters, "Political Choice and Expenditure Change in New Hampshire and Vermont," *Polity* 12(1980), 598-621. In Phoenix, Arizona, as in Vermont, a productive revenue structure is said to promote a notably high level of public sector activity. "The reality in Phoenix for the past thirty years," its officials' conservative philosophy notwithstanding, has been "mostly one of public sector growth rather than constraint." A "diverse, elastic, balanced and sound" revenue structure has made this possible. See John Stuart Hall, "Responses to Retrenchment in Phoenix," paper prepared for the Urban Institute, June 1984, quotations at pp. 5, 6.

[29] The high values on the figures for New Mexico and Wyoming in the 1970s need to be discounted for tax exporting.

and taxes (and annexing revenue by artful means other than taxes), chiefly in the causes of education, public welfare (Medicaid in particular), and pharaonic construction.[30] As a builder of a state public economy Rockefeller may be the only American governor to have equaled or surpassed Huey Long, and what seems to have made his dynamism possible (beyond his considerable talent and drive) raised eyebrows in hearings on his confirmation as Vice President in 1974. The "coupling of his private financial power with public political power" yielded millions of dollars for electoral funding and, probably more important, a lavish program of loans, perquisites, and gifts for staff and top administrators, which created around him a high-priced phalanx of instrumental rationality that Presidents envied.[31]

Entrepreneurs can depress public economies as well as build them. The plunge in California's revenue position from high to average between 1977 and 1980 (see Figures 10.9 and 10.10) is the achievement of Howard Jarvis's Proposition 13, which cut taxes by referendum. New Hampshire's unique transformation from a high-revenue to a low-revenue state—the decline took three decades (see Figures 10.2-10.10)—can no doubt be credited largely to the late William Loeb, working through his *Manchester Union Leader*. Loeb established "the pledge" of no new taxes as the touchstone of the state's gubernatorial politics, harassed unaccommodating politicians, sometimes advanced unlikely candidates for governor or Senator himself, blatantly asserted his own views about candidates in news coverage (evidently with telling electoral effect), and conducted vendettas against state bu-

[30] See Peter D. McClelland and Alan L. Magdovitz, *Crisis in the Making: The Political Economy of New York State since 1945* (New York: Cambridge University Press, 1981), chs. 5, 6, 8; J. Richard Aronson and Arthur E. King, "Is There a Fiscal Crisis Outside of New York?" *National Tax Journal* 31(1978), 153-163; Charles R. Morris, *The Cost of Good Intentions: New York City and the Liberal Experiment* (New York: Norton, 1980); Seymour Sacks, "Financing the State," *Proceedings of the Academy of Political Science* 31(May 1974), 119-130; Robert H. Connery and Gerald Benjamin, *Rockefeller of New York: Executive Power in the Statehouse* (Ithaca: Cornell University Press, 1979), ch. 6. There was also a denominator problem, a significant shrinkage of New York's personal income base (relative to other states') in the 1960s and 1970s. See Roy Bahl, "Fiscal Retrenchment in a Declining State: The New York Case," *National Tax Journal* 32(1979), 277-287.

[31] See James M. Naughton, "Basic Issue Confronted: Rockefeller Decision to Face Question of Wealth Reflects Capital's Concern," *New York Times*, November 14, 1974, pp. 1, 38, quotation at p. 38; Joseph E. Persico, *The Imperial Rockefeller: A Biography of Nelson A. Rockefeller* (New York: Washington Square Press, 1983), ch. 8 and pp. 268-276. On Rockefeller's financial support of his administrators and staff as an issue in the confirmation hearings: "Here was a novel situation in American public life. Countless politicians had been destroyed for being on the take—Nelson Rockefeller was in trouble for being on the give" (p. 272).

reaucrats who took or threatened to take an initiative on policies.[32] Finally, the very low fiscal rank of Virginia among Southern states (in both the revenue and expenditure series) comes as no surprise, given the characteristics of the hegemonic Martin and Byrd organizations.

The instruments of fiscal surge, decline, or constant rank touched on here are impressively heterogeneous. They include a dues-paying, ideologically assertive organization that operated in partisan primaries (the NPL), exceptionally effective demagoguery, a newspaper crafted into a political weapon, a third party rooted in ideology and mass organization (the Farmer-Laborites), a well-conceived referendum campaign, an immense family fortune energetically deployed, and a hegemonic party organization presiding over a miniature electorate. Two points are worth making: (a) In all these cases, policy achievements required skillful maneuvering in electoral processes, yet (b) the basic explanations of the policy achievements have next to nothing to do with electoral competition between Republicans and Democrats as political scientists ordinarily conceive it.

To return to the major statistical relation of the figures and tables, why is having traditional party organizations associated with having relatively small public economies? The macro relation needs a rooting in micro processes. Five lines of argument come to mind, some already developed or implied in earlier discussion. First, in regimes infused by traditional organization the *inherent impulse* to generate ambitious governmental programs is likely to be relatively weak. This is true for two reasons: the sorts of people attracted to organization politics (and perforce government) are relatively unlikely to have much of a program-building bent, given party incentive structures; and the particularism required for organizational maintenance may tend to crowd out other kinds of government activity.[33] There are instances in which organizations in power have used their considerable autonomy to sup-

[32] See Eric P. Veblen, *The* Manchester Union Leader *in New Hampshire Elections* (Hanover, N.H.: University Press of New England, 1975) and Winters, "Political Choice." Winters draws a contrast between the expenditure paths of New Hampshire and Vermont in recent decades, and makes persuasive arguments accounting for the difference.

[33] Edward C. Banfield on the Chicago machine's incentive structure: "The political head is not likely to take a lively interest in the content of policy or to be specially gifted in the development of ideas or in their exposition. If ideas and the content of policy interested him much, or if he were ideologically-minded, he would not have made his career in the machine, for the machine is entirely without interest in such matters" (*Political Influence: A New Theory of Urban Politics* [New York: Free Press, 1961], p. 250). A good crowding-out argument, although it addresses regulatory rather than spending activity, appears in Matthew A. Crenson, *The Un-Politics of Air Pollution: A Study of Non-Decisionmaking in the Cities* (Baltimore: Johns Hopkins University Press, 1971), pp. 135-141.

port expensive programs—urban renewal in New Haven under Lee is an example—but these are probably unusual.

Second, to build on earlier arguments about "autonomy," *interest groups* of a program-building inclination (some unions, for example) seem to have had a hard time exercising influence in a milieu of traditional organization; instances of this, at any rate, can be pointed to.

Third, also building on earlier arguments, the evident relative *issuelessness* of electoral politics in organization environments, a result of both selection (what sorts of people enter politics) and resource arrangements (what people have to do to win office), may leave a mark on government by a dynamic of its own. An electoral politics built on raising and addressing issues may promote governmental action. A politics of high issue density, such as California's, not only gives currency to issues but may also engender among publics and officials a mindset that government activity and electoral relations are and ought to be *about* raising and acting on issues, which—Proposition 13 notwithstanding—is probably on balance expensive.[34]

Fourth, the patronage needs of traditional organizations inhibit the installation of a professionalized *bureaucracy*, and thereby fend off the rationalizing and also expansionary impulses of bureaucracy that are likely to generate both expenditure and revenue in a governmental setting.[35] This argument also accommodates the temporal dimension of

---

[34] "One of the ironies of American city government is that machine politics provides the strongest resources for innovative mayors, but at the same time, in its weak emphasis on issue appeals, is unlikely to attract such leaders *or develop a popular demand for them*" (Raymond E. Wolfinger, *The Politics of Progress* [Englewood Cliffs, N.J.: Prentice-Hall, 1974], p. 121; emphasis added). Crenson (*The Un-Politics of Air Pollution*, pp. 42, 43) on politics in East Chicago, Indiana (organization territory in Lake County): "For East Chicagoans 'politics' has a somewhat different meaning than it does for political scientists. The community definition is probably best illustrated by the comment of a local newspaper editor asked to explain a disagreement that had arisen during the discussion of a local political issue: 'In this town, people don't disagree about *issues*. It's just politics.'" Crenson goes on about "the way in which politically active East Chicagoans regard local politics. For them, political activity appears primarily as a means for private advancement and private revenge. This view is shared even by those citizens who are not active in partisan affairs." The idea of a link between issue density and governmental action has more in common with a Tocquevillean construction of democracy than one emphasizing political parties. A pertinent Tocqueville observation on elections: "When elections quickly follow one another, they keep society in feverish activity, with endless mutability in public affairs." And on government: "There is also in democratic societies a stirring without precise aim; some sort of prevailing feverish excitement finds expression in innovations of all sorts, and innovations are almost always expensive." This sounds more like California than Lake County. Alexis de Tocqueville, *Democracy in America* (Garden City, N.Y.: Doubleday Anchor, 1969), pp. 202, 211, and more generally pp. 202-203, 209-221, 241-250.

[35] Winters, in "Political Choice," p. 606 (and more generally pp. 606-610, 617-620),

American party organization. The movement to professionalize the public sector, which began about a century ago, may have run into resistance varying with, among other things, the incidence of traditional party organization and (where it existed) its strength or deep-rootedness, roughly indexed by how old it was.[36] This suggests a relatively easy move toward bureaucracy in newer states and cities. We know additionally that civil service rules came in early and evidently took hold (though not foreclosing patronage dealing in all environments) in Massachusetts, one of the style-setting older states outside the organization belt.[37]

A fifth line of argument reintroduces *political culture*, not to present an "imprinting" or "bearer" line of ethnocultural explanation but rather to argue that a distinctive American *tradition* of conducting electoral politics grew to high importance in the nineteenth century. Its components were the structure and practices of patronage-based party organization yet also a congruous or complementary public outlook that perhaps came to carry causal weight of its own. This was substantially a national tradition back when patronage-based national parties operated in a nineteenth-century presidential politics centered in the country's northeastern quadrant (roughly Missouri and points north and east), but the putative outlook may well have persisted consequentially afterward in the twentieth century's TPO belt, where state and local organization politics kept on operating in the traditional national

---

writes of "an entrepreneurial and acquisitive style of administration/bureaucracy" in Vermont that has exerted upward pressure on governmental expenditure. Wolfinger on machines (*Politics of Progress*, p. 118): "The machine's appetite for patronage impedes the use of professional talent in government. Skilled professionals are cosmopolitans, moving from city to city as job opportunities become available. Their career patterns are incompatible with the parochial orientations of political machines, which result in pressures for residence requirements for civil servants and other attempts to restrict municipal jobs to city residents." For an economist's perspective see Thomas E. Borcherding, "The Sources of Growth of Public Expenditures in the United States, 1902-1970," ch. 3 in Thomas E. Borcherding (ed.), *Budgets and Bureaucrats: The Sources of Government Growth* (Durham, N.C.: Duke University Press, 1977), pp. 60-64.

[36] Even though at the big-city level, at least, there seems to have been a good deal of commonality across political environments in changes made over pertinent decades toward professionalizing several elements of the public sector. On the late nineteenth century see Jon C. Teaford, *The Unheralded Triumph: City Government in America, 1870-1900* (Baltimore: Johns Hopkins University Press, 1984), ch. 6.

[37] So far as one can tell, patronage networks managed by individual officeholders (usually county officials) in some of the newer metropolitan areas—for example the Phoenix, Houston, Oklahoma City, and Seattle areas—have been insulated and have not barred the construction of administrative instruments in central cities. On Massachusetts see Richard M. Abrams, *Conservatism in a Progressive Era: Massachusetts Politics, 1900-1912* (Cambridge: Harvard University Press, 1964), p. 134.

style.[38] The outlook here is the one given vivid expression by Thomas Nast in his cartoons, Mark Twain in his acid pronouncements on politicians, Finley Peter Dunne via Mr. Dooley in his political anthropology of Chicago, and later Frank R. Kent in his *Great Game of Politics*.[39] It combined an often sardonic appreciation of politics as a spectator sport with a deep pessimism—insufficiently appreciated by students of American politics—about the potential positive use of government. The reform-vs.-regulars cycle gave it a script and a vocabulary—organization politics has at least "reform" as issue content—but reform often meant economy: money given over to government might, after all, end up wasted or stolen.[40] Who thirty years ago would have wanted to pay taxes in New Jersey?[41]

[38] On Republican presidential politics of the late nineteenth century see Robert D. Marcus, *Grand Old Party: Political Structure in the Gilded Age 1880-1896* (New York: Oxford University Press, 1971). Presidential nominating politics in the Republican party consisted largely of maneuvers in the shifting coalitional politics of New York, Pennsylvania, Ohio, and Illinois; the Senatorial combines of Wisconsin and Michigan also drew continual attention. Massachusetts Republicans seem to have had little place in this game. Jesse Macy, writing in 1904, drew an interesting contrast between the Massachusetts and Pennsylvania Republican parties, consigning the former to an expressive (and sanguinary?) past and seeing the latter as an instrumental present: "The Republican party of Massachusetts was founded to promulgate a doctrine. Its creators and leaders were men of profound convictions who were also skilled in the use of argument. They were able to convince their hearers and to move the multitude to action by their powers of speech. Of another sort were the party leaders in Pennsylvania. They were men accustomed to do rather than to talk; they adapted means to ends and looked for direct and tangible results. To the keen-sighted business man the obvious use and purpose of a party organization is to get the right sort of men put into office, and the right sort of man for the office is one who can be relied upon to do the right things" (*Party Organization and Machinery* [New York: The Century Co., 1904], p. 157).

[39] Frank R. Kent, *The Great Game of Politics* (Garden City, N.Y.: Doubleday, Page, 1924).

[40] On reform as issue content: "Reform, it has been said, is what we have in America in place of ideology" (James Reichley in his work on Philadelphia, *The Art of Government: Reform and Organization Politics in Philadelphia* [New York: Fund for the Republic, 1959], p. 107). There are scattered mentions of governments under organization control having difficulty passing bond issues for more or less the reason suggested. On Cincinnati in the 1920s: Richard S. Childs, *Civic Victories: The Story of an Unfinished Revolution* (New York: Harper, 1952), pp. 164-165. On Baltimore at the turn of the century: Alan D. Anderson, *The Origin and Resolution of an Urban Crisis: Baltimore, 1890-1930* (Baltimore: Johns Hopkins University Press, 1977), p. 35. The political culture the Lynds found and characterized in "Middletown" (in fact Muncie, Indiana) in the 1920s and 1930s seems a good instance of the organization culture hypothesized here. See Robert S. Lynd and Helen Merrell Lynd, *Middletown: A Study in Contemporary American Culture* (London: Harcourt, Brace, 1929), ch. 24; and *Middletown in Transition: A Study in Cultural Conflicts* (New York: Harcourt, Brace, 1937), ch. 9.

[41] A recent example of the sort of publicity that can make people reluctant to trust governments with money: "The New Jersey Commission of Investigation urged the Legis-

One way to test these lines of argument against reality is to see whether analysts of particular states or locales supporting traditional organization have come up with evidence or insights that bear out their various logics. Unfortunately this is a difficult assignment. Systematic scholarship investigating the politics of fiscal activity in pertinent states and locales is rare; what writing there is travels mostly on anecdotal evidence. Surprisingly, for example, no one really knows what sort of characteristic fiscal pattern, if any, accompanied the familiar organization-vs.-reform cycle in cities.[42] No consistent message comes through concerning the fiscal records of machines, of which the stronger and more conspicuous seem to have run the gamut from famously cheap to famously extravagant (partly a consequence, perhaps, of their leaders' having enough influence to indulge personal tastes). The Albany machine, for example, has followed a style of providing "a minimum of public services at the lowest possible cost"; Gary before Mayor Hatcher held to "an historic pattern of small budgets, especially for departments dealing with services"; and Memphis's Ed Crump, "committed to having the lowest city taxes in the nation," alienated his business community in the 1940s by refusing to fund expressways, public buildings, or sewage plants.[43] The old Republican machines in

---

lature today to delay passage of bills appropriating more than $100 million for local sewer projects. The commission said the funds should be withheld until legislation could be enacted to insure that the money 'won't be squandered or stolen.' " "More than $1.8 billion has been spent in New Jersey on sewer projects since 1970, and, according to sworn testimony, millions have been wasted or stolen through engineering mistakes, overbilling and kickbacks to local officials." Joseph F. Sullivan, "Jersey Urged to Delay Sewers Pending Study of Corruption," New York Times, July 31, 1982, p. 1.

[42] From a 1982 review essay on urban government: "Basic to all municipal policies, however, is the question of finance, and this topic is one of the most neglected. Around the turn of the century students of public finance published a series of monographs on the history of municipal finance in such cities as New York, Baltimore, Cleveland, Providence, and Boston." However, "few since the Progressive era have delved into the history of municipal expenditures, taxation, and debt. Historians have written blithely about waste, incompetence, and inefficiency in city government without ever testing these generalizations against the municipal ledgers. Likewise, they have characterized bosses as generous in their distribution of funds for public works and patronage jobs, while reformers have assumed the appearance of tight-fisted accountants careful to avoid expense. Yet again there has been no analysis of expenditures to support this view." Jon C. Teaford, "Finis for Tweed and Steffens: Rewriting the History of Urban Rule," Reviews in American History 10(1982), 143. For Teaford's own recent treatment of big-city finance in the late nineteenth century, see The Unheralded Triumph, ch. 10.

[43] On Albany: James Q. Wilson, Varieties of Police Behavior: The Management of Law and Order in Eight Communities (Cambridge: Harvard University Press, 1968), p. 236. "A longstanding joke has it that the city pioneered the use of solar energy by allowing the sun to melt away the copious upstate snows" (Maurice Carroll, "Corning of Al-

Cincinnati and Philadelphia are said to have been low-budget affairs.[44] A student of one of the Appalachian factional regimes points to its notably meager local revenue base.[45]

But at the opposite extreme Leander Perez, using part of a rake-off from oil companies working local wells, built Plaquemines Parish into a welfare state approaching a Persian Gulf sheikdom.[46] Kansas City's Pendergast machine undertook an unusually ambitious construction program during the Depression, avoiding heavy equipment wherever possible in order to employ some 15,000 to 22,000 men in "pick and shovel armies."[47] The Hague machine was an expensive operation,

---

bany Still Thriving in Job," *New York Times*, May 13, 1980, p. B8). Dan O'Connell's "deep-seated conservatism" is said to have had "some strange impacts on Albany. Some time ago, for example, it was proposed to extend a runway at Albany Airport, but the project was stalled year after year. The reason: 'Dan O'Connell does not believe in airplanes.' Renovation of Public School 17 was also deferred for many years, because that was where Dan O'Connell had gone. 'We don't want to renovate it,' explained an official, 'because if it was good enough for Dan, he must think it's good enough now' " (Frank S. Robinson, *Machine Politics: A Study of Albany's O'Connells* [New Brunswick, N.J.: Transaction Books, 1977], p. 113). On Gary: Edward Greer, *Big Steel: Black Politics and Corporate Power in Gary, Indiana* (New York: Monthly Review Press, 1979), p. 161. On Memphis: David M. Tucker, *Memphis Since Crump: Bossism, Blacks, and Civic Reformers, 1948-1968* (Knoxville: University of Tennessee Press, 1980), pp. 67-69, 86, 92, quotation at p. 69. Sewage went directly into streams and rivers, and "in the summer the whole central business district could smell the 'stinking, unsightly and odoriferous mess' " (pp. 68-69).

[44] On Cincinnati: Ralph A. Straetz, *PR Politics in Cincinnati: Thirty-Two Years of City Government through Proportional Representation* (New York: New York University Press, 1958), pp. 223-224; Charles Garrett, *The La Guardia Years: Machine and Reform Politics in New York City* (New Brunswick, N.J.: Rutgers University Press, 1961), p. 86. On Philadelphia: Robert L. Freedman, *A Report on Politics in Philadelphia* (Cambridge: Joint Center for Urban Studies, M.I.T./Harvard, 1963), p. vi:20.

[45] John Gaventa, *Power and Powerlessness: Quiescence and Rebellion in an Appalachian Valley* (Urbana: University of Illinois Press, 1980), pp. 138-141.

[46] Glen Jeansonne, *Leander Perez: Boss of the Delta* (Baton Rouge: Louisiana State University Press, 1977), pp. 69-70, 113-118. For a price: "Judge Leander Perez in the 1930s acquired royalty interests in local public land drilled by major oil companies. In just the past 11 years, Mr. [Luke] Petrovich [president of Plaquemines Parish in 1984] estimates, heirs of the judge (he died in 1969) collected $21 million in royalties from Gulf alone. In 1975, Gulf said in a report to the Securities and Exchange Commission that one of its representatives had given Judge Perez an additional $50,000 in cash annually for years" (Thomas Petzinger, Jr., and George Getschow, "Oil's Legacy: In Louisiana, Big Oil Is Cozy With Officials And Benefit Is Mutual," *Wall Street Journal*, October 22, 1984, p. 26).

[47] "The depression, far from staggering local officials, gave them an opportunity to unite the community toward local improvements and the Pendergast machine. Tom Pendergast and his hand-picked city manager, Henry F. McElroy, came up with the idea of a 'Ten-Year Plan' for Kansas City and Jackson County. The plan called for a bond issue of

though it generated an oddly skewed policy pattern that apparently reflected Hague's own preferences as well as organization needs: a gigantic medical center providing "lavish medical care," a highly paid and extraordinarily overstaffed police deparment, yet poor schools, a "decrepit" sewer system, and horse-drawn wagons collecting garbage along filthy streets lit by arc and gas lamps at night in 1940.[48] New York City's last long stretch of organization government, from 1917 through 1933, drove up the budget and city debt through payroll padding, yet the tax rate stayed even (the 1920s were prosperous) and evidently not much was undertaken in capital improvements. The city's "lack of technical expertise" at the time, due to the way engineers were hired, is said to have "crippled its ability to carry out, or even conceive, complicated public works."[49] As a general matter machines have certainly been labor-intensive, a result that is guaranteed by their internal dynamics and that routinely draws charges of extravagance and waste. Yet this says little about overall cost. On the average, for example, machines may run below the urban norm in capital outlays, making them less expensive in fact than they sometimes appear.

Two works are especially illuminating on organization settings. The first is Sam Bass Warner's *Private City*, a study of Philadelphia over two centuries that pursues a number of themes but gives attention to organization politics.[50] Two groups of professional politicians dealt in or

---

nearly fifty million dollars that would provide the community with a monumental public works program. The unemployed would be put to work, and the city and county would be modernized and beautified" (Lyle W. Dorsett, "Kansas City and the New Deal," pp. 407-419 in John Braeman, Robert H. Bremner, and David Brody [eds.], *The New Deal*, vol. 2, *The State and Local Levels* [Columbus: Ohio State University Press, 1975], p. 408). Companies owned by Pendergast supplied nearly all the concrete. "One of the more interesting construction undertakings of the period was the filling of Brush Creek, which bisects the southern half of the city, with a concrete spillway eighteen feet deep. This must rank as one of the greater political—if not engineering—feats of the twentieth century" (Thomas P. Murphy, *Metropolitics and the Urban County* [Washington, D.C.: Washington National Press, 1970], p. 74).

[48] See Dayton D. McKean, *The Boss: The Hague Machine in Action* (Boston: Houghton Mifflin, 1940), chs. 10, 12, 14, first quotation at p. 166; and Richard J. Connors, *A Cycle of Power: The Career of Jersey City Mayor Frank Hague* (Metuchen, N.J.: Scarecrow Press, 1971), pp. 74-76, 165-168, second quotation at p. 166. Garbage collection "emphasized manpower rather than equipment, with the logic that men vote, trucks don't" (Connors, p. 165).

[49] See Garrett, *The La Guardia Years*, pp. 16-19 and ch. 3 ("An Age of Tammany"); and Robert A. Caro, *The Power Broker: Robert Moses and the Fall of New York* (New York: Knopf, 1974), ch. 18 ("New York City Before Robert Moses"), quotation at p. 328.

[50] Sam Bass Warner, *The Private City: Philadelphia in Three Periods of Its Growth* (Philadelphia: University of Pennsylvania Press, 1968), pp. 86-91, 98, 175, 184, and especially 214-223.

with Philadelphia during roughly the first third of the twentieth century: "the locally oriented [notably the Vare brothers' Republican ma-
chine], and the state and federally oriented. The former sought to create
power in organizing the wards and districts of Philadelphia in order to
control Philadelphia city and county offices and to benefit from the private business done with these governments; the latter, working from a
base outside the city, sought to control the blocks of Philadelphia votes
in order to gain power in state and federal political competition."[51] The
Vare organization did little to foster government activity beyond tasks
at the ward level: "After almost forty years of power and effort the
Vares could boast of very little constructive results for Philadelphia or
Philadelphians."[52] In 1905 the Vares supported a centralization and
bureaucratization of the school system, but this stood out as an exceptional move—"apparently their machine did not depend upon school
jobs and school business for its power"—instituting as it did "the very
kinds of reforms they often fought against in municipal and county
government."[53] Politics at the state level lacked issue content: "The
state party's goals and methods became the focus of all Pennsylvania
politics. The party was the subject of campaigns, not the problems of
Pennsylvania's economy and institutions."[54] Philadelphia had a reform
tradition, but it achieved little and the city's normal political leadership
was such that "the voters of Philadelphia would not trust their government with large sums of money, big projects, or major innovations."[55]
"Municipal politics in [early] twentieth-century Philadelphia can be
summarized as a series of rapidly shifting coalitions of downtown,
ward, and state political groups seeking to control that small fraction
of the Philadelphia patronage and budget which could be varied during
one term of the mayor's office. Such an era was not, nor could it have
been, marked by major undertakings of great novelty or broad social
concern."[56]

The other work is a recent dissertation by Bennett S. Stark on Illinois,

[51] *Ibid.*, pp. 214-215. Warner's judgment: "The most conscientious research would be
required to arrive at a judicious estimate of which of these two groups of professional
political leaders did the most damage to the city of Philadelphia" (p. 215).

[52] *Ibid.*, p. 217, more generally pp. 215-218.

[53] *Ibid.*, p. 218.

[54] "In the twentieth century two issues overshadowed all the rest: honesty in government, and big-business domination of government. The first issue should not have been
a major concern in a well-led democratic society. The second issue prevented the state
from dealing with the difficult and important matters of social welfare and economic development, which became more and more serious as the twentieth century advanced"
(*ibid.*, p. 219).

[55] *Ibid.*, p. 98. See also p. 91.

[56] *Ibid.*, p. 175.

which investigates a century of political history asking the question: why are Illinois's taxes so low?[57] The state's rates are among the lowest, as an examination of the rankings here in Figures 10.2 through 10.10 will suggest. The explanation is complex, not surprisingly, but a central part of it has to do with the maintenance needs of the Chicago organizations—ward organizations of both parties before 1931 and of the Democratic machine since.[58] By the 1890s the ward organizations had become accustomed to "tax-fixing" as a source of revenue—a system wherein ward committeemen and precinct captains set the tax assessments of individuals and corporations by making ad hoc, bilateral deals; the terms were low or zero assessments in return for payoffs to the organization.[59] The tax that allowed this exchange was a state property tax administered in decentralized fashion by amateur assessors; assessments on corporate stock and personal property (stocks, bonds, cash, etc.) provided especially good room for maneuver.[60] On the politicians' side tax-fixing had become an occupational cornerstone: "This whole organization," according to a 1930 analysis, "is built to a large extent upon the present tax system, derives its revenues and resources therefrom, and is therefore vitally dependent upon the continuance of the present tax system."[61] With its amateur administration and low assessments, the Illinois property tax drew criticism as an inadequate supplier of government revenue, but shifting to a more productive tax proved an uphill enterprise: "A partnership in effect existed

[57] Bennett S. Stark, "The Political Economy of State Public Finance: A Model of the Determinants of Revenue Policy: The Illinois Case 1850-1970" (Ph.D. dissertation, University of Wisconsin–Madison, 1982). On Illinois's low rank in recent decades: ch. 8.

[58] See *ibid.*, pp. 8-10, 13-15, 77, 93-94, 103-104, 118, 152, 158, 167, 171-174 (especially illuminating), 180, 214, 229-235, 253-254, 297-298. See also Harold F. Gosnell, *Machine Politics: Chicago Model* (Chicago: University of Chicago Press, 1968), pp. 6-7, 77.

[59] "Political organizations depended upon financial payments for their economic survival in return for substantial underassessment; large business interests preferred such payments to taxation on an accurate assessment" (Stark, "Political Economy of State Public Finance," p. 180).

[60] The Chicago machine is commonly said to be a functional adaptation to the pronounced formal decentralization of governmental authority in Cook County—formal decentralization, that is, caused or causes the machine. Whether or not this is true its near converse is: the ward organizations certainly used to be an important cause of the persistence of decentralization: "Chicago ward-level political machines and those representing their interests opposed the consolidation of governments lying within Chicago's territorial limits, inasmuch as such would alter political constituencies and threaten a principal source of party financing [that is, decentralized tax-fixing]" (*ibid.*, p. 152). See also p. 158.

[61] *Ibid.*, p. 10, quoted from Herbert Simpson, *Tax Racket and Tax Reform in Chicago* (Chicago: Collegiate Press, 1930), pp. 101-107.

between big business interests and the political machines, neither of which desired tax reform."[62] Opposition from Chicago politicians and then a court fended off a state income tax in the early 1930s, a key juncture when several other states moved to an income tax and downstate Illinois representatives strongly favored it.[63] It took until 1969 for a (flat rate) income tax to win state adoption, and by this time a segment of the business community had taken the lead in promoting it.[64] The Chicago machine meanwhile did its best to protect the personal property tax and motored on through the 1970s making deals: "In September 1980 a federal grand jury indicted fourteen officials for illegal assessment reductions involving $33 million dollars."[65]

The Philadelphia case produces elements of four of the five lines of argument presented above (all but the one on interest groups). The Illinois case, an instance of what might be called supply-side particularism helping to keep a public sector small, produces elements of two: lack of an inherent organizational impulse to generate government activity (evident in the Chicago organizations' support of a low-yield revenue system throughout the twentieth century), and resolute protection of a nonbureaucratic mode of administration. Just how significant and widespread tax-fixing has been in the various organization states is impossible to say. The Illinois case does recall an important policy showdown in the 1960s in New Jersey, when the Essex County Democratic organization blocked a Democratic governor's drive for an income tax, though what caused the organization's opposition was unclear.[66] Organization states do nonetheless seem distinctive, for whatever mix of reasons, in the *nature* of their revenue systems as well as in their low burden ratios exhibited in Figures 10.2 through 10.10. Consider the data in Figure 10.20, taken from a standard progressive/liberal statement of the late 1970s that ranked the states according to "tax equity." Each of the summary state rankings reported here was arrived at by taking into account a state's policy or performance on a number of particular tax matters.[67] The "tax equity" measure, when its components

---

[62] Stark, "Political Economy of State Public Finance," p. 10.

[63] *Ibid.*, pp. 229-235.   [64] *Ibid.*, pp. 244-255.

[65] *Ibid.*, pp. 253-254, 297-298, quotation at p. 297.

[66] Governor Richard J. Hughes had won a landslide electoral victory, carrying in large Democratic majorities in both houses of the state legislature. "Despite all this, the death blow to the Governor's income tax was delivered by Dennis F. Carey, the short, stocky Essex County Democratic leader who instructed his nine, hand-picked Democratic Assemblymen and four Senators to vote against the tax" (see Ronald Sullivan, "The Hughes Defeat: Absence of Statewide Identity Makes Governor Less Powerful Than Bosses," *New York Times*, March 25, 1966, p. 47).

[67] Diane Fuchs and Steve A. Rabin, *Tax Equity in the Fifty States* (Washington, D.C.:

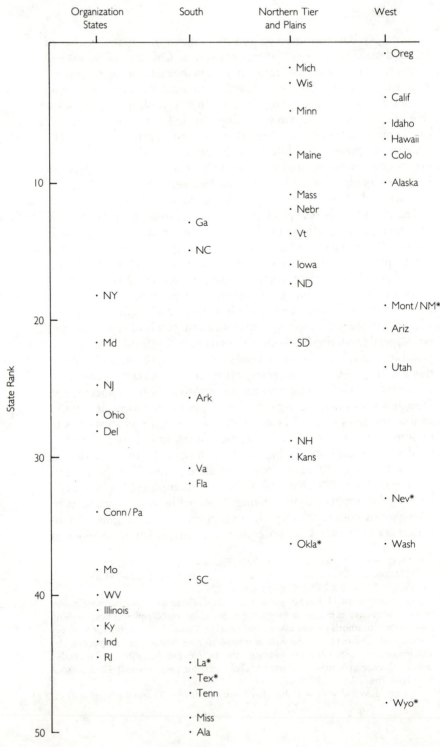

Fig. 10.20 State Rank in Tax Fairness Index, Late 1970s. Asterisks refer to tax-exporting states; see p. 259.

are examined, turns out to award points both for the progressiveness of state (not local) revenue systems and also for what amounts to their adherence to professional standards. Probably both these propensities serve in practice as good generators of revenue (given, in the former case, the productiveness of the income tax).[68] The organization states rank rather low in Figure 10.20—censurable, that is, according to this progressive/liberal rating system—as do most Southern states and also, this time, most states in the business of exporting taxes.[69]

We have considered organization states in general. What about New York, the outlier in the figures and tables? The conspicuously high fiscal rank of (pre-Rockefeller) New York among organization states may well extend back to the beginning of the century or beyond, and it needs explanation.[70] An easy if ad hoc explanation comes to mind: in talent and drive invested in building government instruments and programs over the last century, New York stands unique certainly among organization states and perhaps in the country as a whole. New York City's reform tradition has displayed more energy and resilience than any other large machine city's, and reform in New York since about 1900 has ordinarily meant encouragement of government activity.[71]

Coalition of American Public Employees, 1979). Figure 10.20 omits the District of Columbia.

[68] Though revenue productiveness is not a criterion of "equity" in the study.

[69] The state of Washington, an outlier here, has a tradition of relying heavily on a sales tax. An equation setting up the ordinal-scale tax fairness index as a dependent variable (not a practice highly recommended), and TPO score, a Confederate dummy, and a tax-exporting dummy (score of 1 for each six exporting states) as independent variables, produces the following results (standard-error values in parentheses):

$$\text{TAXFAIRNESS} = 10.6 + 4.49(1.02)\text{TPO}*** + 14.3(3.8)\text{CONFEDERATE}*** + 14.1(4.8)\text{TAXEXPORT}***$$

with adj. $R^2 = .410$ and $N = 49$. Figure 10.20 includes Alaska, but the equation here does not.

[70] The earlier New York rank is an impression. A 1904 source, for example, couples Boston and New York City as especially high-spending cities. Delos F. Wilcox, *The American City: A Problem in Democracy* (New York: Macmillan, 1904), pp. 341-342. New York was one of the early states to adopt an income tax—in 1919. See Clara Penniman, *State Income Taxation* (Baltimore: Johns Hopkins University Press, 1980), pp. 7, 19. In 1937, when income taxes were still not very important sources of revenue at the state level, New York extracted 59% of all revenue extracted anywhere in the country by state income taxes. See U.S. Senate, *Federal, State, and Local Government Fiscal Relations*, 78th Congress, 1st Session, Document no. 69, 1943, p. 431.

[71] A 1910 comparison: "Old New York, under Tammany Hall, which is a Democratic organization, was a synonym for municipal corruption, and yet New York has been overthrowing the Tammany organization off and on ever since the Tweed regime forty years ago. On the other hand, Republican control in Philadelphia has scarcely been contested in that period" (Wilcox, *Great Cities*, p. 252). On twentieth-century reform: Garrett,

The state has specialized in executives with a bent for aggrandizing government: Theodore Roosevelt, Charles Evans Hughes, Franklin D. Roosevelt, Herbert Lehman, Fiorello La Guardia (in New York City), and not least Alfred E. Smith, who of course rose through Tammany but as governor made his administration a powerful instrument of government planning in league with Belle Moskowitz and Robert Moses.[72] Moses, who began as a Progressive reformer, deserves a place himself among the important builders of public economies listed earlier. His maneuvers as bureaucratic entrepreneur and compulsive producer of concrete resulted in construction enterprises that rearranged the New York landscape under six governors, beginning in 1924 with Smith, and under five mayors, beginning in 1933 with La Guardia (Tammany kept Moses out of the city before 1933).[73] As of 1957, for example, two-thirds of all urban renewal money spent anywhere in the country had been spent under Moses's direction in New York City.[74]

New York's governmental expansion has come about against an electoral backdrop of continual and vigorous conflict, in which the various opposing sides have confronted each other in imaginative ways in a number of arenas. The state's conventional election contests between

The La Guardia Years, ch. 2; Augustus Cerillo, Jr., "The Impact of Reform Ideology: Early Twentieth-Century Municipal Government in New York City," ch. 5 in Michael H. Ebner and Eugene M. Tobin (eds.), *The Age of Urban Reform: New Perspectives on the Progressive Era* (Port Washington, N.Y.: Kennikat, 1977). On the administration of reform mayor Seth Low, elected in 1901: Martin J. Schiesl, *The Politics of Efficiency: Municipal Administration and Reform in America, 1800-1920* (Berkeley: University of California Press, 1977), pp. 79-80.

[72] Tammany leader Charles Murphy, proud of Smith, summoned him when he acceded to the governorship and announced that Tammany would make no patronage claims on his administration: "Should Tammany ever ask for anything Smith felt would stand in the way of becoming a great Governor, all Smith had to do was tell him so and the request would be withdrawn" (Caro, *The Power Broker*, p. 128).

[73] "In terms of true building—personal conception and construction—Robert Moses was unique in America. Without including the cost of schools, hospitals, garbage incinerators, sewers and other improvements whose location and design he approved but which were physically constructed by others, without including the amount of money poured by private sources into construction that also had to be approved by him—including, in fact, only those public works that he personally conceived and completed, from first vision to ribbon cutting—Robert Moses built public works costing, in 1968 dollars, twenty-seven billion dollars. In terms of personal conception and completion, no other public official in the history of the United States built public works costing an amount even close to that figure" (*ibid.*, p. 9, and more generally *passim*, with a summary of Moses's achievements at pp. 5-21). On Tammany excluding Moses from city affairs and La Guardia inviting him in: pp. 344-345, 358-362. After La Guardia virtually all top elective officials, including Tammany mayor William O'Dwyer, took advantage of Moses's capacity to generate construction projects. See chs. 32-34.

[74] *Ibid.*, p. 12.

Republicans and Democrats have been rather pallid affairs during most of the twentieth century; rival candidates have ordinarily not differed much on issues. Mario M. Cuomo and Lewis E. Lehrman broke a long tradition in 1982 when they turned an election for governor into a programmatic confrontation—the strong liberal against the strong conservative. The much reduced importance of both sides' county organizations made this possible; Cuomo relied on union support in his primary and general election campaigns, and Lehrman used his own money.[75] The Socialist party, later the American Labor party, and then the Liberal party used to infuse some ideology into New York's general elections, and more recently the Conservative party has done so. But none of these movements has come close to giving ideological confrontation the central role in New York's electoral politics that it had in, say, Minnesota's politics in the 1920s and 1930s; the regular parties' hold on voters has been too strong.[76]

Intense and consequential conflict has nonetheless occurred in three other New York settings. The first is the reform-vs.-regular setting of New York City's mayoral elections, largely ignored by political scientists who study elections, which has generated its own iconography and one of the country's longer runs of electoral competition; one source gives "the years which signalized reform movements in New York City" (through 1920) to be 1844, 1853, 1857, 1861, 1863, 1870-72, 1890, 1894, 1901, 1905, 1909, and 1913, to which a number of others can be appended through 1961.[77] The second setting is the Republican

---

[75] The main Democratic organizations gave their support, by 1982 close to worthless, to Mayor Koch in the primary. Lehrman won his primary easily against a candidate backed by the Nassau County organization.

[76] A substantial Jewish vote went to all three of the left-wing New York parties, and also the Hearst candidacies in 1905 and 1909 and the Progressive candidate for governor in 1912. But Tammany had strong support in the Jewish community too. Until a generation ago, for example, most Jewish members of Congress from Manhattan were organization Democrats. On voting patterns early in the century: Thomas M. Henderson, *Tammany Hall and the New Immigrants: The Progressive Years* (New York: Arno, 1976), chs. 5-9. On Jews entering New York City politics early in the century: Irving Howe, *World of Our Fathers* (New York: Harcourt Brace Jovanovich, 1976), ch. 11.

[77] An imaginative exception to the neglect of New York City elections: Kenneth Finegold, "Progressivism, Electoral Change, and Public Policy in New York City, 1901-1917," Occasional Paper no. 83-1, Center for American Political Studies, Harvard University, October 1983. On 1844 through 1913: Garrett, *The La Guardia Years*, pp. 45, 345. Reform, it should be noted, took on different meanings over time, and Tammany established itself as the authoritative regular organization within the Manhattan Democratic party only in the 1890s. Reform mayors Seth Low (elected 1901) and John Purroy Mitchel (elected 1913) are both said to have brought about a decline in the city's death rate during their terms by imposing professional standards in the health department. On

party during the first decade or so of the twentieth century, when particularly intense controversy occurred within party ranks as Theodore Roosevelt and Charles Evans Hughes presided over the dismantling of the Platt organization.[78] The third setting is the Democratic party, where organization vs. anti-organization conflict persisted from well back in the nineteenth century into the 1960s (and continues in vestigial form today). Major occasions of conflict during the last especially heated decades included the Democratic state convention of 1932, where Franklin Roosevelt (and Al Smith) barely managed to put across Herbert Lehman as nominee for governor against Tammany Hall and the Brooklyn organization's opposition; the 1933, 1937, and 1941 mayoral elections, when Roosevelt as President refused to support Democratic nominees against La Guardia; the 1942 state convention, where the Brooklyn organization carried a nominee for governor over liberal opposition—"some never forgot hearing the jeers of a Democratic assembly directed at [Senator Robert F.] Wagner, Lehman, and Roosevelt"; the 1958 Buffalo convention, where a clash over a Senate nomination resulted in an all-out campaign against "bossism"; organization slating of national convention delegates in 1960 that aroused controversy by denying places to Lehman and Eleanor Roosevelt; and the final wave of primary showdowns between regulars and reform clubs in the 1960s.[79] The bitterness and intensity of the Democrats'

Low: Schiesl, *Politics of Efficiency*, p. 80. On Mitchel: Garrett, p. 44. There may be a discoverable relationship here between an electoral cycle and a policy pattern.

[78] See Harold F. Gosnell, *Boss Platt and His New York Machine* (Chicago: University of Chicago Press, 1924), ch. 11; Robert F. Wesser, *Charles Evans Hughes: Politics and Reform in New York, 1905-1910* (Ithaca: Cornell University Press, 1967).

[79] On the 1932 convention: Edward J. Flynn, *You're the Boss* (New York: Viking, 1947), pp. 105-110. "This is one instance where, notwithstanding the fact that the Leaders of the state were overwhelmingly opposed to a nomination, they were beaten because of the standing of the men they opposed: Roosevelt, Smith, and Lehman" (p. 108). On Roosevelt and La Guardia: Lyle W. Dorsett, *Franklin D. Roosevelt and the City Bosses* (Port Washington, N.Y.: Kennikat, 1977), ch. 4; William Manners, *Patience and Fortitude: Fiorello La Guardia* (New York: Harcourt Brace Jovanovich, 1976), pp. 151-160, 236-240, 254-256. On the 1942 convention: John Syrett, "Roosevelt vs. Farley: The New York Gubernatorial Election of 1942," *New York History* 56(1975), 51-81, quotation at p. 70. On the 1958 convention: Edward N. Costikyan, *Behind Closed Doors: Politics in the Public Interest* (New York: Harcourt, Brace and World, 1966), ch. 12; John F. Davenport, "Skinning the Tiger: Carmine DeSapio and the End of the Tammany Era," *New York Affairs* 3(1975), 87-88. Just after the Buffalo convention, Arthur Schlesinger, Jr., assailed organization Democrats in New York and also in Connecticut and Pennsylvania for their propensity to nominate "mediocre party hacks" for Senate seats. See Arthur Schlesinger, Jr., "Death Wish of the Democrats," *New Republic*, September 15, 1958, pp. 7-8, quotation at p. 7. On slating in 1960: Douglas Dales, "Lehman Is Denied Delegate's Role by State Leaders," *New York Times*, June 17, 1960, pp. 1, 18. The

pro- vs. anti-organization antagonism, fully evident twenty years ago, are hard to bring into focus today.

A promising hypothesis to explain New York's outlier status among organization states in government activity is, perhaps unsurprisingly, the state's tradition of aggressive reform—in New York City's mayoral elections, at a critical juncture in the Republican party, and for over a century in the Democratic party. No other state that had such powerful regular organizations generated anywhere near such forceful and persistent opposition. To make a comparison over the country as a whole, reform is to New York what the Longs were to Louisiana and the Non-partisan League was to North Dakota.

---

regulars backed down under pressure: Douglas Dales, "Lehman Offered Delegate's Post as Leaders Shift," *New York Times*, June 24, 1960, pp. 1, 12.

CHAPTER 11

Progressive Reform and the New Deal Coalition

Patronage networks, material incentives, hierarchical and not easily permeable party organizations, relative issuelessness, sluggish government—this bears a considerable resemblance to a bill of particulars drawn up by reformers early in this century against the American party system at all levels of government. Herbert Croly and others, arguing in terms of problem and solution, brought an unusual lucidity to the nexus of parties, democracy, and government as they assaulted nineteenth-century parties and helped to construct some of this century's basic institutional arrangements. Their blend of normative and explanatory modeling, a common double-purpose role of party models, remains a useful guide to those arrangements. The first part of this concluding chapter discusses this turn-of-the-century reform effort, introducing, besides a few of its spokesmen, some especially imaginative recent scholarship (notably Stephen Skowronek's) that recaptures its logic. But Progressive reform eventuated in a hybrid system—traditional party organizations kept operating for several more generations in much of the country—and the new role the old organizations took on during the middle third of this century (from the New Deal through the Great Society) makes for an interesting and important story. It has to do with relations between different levels of government. The chapter proceeds from Progressive reform through New Deal and post–World War II coalitional politics and closes with comments on the present; its concern throughout is the connection between party structure and assertive government.

What was the American problem with parties around the turn of the century? Skowronek argues, in his recent work on the building of national instruments of government, that the country's nineteenth-century regime of "courts and parties" had proven incapable of managing an industrial order. Parties, in their role as channelers of particularistic goods and favors, had served along with the court system as appropriate societal coordinating instruments during much of the nineteenth century, but industrialization brought pressures and needs on all sides (including the corporate) for "the development of a central bureaucratic apparatus"—a task that "entailed building a qualitatively different kind of state." The party system had become an impediment: "The hold that the party machines had gained over American institutions would have to be broken before new centers of national institutional authority could be built." The United States, with its elaborately organized parties based on mass suffrage, had evolved into a circumstance the opposite of Europe's: "At the very time that parties were developing in Europe to challenge the hegemony of more traditional state institutions, state-building efforts in America aimed at the disintegration of party hegemony as it had developed over the course of a century."[1] Richard L. McCormick has presented an analysis similar to Skowronek's, calling the 1830s through just after 1900 "the party period," a distinctive era in which state and national parties filled a role by delivering "particularistic distributive benefits" generally geared to economic development, but which ended when "new demands" and "fresh needs" brought about a switch to government regulation and administration beyond the old system's capacity: "By the early 1900s the party period's practices no longer matched the country's social circumstances."[2]

Skowronek's argument in particular shares key elements with the case that Herbert Croly presented for Progressivism in 1914, near its height. To Croly also the court and party systems had performed the key institutional roles in the American nineteenth-century regime. The parties had fulfilled a mediating and democratizing function in the country's "do-nothing individualist democracy" before the Civil War. But the industrial age required positive and efficient government. "The overthrow of the two-party system," he concluded, was "indispensable to the success of progressive democracy, because, under American conditions, the vitality of the two-party system had been purchased and must continue to be purchased at the expense of administrative independence and efficiency." One heavy cost had been "an enfeeblement of the administration in the interest of partisan subsistence."[3]

[1] Stephen Skowronek, *Building a New American State: The Expansion of National Administrative Capacities, 1877-1920* (Cambridge: Cambridge University Press, 1982), pp. 1-84, 165-176, 285-292, quotations respectively at pp. 24 (more generally, "The procedural dimension: early America as a state of courts and parties," pp. 24-31), 15, 4, 41, 41.

[2] Richard L. McCormick, "The Party Period and Public Policy: An Exploratory Hypothesis," *Journal of American History* 66(1979), 279-298, quotations at pp. 294, 295.

[3] Herbert Croly, *Progressive Democracy* (New York: Macmillan, 1914), Introduction and chs. 3-6, 15-17, quotations at pp. 100, 349. The long quotation draws on two ar-

Ostrogorski took a somewhat different tack in his work vigorously criticizing American party organization in 1902. The problem with American parties was not that they had lapsed in the late nineteenth century from a former condition of being functional (that is, of fulfilling some valued function), but that their organizations had been fundamentally predatory from the 1830s on. The problem became exacerbated as the early organizations evolved into "the Machine" and took to colluding with private corporations in plundering the public.[4] It is testimony to the American political science community's firmly held belief that American parties somehow or other must be functional that hardly anyone has taken Ostrogorski seriously.[5] He might have profited by writing in a Marxist or Beardian idiom, perhaps treating the nineteenth-century party organization as just another kind of nineteenth-century corporate enterprise.[6] The only notable school of polit-

---

guments against parties, one the obvious one and the other an argument against constraining elective executives by requiring them to work within the frameworks of received party coalitions.

[4] See Moisei Ostrogorski, *Democracy and the Organization of Political Parties*, vol. 2 (New York: Macmillan, 1902). Part 5, Chapter 10 gives a good summary. The end result: "In all the States where the industrial and financial corporations are numerous, the Machine and the boss, fed with their money as with a sap, flourish like a luxuriant plant that overshadows the whole of public life. In these States, where the Machine is supreme, republican institutions are in truth but an idle form, a plaything wherewith to beguile children. It may be that the government of the bosses is not, administratively speaking, more ruinous for the people than plutocracy is oppressive for them from the economic standpoint. But both of them eat out the heart of the commonwealth. It is no longer 'a government of the people, by the people, and for the people' " (p. 576).

[5] See, for example, Arthur W. MacMahon's piece on Ostrogorski in the *Encyclopedia of the Social Sciences* (New York: Macmillan, 1933), vol. 11, pp. 503-504, with its homeostatic language: "Unlike those of his contemporaries in the realistic reorientation of political science who soon proceeded to interpret party abuses as self-corrective adjustments in a defective governmental organism, Ostrogorsky viewed institutional politics as wholly pathological. Despite the apparent sophistication involved in his method of observation, reenforced by some pungency of humor and a racing though repetitious style, the core of his thinking was a vast naiveté, which indeed was the ardent spirit of the man himself."

[6] Friedrich Engels characterized nineteenth-century American parties as "two great gangs of political speculators, who alternately take possession of the state power and exploit it by the most corrupt means and for the most corrupt ends—and the nation is powerless against those two great cartels of politicians, who are ostensibly its servants, but in reality dominate and plunder it" (Quoted in Skowronek, *Building a New American State*, p. 40). Joel A. Tarr on bosses around the turn of the century: "The typical urban boss was a man who regarded politics as a business and who used his power for personal and party gain. He was a businessman whose chief stock in trade was the goods of the political world—influence, laws, government grants, and franchises—which he utilized to make a private profit. In short, he was a 'political entrepreneur.' In the words of boss Richard Croker of Tammany Hall, 'Like a business man in business, I work for my

ical scientists in recent times to stray from the assumption that parties are functional (in fact or in realizable potential) is a group of writers on the left who criticize city machines. The case is that machines have dispensed petty favors to working people at the price of variously petty predation (as in payment of protection money to operate a pushcart), poor overall government programs, the shielding of economic elites from opposition, and a foreclosure of working-class organization.[7] Another Continental scholar besides Ostrogorski who examined American parties at the turn of the century was Werner Sombart, the author of *Why is there no Socialism in the United States?*, and it is interesting that neither of these figures came away with an impression of parties competing against each other in an issue space (in Downsian or some other fashion). What impressed Sombart about the parties was their resources—money (Tammany spent $900,000 in an election for mayor, for example; some $13 million in mid-1980s currency), electoral organization, access to a supply of distributable goods and favors, and control of career opportunities—as well as their capacity to engage strong and persisting voter loyalties that had little or nothing to do with contemporary issues. Having two parties rather than just one seemed a matter of historical accident.[8]

At any rate there seemed to be a serious problem, and the response to it took the form of vigorous drives in and around the Progressive era

---

own pocket all the time' " (Joel A.Tarr, "The Urban Politician as Entrepreneur," *Mid-America* 49[1967], 55).

[7] See Edward Greer, *Big Steel: Black Politics and Corporate Power in Gary, Indiana* (New York: Monthly Review Press, 1979), pp. 27-32; Ira Katznelson, "The Crisis of the Capitalist City: Urban Politics and Social Control," ch. 9 in Willis D. Hawley and Michael Lipsky (eds.), *Theoretical Perspectives on Urban Politics* (Englewood Cliffs, N.J.: Prentice-Hall, 1976), pp. 223-226; Allan Rosenbaum, "Machine Politics, Class Interest and the Urban Poor," paper delivered at the 1973 convention of the American Political Science Association. Rosenbaum draws an interesting contrast between reform mayor Hazen Pingree's handling of relief in Detroit during the depression of the 1890s, and the Chicago machine's handling of it during the depression of the 1930s. Pingree was more impressive. "Indeed Pingree's achievements in Detroit serve in themselves to illustrate not only what the poor and the working class lost as a consequence of the machine but also to demonstrate that the belief that the requirements of commercial progress necessitated the existence of the political machine and its boss as a means to get things accomplished is simply one more erroneous myth" (p. 22).

[8] Werner Sombart, *Why is there no Socialism in the United States?* (London: Macmillan, 1976), pp. 29-54. "The old major parties of America have been correctly compared with giant trusts that control such vast capital and dominate so exclusively all areas of supply and sale that any competition against them by third parties is out of the question" (p. 41). On having two parties rather than one: p. 48. Twice Sombart makes what can be considered Downsian points about competition in an issue space (pp. 38-39, 51-54), but they do not play a very important role in his complicated argument.

(in fact they began earlier and lasted longer) to make parties weaker and governments stronger. The antiparty moves are familiar: direct primaries, detailed regulation of internal party processes, civil service rules, more power and prominence to elected executives, nonpartisan elections in cities, and circumvention of elected officials through use of the initiative, referendum, and recall. On the government side Progressive reform meant at least, by its nature, efforts to inject a capacity to achieve intended ends (instrumental rationality) into governmental institutions. The ends ranged from the narrow ones of eliminating waste and enforcing vice laws through ambitious social engineering. There was a high incidence of ambitious aims: "One of the more fruitful hypotheses to emerge from the recent literature is the view that central to the spirit of Progressive reform was a sustained search for organized political techniques and competence in the management of an urbanized society."[9] Much energy went into constructing government instruments and programs—or mixtures of the two, as in Wisconsin's invention of a state income tax in 1911 that could be successfully administered.[10] A "bureaucratic orientation" took hold, according to Robert H. Wiebe: "A blend of many ideas, the new political theory borrowed its most revolutionary qualities from bureaucratic thought, and the heart of these was continuity. Trained, professional servants would staff a government broadly and continuously involved in society's operations."[11] The era's creativeness in the public sector was accompanied by, among other things, a rise in government expenditure and a sharp and permanent increase in regulatory activity.[12]

[9] Otis A. Pease, "Urban Reformers in the Progressive Era: A Reassessment," *Pacific Northwest Quarterly* 62(1971), 49-58, quotation at p. 52.

[10] See Clara Penniman, *State Income Taxation* (Baltimore: Johns Hopkins University Press, 1980), pp. 6-7; James A. Maxwell and J. Richard Aronson, *Financing State and Local Governments* (Washington, D.C.: Brookings, 1977), pp. 92, 115.

[11] Robert H. Wiebe, *The Search for Order, 1877-1920* (New York: Hill and Wang, 1967), pp. 149, 160, and more generally chs. 6 and 7. Other good sources on government-building in this period: Martin J. Schiesl, *The Politics of Efficiency: Municipal Administration and Reform in America, 1800-1920* (Berkeley: University of California Press, 1977); Kenneth Fox, *Better City Government: Innovation in American Urban Politics, 1850-1937* (Philadelphia: Temple University Press, 1977); Alan D. Anderson, *The Origin and Resolution of an Urban Crisis: Baltimore, 1890-1930* (Baltimore: Johns Hopkins University Press, 1977).

[12] On state and local expenditure: Allan R. Richards, "Half of Our Century," ch. 3 in James W. Fesler (ed.), *The 50 States and Their Local Governments* (New York: Knopf, 1967), p. 83; Thomas E. Borcherding, "One Hundred Years of Public Spending, 1870-1970," ch. 2 in Thomas E. Borcherding (ed.), *Budgets and Bureaucrats: The Sources of Government Growth* (Durham, N.C.: Duke University Press, 1977). On regulatory activity, for which 1905-1915 was the "creative decade": James Willard Hurst, *Law and*

The activation of governments at the expense of parties posed an unusually interesting challenge to the era's political theorists: how to design a mass democracy without parties. The contemporary socialist model was decisively unsuitable, styled as it was—at least in northern Europe—(a) to mobilize newly enfranchised voters (b) for a takeover of well-developed governmental institutions (c) using party as the instrument. Socialists elected mayors in American cities early in this century tended, not surprisingly, to perform like socially oriented Progressives.[13] Ostrogorski's plan for a party-free democracy, which grew from a dislike both of party organization and of parties as constraining channelers of individual opinion, has mostly met with derision. Permanent parties, he argued, should be abandoned in favor of a multiplicity of rising and falling temporary parties that would each advance a position on an issue—"single issue organizations" he calls them at one point, which may be a forgotten first use of the term. His formulation is odd—in 1902 the language and motions of Progressivism had not become clear yet—but if read sympathetically it can be taken to prefigure and approve of referendum campaigns, certain kinds of interest groups, political action committees (PACs), and individual candidacies in primaries and nonpartisan elections.[14] It can be read as a blueprint for much of modern politics in California.

Social Order in the United States (Ithaca, N.Y.: Cornell University Press, 1977), pp. 23-41, 143-154.

[13] In Schenectady, for example: Kenneth E. Hendrickson, Jr., "Tribune of the People: George R. Lunn and the Rise and Fall of Christian Socialism in Schenectady," ch. 3 in Bruce M. Stave (ed.), *Socialism and the Cities* (Port Washington, N.Y.: Kennikat, 1975). In Berkeley: Ira Kipnis, *The American Socialist Movement, 1897-1912* (New York: Columbia University Press, 1952), pp. 347-348. The record in Butte: "Butte, like a number of other cities which maintained solid socialist administrations, enforced housing codes in tenements, cleaned up the city streets, enforced sanitation laws, beefed up the health department and instituted food inspection campaigns, all of which improved the health of those most vulnerable to the miseries of city life" (Richard W. Judd, "Socialist Cities: Explorations into the Grass Roots of American Socialism" [Ph.D. dissertation, University of California–Irvine, 1979], p. 314).

[14] The Ostrogorski argument for issue-specific parties appears in *Democracy and the Organization of Parties*, vol. 2, pp. 658-695, quotation at p. 661. He wanted to build an electoral structure that would generate more interest in public affairs: "The first problem, therefore, which arises in democratic practice is the following: how to so organize political action as to develop spontaneous and regular impulse, to stimulate individual energies and not let them fall asleep" (p. 625). To this end regular parties would give way to "combinations forming and re-forming spontaneously, according to the changing problems of life and the play of opinion brought about thereby" (p. 658). Confronted with campaigns by issue-specific organizations, "the citizen will be enabled and obliged to make up his mind on each of the great questions that will divide public opinion" (p. 659). "Political society will be transformed into a vast school, and democratic government will

Croly's quite different contribution was to propose the strong elective executive as a formula for achieving both more effective democratic processes and more active and effective government. A suitably reformed Crolyan polity (he had the individual American states in mind) would have the following features: One person, elected in a nonpartisan election and subject to recall, would serve as chief executive, and as such would have "full responsibility, both for the management of state business and the enforcement of state laws," the authority to appoint top administrative officials and the right to appeal directly to the electorate on government measures rejected by the legislature.[15] The executive would be elected on the basis of programmatic promises: "When he announced his candidacy, he would have to seek the support of the electorate by making certain specific promises. He would come into office with his work cut out for him and with a yardstick of success or failure definitely established. The electorate would be intrusting the power not to a party, nor to a system, but to a man."[16] The executive was to act as a policy leader and not just as an agent of the electorate: "Public opinion requires to be aroused, elicited, informed, developed, concentrated and brought to an understanding of its own dominant purposes. The value of executive leadership consists in its peculiar serv-

---

become really a government of discussion" (p. 667). In the revised and abridged edition of his volume on the United States, published in 1910, the only pertinent reform of the period that Ostrogorski expressed enthusiasm for was the two-stage nonpartisan election. See Moisei Ostrogorski, *Democracy and the Party System in the United States: A Study in Extra-Constitutional Government* (New York: Macmillan, 1910), pp. 432-436, 441-444. At this point it may have been difficult to see what the referendum and partisan primary would amount to once they became routinized. The most useful treatment of Ostrogorski's views on parties is Austin Ranney, *The Doctrine of Responsible Party Government* (Urbana: University of Illinois Press, 1962), ch. 7.

[15] The features listed here are drawn from Croly, *Progressive Democracy*, chs. 13-17, quotation here at p. 294; and Croly, *The Promise of American Life* (New York: Dutton, 1963), ch. 11. (*Promise* was first published in 1909.) Croly tailors his strong executive plan to fit a government at a subnational level, and suggests it would raise a danger of usurpation at the national level. See Croly, *Promise*, p. 332. Demagogues might occasionally win election as executives at the American state level and "do a great deal of harm," but "could not really damage the foundations of the state" (*ibid.*, p. 340). A discussion of Croly's views on parties appears in Ranney, *Doctrine of Responsible Party Government*, ch. 8.

[16] Croly, *Progressive Democracy*, p. 297. "The chief executive, when supported by public opinion, would become a veritable 'Boss'; and he would inevitably be the sworn enemy of unofficial 'Bosses' who now dominate local politics. . . . The logic of his whole position would convert him into an enemy of the machine, in so far as the machine was using any governmental function for private, special, or partisan purposes. The real 'Boss' would destroy the sham 'Bosses' " (Croly, *Promise*, p. 340). This brings to mind James Michael Curley.

iceability not merely as the agent of a prevailing public opinion, but also as the invigorator and concentrator of such opinion."[17] The executive was also to be a particularly effective popular instrument by virtue of being a human being rather than something else (such as, perhaps, a party, an official institution, or an abstraction): "A vague popular aspiration or a crude and groping popular interest often requires incarnation in a single man, in order to reach a preliminary understanding of its own meaning and purposes." Moreover: "In the case of less sophisticated people, such as compose the majority of a modern democracy, no program is likely to be politically effective unless it is temporarily associated with an effective personality."[18]

In addition there would be a strong nonpartisan legislature, by nature "a talking body, a battleground of opinion," constructed in the spirit (though not by the letter) of J. S. Mill's proportional representation so as to give voice to a diversity of views: "Public opinion in all its vital phases would be aroused and would obtain appropriate means of expression."[19] Legislative support for the executive's proposals would take the shape of freshly forming coalitions issue by issue. There would be a strong, permanent civil service: "The conscientious and competent administrator of an official social program would need and be entitled to the same kind of independence and authority in respect to public opinion as that which has been traditionally granted to a common law judge."[20] The overall result would be a government notably active by nineteenth-century American standards, yet a producer of policies grounded ultimately in public opinion—in a nice phrase, "the decisive temporary result of widespread popular fermentation."[21]

This assemblage of ideas has much in common with Woodrow Wilson's views on reforming American politics at the national level as recently interpreted by James W. Ceaser.[22] Wilson's fixed objectives in his long career as a theorist, according to Ceaser, were "to establish a greater capacity in the government for change through dynamic leadership and to make the relationship between the leader and public opinion the focal point of the new system."[23] When closely analyzed, Wil-

---

[17] Croly, *Progressive Democracy*, p. 304.

[18] *Ibid.*, pp. 313-314.

[19] *Ibid.*, pp. 319, 318.

[20] *Ibid.*, p. 361.

[21] *Ibid.*, p. 283.

[22] James W. Ceaser, *Presidential Selection: Theory and Development* (Princeton: Princeton University Press, 1979), ch. 4 ("Woodrow Wilson and the Origin of the Modern View of Presidential Selection").

[23] *Ibid.*, p. 171.

son's well-known sales pitch for improved American parties offers a surprising product. Party disappears as organization, constraint, persisting creed or mass loyalty and reemerges (every four years) as "an instrument at the leader's command helping to further the principles and programs for which he had won approval in his direct appeal to the people."[24] This is a plan with little more continuity in it than Ostrogorski's.

The Croly (or Croly-Wilson?) model is interesting in a particular way: its components and overall design are such that it might have been conceived specifically as a remedy for the problems of traditional American party organization. It responds to the logics of the links postulated earlier between traditional organization and relatively inactive government (all but the one dealing with interest groups). Croly's executive office carries a powerful inherent impulse to generate government activity; his executive, legislative, and electoral processes serve as nonstop generators of issues; his administrative service seems to be standard twentieth-century bureaucracy; and his political culture, geared to perceiving problems and seeking solutions through government action, brings to mind John Dewey.

Croly's model makes demands on reality that are difficult or impossible to meet—notably on the public's knowledge and attention—but in general its features map rather well onto American twentieth-century political experience. In particular the one-person executive, who draws strength from electoral relations and assumes a basic responsibility for achieving policy ends by assembling and working through an "executive-centered coalition," has served as a paradigmatic (though not the only) energizer of American government at all levels during this century. That the role need not necessarily be partisan is exemplified in the important current array of black big-city mayors, whose electoral successes and governing activity have had little to do with parties.[25]

[24] *Ibid.*, p. 174. "Wilson's 'party' seems . . . to be a temporary organization—perhaps under a traditional party label—that is 'owned' by a particular leader and that exists to promote that leader's interest. Moreover, the real basis of the leader's claim on the party rests not with his acceptance by members of the ongoing organization and not even perhaps with its traditional adherents, but with the mass of voters who take part in the primaries" (pp. 198-199).

[25] That is, parties have not elevated them to power, defined their programs, constituted their supporting coalitions, provided their chief opposition, supplied them with important governing resources, or for that matter preoccupied political scientists who study them. On executive-centered coalitions see Robert A. Dahl, *Who Governs? Democracy and Power in an American City* (New Haven: Yale University Press, 1961), p. 186 and ch. 17.

This was not a well-developed role in the nineteenth century.[26] It seems to have come into its own around 1900 in the Presidency of Theodore Roosevelt, the governorships of such figures as Robert La Follette in Wisconsin, Albert Cummins in Iowa, and Charles Evans Hughes in New York, and reform mayoralties ranging from Seth Low's in New York (based on an upper-bracket electoral coalition) through Hazen Pingree's in Detroit, Thomas L. Johnson's in Cleveland, and Samuel M. "Golden Rule" Jones's in Toledo (pitched to lower-income electorates in drives to enact social programs and to regulate or take over public-service industries).[27]

In general the Progressive reform package, with its strong executives, civil service standards, independent legislators, multiple access routes to government (as in referendum processes), and unmediated relations between politicians and electorates, has probably *fit* actual American

[26] The Civil War and Reconstruction aside. See James Willard Hurst, *The Growth of American Law: The Law-Makers* (Boston: Little, Brown, 1950), pp. 400-405. On state governors: "The Civil War emergency produced strong war governors in some Northern states. But this was an abnormal situation. It was not until the last quarter of the nineteenth century that the stage was set for a lasting trend toward a stronger executive, and it was after 1900 that the governor definitely shouldered responsibility for a legislative program" (p. 402).

[27] The Roosevelt candidacy of 1912 was of course especially appealing to Croly: "Roosevelt progressivism can fairly be charged with many ambiguities, but in one essential respect its meaning is unmistakable. Its advocates are committed to a drastic reorganization of the American political and economic system, to the substitution of a frank social policy for the individualism of the past, and to the realization of this policy, if necessary, by the use of efficient governmental instruments" (*Progressive Democracy*, p. 15). On assertive governors of the time see Wiebe, *Search for Order*, pp. 176-181. For general discussions of the reform mayors who attracted lower-income electorates see Schiesl, *Politics of Efficiency*, pp. 58-60, 81-85; Charles N. Glaab and A. Theodore Brown, *A History of Urban America* (London: Macmillan, 1967), pp. 213-215. On Pingree: Melvin G. Holli, *Reform in Detroit: Hazen S. Pingree and Urban Politics* (New York: Oxford University Press, 1969). On Jones: Donald E. Pitzer, "Revivalism and Politics in Toledo: 1899," *Northwest Ohio Quarterly* 41(Winter 1968-69), 13-24. Mayor George Ellis of Grand Rapids certainly belongs in the same category. See Anthony R. Travis, "Mayor George Ellis: Grand Rapids Political Boss and Progressive Reformer," *Michigan History* 58(1974), 101-130. Mayor Mark Fagan of Jersey City is also sometimes included. See Eugene M. Tobin, "The Progressive as Politician: Jersey City, 1896-1907," *New Jersey History* 91(1973), 5-23. Traditional party organizations do not seem to have amounted to much in the political environments of Detroit, Grand Rapids, or Toledo around the turn of the century. They seem to have been somewhat more important in Cleveland, and much more important in Jersey City. Of these five mayors, sometimes called "reform bosses," Fagan had the least success in building and holding an electoral coalition, and the opposition he ran into in both parties' Hudson County organizations helps to explain why.

twentieth-century electoral politics as well as any other well thought out model—any party model, for example—though, like party models, it remains substantially an idealization. Its components remain available as recourses, as in the Democratic party's reform of its national nominating processes after 1968. And it seems to enjoy substantial public support: outside political science circles such things as independent politicians, direct primaries, civil service rules, and referendum processes are widely thought to be a good idea.

Progressive reform, then, supplied the century's first major strategy for energizing government in an environment of patronage-based parties. Three decades later the New Deal supplied a second and strikingly different strategy. Franklin Roosevelt, taking the offensive as an otherwise highly satisfactory Crolyite executive, approached the still-flourishing stratum of organizations at lower levels not as obstacles that needed to be removed but as possible allies to be mobilized. This considerable turnabout (prefigured in the Wilson administration) issued from a kind of chemical-bonding potential between political actors at different levels in the American federal system. Whatever they amounted to at the local level, it became evident that traditional party organizations could agreeably supply strength to, as well as draw benefits from, politicians who built and tended coalitions at the national level. This contributed a key combinatorial element to the Democratic party's formula for presidential leadership from the mid-1930s through the late 1960s.

This is not to say that the organizations had much to do with bringing about the New Deal or Roosevelt's Presidency in the first place. Democratic presidential nominating in 1932 presented, among other things, a basic reform-vs.-regulars cleavage that had been familiar since the 1870s—a generalizing of New York's widely appreciated Democratic cleavage to the national level—which often favored Eastern blue-ribbon candidates who opposed party organizations in general though especially Tammany Hall.[28] All three Democratic Presidents during

---

[28] Though traditional organizations backed some of the major blue-ribbon candidates at important earlier points in their careers. Tammany backed Samuel J. Tilden and Grover Cleveland for governor in 1874 and 1882 respectively, then in both cases after living with them in office for two years sent trainloads of delegates to national conventions to try to stop their presidential drives. See Alfred Connable and Edward Silberfarb, *Tigers of Tammany: Nine Men Who Ran New York* (New York: Holt, Rinehart and Winston, 1967), pp. 190-191; Allan Nevins, *Grover Cleveland: A Study in Courage* (New York: Dodd, Mead, 1958), pp. 103-104, 150. James Smith, Jr., head of New Jersey's Essex County organization, engineered Wilson's nomination for governor in 1910, expecting that Wilson would carry in the ticket, cooperate with the organization afterward and support Smith for a Senate seat. Once in office Wilson broke with the organi-

these decades—Cleveland, Wilson, and Roosevelt—won their initial nominations over strong Tammany opposition as leaders of coalitions bound together partly by anti-Tammany sentiment. In Cleveland's case, succinctly stated, "The Stop-Cleveland movement was doomed to failure when a Cleveland nominator said of his champion: 'They love him most for the enemies he has made.' All eyes followed his gesture toward the Tammany delegation."[29] Wilson entered presidential politics as an antimachine governor—"The failure of Wilson's managers to win the support of the dominant organizations in most of the states was a result . . . of the fact that Wilson simply had little to offer machine politicians"—and derived significant profit at the 1912 nominating convention from having Tammany against him (though the Chicago and Indiana organizations finally helped to raise him over the two-thirds mark needed to win).[30] Franklin Roosevelt put together an emphatically Bryanesque coalition in winning nomination in 1932. His only important machine support came from Ed Flynn in the Bronx and Ed Crump in Memphis (Al Smith was of course Roosevelt's chief opponent), though the independent Irish mayors of Boston (James Michael Curley) and Detroit (Frank Murphy), both fresh from leading a campaign for federal relief funds, were aboard.[31] Roosevelt had backed

zation and backed somebody else for the Senate, whereupon the Essex County organization and also the rising Hague organization in Hudson County did what they could to derail Wilson's presidential cause in 1912. See Arthur S. Link, *Wilson: The Road to the White House* (Princeton: Princeton University Press, 1947), chs. 5, 7-9, 12. Tom Platt engineered Theodore Roosevelt's nomination for the New York governorship in 1898, seeing him as an attractive candidate, then two years later joined with Matt Quay in the well-known maneuver of Roosevelt into the Vice Presidency, in Platt's case to get him out of New York. See Harold F. Gosnell, *Boss Platt and His New York Machine* (Chicago: University of Chicago Press, 1924), pp. 93-109, 117-123. Quay needed an image overhaul at home in Pennsylvania: "As the champion of the hero of San Juan Hill and an associate of a prominent governor who had developed a reputation for 'honesty in government,' Quay emerged from the [1900] convention as one of its most popular personages, and his home state public was indeed impressed. Several years later he laughingly told Roosevelt that he (Roosevelt) had been responsible for his return to the Senate in 1901: 'When John Wanamaker and others were trying to defeat me, I declared for you for Vice President. Then the anti-Quay movement collapsed.' " James A. Kehl, *Boss Rule in the Gilded Age: Matt Quay of Pennsylvania* (Pittsburgh: University of Pittsburgh Press, 1981), p. 229. Of course nobody expected Roosevelt to accede to the Presidency.

[29] Connable and Silberfarb, *Tigers of Tammany*, p. 195. The importance of the cleavage is confirmed in Nevins, *Grover Cleveland*, ch. 10.

[30] On Wilson's campaign for nomination in 1912: Link, *Wilson: The Road to the White House*, chs. 12, 13, quotation at p. 405.

[31] In general on the Roosevelt coalition: Lyle W. Dorsett, *Franklin D. Roosevelt and the City Bosses* (Port Washington, N.Y.: Kennikat, 1977), ch. 1; Frank Freidel, *Franklin D. Roosevelt: The Triumph* (Boston: Little, Brown, 1956), chs. 19, 20; James A. Farley,

away from attacking machines after an assault on Tammany early in his career, but his campaign leadership in 1932 played the Tammany card for the last time. "We did not hesitate to make it clear that Tammany was opposed to Roosevelt," Flynn later wrote. "This helped him tremendously with many of the delegates throughout the country."[32] The newly assembled Chicago machine had an opportunity to tip the outcome to Roosevelt at the 1932 convention, but its leader Anton J. Cermak refused to assume the role. The deciding votes issued from a Hearst move in California instead.[33] Chicago itself, the site of the convention, is said to have been "enemy ground [for the Roosevelt cause], and the hostility was as open, as crude, and as massive as that city's political reputation would have led anyone to expect."[34] Roosevelt very clearly came into presidential politics from the anti-organization side.

Behind the Ballots: The Personal History of a Politician (New York: Harcourt Brace, 1938), ch. 2. On Curley and Murphy: Sidney Fine, *Frank Murphy: The Detroit Years* (Ann Arbor: University of Michigan Press, 1975), chs. 13, 16; Charles H. Trout, *Boston, the Great Depression, and the New Deal* (New York: Oxford University Press, 1977), ch. 5. It was long accepted that Kansas City's Pendergast machine also supported Roosevelt at the Chicago convention, but this has recently come into question. See J. Christopher Schnell, "Missouri Progressives and the Nomination of F.D.R.," *Missouri Historical Review* 68(1974), 269-279.

[32] On Roosevelt's early tangle with Tammany: James MacGregor Burns, *Roosevelt: The Lion and the Fox* (New York: Harcourt, Brace and World, 1956), pp. 35-41. Flynn's full statement: "Because Tammany was not popular with the country at large, and because in this instance the Roosevelt people were the underdogs [in New York state in 1932], we decided to get as much advantage as possible in that situation. We did not hesitate to make it clear that Tammany was opposed to Roosevelt. This helped him tremendously with many of the delegates throughout the country. We tried further to bring out quietly that most of the decent Democrats in New York were supporting Roosevelt. With this idea in mind, we resolved in no way to contest anything that Tammany wished to do. We wanted to show the rest of the country that Tammany was riding rough-shod over the plain people of New York. I believe that we accomplished this, and that our tactics did more to hold the delegates together—that is, the delegates from all over the country who inclined toward the Roosevelt candidacy—than any other factor" (Edward J. Flynn, *You're the Boss* [New York: Viking, 1947], p. 102).

[33] On the Chicago machine's nonrole see Alex Gottfried, *Boss Cermak of Chicago: A Study of Political Leadership* (Seattle: University of Washington Press, 1962), pp. 297-307. Cermak is said to have stayed with Smith to the end for three reasons: (a) worries about alienating pro-Smith Irish elements in his organization, (b) on a personal plane he liked Smith better than Roosevelt, (c) he thought Smith was more strongly opposed to Prohibition—"Cermak's interest in national policy apparently did not extend beyond this question" (*ibid.*, p. 297). On the California move see W. A. Swanberg, *Citizen Hearst: A Biography of William Randolph Hearst* (New York: Bantam, 1963), pp. 515-518. Hearst had an important place in the John Nance Garner cause, having engineered a Garner victory in the California primary.

[34] R. G. Tugwell, *The Brains Trust* (New York: Viking, 1968), p. 241.

But reaching the Presidency was one thing, using and keeping it another. After he took office Roosevelt came to a quick understanding
with the local Democratic organizations on the terms of support downward in federal money and jobs in exchange for loyalty upward in elections, national conventions, and Congress. This easy and basic accommodation was evidently honored and valued by Democratic Presidents
for three decades.[35] Roosevelt worked around Tammany (which made
political sense in 1933) but otherwise turned the Pendergast, Hague,
Crump, and Kelly-Nash machines into pillars of his administration by
giving out appointments and subsidies—notably WPA money. Federal
support funded, among other things, Pendergast's pick and shovel armies and most of Hague's medical center.[36] Chicago's Ed Kelly took the
initiative in organizing the draft-Roosevelt movement in 1940 and during the Democratic convention (again in Chicago) generated enthusiasm from the galleries that matched the hostility of 1932.[37] The Chicago connection came to take on special importance, offering as it did,
from the White House standpoint, the great virtue of issue-blind support. There was little ideological constraint. It could be called on for
nearly anything, from much-needed support in carrying Henry Wallace's nomination for Vice President in 1940 to backing the Vietnam
War in the 1960s.[38]

The upward transformative effect here is quite interesting. Evidently
through the medium of exchange relations, party organizations geared
on the whole to relatively inactive government at the bottom came to
give vital support to hyperactive government building a welfare state at
the top.[39] One implication is that the country's progressive-liberal pol-

---

[35] The evidence is best on Roosevelt. Woodrow Wilson prefigured this arrangement,
though city machines played a less prominent role in his Presidency than they did later in
Roosevelt's. Once in office in 1913 Wilson abandoned his insurgent supporters over most
of the country, came to terms even with Tammany and agreeably relinquished the New
Jersey party to the Essex and Hudson organizations. See Arthur S. Link, *Wilson: The
New Freedom* (Princeton: Princeton University Press, 1956), pp. 48-53, 157-173.

[36] The authoritative source is Dorsett, *Franklin D. Roosevelt and the City Bosses*, chs.
3-8. See also Flynn, *You're the Boss*, pp. 145-146; Charles W. Van Devander, *The Big
Bosses* (New York: Howell, Soskin, 1944), ch. 13; Gene Delon Jones, "The Origin of the
Alliance Between the New Deal and the Chicago Machine," *Journal of the Illinois State
Historical Society* 67(1974), 253-274. The alliance with Pendergast came to an end during Roosevelt's second term, after some well-publicized election fraud weakened Pendergast's position in Missouri.

[37] Dorsett, *Franklin D. Roosevelt and the City Bosses*, pp. 94-97.

[38] On the 1940 convention see Flynn, *You're the Boss*, pp. 157-158.

[39] A similar general pattern involving levels of government (though evidently not exchange relations) appears in the early twentieth century: many leaders of city machines,
probably not enthusiasts of effective government regulatory activity in their cities, none-

icy agenda of the mid-1930s through the mid-1960s enjoyed systematically better support, on balance, among Washington's governing
elite (the support was purchased in part from below) than it did among
elites at lower levels as they acted on their home grounds. Harold F.
Gosnell noted such a disparity in writing about the Chicago machine's
unwillingness to fund relief during the early years of the Depression:
"One of the curious characteristics of the American form of government is that the local representatives of the party which put these [New
Deal] national policies into effect [as in distributing federal relief
money] operated in accordance with an entirely different political philosophy from that of the nation-wide leaders."[40] Another contemporary analyst wrote of the Hague machine: " 'Dictator' Hague's personal representative in Congress is Mrs. Mary T. Norton, chairman of
the House Committee on Labor. While Hague's police, prosecutors
and judges were driving CIO representatives out of Jersey City, Mrs.
Norton was leading the fight for the Wages and Hours Bill, and was
making her committee a burying ground for anti-labor legislative proposals of all sorts."[41]

E. E. Schattschneider presented a more general analysis in his 1942
work, *Party Government*:

> The parties have a public personality interested in public issues
> and a private personality interested in private objectives reflected
> in the aims and purposes of the state and local machines. Histori-
> cally, the local bosses, interested almost exclusively in patronage,
> have made concessions to the public personality of the parties re-
> luctantly. . . . The distinction between the public and private atti-
> tudes of the party is fundamental. Moreover, it is possible in nearly
> every instance to write the word "central" or "national" in place
> of the word "public" and the word "local" in place of the word
> "private" throughout this discussion without injury to the truth.[42]

theless backed social regulation at the *state* level. Perhaps the position-taking benefits of
doing this outweighed the perceived short- or middle-range costs, given the stage (legislation rather than actual administration) and level (state not local). On Tammany Hall in
1911-1914 under Charles Murphy: J. Joseph Huthmacher, *Senator Robert F. Wagner
and the Rise of Urban Liberalism* (New York: Atheneum, 1971), ch. 3. On the Vares in
Pennsylvania: Sam Bass Warner, *The Private City: Philadelphia in Three Periods of Its
Growth* (Philadelphia: University of Pennsylvania Press, 1968), pp. 217-218. In general:
John D. Buenker, *Urban Liberalism and Progressive Reform* (New York: Scribner's,
1973).

[40] Harold F. Gosnell, *Machine Politics: Chicago Model* (Chicago: University of Chicago Press, 1968), pp. 1-8, quotation at p. 7.

[41] Van Devander, *The Big Bosses*, p. 316.

[42] E. E. Schattschneider, *Party Government* (Westport, Conn.: Greenwood Press,
1970), pp. 136-137 and more generally ch. 6.

It is worth noting that the politics associated with traditional party organization may help to explain not only why New Deal through Great Society activity came to be located at the national level, but also why there may have existed a societal demand for locating it there. Why not locate it at state and local levels instead? The case in a nutshell is that the La Follettes' "Wisconsin idea" and comparably ambitious programmatic undertakings in some other states were hard to carry out in environments such as Pennsylvania's; this may have contributed to a diffuse twentieth-century pressure for action in Washington.

On the familiar question of whether the New Deal strengthened or weakened city machines, without much doubt it strengthened the Democratic machines in the short run (though not Tammany Hall, and Kansas City's Pendergast eventually went to prison).[43] Federal relief money distributed without much constraint shored up old organizations and helped build powerful new ones—in Pittsburgh, Providence, and Lackawanna County (Scranton), for example.[44] But evidently there was a long-run weakening effect too. New social insurance programs, in particular, which were effectively insulated from paronage politics by provisions enacted in 1939-1940, served as models for later federal grant-in-aid programs and also as influential vanguard zones of professionalism in state and local public sectors.[45] Whether social insurance

[43] Dorsett makes the case persuasively in *Franklin D. Roosevelt and the City Bosses*, chs. 3, 5-8.

[44] For an exceptionally good account of federal relief money fueling a new machine, see Kathleen Purcell Munley, "From Minority to Majority: A Study of the Democratic Party in Lackawanna County, 1920-1950" (Ph.D. dissertation, Lehigh University, 1981), part 3, ch. 3 ("Patronage and Power: The Democrats and the New Deal Relief Agencies"). "In Providence the New Deal helped to create a political machine where none existed before. City and relief jobs were utilized to weld the various racial and ethnic groups to the Democratic party." Norma L. Daoust, "The Perils of Providence: Rhode Island's Capital City during the Depression and New Deal" (Ph.D. dissertation, University of Connecticut, 1982), pp. 299-300, 461-463, quotation at p. 461.

[45] "There were basically two different kinds of grants made during the New Deal. One was essentially a relief type grant designed to quickly get assistance to needy individuals. While part of the grants-in-aid system, any national standards included in these grant programs tended to be loosely enforced, if at all. . . . The second, most important and far reaching, type of grant-in-aid of the New Deal period was the permanent, administratively articulated program"—notably the several subsidiary grant programs of the Social Security Act of 1935 (Earl M. Baker et al., *Federal Grants, the National Interest and State Response: A Review of Theory and Research* [Philadelphia: Center for the Study of Federalism, 1974], p. 31). On the effects of planning and merit-personnel requirements lodged against the states in federal grant-in-aid programs: "According to [Deil S.] Wright, the major effects of these criteria have been to catalyze the governor's political power in administrative and budgetary processes, and to create a major new political force in state and for that matter local politics—administrative bureaucracies and their public service professions. Conversely, grants-in-aid have reduced the influence in state politics of political party organizations and state legislatures" (p. 46).

undermined machines by another often-discussed route—by taking over welfare "functions" the machines had performed—is less clear. To demonstrate it would require evidence beyond anecdotes on the actual welfare activities of earlier machines (some serious analysis is in order), and perhaps also an investigation of how such activities were pursued, if at all, in the many cities that had no machines.

City machines were of course not the only major instrument Roosevelt reached for in building an organizational base for the New Deal. Comparably influential and a source of ideological drive in addition was the CIO—a new incentive structure harnessed to the Democratic party in the 1930s that brings to mind Theodore Roosevelt's reach for Progressive activism in 1912 as a supplement to the normal American incentives to work in politics.[46] The result of Franklin Roosevelt's maneuvering, if one thinks in terms of structure and takes into account associated organizations as well as parties proper, was a Democratic party in the 1940s and 1950s made up largely of machines and unions. A striking and unusual asymmetry had come about between the Democratic and Republican parties in the *kinds* of organizations they had in their national mixes of party and associated structures. (In a relation of perfect symmetry the mixes would have the same amounts of such ingredients as machines, "amateur" clubs, other forms of party organization, newspapers, and politically active unions and corporations.) The continued Republican leanings of most corporations and newspapers provided familiar elements of structural asymmetry between the parties during and after the New Deal, but it was new for the Democrats to rely so heavily on unions or for city machines to cluster so disproportionately on the Democratic side. Machines in the especially large cities, following switches in party management in Pittsburgh (in the mid-1930s) and Philadelphia (in 1951), became an entirely Democratic phenomenon for the first time. If one considers solely the clienteles of machines and unions (it is another matter whose interests were

[46] Looked at as an organizational array, the New Deal coalition of the mid-1930s included other instruments besides the CIO that were outside the Democratic party proper: the La Guardia mayoralty, New York's American Labor party, Minnesota's Farmer-Labor party, and Wisconsin's Progressive party. For brief statements on Roosevelt's dealings with the Minnesota and Wisconsin parties see Donald R. McCoy, *Angry Voices: Left-of-Center Politics in the New Deal Era* (Lawrence: University of Kansas Press, 1958), pp. 17, 49, 71. For a full treatment of the Wisconsin relationship see John E. Miller, *Governor Philip F. La Follette, the Wisconsin Progressives, and the New Deal* (Columbia: University of Missouri Press, 1982). On CIO activity in electoral politics under the late Roosevelt, Truman, and early Eisenhower administrations, see James C. Foster, *The Union Politic: The CIO Political Action Committee* (Columbia: University of Missouri Press, 1975).

being served), there was a better case in 1951 for the existence of class-related structural symmetry between the American parties than Duverger writing at the time thought. The asymmetry narrowed some in the 1950s and 1960s as influential activist organizations arose at the local level in both parties; liberal Democratic and conservative Republican "amateur" groups resembled each other in structure however much they differed in views. By Johnson's Presidency the national Democratic party had three distinct organizational bases—machines, unions, and liberal activist groups.

It seems a good bet that the structural side of the Democrats' coalition from Roosevelt through Johnson was quite important. The coalition's organizational components and relations among them probably brought about distinctive effects in Presidential nominating contests, general elections, and the party's programmatic activity in Washington. To make a more specific political scientist's argument, such effects are probably underappreciated in analyses of the era's politics that treat parties as abstractions, voter coalitions as sufficient evidence of parties, government policies as likely to be deposits of election returns or conventionally measured public opinion, or voter preferences as exogenously caused (that is, caused outside the sphere of electoral politics). The innovatively organized CIO supplied critical campaign money to Democratic candidates, mobilized voters, and probably also crystallized, intensified, stimulated, or simply created a substantial amount of voter opinion. "Amateur" activists gave the party an ideological edge in the 1960s (as their counterparts did in the Republican party).

More pertinent here is the ability of traditional party organizations at the local level, through manipulation of blocs of voters, convention delegates, and members of Congress, to contribute influence to, or exercise influence in behalf of, Democratic Presidents and Presidential candidates. Two points are worth emphasizing about such transferable influence: First, it could evidently be converted in Washington into liberal policy leeway and often was, as argued earlier in the discussion of exchange relations. Second, it could evidently add up to significantly more than the population bases controlled by its donors would have seemed to allow. This is the phenomenon of amplified influence at an upper governmental level—achievable no doubt by a local organization's ability to manipulate blocs of people—which came to light earlier in the capacities of the Hague, Pendergast, Crump, Perez, and Parr machines to swing weight at the state level. It is best exemplified here in the influence of the Chicago machine at the national level. Succeeding Tammany Hall in the 1930s as the Democratic party's unquestionably front-ranking metropolitan organization, the Chicago machine took on roles Tammany had never assumed—as effective national power broker and loyal ally of Democratic Presidents. Traces of Chicago influence appear in accounts of national affairs from the 1930s on: in Roosevelt's reaching through the Kelly organization in 1937, for example, to help tip a close contest for Senate Democratic majority leader to Alben Barkley; in the already mentioned nominating of Roosevelt and Wallace for President and Vice President in 1940; in close, vital Democratic victories in Illinois in presidential balloting in 1948 and 1960 (very likely the results of at least resourceful voter mobilization, fraud aside); the organization's important role in the nominating of Stevenson in 1952, Kennedy in 1960, and Humphrey in 1968, and in giving the divisive 1968 convention much of its character; and later in 1976—after the Democratic party had lost much of its effectiveness as a national instrument—in Mayor Daley's authoritative declaration at a pertinent point that the Democratic nominating contest was over and Carter had won.[47] It must be true if he said so, the surprisingly widespread reaction seemed to be.

[47] On Barkley's election as Senate Democratic majority leader in 1937 (by a vote of 38 to 37) see Martha H. Swain, *Pat Harrison: The New Deal Years* (Jackson: University Press of Mississippi, 1978), pp. 158-159; James F. Byrnes, *All in One Lifetime* (New York: Harper, 1958), pp. 99-100; Grace Tully, *F.D.R., My Boss* (New York: Scribner's, 1949), p. 225. Did the Daley machine steal Illinois in November 1960 for Kennedy? It seems (according to a recent judicious treatment) that the machine was much more interested in the election for Cook County state's attorney than for President (the attorney's office controlled prosecutions), and that machine operatives almost certainly stole the state's attorney election and may actually have stolen Illinois in the Presidential column as a byproduct. But estimations of what the correct Presidential vote may have been give the result as about a tossup (down from Kennedy's official edge of about 9,000). The author's conclusion: "The fact is that no one can say certainly who 'really' carried Illinois in 1960." See Edmund F. Kallina, "The State's Attorney and the President: The Inside Story of the 1960 Presidential Election in Illinois," *Journal of American Studies* 12(1978), 147-160, quotation at p. 160. Again, as a general matter fraud was probably frosting on top of the organization's capacity to mobilize legitimate votes. On the Chicago and other organizations' role in nominating Kennedy in 1960 see Theodore H. White, *The Making of the President 1960* (New York: Atheneum, 1961), chs. 5, 6. Relations between machines and Presidents notwithstanding, Kennedy was the first and also last Democratic President (since the Civil War, anyway) to win a nonincumbent nomination by way of a coalition prominently including machines. On the Chicago connection under Johnson see Martin I. Elzy, "Illinois Viewed from the Johnson White House," *Journal of the Illinois State Historical Society* 74(1981), 2-16. The Chicago role of supporting Presidents (though not in this case liberal propensities) turned up at the Democrats' midterm convention in Memphis in 1978, where the Carter administration won a showdown vote against liberals on budgeting for social expenditures. Illinois came through, 72 to 0. "Illinois is always that way," the administration's floor manager explained. See Elizabeth B. Drew, "Reporter at Large," *The New Yorker*, January 15, 1979,

A major product of the Democrats' coalition extending from the New Deal through the Great Society was, of course, much of the American version of a welfare state. This came late and is modest and somewhat vulnerable by Northern European standards, probably in large part because neither a socialist movement nor an authoritative, nationally centered bureaucracy was available in this country to construct and defend the relevant programs. American patronage-based parties, which filled organizational niches that might have accommodated in different fashions both socialism and bureaucracy, may have affected the construction and functioning of a modern welfare state in two ways. First, there is a good case that city machines were essential to the programmatic efforts of Democratic Presidents from Roosevelt through Johnson. Second, it is nonetheless possible that traditional organizations have contributed in recent decades to the overall vulnerability of government programs by helping to keep alive a nineteenth-century view that government activity is inherently seedy and incompetent. Local administration of some federal programs, from the WPA in the 1930s through CETA in the 1970s, frequently aided the case.

It seems another good bet that the example of the New Deal coalition helped to stimulate a school of political analysis in the 1940s and 1950s that linked electoral processes to government in new ways. Models followed the evident political reality.[48] Parties themselves, rather than as in Croly's earlier analysis, victors over them, could assume a central theoretical role as energizers of government. Key and Schattschneider, crossing an assumption of party competition with a Beardian sensitiv-

---

pp. 80-81. The contemporary Chicago organization under Edward "Fast Eddie" Vrdolyak, no longer holding the mayoralty, evidently tried in 1983 to switch its traditional national dealing over to the Republican party, but the Reagan administration seems to have shown no interest. See " 'Fast Eddie' Pulls a Fast One," *Newsweek*, December 5, 1983, pp. 68, 71.

[48] The Committee on Political Parties of the American Political Science Association referred to changes in underlying political reality in its report in 1950 advocating renovation of American parties, *Toward a More Responsible Two-Party System* (New York: Rinehart, 1950): "If public esteem of the parties is much less high than it might be, the depressed state of their reputation has resulted in the main from their past indifference to broadly conceived public policy. This indifference has fixed in the popular mind the idea of spoils, patronage and plunder. It is hence not astonishing when one hears a chosen representative assert for the public ear that in his state 'people put principles above party.' Much of the agitation for nonpartisanship—despite the impossibility of nonpartisan organization on a national level—is rooted in the same attitudes. Bad reputations die hard, but things are no longer what they used to be. Certainly success in presidential campaigns today is based on broad national appeals to the widest possible constituencies. To a much greater extent than in the past, elections are won by influences and trends that are felt throughout the country" (p. 16).

ity to socioeconomic cleavage among voters, developed theories in which parties winning elections in suitable circumstances would do New Deal–like things. In Key's argument, rivalry induced by close electoral competition (specifically at the American state level) would cause winning parties to serve society's "have-nots."[49] In Schattschneider's argument, cleavages between parties—how they divide the electorate—made a difference by setting issue agendas and influencing government response. Pre–New Deal American politics, for example, in which Republicans were weak in the South and Democrats in the North, had an overall conservative tilt to it since "one-party politics tends strongly to vest political power in the hands of people who already have economic power." The less sectional New Deal cleavage of the 1930s and after diminished the tilt.[50]

How valid were these theoretical claims? It is easy to see how they could make sense in the climate of the national New Deal coalition, but it is another matter whether they have offered much explanatory power if applied to earlier, later, or subnational settings. What sorts of party or quasi-party structure, if any, did they require to do the work of mobilizing voters, organizing politicians, or activating governments as policy instruments? This is a particularly pertinent question to ask in connection with American subnational electoral settings of, say, the first two-thirds of the twentieth century, where the most elaborately organized parties were uncertain policy instruments, and the least organized—little more than arenas for competing candidate organizations, in parts of both North and South—were hardly instruments at all. Little has resulted from efforts following Key to find relationships between state policy patterns and levels of interparty competition—studies in which "party" and "competition" have ordinarily been indexed by using only general election returns.[51] The null results are understandable. For one thing there is no good reason to suppose, or evidence to suggest, that strong governors and mayors—probably the chief sources of state and local policy initiative during this century—have served in dis-

[49] V. O. Key, Jr., *Southern Politics in State and Nation* (New York: Vintage, 1949), ch. 14.

[50] E. E. Schattschneider, *The Semi-Sovereign People: A Realist's View of Democracy in America* (New York: Holt, Rinehart and Winston, 1960), especially ch. 5, quotation at p. 80.

[51] Key gave considerable attention to parties as organized entities in his statement on party competition in *Southern Politics* (ch. 14). The concern is also evident later in *American State Politics: An Introduction* (New York: Knopf, 1956), for example in his treatment of Massachusetts Democrats (pp. 154-163). Other scholars, however, quickly (and understandably, given data problems) reached for operational definitions of party competition dependent entirely on general election returns.

proportionate numbers or enjoyed disproportionate success in environments where Democrats and Republicans have run neck and neck in elections. On balance Croly, given his emphasis on the elective executive, is probably a better theoretical guide to twentieth-century state and local politics than the literature on party competition. What of Schattschneider's claim, directed in particular to the lasting "1896 system" that featured Republican and Democratic one-partyism in North and South respectively, that lack of party competition goes hand in hand with greater business influence in politics? At the state level at least, around the turn of the century, this is very likely false. A carefully framed study would probably turn up no such pattern, either longitudinally within states or synchronically at pertinent times across states. This is not what was going on.[52] Among other things, resourceful corporations seem to have had little difficulty exercising decisive influence in some of the toss-up states.[53] In general, patterns of electoral competition taken alone seem questionable guides to political reality; they convey too little information.

This chapter began with the Progressive era and can appropriately end with comments on the last decade and a half or so of comparably striking change in American party structure—also comparable in that relying on voter "realignments" to index change largely misses it. One clear conclusion is that local party organizations of several kinds have decisively declined since the 1960s in their ability to influence nominating processes for local, state, or national offices, bringing to an end

[52] In some states another kind of environmental change around 1900 did evidently alter the conduct of politics and generate a sense of corporate oppression. This was corporate consolidation that resulted in monopoly in a state's major industry. The clear instances are railroads in the mid-1890s in New Hampshire and copper just after 1900 in Montana. But this has nothing to do with patterns of party competition.

[53] There is the exquisite case (again) of West Virginia, in the late 1890s: "During 1898 and 1900, Davis, Elkins, and Scott consolidated their power within each political party in West Virginia and at the same time engaged in noisy and expensive two-party competition—within certain limits. The objectives of this bipartisan conservative leadership were less precisely defined than those of the B&O lobby or the Santa Fe ring [earlier ventures]. Its activities were less the result of conscious conspiracy across party lines—at least none has come to light—than of several individuals involved simply 'doing what came naturally' as businessmen and politicians. And the limits of partisan competition between the conservatives were sometimes overstepped in the excitement of campaigns. But regardless of these differences, the new West Virginia leadership worked in much the same way as had these earlier, more deliberately exploitative political arrangements." One of the limits sometimes overstepped: "As nearly as can be determined, it was tacitly understood within the Davis-Elkins family that family members belonging to one party would remain 'passive' if there were family candidates of the opposite party in the field" (John Alexander Williams, *West Virginia and the Captains of Industry* [Morgantown: West Virginia University Library, 1976], pp. 78, 87).

practices in some cases a century or more old.[54] The 1950s and 1960s were a golden age of sorts for American local organization. Traditional patronage organizations hung on quite successfully, Democratic and Republican "amateur" organizations appeared and thrived, and some especially strong municipal parties (as in San Antonio, Dallas, and Phoenix) enjoyed perfect or nearly perfect records of slating success. All these forms of structure fared very badly in the 1970s, largely losing out to candidate organizations that introduced capital-intensive campaigns. Most of the more important municipal parties faded or folded, the traditional organizations followed downward trajectories reported in the state sketches in Part I (though some are unquestionably still in business), and at least on the Democratic side (it is harder to tell on the Republican) the amateur organizations declined also. Democratic liberal or liberal-labor organizations suffered more than other structures from infighting in the late 1960s over Vietnam—a problem in Minnesota's Democratic-Farmer-Labor party, the California Democratic Council, and Houston's Harris County Democrats—but candidate organizations were a greater threat, as evidenced in the Manhattan clubs' inability to nominate a talented third-generation Wagner for borough president in 1977, and the Denver liberal organization's helplessness when confronted by Gary Hart's media campaign for a Senate nomination in 1974.[55] Organizational decay in the Democratic party has been masked somewhat by attention given to reforms in presidential nominating processes, but rules changes or no rules changes, it is hard to see how the party at the presidential level could have entered the 1980s as much more than an arena for competing candidate organizations. Who was still capable of packaging the delegates? In particular, it is hard to believe that local organizations of any sort could have shielded some key presidential primaries that local party regulars once

[54] Evidently the only type of local slating organization to rise and flourish in recent years is the neoradical type operating in California cities of appropriate demography. Also bucking the trend or at least unusual: Democratic nominating in Virginia, for statewide down through state legislative offices, shifted (by sizable proportions within office levels) from primaries to conventions in the 1970s. See Larry Sabato, *The Democratic Party Primary in Virginia: Tantamount to Election No Longer* (Charlottesville: University Press of Virginia, 1977), chs. 8-10.

[55] Alan Ware, "The End of Party Politics? Activist-Officeseeker Relationships in the Colorado Democratic Party," *British Journal of Political Science* 9(1979), on Denver, gives an especially good account of the decline in influence of an amateur Democratic organization. Organized liberal activists exercised considerable influence in the Denver party around 1970, but their vulnerability to technological incursion became evident when Hart won the 1974 Senate primary (and then election) by making an end-run around them. "Gary Hart's campaign in 1974 was perhaps the most self-consciously media-based one in Democratic party history in Colorado" (p. 248).

could control—notably in New York, New Jersey, Pennsylvania, and Illinois—from incursion by candidates' campaign technologies.

American electoral politics today, if compared with the 1960s and earlier, seems at once more distant (local organizational influence in nominating processes is down), more ideological (the appeals needed in direct-mail fund raising may be one cause), more capital-intensive (money has been replacing the mobilizing powers of patronage-based and membership organizations), and certainly more expensive. Its structural components now include aggressive, self-propelled candidate organizations, party organizations in general more simply instrumental (geared to winning November elections), proliferating political action committees (especially corporate), unprecedentedly elaborate and effective national party organization on the Republican side, and a Christian Right newly mobilized for politics—largely a mailing-list side product, it seems, of fundamentalist ministers' discovery of the potential of Sunday-morning television. At one remove from electoral politics, corporate-funded foundations and think tanks generate and circulate well-prepared assertions such as that government regulation is a mistake, reduction of high-bracket taxes produces economic growth, government social programs cause poverty, and religion and capitalism go hand in hand.[56] All three Democratic organizational bases of the 1960s (traditional party organizations, liberal activist groups, and labor unions) have deteriorated—unions have declined in membership, mobilizing power in elections, and influence in Congress as evidenced under Carter—and the party's procedures for nominating presidential candidates have not worked well since the 1960s.

The resulting overall pattern, which may in turn be engendering distinctive public policies, is a pronounced new asymmetry between Re-

---

[56] For a thought-provoking general treatment of the structural environment of the 1970s and 1980s see Thomas B. Edsall, *The New Politics of Inequality* (New York: W. W. Norton and Co., 1984). Frances FitzGerald, in "A Reporter at Large: A Disciplined, Charging Army," *The New Yorker*, May 18, 1981, at pp. 53-54, 59, 60, 63-64, 122, and 124 traces the Moral Majority to television's new "electric church." For an excellent discussion of the influence of Republican national oranizations in congressional elections in the early 1980s see Gary C. Jacobson and Samuel Kernell, "Party Organization and the Efficient Distribution of Congressional Campaign Resources: Republicans and Democrats in 1982," Caltech conference paper, February 1984. Two instances of recent scholarship that approach subnational party organization as largely an instrument for winning general elections (an emphasis that would have been inappropriate in discellent discussion of the influence of Republican national organizations in congressional club): James L. Gibson et al., "Assessing Party Organizational Strength," *American Journal of Political Science* 27(1983), 193-222; Timothy Conlan, Ann Martino, and Robert Dilger, "State Parties in the 1980s: Adaptation, Resurgence and Continuing Constraints," *Intergovernmental Perspective* 10(Fall 1984), 6-13.

publans and Democrats in their arrays of party and associated structures. The last time the party causes differed so decisively in structure
was around the middle of this century as a consequence of Roosevelt's
joining together machines and unions on the Democratic side, but this
time the innovation and advantage are on the Republican side.[57] Still,
the opportunities available in a politics unanchored in traditional local
organizations are just beginning to be explored.

[57] In some respects the Moral Majority as a mobilizing agent is an analogue of the aggressive, ideological CIO of the 1930s, 1940s, and 1950s: it aims at a mass population,
uses one of the two appeals conventional in Europe for building mass parties (that is, religion and class), adds ideological flavor to one of the American parties, and arouses considerable controversy. But the location of mobilization has shifted from the workplace to
television sermons and direct mail.

Appendices

Candidate Activity in Primaries

Taking into account the varying attractiveness of public offices, the idiosyncrasies of electoral systems, and the varying value of nominations for the elections in November (is a Republican assembly nomination worth much in this district?), what differences are there among American states in levels of candidate activity in primaries? To put it another way, what state-specific *propensities* to generate distinctive levels of candidate activity can be made to shine through actual state-specific primary data cluttered (so to speak) by particularities of office attractiveness, electoral system, and November nomination value? This is a question I sought to answer by assembling and manipulating data on candidate activity in primaries for all fifty states. More specifically, I used a mixture of election returns for U.S. House, state senate, and state assembly primaries for each state, drawn from at least two election years (1970 and 1968 if possible and often extending backward), covering in principle primaries of both parties (the returns were handled separately) in all instances of "open seats" (that is, neither party had an incumbent seeking renomination). Data for runoff states are for first-round primaries (not runoffs). *A party's primary for an office*, each generating in principle one *observation*, can in principle be unentered (zero candidates), uncontested (one candidate; or else a caucus, convention, or other process aside from a primary election confers the nomination), or contested (two or more candidates).[1] I coded each instance of a party's primary for an office in two ways: *number of candidates* (NCAND) who sought the nomination, which can take on values from zero through N; and *fragmentation of the vote* (FRAG), or $1 - \Sigma p_i^2$, where p_i is the proportion of the primary vote won by the ith

---

[1] All states decided at least some legislative nominations by primary in the late 1960s, but in a few states parties could decide how to nominate and sometimes steered clear of primaries, and in a few others legally prescribed convention, caucus, or assembly processes at least preceded and commonly foreclosed primaries. All nominations decided by processes not involving contests in primaries count here as instances of uncontested primaries.

candidate.[2] The fragmentation index cannot be calculated for unentered primaries. The national data set for NCAND includes 9,220 observations (a mean of 184 per state), and the data set for FRAG contains 8,376 observations (a mean of 168 per state, ranging from a low of 61 to a high of 339).

Consider a notional example. Democrat Smith retires in the Missouri 310th assembly district, producing an open seat. Four candidates enter the Democratic primary and draw respectively 400, 300, 200, and 100 votes. The Republicans nominate no one. The coding result: two NCAND observations, generating values of 4 for the Democrats and 0 for the Republicans; but only one FRAG observation, generating a reading of .7 for the Democrats.

Next I constructed two complicated regression equations, using as dependent variables NCAND in one (9,220 data readings) and FRAG in the other (8,376 readings). The independent variables (same in both equations) sort into four subsets: (a) *Attractiveness of office*, which includes variables for the salary of the office at stake in the primary (high salary may draw more candidates and fragment the vote more), size of the pertinent legislature and the level of personnel turnover in it, and dummy variables for U.S. House and state senate (positions in these perhaps differ in attractiveness from positions in a state assembly). (b) *Electoral structure*, which includes suitable variables for population size of district and to accommodate election at-large by "position" or in multimember districts (the last also required tailored definitions of NCAND and FRAG, as did Minnesota's and Nebraska's nonpartisan first-round legislative elections). (c) *November value of nomination*, in principle the pertinent party's vote percentage for the pertinent office in the last November election, entered in linear, quadratic, and also cubic formulations to allow for a predictable (and materializing) curvilinear relation between "November value" and either NCAND or FRAG: the difference between a district being 40 or 60 percent Democratic affects candidate activity more than the difference between being, say, 60 as opposed to 80 percent Democratic. It is the introduction of "November value" here that allows simultaneous inclusion of both parties' primary data for the same office in one equation's data set (even if one party is lopsidedly the majority party in the pertinent district). (d) *Dummy variables for the states*, more specifically one for each of forty-nine states; Connecticut is left out and serves as a baseline for the rest. Technically, a coefficient for any state gives the difference between its own level of candidate activity and Connecticut's. The important prod-

[2] The fragmentation index is taken from Douglas W. Rae and Michael Taylor, *The Analysis of Political Cleavages* (New Haven: Yale University Press, 1970), ch. 2.

ucts of these equations, again, are the forty-nine state coefficients. A list of these expresses, within the constraints of data, assumption, and measurement, for a range of legislative offices in the late 1960s, what differences there were among states in levels of candidate activity in their primaries—controlling as planned for varying attractiveness of public offices, idiosyncrasies of electoral systems, and varying November value of nominations.

Table A.1 provides the two equations' lists of state coefficients. Connecticut, with its artifactual zero scores, heads up both (that is, its propensity to generate candidate activity in primaries is uniquely low). The "number of candidates" equation produces a Connecticut-through-California dimension. California's coefficient of 2.11 means that (all else equal) a California legislative primary generates 2.11 more candidates than a Connecticut primary (again, Connecticut's many nomi-

Table A.1   Measures of Candidate Activity in Legislative Primaries

Number of Candidates		Fragmentation of Vote	
1. Connecticut	.00	1. Connecticut	.00
2. New York	.08	2. North Dakota	.05
3. Colorado	.17	3. Colorado	.05
4. North Dakota	.20	4. Rhode Island	.06
5. Delaware	.21	5. New York	.06
6. Utah	.21	6. Virginia	.07
7. Rhode Island	.22	7. Delaware	.10
8. Virginia	.24	8. Iowa	.11
9. Iowa	.31	9. Utah	.12
10. North Carolina	.32	10. South Dakota	.13
11. Arizona	.33	11. Idaho	.13
12. South Dakota	.34	12. North Carolina	.13
13. Georgia	.35	13. Maine	.14
14. South Carolina	.35	14. Georgia	.15
15. Maine	.37	15. New Jersey	.15
16. New Jersey	.41	16. Arkansas	.16
17. Idaho	.43	17. South Carolina	.16
18. Montana	.44	18. Illinois	.16
19. Arkansas	.44	19. Montana	.16
20. Wyoming	.44	20. Minnesota	.16
21. Kansas	.47	21. Kansas	.17
22. Hawaii	.51	22. Wyoming	.17
23. Tennessee	.52	23. Arizona	.17
24. Minnesota	.58	24. Vermont	.18

Table A.1   (cont.)

Number of Candidates		Fragmentation of Vote	
25. Illinois	.58	25. Pennsylvania	.19
26. Florida	.60	26. Hawaii	.20
27. Vermont	.61	27. Florida	.20
28. Texas	.62	28. Missouri	.20
29. Alabama	.63	29. Tennessee	.20
30. Pennsylvania	.74	30. Nevada	.21
31. Mississippi	.78	31. Alabama	.22
32. Oklahoma	.81	32. Oklahoma	.22
33. Washington	.83	33. Washington	.23
34. Alaska	.84	34. New Mexico	.24
35. New Mexico	.87	35. Texas	.26
36. Missouri	.88	36. New Hampshire	.28
37. Nevada	.94	37. Ohio	.28
38. West Virginia	.98	38. Nebraska	.28
39. Wisconsin	1.00	39. Wisconsin	.29
40. New Hampshire	1.02	40. Oregon	.29
41. Kentucky	1.14	41. Alaska	.30
42. Oregon	1.14	42. Mississippi	.31
43. Ohio	1.14	43. Massachusetts	.32
44. Nebraska	1.27	44. West Virginia	.32
45. Indiana	1.32	45. Kentucky	.33
46. Maryland	1.37	46. Maryland	.33
47. Massachusetts	1.42	47. Indiana	.34
48. Louisiana	1.57	48. Michigan	.36
49. Michigan	1.75	49. California	.39
50. California	2.11	50. Louisiana	.40

nations made without resort to primaries count as uncontested primaries). The "fragmentation of vote" equation generates an analogous Connecticut-through-Louisiana dimension; Louisiana leads (all else equal) in fragmentation of the primary vote. Some notable patterns in the lists: (a) States whose parties have official endorsing powers (at the legislative level) understandably score low in candidate activity: see Connecticut, Rhode Island, North Dakota, Colorado, and Utah, which provide for conventions, assemblies, ballot asterisks, etc., and also Virginia, whose parties can choose to nominate by convention and often do. New York's uniquely burdensome signature requirement for prospective candidates probably cuts down on primary competition (though in general variables for fee and signature requirements do not perform well in equations explaining candidate activity). (b) The Southern states vary among themselves nearly as much as the country as a whole varies in candidate activity; the range runs from very low in Virginia through very high in Louisiana with most states not far from the national median. (c) States with high TPO scores also differ a great deal among themselves in candidate activity, several ranking either very low or very high. "Factional" states in particular cluster in the very high range (West Virginia, Kentucky, Maryland, Indiana, and also Louisiana, though Missouri is somewhat lower).

Three of these patterns (and one other) emerge in appropriate equations. Table A.2 reports the results of two equations that use, respectively, the "number of candidates" and "fragmentation of vote" coefficients ($N = 50$ in each case) of Table A.1 as dependent variables. What explains variation among the states in these extracted measures of candidate activity? (a) *Official processes*, a variable that suitably accommodates official party endorsing powers of various sorts, decisively

Table A.2 State Levels of Candidate Activity in Primaries as a Function of Organizational Form

Independent Variable	Regression Coefficient	Standard Error	t Ratio
Number of candidates as dependent variable:			
Official processes	−189	50	−3.77***
% population SMSA	.673	.216	3.12***
TPO score (regular)	−92.7	42.8	−2.17**
TPO score (factional)	99.2	48.5	2.04**
Constant	466		
$N = 50$			
Adj. R^2 = .428			
Fragmentation of vote as dependent variable:			
Official processes	−45.9	9.7	−4.76***
% population SMSA	.091	.042	2.19**
TPO score (regular)	−19.2	8.2	−2.34**
TPO score (factional)	24.3	9.3	2.60**
Constant	182		
$N = 50$			
Adj. R^2 = .516			

NOTE: Two asterisks indicate a .01 level of significance; three indicate a .001 level. SMSA stands for "standard metropolitan statistical area."

depresses candidate activity. (b) *Percent population SMSA*, which gives the proportion of each state's population living in standard metropolitan statistical areas in 1970, enhances candidate activity. The more urban the population, the heavier the candidate activity—a result that squares with the generally low scores of rural states in the South, plains, and northern mountain region in Table A.1. (c) *TPO score (regular)*, a variable that registers TPO scores for monopolistic but not factional states (New Jersey scores 5, but Maryland like California scores 1), significantly depresses candidate activity; but (d) *TPO score (factional)*, which registers TPO scores for factional but not monopolistic states (Maryland scores 5, but New Jersey like California scores 1), significantly enhances it. Regular organization evidently cuts down on candidate activity, but factional organization drives it up.[3] A relation emerges after all between organization and candidate activity, though it is more complex than one might expect.

A final set of relations can be teased from the state coefficients. "Number of candidates" used as a variable correlates very highly, of course, with "fragmentation of vote"—both are measures of candidate activity for each state based more or less on the same data. But they stop short of mapping perfectly onto each other, and NCAND can be entered in combination with other variables to *explain* FRAG (again in equations of $N = 50$ states). NCAND accounts for the lion's share of the variance in FRAG (knowing the number of candidates goes a long way toward predicting fragmentation of the vote), but additional independent variables can be introduced using the logic: given numbers of candidates entering primaries, what considerations are likely to push their vote shares toward or away from equality? Table A.3 is the product of such an equation explaining "fragmentation of vote." The explanatory power of the *number of candidates* variable can be seen. The variable *official processes*, used earlier, pushes vote shares significantly toward *inequality*. (It produces a sturdy coefficient with a minus sign.)

---

[3] An indirect confirmation of the latter effect: Jewell found, in comparing patterns in Louisiana assembly districts, that in the elections of 1948-1956 "there was more [primary] competition in the races involving slates, and throughout the five elections [of 1948-1964] the levels of competition were higher in districts where slating was a well-established practice. We conclude that the frequent use of legislative slates and alliances between legislative and gubernatorial candidates probably helps to account for the extremely high levels of competition found in Louisiana during the period under study" (Malcolm E. Jewell, *Legislative Representation in the Contemporary South* [Durham: Duke University Press, 1967], pp. 45-47, quotation at p. 47). Recall the relation posited earlier, in discussing "persistent factionalism," between the incidence of factional TPOs and the incidence of Jewell's slating tie-ins between candidates for governor and for lower offices in Democratic primaries.

Table A.3   Fragmentation of Vote in Primaries as a Function of Number of Candidates and Organizational Form

Independent Variable	Regression Coefficient	Standard Error	t Ratio
N of candidates	.167	.011	14.65***
Official processes	−14.3	4.7	−3.06***
Runoffs held	3.24	1.08	2.99***
TPO score (regular)	−4.15	3.31	−1.25
TPO score (factional)	8.36	4.28	1.95*
Constant	86.2		
N = 50			
Adj. R² = .908			

NOTE: One asterisk indicates a .05 level of significance; three indicate a .001 level.

This makes sense: official party endorsements in, say, Colorado or Connecticut are likely on the average to generate lopsided wins by endorsees over challengers. *Runoffs held* is a dummy variable reading 1 for states holding runoff primaries in the late 1960s (the eleven Confederate states plus Oklahoma minus Tennessee and Virginia at pertinent levels of office), zero otherwise.[4] Data here for the ten runoff states derive from first-round primaries whose candidates had to place first or second in order to progress to a runoff; candidates in primaries elsewhere in the country had to place first or lose. The result reported in Table A.3 suggests that the prospect of runoffs spreads out first-round vote shares toward *equality*. *TPO score (regular)* should push vote shares toward *inequality* if organization slating power produces lopsided primary victories. The coefficient in Table A.3 has the expected minus sign but a high standard error. *TPO score (factional)* should push vote shares toward *equality*, given patterns of competitive factional slating, and it does this well enough to meet a .05 significance test.

In gathering data on primaries I recorded the large metropolitan counties they took place in, if any, as well as their states. This was done on the assumption that patterns of candidate activity specific to metropolitan centers might prove interesting in their own right. Variables for counties can be used in equations covering the whole country in

---

[4] A variable for runoffs could have gone into the large equations generating Table A.1 (and in fact this was tried), but it comes so close to being a variable for the South that its meaning is clouded.

more or less the fashion of the state dummies. Results of two such equations, which employ "number of candidates" and "fragmentation of
vote," respectively, as dependent variables are reported in Tables A.4
and A.5. The coefficients for individual counties are identical in prove-
nance to the coefficients for states in Table A.1, with the qualification
that readings "left out" here from dummy-variable coverage attach not
to Connecticut (at an extreme of candidate activity) but to the entire
remainder of the country (all rural and many urban and suburban
areas) not encompassed by the metropolitan units listed. As a consequence Tables A.4 and A.5 have to be read differently than Table A.1.
Counties whose coefficients have negative signs generate *less* candidate
activity than the left-out remainder of the country; those whose coefficients have positive signs generate *more*. A Suffolk County (N.Y.)–Los
Angeles NCAND dimension emerges in Table A.4. The Los Angeles
County coefficient of 1.86 means that (all else equal) a Los Angeles legislative primary generates 1.86 more candidates than a primary in the
left-out remainder of the country; a Suffolk County primary generates
1.08 fewer candidates. A Suffolk County–Kanawha County dimension
emerges in the "fragmentation of vote" equation reported in Table A.5.

Some particular patterns in Tables A.4 and A.5 are of interest: (a)
Ohio stands out for the considerable range of its metropolitan counties'
coefficients; Hamilton County (Cincinnati) ranks near the bottom in
candidate activity and Cuyahoga County (Cleveland) and other units
appear well on the Los Angeles side of average. In the cases of the Cincinnati and Cleveland areas this is in accord with reports on their organizational settings discussed in Part I. (b) Several counties scoring
especially high in candidate activity have supported factional organizations—notably Marion County (Indianapolis), Lake County (Gary),
Baltimore County, New Orleans, Jefferson County (Louisville), and
the prize exhibit perhaps, Kanawha County (Charleston). (c) But other
metropolitan centers with especially high scores—notably the Los Angeles, Detroit, and Boston areas—have set an American standard for
free-wheeling, candidate-centered primaries in which well-known surnames have great value.[5]

[5] On the Boston area: V. O. Key, Jr., *American State Politics: An Introduction* (New
York: Knopf, 1956), pp. 160-163; Edward C. Banfield and Martha Derthick (eds.), *A
Report on the Politics of Boston* (Cambridge: Joint Center for Urban Studies, M.I.T./
Harvard, 1960), p. II:21. On the Detroit area: Maurice M. Ramsey, *Name Candidates
in Detroit Elections* (Detroit: Detroit Bureau of Governmental Research, Report No.
158, 1941); J. David Greenstone, *A Report on the Politics of Detroit* (Cambridge: Joint
Center for Urban Studies, M.I.T./Harvard, 1961), pp. II:2-3. On the Los Angeles area:
John E. Mueller, "Choosing among 133 Candidates," *Public Opinion Quarterly*
34(1970), 395-402.

Table A.4 Measure of Number of Candidates in Legislative Primaries of Metropolitan Counties

1. Suffolk, N.Y.	−1.08	40. Mobile (Mobile), Ala.	.11
2. Westchester (Yonkers), N.Y.	−.99	41. Hillsborough (Tampa), Fla.	.15
3. Nassau, N.Y.	−.91	42. Shelby (Memphis), Tenn.	.16
4. Kings (Brooklyn), N.Y.	−.76	43. Sedgwick (Wichita), Kans.	.16
5. Queens, N.Y.	−.68	44. Jackson (Kansas City), Mo.	.16
6. Erie (Buffalo), N.Y.	−.63	45. City of St. Louis, Mo.	.17
7. New York (Manhattan), N.Y.	−.61	46. City of Pittsburgh, Pa.	.17
8. Hamilton (Cincinnati), Ohio	−.60	47. Fulton (Atlanta), Ga.	.24
9. City of Chicago, Ill.	−.56	48. Hinds (Jackson), Miss.	.27
10. Delaware, Pa.	−.53	49. Davidson (Nashville), Tenn.	.29
11. City of New Haven, Conn.	−.50	50. Montgomery, Md.	.32
12. Dallas (Dallas), Tex.	−.49	51. Tulsa (Tulsa), Okla.	.33
13. Pima (Tucson), Ariz.	−.48	52. Dade (Miami), Fla.	.44
14. Richmond SMSA, Va.	−.45	53. Jefferson (Louisville), Ky.	.46
15. Chatham (Savannah), Ga.	−.42	54. Franklin (Columbus), Ohio	.51
16. City of Hartford, Conn.	−.40	55. City of Manchester, N.H.	.53
17. Denver (Denver), Colo.	−.39	56. King (Seattle), Wash.	.53
18. Bronx, N.Y.	−.37	57. Milwaukee (Milwaukee), Wis.	.57
19. Montgomery, Pa.	−.34	58. San Francisco Bay area, Calif.	.59
20. Norfolk SMSA, Va.	−.31	59. Allegheny (outside Pittsburgh), Pa.	.74
21. Cook (outside Chicago), Ill.	−.25	60. City of Baltimore, Md.	.76
22. Montgomery (Dayton), Ohio	−.25	61. Clark (Las Vegas), Nev.	.76
23. Mecklenburg (Charlotte), N.C.	−.22	62. Cuyahoga (Cleveland), Ohio	.89
24. City of Providence, R.I.	−.16	63. Prince Georges, Md.	.96
25. Duval (Jacksonville), Fla.	−.14	64. Summit (Akron), Ohio	.98
26. Jefferson (Birmingham), Ala.	−.14	65. East Baton Rouge (Baton Rouge), La.	.98
27. Harris (Houston), Tex.	−.14	66. Marion (Indianapolis), Ind.	1.18
28. Salt Lake (Salt Lake City), Utah	−.13	67. Bernalillo (Albuquerque), N. Mex.	1.23
29. Philadelphia (Philadelphia), Pa.	−.12	68. Oklahoma (Oklahoma City), Okla.	1.27
30. Maricopa (Phoenix), Ariz.	−.09	69. Orleans (New Orleans), La.	1.33
31. Hudson (Jersey City), N.J.	−.07	70. Kanawha (Charleston), W.Va.	1.36
32. Oahu (Honolulu), Hawaii	−.06	71. City of Boston, Mass.	1.40
33. Essex (Newark), N.J.	−.05	72. Multnomah (Portland), Oreg.	1.48
34. Polk (Des Moines), Iowa	−.04	73. Lake (Gary), Ind.	1.50
35. Washington suburbs, Va.	−.03	74. Baltimore County, Md.	1.54
36. Bexar (San Antonio), Tex.	.02	75. Wayne (Detroit), Mich.	1.61
37. Lucas (Toledo), Ohio	.05	76. Orange, Calif.	1.64
38. Pulaski (Little Rock), Ark.	.05	77. Los Angeles (Los Angeles), Calif.	1.86
39. San Diego (San Diego), Calif.	.08		

NOTE: Values are for counties unless otherwise indicated. Places in parentheses are major cities within specified counties. SMSA stands for "standard metropolitan statistical area."

Table A.5 Measures of Fragmentation of Vote in Legislative Primaries of Metropolitan Counties

1. Suffolk, N.Y.	− .31	40. City of Boston, Mass.	.04
2. Westchester (Yonkers), N.Y.	− .23	41. Jackson (Kansas City), Mo.	.05
3. City of New Haven, Conn.	− .19	42. Pulaski (Little Rock), Ark.	.05
4. Kings (Brooklyn), N.Y.	− .18	43. Fulton (Atlanta), Ga.	.05
5. Nassau, N.Y.	− .18	44. Hinds (Jackson), Miss.	.05
6. Erie (Buffalo), N.Y.	− .18	45. Milwaukee (Milwaukee), Wis.	.07
7. City of Chicago, Ill.	− .17	46. Tulsa (Tulsa), Okla.	.07
8. Chatham (Savannah), Ga.	− .16	47. Montgomery, Md.	.07
9. City of Hartford, Conn.	− .15	48. Lucas (Toledo), Ohio	.08
10. New York (Manhattan), N.Y.	− .15	49. Shelby (Memphis), Tenn.	.08
11. Hamilton (Cincinnati), Ohio	− .15	50. Cuyahoga (Cleveland), Ohio	.08
12. Denver (Denver), Colo.	− .14	51. Clark (Las Vegas), Nev.	.09
13. Queens, N.Y.	− .14	52. King (Seattle), Wash.	.09
14. Richmond SMSA, Va.	− .13	53. San Francisco Bay area, Calif.	.09
15. Delaware, Pa.	− .12	54. Bexar (San Antonio), Tex.	.09
16. Pima (Tucson), Ariz.	− .12	55. Harris (Houston), Tex.	.10
17. Philadelphia (Philadelphia), Pa.	− .12	56. Sedgwick (Wichita), Kans.	.10
18. City of Providence, R.I.	− .10	57. Davidson (Nashville), Tenn.	.10
19. Bronx, N.Y.	− .08	58. Allegheny (outside Pittsburgh), Pa.	.11
20. Cook (outside Chicago), Ill.	− .08	59. San Diego (San Diego), Calif.	.11
21. City of St. Louis, Mo.	− .06	60. City of Manchester, N.H.	.12
22. Jefferson (Birmingham), Ala.	− .06	61. City of Baltimore, Md.	.14
23. Montgomery, Pa.	− .05	62. Los Angeles (Los Angeles), Calif.	.15
24. Norfolk SMSA, Va.	− .05	63. Franklin (Columbus), Ohio	.15
25. City of Pittsburgh, Pa.	− .05	64. Wayne (Detroit), Mich.	.16
26. Duval (Jacksonville), Fla.	− .04	65. Jefferson (Louisville), Ky.	.17
27. Hudson (Jersey City), N.J.	− .02	66. Oklahoma (Oklahoma City), Okla.	.18
28. Polk (Des Moines), Iowa	− .01	67. Prince Georges, Md.	.19
29. Dallas (Dallas), Tex.	− .01	68. East Baton Rouge (Baton Rouge), La.	.19
30. Montgomery (Dayton), Ohio	− .01	69. Summit (Akron), Ohio	.19
31. Mecklenburg (Charlotte), N.C.	.00	70. Marion (Indianapolis), Ind.	.20
32. Washington suburbs, Va.	.00	71. Orleans (New Orleans), La.	.22
33. Oahu (Honolulu), Hawaii	.00	72. Bernalillo (Albuquerque), N.Mex.	.23
34. Essex (Newark), N.J.	.01	73. Baltimore County, Md.	.23
35. Hillsborough (Tampa), Fla.	.01	74. Orange, Calif.	.25
36. Salt Lake (Salt Lake City), Utah	.01	75. Multnomah (Portland), Oreg.	.25
37. Mobile (Mobile), Ala.	.02	76. Lake (Gary), Ind.	.28
38. Maricopa (Phoenix), Ariz.	.03	77. Kanawha (Charleston), W.Va.	.30
39. Dade (Miami), Fla.	.03		

NOTE: Values are for counties unless otherwise indicated. Places in parentheses are major cities within specified counties. SMSA stands for "standard metropolitan statistical area."

Expenditure and Revenue Data for 1942

Solomon Fabricant pioneered in the cross-sectional study of state and local expenditure patterns by employing exceptionally comprehensive and accurate data gathered by the Census Bureau for 1942.[1] He sorted the data differently than the Census Bureau did in the 1940s or has since; he included in overall spending totals items the Census Bureau partly or wholly excluded and excluded things the Bureau partly or wholly counted: he excluded capital outlays, for example.[2] In setting up his cross-state equations, Fabricant used state (cum local) expenditures per capita as his dependent variable (rather than, as done here, a ratio of per capita expenditure over per capita personal income), and introduced per capita personal income (averaged over 1938-1942 in an effort to even out idiosyncrasies) as one among several independent variables—making it, that is, solely a variable on the right-hand side rather than, as here, the denominator of a ratio on the left-hand side and also in a lesser role a variable by itself on the right-hand side. Not surprisingly, Fabricant's variation in per capita personal income explained much of his variation in per capita government spending; rich states spend more per capita than poor states. Variables for population density and percent urban performed modestly well.[3]

Tailoring Fabricant's money data to the standard treatment here (per capita personal income enters as a left-hand-side denominator) generates Figure B.1 and Table B.1. The pattern is rather like expenditure patterns for the 1950s covered earlier here in the text (see Figures 10.12 and 10.13 and Table 10.4).[4] Running the Census Bureau's 1942 data through the Bureau's conventional post-1950 sorting categories (but still using Fabricant's 1938-1942 measure of per capita personal in-

---

[1] *The Trend of Government Activity in the United States since 1900* (New York: National Bureau of Economic Research, 1952), ch. 6 and appendixes D, E.

[2] *Ibid.*, pp. 112 (footnote 3), 115 (footnote c).

[3] *Ibid.*, pp. 122-131, 261.

[4] For whatever particular reasons in 1942, Utah, Colorado, and Arizona score very high in Figure B.1 largely because of exceptional expenditure in the "public welfare" category.

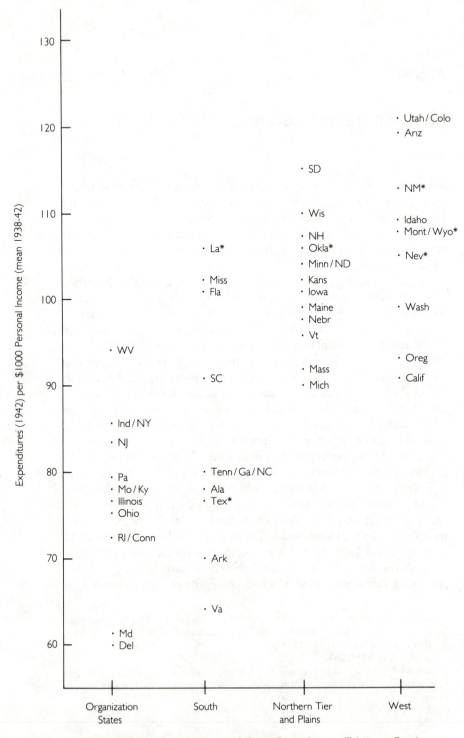

Fig. B.1 Traditional Party Organization and State Expenditures (Fabricant Data) per $1,000 Personal Income, 1942. Asterisks in figures refer to tax-exporting states; see p. 259.

Table B.1   Determinants of State Variation in Expenditures (Fabricant Data) per
$1,000 Personal Income, 1942

Independent Variable	Regression Coefficient	Standard Error	t Ratio
TPO score	−6.20	1.05	−5.93***
Confederate	−21.2	4.5	−4.69***
Per capita income	−.025	.011	−2.22**
Constant	125.1		
N = 48			
Adj. R² = .577			
TPO score	−6.14	1.19	−5.17***
Confederate	−21.0	4.6	−4.56***
Per capita income	−.037	.016	−2.35**
Percent urban	23.9	17.6	1.36
Population density	−.015	.017	−.91
Constant	122.3		
N = 48			
Adj. R² = .576			

NOTE: Per capita income is an average for the five years 1938-1942. Two asterisks indicate a
.01 level of significance; three indicate a .001 level.

come) generates Figure B.2 and Table B.2 for "general expenditure,"
and Figure B.3 and Table B.3 for "general revenue."[5] Again the 1942
patterns are familiar, though some major urban states (California,
Michigan, Massachusetts, and New York) appear in rather low ratio
positions by postwar standards. (There are ways of putting together
equations for these 1942 Census Bureau data that produce stable negative coefficients for the urban variable, though the TPO variable holds
up.) It is worth saying in the Michigan case that the full force of labor
mobilization had not yet registered in 1942 in state politics; the liberal-
UAW alliance's upward pressure on the budget came later, as did the
state income tax.[6] But war mobilization after Pearl Harbor drove gov-

[5] The required money data appear in Bureau of the Census, *State and Local Government Finances in 1942 and 1957*, State and Local Government Special Studies, no. 43
(release date December 11, 1959), tables 2 and 9.

[6] For a treatment of Michigan's budgetary politics in the 1950s and 1960s see Dudley
W. Buffa, *Union Power and American Democracy: The UAW and the Democratic Party,
1935-72* (Ann Arbor: University of Michigan Press, 1984), ch. 4.

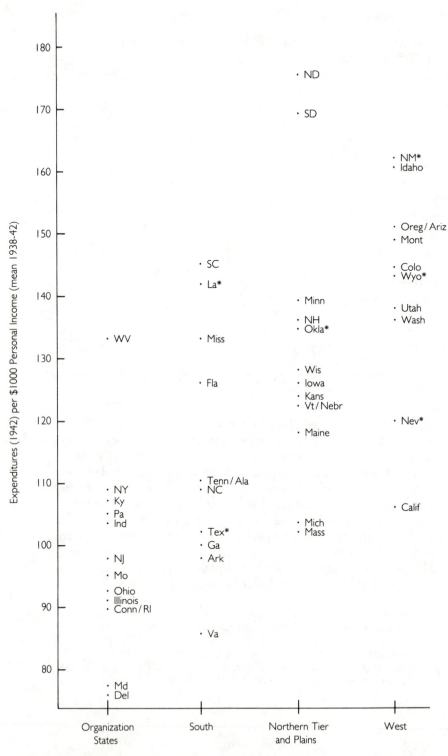

Fig. B.2 Traditional Party Organization and State General Expenditures per $1,000 Personal Income, 1942

Table B.2   Determinants of State Variation in General Expenditures per $1,000 Personal Income, 1942

Independent Variable	Regression Coefficient	Standard Error	t Ratio
TPO score	−7.76	1.67	−4.65***
Confederate	−30.4	7.2	−4.23***
Per capita income	−.066	.018	−3.76***
Constant	183.0		
N = 48			
Adj. R^2 = .543			
TPO score	−7.23	1.91	−3.77***
Confederate	−29.7	7.4	−3.99***
Per capita income	−.048	.025	−1.89*
Percent urban	−25.1	28.4	−.88
Population density	.014	.027	.05
Constant	182.7		
N = 48			
Adj. R^2 = .533			

NOTE: Per capita income is an average for the five years 1938-1942. One asterisk indicates a .05 level of significance; three indicate a .001 level.

ernment activity during much of fiscal 1942, so there are limits on what can be made of the year's data. Nonmilitary public construction in particular fell off sharply.[7]

[7] See Bureau of the Census, *State and Local Government Finances in 1942 and 1957*, p. 2; and Bureau of the Census, *Governmental Finances in the United States, 1942* (Washington, D.C.: GPO, 1945), p. 3. The Bureau's state-specific revenue and expenditure data are good for 1932 (though not so detailed as for 1942), but 1932 was also an abnormal year. One thing that seems to have happened is that the Depression's collapse in farm income elevated both government revenue and government spending to a startlingly high proportion of personal income in some of the agricultural states. See *ibid.*, pp. 3, 134; and Bureau of the Census, *Historical Review of State and Local Government Finances*, State and Local Government Special Studies, no. 25 (June 1948) table 22.

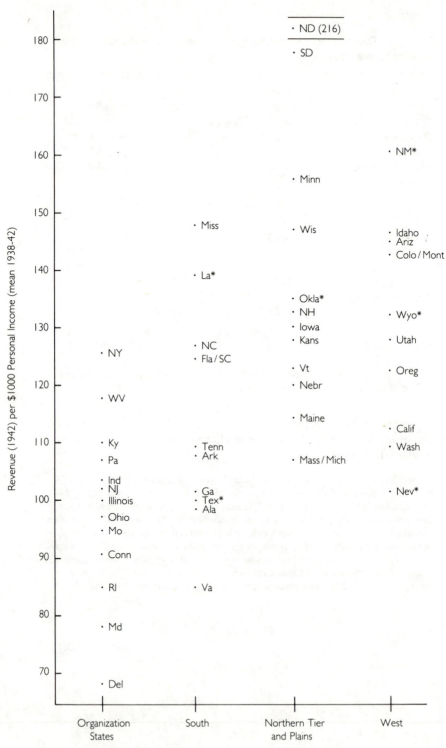

Fig. B.3   Traditional Party Organization and State General Revenue per $1,000 Personal Income, 1942

Table B.3 Determinants of State Variation in General Revenue per $1,000 Personal Income, 1942

Independent Variable	Regression Coefficient	Standard Error	t Ratio
TPO score	−6.51	1.96	−3.32***
Confederate	−32.4	8.5	−3.83***
Per capita income	−.080	.021	−3.86***
Constant	188.7		
N = 48			
Adj. R^2 = .457			
TPO score	−6.76	2.28	−2.97***
Confederate	−32.8	8.8	−3.72***
Per capita income	−.076	.030	−2.53**
Percent urban	−11.4	33.8	−.34
Population density	.013	.033	.40
Constant	191.2		
N = 48			
Adj. R^2 = .433			

NOTE: Per capita income is an average for the five years 1938-1942. Two asterisks indicate a .01 level of significance; three indicate a .001 level.

Library of Congress Cataloging-in-Publication Data

Mayhew, David R.
Placing parties in American politics.

Includes indexes.
1. Political parties—United States. 2. Elections—
United States. I. Title.
JK2261.M37 1986   324.273   85-43298
ISBN 0-691-07707-X   ISBN 0-691-02249-6 (pbk.)

David R. Mayhew is Alfred Cowles Professor of
Government at Yale University. He is the author of
*Party Loyalty among Congressmen: The Difference be-
tween Democrats and Republicans, 1947-1962* (Harvard) and *Congress: The Electoral Connection* (Yale).